USB Complete

Everything You Need
to Develop Custom USB Peripherals

Third Edition

Jan Axelson

Lakeview Research LLC
Madison, WI 53704

USB Complete: Everything You Need to Develop USB Peripherals, Third Edition
by Jan Axelson

Copyright 1999-2005 by Janet L. Axelson

Published by Lakeview Research LLC, 5310 Chinook Ln., Madison WI 53704

On the web at **www.Lvr.com**

Distributed by Independent Publishers Group (www.ipgbook.com).

Cover by Rattray Design. Cover Photo by Bill Bilsley Photography.

Index by Julie Kawabata.

14 13 12 11 10 9 8 7 6 5 4 3 2

Printed and bound in the United States of America

ISBN13 978-1-931448-02-4

ISBN10 1-931448-02-7

Contents

Contents

Contents

Contents

11. Human Interface Devices: Using Control and Interrupt Transfers 319

12. Human Interface Devices: Reports 351

Contents

Contents

Contents

Introduction

This book is for developers who design and program devices that use the Universal Serial Bus (USB) interface. My goal is to introduce you to USB and to help you get your devices up and communicating as quickly and easily as possible.

The USB interface is versatile enough for a wide range of peripheral devices. Standard peripherals that use USB include mice, keyboards, drives, printers, and audio/video devices. USB is also suitable for data-acquisition units, control systems, and other devices with specialized functions, including one-of-a-kind designs.

To develop a device with a USB interface, you need to know something about how the interface works, what tasks your device firmware must perform to communicate on the bus, and what class drivers and other support are available on the host computers that your device will attach to. The right choices of device hardware, device class, and development tools and techniques can go a long way in avoiding snags and simplifying what needs to be done.

If you're involved with designing USB devices, writing the firmware that resides inside USB devices, or writing applications that communicate with USB devices, this book will help you along the way.

What's Inside

These are some of questions the book answers:

- *How do USB devices communicate?* The USB interface can seem daunting at first. The USB 2.0 specification is over 600 pages, not counting the class specifications and other supplementary documents. This book doesn't attempt to restate everything in the specifications. Instead, the focus is on what you'll need to know to enable your devices to communicate efficiently and reliably.

- *How can I decide if my device should use a USB interface?* USB isn't the best choice for every application. Find out whether your design should use USB or another interface. The chances are good that you will choose USB, however, and if so, you'll learn how to decide which of USB's three speeds and four transfer types are appropriate for your application.

- *What controller chip should my device use?* Every USB device must contain an intelligent controller to implement the USB interface. Dozens of manufacturers offer controller chips with differing architectures and abilities. This book includes descriptions of popular chips and tips to help you select a controller based on your project's needs and your background and preferences.

- *How do applications communicate with USB devices?* PC applications access a USB device by communicating with the device driver the operating system has assigned to the device. Some devices can use class drivers that are included with Windows. Others devices require custom drivers. This book will introduce you to the classes and will help you determine if a defined class is appropriate for your device. If your device requires a custom driver, you'll learn what's involved in writing a driver, what tools can help speed up the process, and options for obtaining drivers from other sources. Example code shows how to detect and communicate with devices in Visual Basic .NET and Visual C++ .NET applications.

- *What firmware does my device need to support USB communications?* Learn how to write device firmware that enables your device to respond to received requests and exchange other data on the bus.

- *How do I decide whether my device can use bus power or needs its own supply?* Many USB devices can be powered entirely from the bus. Find out whether your device can use bus power. Learn how to ensure that your device meets USB's requirement to limit the use of bus current when the host computer suspends the bus.

- *Can I connect other USB peripherals to my device?* Find out how to use USB On-The-Go to enable your device to act as a limited-capability host that can access other USB peripherals.

- *How can I ensure that my device will communicate without problems?* At the device, writing bugfree firmware requires understanding what your device must do to meet the requirements of the USB specifications. At the host computer, Windows must have the information needed to identify the device and locate a driver to communicate with the device. This book has tips, example code, and information about debugging software and hardware to help with these tasks.

To understand the material in the book, it's helpful to have basic knowledge in a few areas. I assume you have some experience with digital logic, application programming for PCs and writing embedded code for peripherals. You don't have to know anything at all about USB.

What's New in the Third Edition?

Since the publication of *USB Complete Second Edition*, much has happened in the world of USB. Additions to the USB specifications include many updated and expanded device-class specifications and the USB On-The-Go supplement. Many new device-controller chips have been released. New tools for debugging and compliance testing are available. Support for USB device classes under Windows has improved. And Microsoft's .NET Framework has become a popular platform for developing host applications.

These developments prompted me to write *USB Complete Third Edition*. The material is revised and updated from start to finish to reflect these and other developments related to USB hardware and programming.

More Information, Updates, and Corrections

To find out more about developing USB devices and the software that communicates with them, I invite you to visit my USB Central page at Lakeview Research's Web site (*www.Lvr.com*). You'll find code examples and links to articles, products, tools, and other information related to developing USB devices. If you have a suggestion, code, or other information that you'd like me to post or link to, let me know at *jan@Lvr.com*.

Corrections and updates will also be available at *www.Lvr.com*. If you find an error, please let me know and I'll post it.

Acknowledgements

USB is too big a topic to write about without help. I have many people to thank.

I owe a big thanks to my technical reviewers, who provided feedback that has greatly improved the book. (With that said, every error in this book is mine and mine alone.)

Thanks first to Paul E. Berg, MCCI Vice President, Architecture and USB-IF Device Working Group Chair. Thanks also to David Goll of the USB-IF's Video Device Working Group, Lucio DiJasio and Rawin Rojvanit of Microchip Technology, John Hyde of *usb-by-example.com,* Geert Knapen of the USB-IF's Audio Device Working Group, Walter Oney of Walter Oney Software, and Marc Reinig of System Solutions.

Others I want to thank for their support are Glenn M. Roberts of Cypress Semiconductor, Fred Dart and Keith Dingwall of FTDI Chip, Wendy Dee of Keil Software, Michael DeVault of DeVaSys Embedded Systems, Alan Lowne of Saelig Company Inc., Laurent Guinnard of Ellisys, Rich Moran of RPM Systems Corporation, and Bob Nathan of NCR Corporation.

For help and support with the previous editions that this edition builds on, thanks to Joshua Buergel, Gary Crowell, Dave Dowler, Mike Fahrion, John M. Goodman, Lane Hauck, David James, Christer Johansson, Kosta Koeman, Jon Lueker, Brad Markisohn, Amar Rajan, Robert Severson, Craig R. Smith, and Dave Wright.

I hope you find the book useful. Comments invited!

Jan Axelson
jan@Lvr.com

1

USB Basics

What if you had the chance to design a peripheral interface from scratch? Your wish list would likely include these qualities:

- Easy to use, so there's no need to fiddle with configuration and setup details.
- Fast, so the interface doesn't become a communications bottleneck.
- Reliable, so that errors are rare, with automatic retries when errors occur.
- Versatile, so many kinds of peripherals can use the interface.
- Inexpensive, so manufacturers and users don't balk at the price.
- Power-conserving, to save energy and extend battery life in portable computers and devices.
- Supported by the Windows and other operating systems, so developers don't have to write low-level drivers to communicate with the peripherals.

The Universal Serial Bus (USB) has all of these qualities. USB was designed from the ground up to be an interface for communicating with many types of peripherals without the limits and frustrations of older interfaces.

Every recent PC and Macintosh computer includes USB ports that can connect to standard peripherals such as keyboards, mice, scanners, cameras, printers, and drives as well as custom hardware for just about any purpose.

This chapter introduces USB, including its advantages and limits, some history about the interface and recent enhancements to it, and a look at what's involved in designing and programming a device with a USB interface.

What USB Can Do

USB is a likely solution any time you want to use a computer to communicate with a device outside of the computer. The interface is suitable for mass-produced, standard peripheral types as well as small-volume designs, including one-of-a-kind projects.

To be successful, an interface has to please two audiences: the users who want to use the peripherals and the developers who design the hardware and write the code that communicates with the device. USB has features to please both.

Benefits for Users

From the user's perspective, the benefits of USB are ease of use, fast and reliable data transfers, flexibility, low cost, and power conservation. Table 1-1 compares USB with other popular interfaces.

Ease of Use

Ease of use was a major design goal for USB, and the result is an interface that's a pleasure to use for many reasons:

One interface for many devices. USB is versatile enough to be usable with a variety of peripheral types. Instead of having a different connector type and supporting hardware for each peripheral, one interface serves many.

Table 1-1: Comparison of popular computer interfaces. Where a standard doesn't specify a maximum, the table shows a typical maximum.

Interface	Format	Number of Devices (maximum)	Distance (maximum, feet)	Speed (maximum, bits/sec.)	Typical Use
USB	asynchronous serial	127	16 (up to 96 ft. with 5 hubs)	1.5M, 12M, 480M	Mouse, keyboard, drive, audio, printer, other standard and custom peripherals
Ethernet	serial	1024	1600	10G	General network communications
IEEE-1394b (FireWire 800)	serial	64	300	3.2G	Video, mass storage
IEEE-488 (GPIB)	parallel	15	60	8M	Instrumentation
IrDA	asynchronous serial infrared	2	6	16M	Printers, hand-held computers
I²C	synchronous serial	40	18	3.4M	Microcontroller communications
Microwire	synchronous serial	8	10	2M	Microcontroller communications
MIDI	serial current loop	2 (more with flow-through mode)	50	31.5k	Music, show control
Parallel Printer Port	parallel	2 (8 with daisy-chain support)	10–30	8M	Printers, scanners, disk drives
RS-232 (EIA/TIA-232)	asynchronous serial	2	50-100	20k (115k with some hardware)	Modem, mouse, instrumentation
RS-485 (TIA/EIA-485)	asynchronous serial	32 unit loads (up to 256 devices with some hardware)	4000	10M	Data acquisition and control systems
SPI	synchronous serial	8	10	2.1M	Microcontroller communications

Automatic configuration. When a user connects a USB peripheral to a PC, Windows detects the peripheral and loads the appropriate software driver. The first time the peripheral connects, Windows may prompt the user to insert a disk with driver software, but other than that, installation is automatic. There's no need to restart the system before using the peripheral.

Easy to connect. With USB, there's no need to open the computer's enclosure to add an expansion card for each peripheral. A typical PC has four or more USB ports. You can expand the number of ports by adding hubs with additional ports.

Easy cables. USB cable connectors are keyed so you can't plug them in wrong. A cable segment can be as long as 5 meters. With hubs, a peripheral can be as far as 30 meters from its host PC. USB connectors are small and compact in contrast to typical RS-232 and parallel connectors. To ensure reliable operation, the USB specification includes detailed requirements that all cables and connectors must meet.

Hot pluggable. You can connect and disconnect a USB peripheral whenever you want, whether or not the system and peripheral are powered, without damaging the PC or device. The operating system detects when a peripheral is attached and readies it for use.

No user settings. USB peripherals don't have user-selectable settings such as port addresses and interrupt-request (IRQ) lines so there are no jumpers to set or configuration utilities to run.

Frees hardware resources for other devices. Using USB for as many peripherals as possible frees up IRQ lines for the peripherals that require them. The PC dedicates a series of port addresses and one IRQ line to the USB host controller, but individual peripherals don't require additional resources or any PC programming that involves specifying port addresses or detecting hardware interrupts. In contrast, peripherals with other interfaces may require dedicated port addresses, an IRQ line, and an expansion slot.

No power supply required (sometimes). The USB interface includes power-supply and ground lines that provide a nominal +5V from the computer's or hub's power supply. A peripheral that requires up to 500 milliamperes can draw all of its power from the bus instead of having to provide a power supply. In contrast, peripherals that use other interfaces may have to choose between including a power supply inside the device or using a bulky and inconvenient external supply.

Speed

USB supports three bus speeds: high speed at 480 Megabits/sec., full speed at 12 Megabits/sec., and low speed at 1.5 Megabits/sec. The USB host controllers in recent PCs support all three speeds.

The bus speeds describe the rate that information travels on the bus. In addition to data, the bus must carry status, control, and error-checking signals. Plus, all peripherals must share the bus. So the rate of data transfer that an individual peripheral can expect will be less than the bus speed. The theoretical maximum rate for a single data transfer is about 53 Megabytes/sec. at high speed, 1.2 Megabytes/sec. at full speed, and 800 bytes/sec. at low speed.

The USB 1.0 specification defined low and full speeds. Low speed was included for two reasons. Mice require flexible cables to make the devices easy to move around. Low-speed cables don't require twisted pairs or as much shielding and thus can be more flexible than full/high-speed cables. Also, low-speed devices can often be manufactured more cheaply. Full speed was intended to replace most other peripherals that used RS-232 (serial) and parallel ports. The data-transfer rates attainable at full speed are comparable to or better than the speeds attainable with earlier interfaces. High speed became an option with the release of version 2.0 of the USB specification.

Reliability

The reliability of USB is due to both the hardware and the protocols for data transfer. The hardware specifications for USB drivers, receivers, and cables ensure a quiet interface that eliminates most noise that could cause data errors. The USB protocol enables the detecting of errors in received data and notifying the sender so it can retransmit. The detecting, notifying, and retransmitting are done in hardware and don't require any programming or user intervention.

Low Cost

Even though USB is more complex than earlier interfaces, the components and cables are inexpensive. A device with a USB interface is likely to cost the same or less than an equivalent device with an older interface or a more recent interface such as IEEE-1394.

Low Power Consumption

Power-saving circuits and code can automatically power down USB peripherals when not in use yet keep them ready to respond when needed. The reduced power consumption saves money, is environmentally friendly, and for battery-powered devices, allows a longer time between recharges.

Wireless Communications

USB originated as a wired interface, but options now exist for wireless devices that use USB to communicate with PCs.

Benefits for Developers

Many of the user advantages described above also make things easier for developers. For example, USB's defined cable standards and automatic error checking mean that developers don't have to worry about specifying cable characteristics or providing error checking in software.

USB has other advantages that benefit developers. The developers include the hardware designers who select components and design the circuits in devices, the programmers who write the software embedded in the devices, and the programmers who write the PC software that communicates with the devices.

The benefits to developers result from the flexibility built into the USB protocol, the support in the controller chips and operating system, and the support available from the USB Implementers Forum.

Versatility

USB's four transfer types and three speeds make the interface feasible for many types of peripherals. There are transfer types suited for exchanging large and small blocks of data, with and without time constraints. For data that can't tolerate delays, USB can guarantee bandwidth or a maximum time between transfers. These abilities are especially welcome under Windows, where accessing peripherals in real time is often a challenge. Although the operating system, device drivers, and application software can introduce unavoidable delays, USB makes it as easy as possible to achieve transfers that are close to real time.

Unlike other interfaces, USB doesn't assign specific functions to signal lines or make other assumptions about how the interface will be used. For example, the status and control lines on the PC's parallel port were defined with the intention of communicating with line printers. There are five input lines with assigned functions such as indicating a busy or paper-out condition. When developers began using the port for scanners and other peripherals that send large amounts of data to the PC, having just five inputs was a limitation. (Eventually the interface was enhanced to allow eight bits of input.) USB makes no such assumptions and is suitable for just about any peripheral type.

For communicating with common peripheral types such as printers, keyboards, and drives, USB has defined classes that specify device requirements and protocols. Developers can use the classes as a guide instead of having to reinvent everything from the ground up.

Operating System Support

Windows 98 was the first Windows operating system with reliable support for USB, and the editions that have followed, including Windows 2000, Windows Me, Windows XP, and Windows Server 2003, support USB as well. This book focuses on Windows programming for PCs, but other computers and operating systems also have USB support, including Apple Computer's Macintosh and the Linux operating system for PCs. Some real-time kernels also support USB.

A claim of operating-system support for USB can mean many things. At the most basic level, an operating system that supports USB must do three things:

- Detect when devices are attached to and removed from the system.

- Communicate with newly attached devices to find out how to exchange data with them.

- Provide a mechanism that enables software drivers to communicate with the computer's USB hardware and the applications that want to access USB peripherals.

At a higher level, operating system support may also mean the inclusion of class drivers that enable application programmers to access devices. If the operating system doesn't include a driver appropriate for a specific peripheral, the peripheral vendor must provide the driver.

With each new edition of Windows, Microsoft has added class drivers. Supported device types in recent Windows editions include human interface devices (keyboards, mice, game controllers), audio devices, modems, still-image and video cameras, scanners, printers, drives, and smart-card readers. Filter drivers can support device-specific features and abilities within a class. Applications use Application Programming Interface (API) functions or other operating-system components to communicate with device drivers.

For devices that aren't in supported classes, some vendors of USB peripheral controllers provide drivers that developers can use with the vendor's controllers.

USB device drivers use the Windows Driver Model (WDM), which defines an architecture for drivers that run under Windows 98 and later Windows editions. The aim is to enable developers to support multiple Windows editions with a single driver, though some devices may require different drivers for Windows 98/Windows Me and for Windows 2000/Windows XP. Because Windows includes low-level drivers that handle communications with the USB hardware, writing a USB device driver is typically easier than writing drivers for devices that use other interfaces.

Peripheral Support

On the peripheral side, each USB device's hardware must include a controller chip that manages the details of USB communications. Some controllers are complete microcontrollers that include a CPU, program and data memory, and a USB interface. Other controllers must interface to an external CPU that communicates with the USB controller as needed.

The peripheral is responsible for responding to requests to send and receive data used in identifying and configuring the device and for reading and writing other data on the bus. In some controllers, some functions are microcoded in hardware and don't need to be programmed.

Many USB controllers are based on popular architectures such as Intel Corporation's 8051 or Microchip Technology's PICMicro®, with added circuits and machine codes to support USB communications. If you're already familiar with a chip architecture that has a USB-capable variant, you don't need to learn an entirely new architecture. Most peripheral manufacturers provide sample code for their chips. Using this code as a starting point can save much time.

USB Implementers Forum

With some interfaces, you're pretty much on your own when it comes to getting a design up and running. With USB, you have plenty of help via the USB Implementers Forum, Inc. (USB-IF) and its Web site (*www.usb.org*). The USB-IF is the non-profit corporation founded by the companies that developed the USB specification.

The USB-IF's mission is to support the advancement and adoption of USB technology. To that end, the USB-IF offers information, tools, and tests. The information includes the specification documents, white papers, FAQs, and a Web forum where developers can discuss USB-related topics. The tools provided by the USB-IF include software and hardware to help in developing and testing products. The support for testing includes developing compliance tests to verify proper operation and holding compliance workshops where developers can have their products tested and earn the rights for their devices to display the USB logo.

Beyond the Hype

All of USB's advantages mean that it's a good candidate for use on many peripherals. But a single interface can't handle every task.

Interface Limits

Every interface has limits that make the interface impractical for some applications. For USB, limits to be aware of include speed and distance, lack of support for peer-to-peer communications, no ability to broadcast, and lack of support in older hardware and operating systems.

Speed. USB is versatile, but it's not designed to do everything. USB's high speed makes it competitive with the IEEE-1394a (Firewire) interface's 400 Megabits/sec., but IEEE-1394b is faster still, at 3.2 Gigabits/sec.

Distance. USB was designed as a desktop-expansion bus with the expectation that peripherals would be relatively close at hand. A cable segment can be as long as 5 meters. Other interfaces, including RS-232, RS-485, IEEE-1394b, and Ethernet, allow much longer cables. You can increase the length of a USB link to as much as 30 meters by using cables that link five hubs and a device.

To extend the range beyond 30 meters, an option is to use a USB interface on the PC, then convert to RS-485 or another interface for the long-distance cabling and peripheral interface.

Peer-to-Peer Communications. Every USB communication is between a host computer and a peripheral. The host is a PC or other computer with host-controller hardware. The peripheral contains device-controller hardware. Hosts can't talk to each other directly, and peripherals can't talk to each other directly. Other interfaces, such as IEEE-1394, allow direct peripheral-to-peripheral communications.

USB provides a partial solution with USB On-The-Go. An On-The-Go device can function both as a peripheral and as a limited-capability host that can communicate with other devices. Two hosts can communicate with each other via a PC-to-PC network bridge cable, which contains two devices that each connect to a different PC and pass data between the PCs.

Broadcasting. USB provides no way to send a message simultaneously to multiple devices on the bus. The host must send the message to each device individually. If you must have broadcasting ability, use IEEE-1394 or Ethernet.

Legacy Hardware. Older ("legacy") computers and peripherals don't have USB ports. If you want to connect a legacy peripheral to a USB port, a solution is a converter that translates between USB and the older interface. Several sources have converters for use with peripherals with RS-232, RS-485, and Centronics-type parallel ports. But the converter solution is useful only for peripherals that use conventional protocols supported by the converter's device driver. For example, most parallel-port converters support communications only with printers. Converters that will work with most devices that have RS-232 interfaces are available, however.

If you want to use a USB peripheral with a PC that doesn't support USB, a solution is to add USB capabilities to the PC. To do so, you'll need to add USB host-controller hardware and install an operating system that supports USB. The hardware is available on expansion cards that plug into a PCI slot or on a replacement motherboard. The Windows edition must be Windows 98 or later. Hardware that doesn't meet Windows 98's minimum requirements will need upgrades that may cost more than a new system.

If upgrading the PC to support USB isn't feasible, you might think a converter would be available to translate a peripheral's USB interface to the PC's RS-232, parallel, or other interface. But a converter isn't normally an option when the PC has the legacy interface. Creating a converter that contains the host-controller hardware and code that normally resides in the PC would cost too much to be practical.

Even on new systems, users may occasionally run applications on older operating systems such as MS-DOS. But for the most part, the drivers that Windows applications use to communicate with USB devices are specific to Windows. Without a driver, there's no way to access a USB peripheral. Although it's possible to write a USB driver for DOS, few peripheral vendors provide one. An exception is the mouse and keyboard, where a system's BIOS may include support to ensure that the peripherals are usable any time, including from within DOS, from the BIOS screens that you can view on bootup, and from Windows' Safe mode.

Of course, the problem of supporting legacy hardware and operating systems is diminishing as these systems are replaced.

Developer Challenges

From the developer's perspective, the main challenges to USB are the complexity of the programming and for small-scale developers, the need to obtain a Vendor ID.

Protocol Complexity. A USB peripheral is an intelligent device that knows how to respond to requests and other events on the bus. Chips vary in how much firmware support they require to perform USB communications. In most cases, to program a USB peripheral, you need to know a fair amount about the USB's protocols, or rules for exchanging data on the bus. On the PC side, the device driver insulates application programmers from having to know many of the details, but device-driver writers need to be familiar with USB protocols and the driver's responsibilities.

In contrast, some older interfaces can connect to very simple circuits with very basic protocols. For example, the PC's original parallel printer port is just a series of digital inputs and outputs. You can connect to basic input and output circuits such as relays, switches, and analog-to-digital converters, with no computer intelligence required on the peripheral side. The PC software can monitor and control the individual bits on the ports.

With USB, applications can't just read and write to port addresses, and devices can't just present a series of inputs and outputs to read and write to directly. To access a USB device, applications must communicate with a class or device driver that in turn communicates with the lower-level USB drivers that manage communications on the bus. The device must implement the protocols that enable the PC to detect, identify, and communicate with the device.

Evolving Support in the Operating System. The class drivers included with Windows enable applications to communicate with many devices. Often, you can design your device to use one of the provided drivers. If not, you may be able to use or adapt a driver provided by the controller-chip vendor. If you need to provide your own driver, there are toolkits that make the job of writing USB drivers easier.

Fees. The USB-IF provides the USB specification, related documents, software for compliance testing, and much more, all for free on its Web site. Anyone can develop USB software without paying a licensing fee.

However, anyone who distributes a device with a USB interface must obtain the rights to use a Vendor ID. At this writing, the administrative fee for obtaining a Vendor ID from the USB-IF is $1500. If you join the USB-IF (currently $2500/year), a Vendor ID is included along with other benefits such as admittance to compliance workshops. The Vendor ID and a Product ID assigned by the vendor are embedded in each device to identify the device to the operating system.

The fee is no problem for developers of high-volume products but can be an impediment to developers who expect to sell small quantities of inexpensive devices. With a few controllers that use the chip vendor's driver and require no vendor programming for the USB interface, peripheral developers can use the chip manufacturer's Vendor ID and a Product ID that the chip manufacturer assigns to the peripheral developer.

Evolution of an Interface

The main reason that new interfaces don't come around very often is that existing interfaces have the irresistible pull of all of the peripherals that users don't want to scrap. Using an existing interface also saves the time and expense of designing a new interface. This is why the designers of the original IBM PC chose compatibility with the existing Centronics parallel interface and the RS-232 serial-port interface—to speed up the design process and enable users to connect to printers and modems already on the market. These interfaces proved serviceable for close to two decades. But as computers became more powerful and the number and kinds of peripherals increased, the older interfaces became a bottleneck of slow communications with limited options for expansion.

A break with tradition is justified when the desire for enhancements is greater than the inconvenience and expense of change. This is the situation that prompted the development of USB.

The copyright on the USB 2.0 specification is assigned jointly to seven corporations, all heavily involved with PC hardware or software: Compaq, Hewlett-Packard, Intel, Lucent, Microsoft, NEC, and Philips. The USB-IF's Web site has the USB 2.0 specification, related documents, and other information for developers and end users.

Original USB

Version 1.0 of the USB specification was released in January 1996. Version 1.1 is dated September 1998. USB 1.1 added one new transfer type (interrupt OUT). In this book, *USB 1.x* refers to USB 1.0 and 1.1. April 2000 saw the release of USB 2.0 which added the option to use high speed. Engineering Change Notices (ECNs) contain revisions and additions to the specification, including defining a new mini-B connector, specifying a way for devices to use bus pull-up and pull-down resistors with looser tolerances, and defining a new descriptor type (the Interface Association Descriptor).

USB capability first became available on PCs with the release of Windows 95's OEM Service Release 2, available only to vendors installing Windows 95 on the PCs they sold. The USB support in these versions was limited and buggy, and there weren't a lot of USB peripherals available, so use of USB was limited in this era.

Things improved with the release of Windows 98 in June 1998. By this time, many more vendors had USB peripherals available, and USB began to take hold as a popular interface. Windows 98 Second Edition (SE) fixed some bugs and further enhanced the USB support. The original version of Windows 98 is called Windows 98 Gold, to distinguish it from Windows 98 SE.

This book concentrates on PCs running Windows 98 and later Windows editions. Windows NT4 preceded Windows 98 and doesn't support USB. Windows 2000, Windows Me, Windows XP, and Windows Server 2003 all support USB.

In this book, the term *PC* includes all of the various computers that share the common ancestor of the original IBM PC. The expression *Windows 98 and later* means Windows 98, Windows 98 SE, Windows 2000, Windows Me, Windows XP, and Windows Server 2003, and is also likely to apply to any Windows editions that follow. A USB-capable PC is assumed to be using Windows 98 or later. A host computer is any computer that can communicate with USB peripherals.

USB 2.0

As USB 1.x gained in popularity, it became clear that a faster bus speed would be useful. Investigation showed that a bus speed forty times faster than full speed could remain backwards-compatible with the low- and full-speed interfaces. Version 2.0's support for a bus speed of 480 Megabits/sec. makes USB much more attractive for peripherals such as printers, scanners, disk drives, and video.

An external USB 2.0 hub must support all three speeds. Other USB 2.0 devices can support low, full, or high speed or a combination. USB 2.0 is backwards compatible with USB 1.1. In other words, USB 2.0 peripherals can use the same connectors and cables as 1.x peripherals, and a USB 2.0 peripheral works when connected to a PC that supports USB 1.x or 2.0. To use high speed, a high-speed-capable device must connect under a 2.0 host computer, and all hubs between the host computer and the device must be 2.0 hubs. Version 2.0 hosts and hubs can also communicate with 1.x peripherals. A 2.0-compliant hub with a slower device attached converts between speeds as needed. This ability increases the complexity of 2.0 hubs but conserves bus bandwidth without requiring different hubs for different speeds.

When USB 2.0 devices first became available, there was confusion among users about whether all USB 2.0 devices supported high speed. In an attempt to reduce the confusion, the USB-IF released naming and packaging recommendations that emphasize speed and compatibility rather than USB version numbers. The recommendations say that a product that supports high speed should be labeled a "Hi-Speed USB" product, and messages on the packaging might include "Fully compatible with Original

USB" and "Compatible with the USB 2.0 Specification." A product that supports low or full speed only is a "USB" product, and the recommended messages on packaging are "Compatible with the USB 2.0 Specification" and "Works with USB and Hi-Speed USB systems, peripherals and cables." Manufacturers should avoid references to low or full speed on consumer packaging.

USB On-The-Go

As USB became the interface of choice for all kinds of peripherals, developers began to ask for a way to connect their peripherals directly to each other and to other USB peripherals. For example, a user might want to attach a printer directly to a camera or connect two drives together to exchange files. The On-The-Go (OTG) Supplement to the USB 2.0 Specification released in 2001 defines a limited-capability host function that devices can implement to enable communicating with peripherals.

Wireless USB

An enhancement under development for USB is a Wireless USB specification to enable wireless communications with devices at up to 480 Megabits/sec. The specification should be available in 2005.

USB versus IEEE-1394

Another popular interface choice for new peripherals is IEEE-1394. Apple Computer's implementation of the interface is called Firewire. Generally, IEEE-1394 can be faster and more flexible than USB but is more expensive to implement. With USB, a single host controls communications with many devices. The host handles most of the complexity, so the devices' electronics can be relatively simple and inexpensive. IEEE-1394 devices can communicate with each other directly, and a single communication can be directed to multiple receivers. The result is a more flexible interface, but the devices' electronics are more complex and expensive.

IEEE-1394 is best suited for applications that require extremely fast communications or broadcasting to multiple receivers. USB is best suited for common peripherals such as keyboards, printers, and scanners, as well as low- to moderate-speed and cost-sensitive applications. For many devices, such as drives, either interface works well, and in fact some devices include both interfaces.

USB versus Ethernet

For some applications, the choice is between USB and Ethernet. Ethernet's advantages include the ability to use very long cables, broadcasting ability, and support for Internet protocols in PCs and Ethernet-capable development systems. Like IEEE-1394, however, the hardware required to support Ethernet is more complex and expensive than typical USB peripheral hardware. USB is also more versatile with four transfer types and a variety of defined classes for different purposes.

Bus Components

The physical components of the Universal Serial Bus consist of the circuits, connectors, and cables between a host and one or more devices.

The host is a PC or other computer that contains a USB host controller and a root hub. These components work together to enable the operating system to communicate with the devices on the bus. The host controller formats data for transmitting on the bus and translates received data to a format that operating-system components can understand. The host controller also performs other functions related to managing communications on the bus. The root hub has one or more connectors for attaching devices. The root hub, in combination with the host controller, detects attached and removed devices, carries out requests from the host controller, and passes data between devices and the host controller.

The devices are the peripherals and additional hubs that connect to the bus. A hub has one or more ports for connecting devices. Each device must contain circuits and code that know how to communicate with the host. The USB specification defines the cables and connectors that connect devices to hubs.

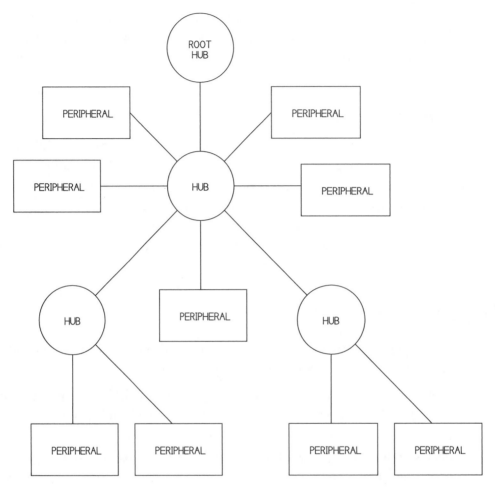

Figure 1-1: USB uses a tiered star topology, where each hub is the center of a star that can connect to peripherals or additional hubs.

Topology

The topology, or arrangement of connections, on the bus is a tiered star (Figure 1-1). At the center of each star is a hub. Each point on a star is a device that connects to a port on a hub. The number of points on each star can vary, with a typical hub having two, four, or seven ports. When there are multiple hubs in series, you can think of them as connecting in a tier, or series, one above the next.

The tiered star describes only the physical connections. In programming, all that matters is the logical connection. To communicate, the host and device don't need to know or care how many hubs the communication passes through.

Only one device at a time can communicate with a host controller. To increase the available bandwidth for USB devices, a PC can have multiple host controllers.

Figure 1-2 shows a few possible configurations for a PC with two USB connectors. Some devices are compound devices that contain both a peripheral and a hub. You can cascade up to five external hubs in series, up to a total of 127 peripherals and hubs including the root hub. However, it may be impractical to have this many devices communicating with a single host controller.

In some cases, especially with compound devices where the hubs are hidden inside the peripherals, the peripherals may appear to be using a daisy-chain type of connection, where each new peripheral hooks to the last one in a chain. But the USB's topology is more flexible and complicated than a daisy chain. Each peripheral connects to a hub that manages communications with the host, and the peripherals and hubs aren't limited to connecting in a single chain.

Defining Terms

In the universe of USB, several everyday words have specific meanings. Along with *host*, defined earlier as the computer that controls the interface, three other such terms are *function, hub,* and *device.* It's also important to understand the concept of a USB port and how it differs from other ports such as RS-232.

Function

The USB specification defines a function as a device that provides a capability to the host. Examples of functions are a mouse, a set of speakers, or a

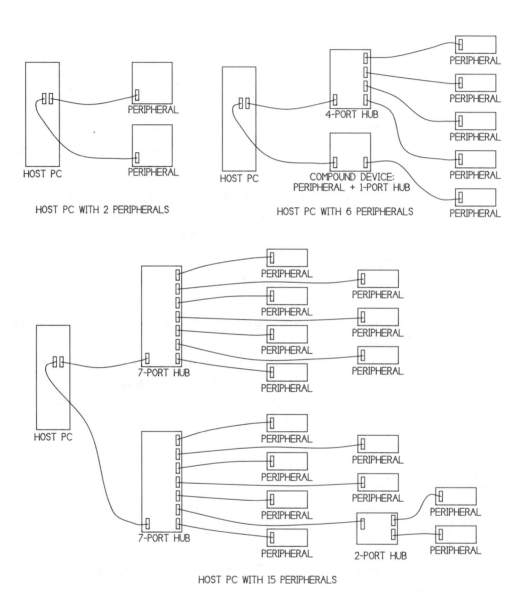

Figure 1-2: There are many possible configurations for connecting USB devices to a host PC. These are a few of the options for a host with two ports.

data-acquisition unit. A single physical device can contain more than one function.

Hub

A hub has one upstream connector for communicating with the host and one or more downstream connectors or internal connections to embedded devices. Each downstream connector or internal connection represents a USB port.

A 1.x hub repeats received USB traffic in both directions, manages power, and sends and responds to status and control messages. A 2.0 hub does all of this and also supports high speed, converting as needed between speeds.

Device

The USB specification's definition of a device is a function or a hub, except for the special case of the compound device, which contains a hub and one or more functions. The host treats a compound device in much the same way as if the hub and its functions were separate physical devices. Every device on the bus has a unique address, except again for a compound device, whose hub and functions each have unique addresses.

A composite device is a multi-function device with multiple, independent interfaces. The interfaces are defined by interface descriptors stored in the device. A composite device has one address on the bus but each interface has a different function and specifies its own device driver on the host. For example, a composite device could have one interface for an audio device and another interface for a control panel. Some Microsoft documentation uses the term composite device to refer to any device whose function is defined by its interface descriptor, rather than its device descriptor, whether or not there is more than one active interface.

Port

In a general sense, a computer port is an addressable location that is available for attaching additional circuits. Usually the circuits terminate at a connector that enables attaching a cable to a peripheral. Some peripheral circuits are hard-wired to a port. Software can monitor and control the port circuits by reading and writing to the port's address. Computer memory also consists of addressable locations, but the CPU typically accesses memory with different machine instructions than are used for accessing ports.

USB ports differ from many other ports because all of the ports on a bus share a single path to the host and aren't directly addressable. With the RS-232 interface, each port is on the PC and independent from the others. If you have two RS-232 ports, each has its own data path, and each cable carries its own data and no one else's. The two ports can send and receive data at the same time.

With USB, each host controller manages a single bus, or data path. Each connector on a bus represents a USB port, but unlike RS-232, all devices share the bus's bandwidth. So even though a USB host controller can communicate with multiple ports, each with its own connector and cable, one data path serves all. Only one device or the host may transmit at a time. A single computer can have multiple USB host controllers, however, each with its own bus. Other interfaces where multiple devices can share a data path include IEEE-1394, SCSI, and Ethernet.

Another difference with USB is that a bus can have ports on hubs that are external to the host controller's PC.

Division of Labor

The host and its devices each have defined responsibilities. The host bears most of the burden of managing communications, but a device must have the intelligence to respond to communications and other bus events from the host and the hub the device attaches to.

The Host's Duties

To communicate with USB devices, a computer needs hardware and software support that enable the computer to function as a USB host. The hardware consists of a USB host controller and a root hub with one or more USB ports. The software support is an operating system that provides a mechanism for drivers to communicate with the USB hardware.

Just about any recent PC will have a USB host controller and two or more USB-port connectors. Many PCs have multiple host controllers. If a computer doesn't have USB support built into its motherboard, you can add a host controller on an expansion card that plugs into a slot on the PCI bus. For portable computers, USB controllers on PC cards are available.

The host is in charge of the bus. The host has to know what devices are on the bus and the capabilities of each device. The host must also do its best to ensure that all devices on the bus can send and receive data as needed. A bus may have many devices, each with different requirements, and all wanting to transfer data at the same time. The host's job is not trivial.

Fortunately, the host-controller hardware and the host-controller drivers in Windows do much of the work of managing the bus. Each device attached to the host must also have a device driver that enables applications to communicate with the device. Some peripherals can use device drivers included with Windows. Other devices use drivers provided by the device manufacturer. Various system-level software components manage communications between the device driver and the host-controller and root-hub hardware.

Applications don't have to worry about the USB-specific details of communicating with devices. All the application has to do is send and receive data using standard operating-system functions that are accessible from just about all programming languages. Often the application doesn't have to know or care whether the device uses USB or another interface.

The host performs the tasks below. The descriptions are in general terms. Later chapters have more specifics.

Detect Devices

On power-up, the hubs make the host aware of all attached USB devices. In a process called enumeration, the host assigns an address and requests additional information from each device. After power-up, whenever a device is removed or attached, the host learns of the event and enumerates any newly attached device and removes any detached device from its list of devices available to applications.

Manage Data Flow

The host manages the flow of data on the bus. Multiple peripherals may want to transfer data at the same time. The host controller divides the available time into segments called frames and microframes and gives each transmission a portion of a frame or microframe.

Transfers that must occur at specific rate are guaranteed to have the amount of time they need in each frame. During enumeration, a device's driver requests the bandwidth it will need for any transfers that must have guaranteed timing. If the bandwidth isn't available, the host doesn't allow communications to begin. The driver must then request a smaller portion of the bandwidth or wait until the requested bandwidth is available. Transfers that have no guaranteed timing use the remaining portion of the frames and must wait if the bus is busy.

Error Checking

When transferring data, the host adds error-checking bits. On receiving data, the device performs calculations on the data and compares the results with the received error-checking bits. If the results don't match, the device doesn't acknowledge receiving the data and the host knows that it should retransmit. USB also supports one transfer type that doesn't allow re-transmitting, in the interest of maintaining a constant transfer rate. In a similar way, the host error-checks the data received from devices.

The host may receive other indications that a device can't send or receive data. The host can then inform the device's driver of the problem, and the driver can notify the application so it can take appropriate action.

Provide Power

In addition to its two signal wires, a USB cable has +5V and ground wires. Some devices draw all of their power from these wires. The host provides power to all devices on power-up or attachment, and works with the devices to conserve power when possible. A high-power, bus-powered device can draw up to 500 milliamperes. The ports on a battery-powered host or hub may support only low-power devices, which are limited to 100 milliamperes. A device may also have its own power supply.

Exchange Data with Peripherals

All of the above tasks support the host's main job, which is to exchange data with peripherals. In some cases, a device driver requests the host to attempt to send or receive data at defined intervals, while in others the host communicates only when an application or other software component requests a transfer. The device driver reports any problems to the appropriate application.

The Peripheral's Duties

In many ways, the peripheral's duties are a mirror image of the host's. When the host initiates communications, the peripheral must respond. But peripherals also have duties that are unique. A peripheral can't begin USB communications on its own. Instead, the peripheral must wait and respond to a communication from the host. (An exception is the remote wakeup feature, which enables a peripheral to request communications from the host.)

The USB controller in the peripheral handles many of the device's responsibilities in hardware. The amount of support required by device firmware varies with the chip.

The peripheral must perform all of the tasks described below. The descriptions are in general terms. Later chapters have more specifics.

Detect Communications Directed to the Chip

Each device monitors the device address contained in each communication on the bus. If the address doesn't match the device's stored address, the device ignores the communication. If the address matches, the device stores the data in its receive buffer and triggers an interrupt to indicate that data has arrived. In almost all chips, these functions are built into the hardware and require no support in code. The firmware doesn't have to take action or make decisions until the chip has detected a communication containing the device's address.

Respond to Standard Requests

On power-up, or when the device attaches to a powered system, a device must respond to standard requests sent by the host during enumeration. The host may also send requests any time after enumeration completes.

All devices must respond to these requests, which query the capabilities and status of the device or request the device to take other action. On receiving a request, the device places data or status information in a transmit buffer to send to the host. For some requests, such as selecting a configuration, the device takes other action in addition to responding with information.

The USB specification defines eleven requests, and a class or vendor may define additional requests. A device doesn't have to carry out every request, however; the device just has to respond to the request in an understandable way. For example, when the host requests a configuration that the device doesn't support, the device responds with a code that indicates that the configuration isn't supported.

Error Check

Like the host, a device adds error-checking bits to the data it sends. On receiving data that includes error-checking bits, the device does the error-checking calculations. The device's response or lack of response tells the host whether to re-transmit. These functions are typically built into the controller's hardware and don't need to be programmed. When appropriate, the device also detects the acknowledgement the host returns on receiving data from the device.

Manage Power

A device may be bus-powered or have its own power supply. For devices that use bus power, when there is no bus activity, the device must limit its use of bus current. When the host enters a low-power state, all communications on the bus cease, including the periodic timing markers the host normally sends. On detecting the absence of bus activity for three milliseconds, a device must enter the Suspend state and limit the current drawn from the bus. While in the Suspend state, the device must continue to monitor the bus and exit the Suspend state when bus activity resumes.

Devices that don't support the remote-wakeup feature should consume no more than 500 microamperes from the bus in the Suspend state. If a device supports the remote-wakeup feature and the host has enabled the feature, the limit is 2.5 milliamperes. These are average values over 1 second; the peak current can be greater.

Exchange Data with the Host

All of the above tasks support the main job of the device's USB port, which is to exchange data with the host. After being configured, the device must respond to communications that may contain data and may require the device to return data or status information. The device's capabilities, the host's device driver, and the applications that use the device together determine the type of communications and when they occur.

For most transfers where the host sends data to the device, the device must respond to each transfer attempt by sending a code that indicates whether the device accepted the data or was too busy to handle it. For most transfers where the device sends data to the host, the device must respond to each attempt by returning data or a code indicating there was no data to send or the device was busy. Typically, the hardware responds automatically according to settings made previously in firmware. Some transfers don't use acknowledgements and the sender assumes the receiver has received all transmitted data.

The controller chip's hardware handles the details of formatting the data for the bus. The formatting includes adding error-checking bits to data to transmit, checking for errors in received data, and sending and receiving the individual bits on the bus.

Of course, the device must also do anything else it's responsible for. For example, a mouse must be ready to detect movement and button clicks, a data-acquisition unit has to read the data from its sensors, and a printer must translate received data into images on paper.

What about Speed?

A device controller may support one or more bus speeds. Virtually all hubs support low- and full-speed devices. The exception is a hub in a compound device whose functions use a single speed. A low- or full-speed peripheral can connect to any USB hub. Users don't have to know whether a device is low or full speed because there are no user settings or configurations for different speeds.

High-speed peripherals are likely to be dual-speed devices that also function at full speed. A 1.x host or hub doesn't support high speed because high speed didn't exist when the 1.x specifications were written. To ensure that high-speed devices don't confuse 1.x hosts and hubs, all high-speed devices must at least respond to standard enumeration requests at full speed. Any host can thus identify any attached device.

Other than responding to bus reset and standard requests at full speed, a high-speed device doesn't have to function at full speed. But because adding support for full speed is easy to do and is required to pass the USB IF's compliance tests, most high-speed devices also function at full speed.

The actual rate of data transfer between a peripheral and host is less than the bus speed and isn't always predictable. Some of the transmitted bits are used for identifying, synchronizing, and error-checking, and the data rate also depends on the type of transfer and how busy the bus is.

For time-sensitive data, USB supports transfer types that have a guaranteed rate or guaranteed maximum latency. Isochronous transfers have a guaranteed rate, where the host can request a specific number of bytes to transfer to or from a peripheral at defined intervals. The intervals can be as often as every millisecond at full speed or every 125 microseconds at high speed. Isochronous transfers have no error correcting, however. Interrupt transfers have error correcting and guaranteed maximum latency, which means that a precise rate isn't guaranteed, but the time between transfer attempts will be no greater than a specified period. At low speed, the requested maximum interval can range from 10 to 255 milliseconds. At full speed, the range is 1 to 255 milliseconds. At high speed, the range is 125 microseconds to 4.096 seconds.

Because the bus is shared, there's no guarantee that a particular rate or maximum latency will be available to a device. If the bus is too busy to allow a requested rate or maximum latency, the host refuses to complete the configuration process that enables the host to attempt the transfers. To take full advantage of reserved bandwidth, the device driver and application software or device firmware must ensure that data is available to send when the host controller is ready to initiate the transfer. The receiver of the data must also be ready to accept the data when it arrives.

At full and high speeds, the fastest transfers on an otherwise idle bus are bulk transfers, with a theoretical maximum of 1.216 Megabytes/sec. at full speed and 53.248 Megabytes/sec. at high speed. The host controller may limit a single bulk transfer to a slower rate, however. The transfers with the most guaranteed bandwidth are high-speed interrupt and isochronous transfers at 24.576 Megabytes/second.

Although the low-speed bus speed is 1.5 Megabits/sec., the fastest guaranteed delivery for the data in a single transfer is 8 bytes every 10 milliseconds, or just 800 bytes/sec.

Developing a Device

Designing a USB product for PCs involves both getting the peripheral up and running and developing or obtaining PC software needed to communicate with the peripheral.

Elements in the Link

A USB peripheral needs all of the following:

- A controller chip with a USB interface.
- Code in the peripheral to carry out the USB communications.
- Whatever hardware and code the peripheral needs to carry out its other functions (processing data, reading inputs, writing to outputs).
- A host that supports USB.

- Device-driver software on the host to enable applications to communicate with the peripheral.

- If the peripheral isn't a standard type supported by the operating system, the host must have application software to enable users to access the peripheral. For standard peripheral types such as a mouse, keyboard, or disk drive, you don't need custom application software, though you may want to write a test application.

Tools for Developing

To develop a USB peripheral, you need the following tools:

- An assembler or compiler to create the device firmware (the code that runs inside the device's controller chip).

- A device programmer or development kit that enables you to store the assembled or compiled code in the controller's program memory.

- A programming language and development environment on the host for writing and debugging the host software. The host software may include a device driver or filter driver and/or application code. To write a device driver, you'll need Microsoft's Windows Driver Development Kit (DDK).

- Also recommended are a monitor program for debugging the device firmware and a protocol analyzer to enable viewing USB traffic.

Steps in Developing a Project

For a project of any size, you'll want to create the project in modules and get each piece working before moving on to the next. In writing the firmware, you can begin by writing just enough code to enable Windows to detect and enumerate the device. When that code is working, you can move on to exchanging small blocks of data with applications. From there you can add specific code for your application. The steps in project development include initial decisions, enumerating, and exchanging data.

Initial Decisions

Before you begin the developing, you need to gather data and make some decisions:

1. Specify the requirements of your device. For the USB interface, how much data does it need to transfer, and how fast? Do you need error correcting? How much power will the device draw? What else does the device need to do?

2. From your requirements, decide whether the PC will communicate with the peripheral using Windows' built-in drivers, a generic device driver from another source, or a custom driver.

3. Select a controller chip that matches your requirements.

Enumerating

Here's what you need to do to get Windows to enumerate your device:

1. Write the code the controller chip needs to be enumerated by its host. The details vary with the chip, but every chip must be able send a series of descriptors to the host. The descriptors are data structures that describe the device's USB capabilities and how they'll be used. The chip must have program code or hardware that decodes and responds to the requests that the host sends and other events that occur when the host enumerates the device. Chip vendors generally provide example code that you can modify. A few controllers can enumerate with no user code required.

2. Identify or create a device driver and INF (information) file so that Windows can identify the device and assign a driver. The INF file is a text file that names the driver the device will use on the host computer. If your device fits a class supported by Windows, you may be able to use an INF file included with Windows.

3. If necessary, design and build a circuit to enable testing the chip and your firmware. In many cases, you can use a development board available from the chip's manufacturer.

4. Load the code into the device and plug the device into the host's bus. Windows should enumerate the device, adding it to the Control Panel and identifying it correctly.

5. Debug and repeat as needed!

Exchanging Data

When the device enumerates successfully, you can add components and code to enable the device to carry out its intended function. If needed, write application code to communicate with and test the device. When the code is debugged, you're ready to program the code into the chip and test on your final hardware.

But before you begin, it's useful to know a little more about how the host enumerates and transfers data with devices, so you can make the right choices about controller chips and drivers. This is the purpose of the following chapters.

2

Inside USB Transfers

This and the next three chapters are a tutorial on USB transfers. This chapter has essentials that apply to all transfers. The following chapters cover the four transfer types supported by USB, the enumeration process, and the standard requests used in control transfers.

You don't need to know every bit of this information to get a project up and running, but understanding something about how transfers work can help in deciding which transfer types to use, writing device firmware, and debugging.

The information in these chapters is dense. If you don't have a background in USB, you won't absorb it all in one reading. You should, however, get a feel for how USB works, and will know where to look later when you need to check the details.

The ultimate authority on the USB interface is the specification document, *Universal Serial Bus Specification,* available on the USB-IF's Web site. By design, the specification omits information and tips that are unique to any operating system or controller chip. This type of information is essential when you're designing a product for the real world, so I include this information where relevant.

Transfer Basics

You can divide USB communications into two categories: communications used in enumerating the device and communications used by the applications that carry out the device's purpose. During enumeration, the host learns about the device and prepares it for exchanging data. Application communications occur when the host exchanges data that performs the functions the device is designed for. For example, for a keyboard, the application communications are the sending of keypress data to the host to tell an application to display a character or perform another action.

Enumeration Communications

During enumeration, the device's firmware responds to a series of standard requests from the host. The device must identify each request, return requested information, and take other actions specified by the requests.

On PCs, Windows performs the enumeration, so there's no user programming involved. However, to complete the enumeration, on first attachment, Windows must locate an INF file that identifies the file name and location of the device's driver. If the required files are available and the firmware functions correctly, the enumeration process is generally invisible to users. Chapter 9 has more details about device drivers and INF files.

Application Communications

After the host has exchanged enumeration information with the device and a device driver has been assigned and loaded, the application communications can begin. At the host, applications can use standard Windows API functions or other software components to read and write to the device. At the device, transferring data typically requires either placing data to send in the USB controller's transmit buffer or retrieving received data from the receive buffer, and on completing a transfer, ensuring that the device is ready

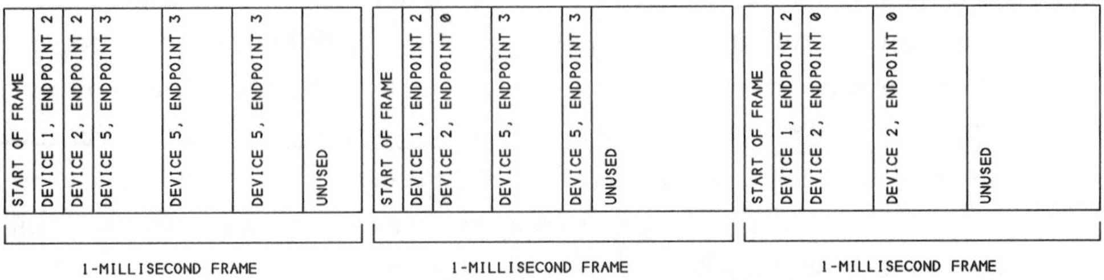

Figure 2-1: At low and full speeds, the host schedules transactions within 1-millisecond frames.The host may schedule transactions anywhere it wants within a frame. The process is similar at high speed, but using 125-microsecond microframes.

for the next transfer. Most devices also require additional firmware support for handling errors and other events. Each data transfer uses one of the four transfer types: control, interrupt, bulk, or isochronous. Each has a format and protocol to suit different needs.

Managing Data on the Bus

USB's two signal lines carry data to and from all of the devices on the bus. The wires form a single transmission path that all of the devices must share. (As explained later in this chapter, an exception is a cable segment between a 1.x device and a 2.0 hub on a high-speed bus, but even here, all data shares a path between the hub and host.) Unlike RS-232, which has a TX line to carry data in one direction and an RX line for the other direction, USB's pair of wires carries a single differential signal, with the directions taking turns.

The host is in charge of seeing that all transfers occur as quickly as possible. The host manages the traffic by dividing time into chunks called frames (at low and full speeds) or microframes (at high speed). The host allocates a portion of each frame or microframe to each transfer (Figure 2-1). A frame has a period of one millisecond. For high speed traffic, the host divides each frame into eight 125-microsecond microframes. Each frame or microframe begins with a Start-of-Frame timing reference.

Each transfer consists of one or more transactions. Control transfers always have multiple transactions because they have multiple stages, each consisting of one or more transactions. Other transfer types use multiple transactions when they have more data than will fit in a single transaction. Depending on how the host schedules the transactions and the speed of a device's response, a transfer's transactions may all be in a single frame or microframe, or they may be spread over multiple (micro)frames.

Because all of the traffic shares a data path, each transaction must include a device address that identifies the transaction's destination. Every device has a unique address assigned by the host, and all data travels to or from the host. Each transaction begins when the host sends a block of information that includes the address of the receiving device and a specific location, called an endpoint, within the device. Everything a device sends is in response to receiving a packet sent by the host.

Host Speed and Bus Speed

USB 2.0 hosts in general-purpose PCs support low, full, and high speeds. A 1.x host supports low and full speeds only. (Special-purpose hosts, typically found in small embedded systems, don't always support all speeds.)

A 1.x hub doesn't convert between speeds; it just passes received traffic up or down the bus, changing only the edge rate and signal polarity of traffic to and from attached low-speed devices. In contrast, a 2.0 hub acts as a remote processor with store-and-forward capabilities. The hub converts between high speed and low or full speed as needed and performs other functions that help make efficient use of the bus time. The added intelligence of 2.0 hubs is a major reason why the high-speed bus remains compatible with 1.x hardware.

The traffic on a bus segment is high speed only if the device is high speed and the host controller and all hubs between the host and device are 2.0-compliant. Figure 2-2 illustrates. A high-speed bus may also have 1.x hubs, and if so, any bus segments downstream from this hub (away from the host) are low or full speed. Traffic to and from low- and full-speed devices travels at high speed between the host and any 2.0 hubs that connect to the host with no 1.x hubs between. Traffic between a 2.0 hub and a 1.x hub or another low- or full-speed device travels at low or full speed. A bus with only a 1.x host controller supports only low and full speeds, even if the bus has 2.0 hubs and high-speed-capable devices.

Elements of a Transfer

Every USB transfer consists of one or more transactions, and each transaction in turn contains packets that contain information. To understand transactions, packets, and their contents, you also need to know about endpoints and pipes. So that's where we'll begin.

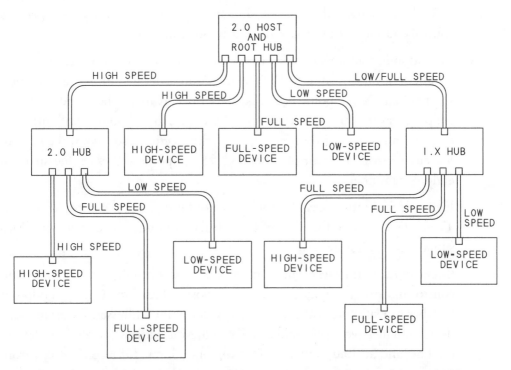

Figure 2-2: A USB 2.0 hub uses high speed whenever possible, switching to low and full speeds when necessary.

Device Endpoints: the Source and Sink of Data

All bus traffic travels to or from a device endpoint. The endpoint is a buffer that stores multiple bytes. Typically the endpoint is a block of data memory or a register in the controller chip. The data stored at an endpoint may be received data or data waiting to transmit. The host also has buffers that hold received data and data waiting to transmit, but the host doesn't have endpoints. Instead, the host serves as the start and finish for communications with device endpoints.

The USB specification defines a device endpoint as "a uniquely addressable portion of a USB device that is the source or sink of information in a communication flow between the host and device." This definition suggests that an endpoint carries data in one direction only. However, as I'll explain, a control endpoint is a special case that is bidirectional.

An endpoint's address consists of an endpoint number and direction. The number is a value from 0 to 15. The direction is defined from the host's perspective: an IN endpoint providess data to send to the host and an OUT endpoint stores data received from the host. An endpoint configured for control transfers must transfer data in both directions, so a control endpoint actually consists of a pair of IN and OUT endpoint addresses that share an endpoint number.

Every device must have Endpoint 0 configured as a control endpoint. There's rarely a need for additional control endpoints. Some controller chips support them, however.

Other types of transfers send data in one direction only, though status and control information may flow in the opposite direction. A single endpoint number can support both IN and OUT endpoint addresses. For example, a device might have an Endpoint 1 IN endpoint address for sending data to the host and an Endpoint 1 OUT endpoint address for receiving data from the host.

In addition to Endpoint 0, a full- or high-speed device can have up to 30 additional endpoint addresses (1 through 15, with each supporting both IN and OUT transfers). A low-speed device is limited to two additional endpoint addresses in any combination of directions (for example, Endpoint 1 IN and Endpoint 1 OUT or Endpoint 1 IN and Endpoint 2 IN).

Every transaction on the bus begins with a packet that contains an endpoint number and a code that indicates the direction of data flow and whether or not the transaction is initiating a control transfer. The codes are IN, OUT, and Setup:

Transaction Type	Source of Data	Types of Transfers that Use this Transaction Type	Contents
IN	device	all	data or status information
OUT	host	all	data or status information
Setup	host	control	a request

As with the endpoint directions, the naming convention for IN and OUT transactions is from the perspective of the host. In an IN transaction, data travels from the device to the host. In an OUT transaction, data travels from the host to the device.

A Setup transaction is like an OUT transaction because data travels from the host to the device, but a Setup transaction is a special case because it initiates a control transfer. Devices need to identify Setup transactions because these are the only type of transactions that devices must always accept and because the device needs to identify and respond to the request contained in the received data. Any transfer type may use IN or OUT transactions.

Each transaction contains a device address and an endpoint address. When a device receives an OUT or Setup packet containing the device's address, the endpoint stores the data that follows the OUT or Setup packet and the hardware typically triggers an interrupt. An interrupt-service routine in the device can then process the received data and take any other required action. When a device receives an IN packet containing its device address, if the device has data ready to send to the host, the hardware sends the data from the specified endpoint onto the bus and typically triggers an interrupt. An interrupt-service routine in the device can then do whatever is needed to get ready for the next IN transaction.

Pipes: Connecting Endpoints to the Host

Before a transfer can occur, the host and device must establish a pipe. A USB pipe is an association between a device's endpoint and the host controller's software.

The host establishes pipes during enumeration. If the device is removed from the bus, the host removes the no-longer-needed pipes. The host may also request new pipes or remove unneeded pipes at other times by requesting an alternate configuration or interface for a device. Every device has a Default Control Pipe that uses Endpoint 0.

The configuration information received by the host includes an endpoint descriptor for each endpoint that the device wants to use. Each endpoint descriptor is a block of information that tells the host what it needs to know about the endpoint in order to communicate with it. The information includes the endpoint address, the type of transfer to use, the maximum size of data packets, and, when appropriate, the desired interval for transfers.

Types of Transfers

USB is designed to handle many types of peripherals with varying requirements for transfer rate, response time, and error correcting. The four types of data transfers each handle different needs, and a device can support the transfer types that are best suited for its purpose. Table 2-1 summarizes the features and uses of each transfer type.

Control transfers are the only type that have functions defined by the USB specification. Control transfers enable the host to read information about a device, set a device's address, and select configurations and other settings. Control transfers may also send vendor-specific requests that send and receive data for any purpose. All USB devices must support control transfers.

Table 2-1: Each of the USB's four transfer types is suited for different uses.

Transfer Type	Control	Bulk	Interrupt	Isochronous
Typical Use	Identification and configuration	Printer, scanner, drive	Mouse, keyboard	Streaming audio, video
Required?	yes	no	no	no
Low speed allowed?	yes	no	yes	no
Data bytes/millisecond per transfer, maximum possible per pipe (high speed).*	15,872 (thirty-one 64-byte transactions/ microframe)	53,248 (thirteen 512-byte transactions/ microframe)	24,576 (three 1024-byte transactions/ microframe)	24,576 (three 1024-byte transactions/ microframe)
Data bytes/millisecond per transfer, maximum possible per pipe (full speed).*	832 (thirteen 64-byte transactions/ frame)	1216 (nineteen 64-byte transactions/ frame)	64 (one 64-byte transaction/ frame)	1023 (one 1023-byte transaction/ frame)
Data bytes/millisecond per transfer, maximum possible per pipe (low speed).*	24 (three 8-byte transactions)	not allowed	0.8 (8 bytes per 10 milliseconds)	not allowed
Direction of data flow	IN and OUT	IN or OUT	IN or OUT (USB 1.0 supports IN only)	IN or OUT
Reserved bandwidth for all transfers of the type (percent)	10 at low/full speed, 20 at high speed (minimum)	none	90 at low/full speed, 80 at high speed (isochronous & interrupt combined, maximum)	
Error correction?	yes	yes	yes	no
Message or Stream data?	message	stream	stream	stream
Guaranteed delivery rate?	no	no	no	yes
Guaranteed latency (maximum time between transfers)?	no	no	yes	yes
*Assumes transfers use maximum packet size.				

Bulk transfers are intended for situations where the rate of transfer isn't critical, such as sending a file to a printer, receiving data from a scanner, or accessing files on a drive. For these applications, quick transfers are nice but the data can wait if necessary. If the bus is very busy, bulk transfers are delayed, but if the bus is otherwise idle, bulk transfers are very fast. Only full- and high-speed devices can do bulk transfers. Devices aren't required to support bulk transfers, but a specific device class might require them.

Interrupt transfers are for devices that must receive the host's or device's attention periodically. Other than control transfers, interrupt transfers are the only way that low-speed devices can transfer data. Keyboards and mice use interrupt transfers to send keypress and mouse-movement data. Interrupt transfers can use any speed. Devices aren't required to support interrupt transfers, but a specific device class might require them.

Isochronous transfers have guaranteed delivery time but no error correcting. Data that might use isochronous transfers incudes audio or video to be played in real time. Isochronous is the only transfer type that doesn't support automatic re-transmitting of data received with errors, so occasional errors must be acceptable. Only full- and high-speed devices can do isochronous transfers. Devices aren't required to support isochronous transfers, but a specific device class might require them.

Stream and Message Pipes

In addition to classifying a pipe by the type of transfer it carries, the USB specification defines pipes as either stream or message, according to whether or not information travels in one or both directions. Control transfers use bidirectional message pipes; all other transfer types use unidirectional stream pipes.

Control Transfers Use Message Pipes

In a message pipe, each transfer begins with a Setup transaction containing a request. To complete the transfer, the host and device may exchange data and status information, or the device may just send status information. Each control transfer has at least one transaction that sends information in each direction.

If a device supports a received request, the device takes the requested action. If a device doesn't support the request, the device responds with a code to indicate that the request isn't supported.

All Other Transfers Use Stream Pipes

In a stream pipe, the data has no structure defined by the USB specification. The receiving host or device just accepts whatever arrives. The device firmware or host software can then process the data in whatever way is appropriate for the application.

Of course, even with stream data, the sending and receiving devices will need to agree on a format of some type. For example, a host application may define a code that requests a device to send a series of bytes indicating a temperature reading and the time of the reading. Although the host could use control transfers with a vendor-defined Get_Temperature request, interrupt transfers may be preferable because of their guaranteed bandwidth.

Initiating a Transfer

When a device driver in the host wants to communicate with a device, the driver initiates a transfer. The USB specification defines a transfer as the process of making and carrying out a communication request. A transfer may be very short, sending as little as a byte of application data, or very long, sending the contents of a large file.

A Windows application can open communications with a device using a handle retrieved using standard API functions. To begin a transfer, an application may use the handle in calling an API function to request the transfer from the device's driver. An application might request to "send the contents of the file *data.txt* to the device" or "get the contents of Input Report 1 from the device." When an application requests a transfer, the operating system passes the request to the appropriate device driver, which in turn passes the request to other system-level drivers and on to the host controller. The host controller then initiates the transfer on the bus.

For devices in standard classes, a programming language can provide alternate ways to access a device. For example, the .NET Framework includes Directory and File classes for accessing files on drives. A vendor-supplied driver can also define its own API functions. For example, devices that use controllers from FTDI Chip can use FTDI's D2XX driver, which exposes a series of functions for setting communications parameters and exchanging data.

In some cases, a driver is configured to request periodic transfers, and applications can read the retrieved data or provide data to send in these transfers. During enumeration, the operating system initiates transfers. Other transfers require an application to request to send or receive data.

Transactions: the Building Blocks of a Transfer

Figure 2-3 shows the elements of a typical transfer. A lot of the terminology here begins to sound the same. There are transfers and transactions, stages and phases, data transactions and data packets, Status stages and handshake

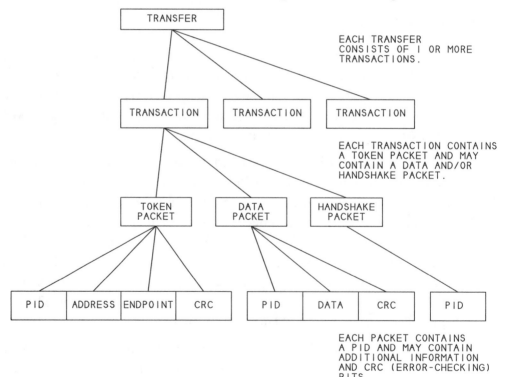

Figure 2-3: A USB transfer consists of transactions. The transactions in turn contain packets, and the packets contain a packet identifier (PID), PID-check bits, and sometimes additional information.

phases. Data stages have handshake packets and Status stages have data packets. It can take a while to absorb it all. Table 2-2 lists the elements that make up each of the four transfer types and may help in keeping the terms straight.

Each transfer consists of one or more transactions, and each transaction in turn consists of one, two, or three packets.

The three transaction types are defined by their purpose and direction of data flow. Setup transactions send control-transfer requests to a device. OUT transactions send other data or status information to the device. IN transactions send data or status information to the host.

The USB specification defines a transaction as the delivery of service to an endpoint. *Service* in this case can mean either the host's sending information to the device, or the host's requesting and receiving information from the device.

Each transaction includes identifying, error-checking, status, and control information as well as any data to be exchanged. A complete transfer may take place over multiple frames or microframes, but a transaction must complete uninterrupted. No other communication on the bus can break into the middle of a transaction. Devices thus must be able to respond quickly with requested data or status information in a transaction. Device firmware typically configures, or arms, an endpoint to respond to received packets, and the hardware responds to the packets when they arrive.

A transfer with a small amount of data may require just one transaction. Other transfers require multiple transactions with a portion of the data in each.

Transaction Phases

Each transaction has up to three phases, or parts that occur in sequence: token, data, and handshake. Each phase consists of one or two transmitted packets. Each packet is a block of information with a defined format. All packets begin with a Packet ID (PID) that contains identifying information (shown in Table 2-3). Depending on the transaction, the PID may be fol-

Table 2-2: Each of the four transfer types consists of one or more transactions, with each transaction containing two or three phases. (This table doesn't show the additional transactions required for the split transactions and PING protocol used in some transfers.)

Transfer Type		Transactions	Phases (packets). Each downstream, low-speed packet is also preceded by a PRE packet.
Control	Setup Stage	One transaction	Token
			Data
			Handshake
	Data Stage	Zero or more transactions (IN or OUT)	Token
			Data
			Handshake
	Status Stage	One transaction (opposite direction of transaction(s) in the Data stage or IN if there is no Data stage)	Token
			Data
			Handshake
Bulk		One or more transactions (IN or OUT)	Token
			Data
			Handshake
Interrupt		One or more transactions (IN or OUT)	Token
			Data
			Handshake
Isochronous		One or more transactions (IN or OUT)	Token
			Data

lowed by an endpoint address, data, status information, or a frame number, along with error-checking bits.

In the token phase of a transaction, the host initiates a communication by sending a token packet. The PID indicates the transaction type, such as Setup, IN, OUT, or Start-of-Frame.

In the data phase, the host or device may transfer any kind of information in a data packet. The PID includes a data-toggle or data-sequencing value used to guard against lost or duplicated data when a transfer has multiple data packets.

Table 2-3: The PID (packet identifier) provides information about a transaction. (Sheet 1 of 2)

Packet Type	PID Name	Value	Transfer types used in	Source	Bus Speed	Description
Token (identifies transaction type)	OUT	0001	all	host	all	Device and endpoint address for OUT (host-to-device) transaction.
	IN	1001	all	host	all	Device and endpoint address for IN (device-to-host) transaction.
	SOF	0101	Start-of-Frame	host	all	Start-of-Frame marker and frame number.
	SETUP	1101	control	host	all	Device and endpoint address for Setup transaction.
Data (carries data or status code)	DATA0	0011	all	host, device	all	Data toggle, data PID sequencing
	DATA1	1011	all	host, device	all	Data toggle, data PID sequencing
	DATA2	0111	isoch.	host, device	high	Data PID sequencing
	MDATA	1111	isoch., split transac- tions	host, device	high	Data PID sequencing
Handshake (carries status code)	ACK	0010	all	host, device	all	Receiver accepts error-free data packet.
	NAK	1010	control, bulk, interrupt	device	all	Receiver can't accept data or sender can't send data or has no data to transmit.
	STALL	1110	control, bulk, interrupt	device	all	A control request isn't sup- ported or the endpoint is halted.
	NYET	0110	control Write, bulk OUT, split transac- tions	device	high	Device accepts error-free data packet but isn't yet ready for another or a hub doesn't yet have complete-split data.

Table 2-3: The PID (packet identifier) provides information about a transaction. (Sheet 2 of 2)

Packet Type	PID Name	Value	Transfer types used in	Source	Bus Speed	Description
Special	PRE	1100	control, interrupt	host	full	Preamble issued by host to indicate that the next packet is low speed.
	ERR	1100	all	hub	high	Returned by a hub to report a low- or full-speed error in a split transaction.
	SPLIT	1000	all	host	high	Precedes a token packet to indicate a split transaction.
	PING	0100	control Write, bulk OUT	host	high	Busy check for bulk OUT and control Write data transactions after NYET.
	reserved	0000	–	–	–	For future use.

In the handshake phase, the host or device sends status information in a handshake packet. The PID contains a status code (ACK, NAK, STALL, or NYET). The USB specification sometimes uses the terms *status phase* and *status packet* to refer to the handshake phase and packet.

The token phase has one additional use. A token packet may carry a Start-of-Frame (SOF) marker, which is a timing reference that the host sends at 1-millisecond intervals at full speed and at 125-microsecond intervals at high speed. This packet also contains a frame number that increments and rolls over on reaching the maximum. The number indicates the frame count, so the eight microframes within a frame all have the same number. An endpoint may synchronize to the Start-of-Frame packet or use the frame count as a timing reference. The Start-of-Frame marker also keeps devices from entering the low-power Suspend state when there is no other USB traffic.

Low-speed devices don't see the SOF packet. Instead, the hub that the device attaches to uses a simpler End-of-Packet (EOP) signal called the low-speed keep-alive signal, sent once per frame. As the SOF does for full-speed devices, the low-speed keep-alive keeps low-speed devices from entering the Suspend state.

Of the four special PIDs, one is used only with low-speed devices, one is used only with high-speed devices, and two are used when a low- or full-speed device's 2.0 hub communicates at high speed with the host.

The special low-speed PID is PRE, which contains a preamble code that tells hubs that the next packet is low speed. On receiving a PRE PID, the hub enables communications with any attached low-speed devices. On a low- and full-speed bus, the PRE PID precedes all token, data, and handshake packets directed to low-speed devices. High-speed buses encode the PRE in the SPLIT packet, rather than sending the PRE separately. Low-speed packets sent by a device don't require a PRE PID.

The PID used only with high-speed devices is PING. In a bulk or control transfer with multiple data packets, before sending the second and any subsequent data packets, the host may send a PING to find out if the endpoint is ready to receive more data. The device responds with a status code.

The SPLIT PID identifies a token packet as part of a split transaction, as explained later in this chapter. The ERR PID is used only in split transactions. A 2.0 hub uses this PID to report an error to the host in a low- or full-speed transaction. The ERR and PRE PIDs have the same value but won't be confused because a hub never sends a PRE to the host or an ERR to a device. Also, ERR is used only on high-speed segments and PRE is never used on high-speed segments.

Packet Sequences

Every transaction has a token packet. The host is always the source of this packet, which sets up the transaction by identifying the packet type, the receiving device and endpoint, and the direction of any data the transaction will transfer. For low-speed transactions on a full-speed bus, a PRE packet precedes the token packet. For split transactions, a SPLIT packet precedes the token packet.

Depending on the transfer type and whether the host or device has information to send, a data packet may follow the token packet. The direction specified in the token packet determines whether the host or device sends the data packet.

In all transfer types except isochronous, the receiver of the data packet (or the device if there is no data packet) returns a handshake packet containing a code that indicates the success or failure of the transaction. The absence of an expected handshake packet indicates a more serious error.

Timing Constraints and Guarantees

The allowed delays between the token, data, and handshake packets of a transaction are very short, intended to allow only for cable delays and switching times plus a brief time to allow the hardware to prepare a response, such as a status code, in response to a received packet.

A common mistake in writing firmware is to assume that the firmware should wait for an interrupt before providing data to send to the host. Instead, before the host requests the data, the firmware must copy the data to send into the endpoint's buffer and configure the endpoint to send the data on receiving an IN token packet. The interrupt occurs after the transaction completes, to tell the firmware that the endpoint's buffer can store data for the next transaction. If the firmware waits for an interrupt before providing the initial data, the interrupt never happens and no data is transferred.

A single transaction can carry an amount of data up to the maximum packet size specified for the endpoint. A data packet that is less than the maximum packet size is a *short packet*. A transfer with multiple transactions may take place over multiple frames or microframes, which don't have to be contiguous. For example, in a full-speed bulk transfer of 512 bytes, the maximum number of bytes in a single transaction is 64, so transferring all of the data requires at least 8 transactions, which may occur in one or more (micro)frames.

Split Transactions

A 2.0 hub communicates with a 2.0 host at high speed unless a 1.x hub lies between them. When a low- or full-speed device is attached to a 2.0 hub, the hub converts between speeds as needed. But speed conversion isn't the only thing a hub does to manage multiple speeds. High speed is 40 times faster than full speed and 320 times faster than low speed. It doesn't make sense for the entire bus to wait while a hub exchanges low- or full-speed data with a device.

The solution is split transactions. A 2.0 host uses split transactions when communicating with a low- or full-speed device on a high-speed bus. What would be a single transaction at low or full speed usually requires two types of split transactions: one or more start-split transactions to send information to the device and one or more complete-split transactions to receive information from the device. The exception is isochronous OUT transactions, which don't use complete-split transactions because the device has nothing to send.

Even though they require more transactions, split transactions make better use of bus time because they minimize the amount of time spent waiting for a low- or full-speed device to transfer data. The USB 2.0 host controller and the closest 2.0 hub upstream from the low- or full-speed device are entirely responsible for performing split transactions. The device and its firmware don't have to know or care whether the host is using split transactions. The transactions at the device are identical whether the host is using split transactions or not. At the host, device drivers and application software don't have to know or care whether the host is using split transactions because the protocol is handled at a lower level. Chapter 15 has more about how split transactions work.

Ensuring that Transfers Are Successful

USB transfers use handshaking and error-checking to help ensure that data gets to its destination as quickly as possible and without errors.

Handshaking

Like other interfaces, USB uses status and control, or handshaking, information to help to manage the flow of data. In hardware handshaking, dedicated lines carry the handshaking information. An example is the RTS and

CTS lines in the RS-232 interface. In software handshaking, the same lines that carry the data also carry handshaking codes. An example is the XON and XOFF codes transmitted on the data lines in RS-232 links.

USB uses software handshaking. A code indicates the success or failure of all transactions except in isochronous transfers. In addition, in control transfers, the Status stage enables a device to report the success or failure of an entire transfer.

Handshaking signals transmit in the handshake or data packet. The defined status codes are ACK, NAK, STALL, NYET, and ERR. The absence of an expected handshake code indicates a more serious error. In all cases, the expected receiver of the handshake uses the information to help decide what to do next. Table 2-4 shows the status indicators and where they transmit in each transaction type.

ACK

ACK (acknowledge) indicates that a host or device has received data without error. Devices must return ACK in the handshake packets of Setup transactions when the token and data packets were received without error. Devices may also return ACK in the handshake packets of OUT transactions. The host returns ACK in the handshake packets of IN transactions.

NAK

NAK (negative acknowledge) means the device is busy or has no data to return. If the host sends data at a time when the device is too busy to accept the data, the device returns a NAK in the handshake packet. If the host requests data from the device when the device has nothing to send, the device returns a NAK in the data packet. In either case, NAK indicates a temporary condition, and the host retries later.

Hosts never send NAK. Isochronous transactions don't use NAK because they have no handshake packet for returning a NAK. If a device or the host doesn't receive transmitted isochronous data, it's gone.

Table 2-4: The location, source, and contents of the handshake signal depend on the type of transaction.

Transaction type or PING query	Data packet source	Data packet contents	Handshake packet source	Handshake packet contents
Setup	host	data	device	ACK
OUT	host	data	device	ACK, NAK, STALL, NYET (high speed only), ERR (from hub in complete split)
IN	device	data, NAK, STALL, ERR (from hub in complete split)	host	ACK
PING (high speed only)	none	none	device	ACK, NAK, STALL

STALL

The STALL handshake can have any of three meanings: unsupported control request, control request failed, or endpoint failed.

When a device receives a control-transfer request that the device doesn't support, the device returns a STALL to the host. The device also returns a STALL if the device supports the request but for some reason can't take the requested action. For example, if the host sends a Set_Configuration request that requests the device to set its configuration to 2, and the device supports only configuration 1, the device returns a STALL. To clear this type of stall, the host just needs to send another Setup packet to begin a new control transfer. The USB specification calls this type of stall a protocol stall.

Another use of STALL is to respond when the endpoint's Halt feature is set, which means that the endpoint is unable to send or receive data at all. The USB specification calls this type of stall a functional stall.

Bulk and interrupt endpoints must support the functional stall. Although control endpoints may also support this use of STALL, it's not recommended. A control endpoint in a functional stall must continue to respond normally to other requests related to controlling and monitoring the stall condition. And an endpoint that is capable of responding to these requests is clearly capable of communicating and shouldn't be stalled. Isochronous transactions don't use STALL because they have no handshake packet for returning the STALL.

On receiving a functional STALL, the host drops all pending requests to the device and doesn't resume communications until the host has sent a successful request to clear the Halt feature on the device. Hosts never send STALL.

NYET

Only high-speed devices use NYET, which stands for *not yet*. High-speed bulk and control transfers have a protocol that enables the host to find out before sending data if a device is ready to receive the data. At full and low speeds, when the host wants to send data in a control, bulk, or interrupt transfer, the host sends the token and data packets and receives a reply from the device in the handshake packet of the transaction. If the device isn't ready for the data, the device returns a NAK and the host tries again later. This can waste a lot of bus time if the data packets are large and the device is often not ready.

High-speed bulk and control transactions with multiple data packets have a better way. After receiving a data packet, a device endpoint can return a NYET handshake, which says that the endpoint accepted the data but is not yet ready to receive another data packet. When the host thinks the device might be ready, the host can send a PING token packet, and the endpoint returns either an ACK to indicate the device is ready for the next data packet or NAK or STALL if the device isn't ready. Sending a PING is more efficient than sending the entire data packet only to find out the device wasn't ready and having to resend later. Even after responding to a PING or OUT with ACK, an endpoint is allowed to return NAK on receiving the data packet that follows but should do so rarely. The host then tries again with another PING. The use of PING by the host is optional.

A 2.0 hub may also use NYET in complete-split transactions. Hosts and low- and full-speed devices never send NYET.

ERR

The ERR handshake is used only by high-speed hubs in complete-split transactions. ERR indicates the device didn't return an expected handshake in the transaction the hub is completing with the host.

No Response

Another type of status indication occurs when the host or a device expects to receive a handshake but receives nothing. This lack of response can occur if the receiver's error-checking calculation detected an error. On receiving no response, the sender knows that it should try again. If if multiple tries fail, the sender can take other action. (If the receiver ACKs the data but doesn't use it, the problem is probably in the data-toggle value.)

Reporting the Status of Control Transfers

In addition to reporting the status of transactions, the same ACK, NAK, and STALL codes report the success or failure of complete control transfers. An additional status code is a zero-length data packet (ZLP), which reports successful completion of a control transfer. A transaction with a zero-length data packet is a transaction whose Data phase consists of a Data PID and error-checking bits but no data. Table 2-5 shows the status indicators for control transfers.

For control Write transfers, where the device receives data in the Data stage, the device returns the transfer's status in the data packet of the Status stage. A zero-length data packet means the transfer was successful, a STALL indicates that the device can't complete the transfer, and a NAK indicates that the device isn't ready to complete the transfer. The host returns an ACK in the handshake packet of the Status stage to indicate that the host received the response.

For control Read transfers, where the host receives data in the Data stage, the device returns the status of the transfer in the handshake packet of the

Table 2-5: Depending on the direction of the Data stage, the status information for a control transfer may be in the data or handshake packet of the Status stage.

Transfer Type and Direction	Status Stage Direction	Status stage's data packet	Status stage's handshake packet
Control Write (Host sends data to device or no Data stage)	IN	Device sends status: zero-length data packet (success), NAK (busy), or STALL (failed)	Host returns ACK
Control Read (Device sends data to host)	OUT	Host sends zero-length data packet	Device sends status: ACK (success), NAK (busy), or STALL (failed)

Status stage. The host normally waits to receive all of the packets in the Data stage, then returns a zero-length data packet in the Status stage. The device responds with ACK, NAK, or STALL. However, if the host begins the Status stage before all of the requested data packets have been sent, the device must abandon the Data stage and return a status code.

Error Checking

The USB specification spells out hardware requirements that ensure that errors due to line noise will be rare. Still, there is a chance that a noise glitch or unexpectedly disconnected cable could corrupt a transmission. For this reason, USB packets include error-checking bits that enable a receiver to identify just about any received data that doesn't match what was sent. In addition, for transfers that require multiple transactions, a data-toggle value keeps the transmitter and receiver synchronized to ensure that no transactions are missed entirely.

Error-checking Bits

All token, data, and Start-of-Frame packets include bits for use in error-checking. The bit values are calculated using a mathematical algorithm called the cyclic redundancy check (CRC). The USB specification explains how the CRC is calculated. The hardware handles the calculations, which must be done quickly to enable the device to respond appropriately.

The CRC is applied to the data to be checked. The transmitting device performs the calculation and sends the result along with the data. The receiving device performs the identical calculation on the received data. If the results match, the data has arrived without error and the receiving device returns an ACK. If the results don't match, the receiving device sends no handshake. The absence of the expected handshake tells the sender to retry.

Typically, the host tries a total of three times, but the USB specification gives the host some flexibility in determining the number of retries. On giving up, the host informs the driver of the problem.

The PID field in token packets uses a simpler form of error checking. The lower four bits in the field are the PID, and the upper four bits are its complement. The receiver can check the integrity of the PID by complementing the upper four bits and ensuring that they match the PID. If not, the packet is corrupted and is ignored.

The Data Toggle

In transfers that require multiple transactions, the data-toggle value can ensure that no transactions are missed by keeping the transmitting and receiving devices synchronized. The data-toggle value is included in the PID field of the token packets for IN and OUT transactions. DATA0 is a code of 0011, and DATA1 is 1011. In controller chips, a register bit often indicates the data-toggle state, so the data-toggle value is often referred to as the data-toggle bit. Each endpoint maintains its own data toggle.

Both the sender and receiver keep track of the data toggle. A Windows host handles the data toggles without requiring any user programming. Some device controller chips also handle the data toggles completely automatically, while others require some firmware control. If you're debugging a device where it appears that the proper data is transmitting on the bus but the receiver is discarding the data, chances are good that the device isn't sending or expecting the correct data toggle.

When the host configures a device on power up or attachment, the host and device each set their data toggles to DATA0 for all except some high-speed isochronous endpoints. On detecting an incoming data packet, the host or device compares the state of its data toggle with the received data toggle. If the values match, the receiver toggles its value and returns an ACK hand-shake packet to the sender. The ACK causes the sender to toggle its value for the next transaction.

The next received packet in the transfer should contain a data toggle of DATA1, and again the receiver toggles its bit and returns an ACK. The data toggle continues to alternate until the transfer completes. (An exception is control transfers, where the Status stage always uses DATA1.)

If the receiver is busy and returns a NAK, or if the receiver detects corrupted data and returns no response, the sender doesn't toggle its bit and instead tries again with the same data and data toggle.

If a receiver returns an ACK but for some reason the sender doesn't see the ACK, the sender will think that the receiver didn't get the data and will try again using the same data and data-toggle bit. In this case, the receiver of the repeated data doesn't toggle the data toggle and ignores the data but returns an ACK. The ACK re-synchronizes the data toggles. The same thing happens if the sender mistakenly sends the same data toggle twice in a row.

Control transfers always use DATA0 in the Setup stage, use DATA1 in the first transaction of the Data stage, toggle the bit in any additional Data-stage transactions, and use DATA1 in the Status stage. Bulk endpoints toggle the bit in every transaction, resetting the data toggle only after completing a Set_Configuration, Set_Interface, or Clear_Feature(ENDPOINT HALT) request. Interrupt endpoints can behave the same as bulk endpoints. Or an interrupt IN endpoint can toggle its data toggle in each transaction without checking for the host's ACKs, at the risk of losing some data. Full-speed iso-chronous transfers always use DATA0. Isochronous transfers can't use the data toggle to correct errors because there is no handshake packet for return-ing an ACK or NAK and no time to resend missed data.

Some high-speed isochronous transfers use DATA0, DATA1, and additional PIDs of DATA2 and MDATA. High-speed isochronous IN transfers that have two or three transactions per microframe use DATA0, DATA1, and DATA2 encoding to indicate a transaction's position in the microframe:

Number of IN Transactions in the Microframe	Data PID		
	First Transaction	Second Transaction	Third Transaction
1	DATA0	–	–
2	DATA1	DATA0	–
3	DATA2	DATA1	DATA0

High-speed isochronous OUT transfers that have two or three transactions per microframe use DATA0, DATA1, and MDATA encoding to indicate whether more data will follow in the microframe:

Number of OUT Transactions in the Microframe	Data PID:		
	First Transaction	Second Transaction	Third Transaction
1	DATA0	–	–
2	MDATA	DATA1	–
3	MDATA	MDATA	DATA2

This use of the data toggle and other PIDs is called data PID sequencing.

USB Complete

3

A Transfer Type for Every Purpose

This chapter takes a closer look at USB's four transfer types: control, bulk, interrupt, and isochronous. Each transfer type has abilities and limits that make the transfers suitable for different purposes. Table 3-1 compares the amount of data that each transfer type can move at each of the three speeds.

Control Transfers

Control transfers have two uses. Control transfers carry the requests that are defined by the USB specification and used by the host to learn about and configure devices. Control transfers can also carry requests defined by a class or vendor for any purpose.

Table 3-1: The maximum possible rate of data transfer varies greatly with the transfer type and bus speed.

Transfer Type	Maximum data-transfer rate per endpoint (kilobytes/sec. with data payload/transfer = maximum packet size allowed for the speed)		
	Low Speed	Full Speed	High Speed
Control	24	832	15,872
Interrupt	0.8	64	24,576
Bulk	not allowed	1216	53,248
Isochronous		1023	24,576

Availability

Every device must support control transfers over the default pipe at End-point 0. A device may also have additional pipes for control transfers, but in reality there's no need for more than one. Even if a device needs to send a lot of control requests, hosts allocate bandwidth for control transfers according to the number and size of requests, not by the number of control endpoints, so additional control endpoints offer no advantage.

Structure

Chapter 2 introduced control transfers and their stages: Setup, Data (optional), and Status. Each stage consists of one or more transactions.

Every control transfer must have a Setup stage and a Status stage. The Data stage is optional, though a particular request may require a Data stage. Because every control transfer requires transferring information in both directions, the control transfer's message pipe uses both the IN and OUT endpoint addresses.

In a control Write transfer, the data in the Data stage travels from the host to the device. Control transfers that have no Data stage are also considered to be control Write transfers. In a control Read transfer, the data in the Data stage travels from the device to the host. Figure 3-1 and Figure 3-2 show the stages of control Read and control Write transfers at low and full speeds on a low/full-speed bus. There are differences, described later in this chapter, for

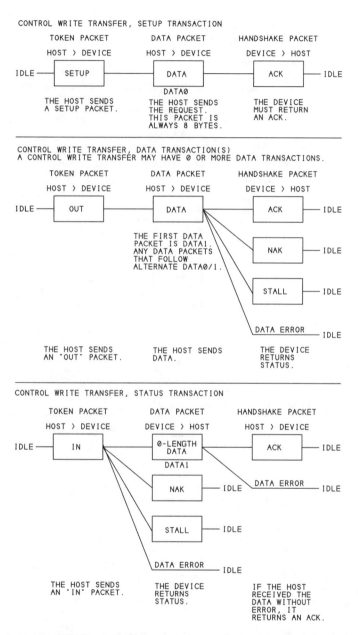

Figure 3-1: A control Write transfer contains a Setup transaction, zero or more Data transactions, and a Status transaction. Not shown are the PING protocol used in some high-speed transfers with multiple data packets and the split transactions used with low- and full-speed devices on a high-speed bus.

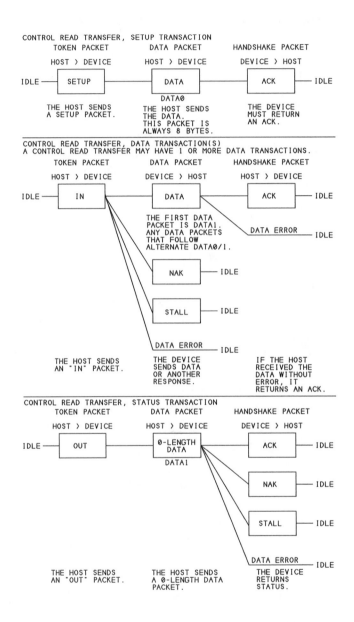

Figure 3-2: A control Read transfer contains a Setup transaction, one or more data transactions, and a status transaction. Not shown are the split transactions used with low- and full-speed devices on a high-speed bus.

USB Complete

some high-speed transfers and for low- and full-speed transfers with 2.0 hubs on high-speed buses.

In the Setup stage, the host begins a Setup transaction by sending information about the request. The token packet contains a PID that identifies the transfer as a control transfer. The data packet contains information about the request, including the request number, whether or not the transfer has a Data stage, and if so, in which direction the data will travel.

The USB 2.0 specification defines 11 standard requests. Successful enumeration requires specific responses to some requests, such as the request that sets a device's address. For other requests, a device can return a code that indicates that the request isn't supported. A specific class may require a device to support class-specific requests, and any device may support vendor-specific requests defined by a vendor-specific driver.

When present, the Data stage consists of one or more Data transactions, which may be IN or OUT transactions. Depending on the request, the host or peripheral may be the source of these transactions, but all data packets in this stage are in the same direction.

As described in Chapter 2, if a high-speed control Write transfer has more than one data packet in the Data stage, and if the device returns NYET after receiving a data packet, the host may use the PING protocol before sending the next data packet.

The Status stage consists of one IN or OUT transaction, also called the status transaction. In the Status stage, the device reports the success or failure of the previous stages. The source of the Status stage's data packet is the receiver of the data in the Data stage. When there is no Data stage, the device sends the Status stage's data packet. The data or handshake packet sent by the device in the Status stage contains a code that indicates the success or failure of the request.

If a host is performing a control transfer with a low- or full-speed device on a high-speed bus, the host uses the split transactions introduced in Chapter 2 for all of the transfer's transactions. To the device, the transaction is no different than a transaction with a 1.x host. The device's hub carries out the transaction with the device and reports back to the host when requested.

Data Size

The maximum size of the data packet in the Data stage varies with the device's speed. For low-speed devices, the maximum is 8 bytes. For full speed, the maximum may be 8, 16, 32, or 64 bytes. For high speed, the maximum must be 64 bytes. These bytes include only the information transferred in the data packet, excluding the PID and CRC bits.

In the Data stage, all data packets except the last must be the maximum packet size for the endpoint. The maximum packet size for the Default Control Pipe is in the device descriptor that the host retrieves during enumeration. If there are other control endpoints (this is rare), the size is in the endpoint descriptor. If a transfer has more data than will fit in one data transaction, the host sends or receives the data in multiple transactions.

In some control Read transfers, the amount of data returned by the device can vary. If the amount is less than the requested number of bytes and is an even multiple of the endpoint's maximum packet size, the device should indicate when it has no more data to send by returning a zero-length data packet in response to the next IN token packet that arrives after all of the data has been sent.

Speed

The host must make its best effort to ensure that all control transfers get through as quickly as possible. The host controller reserves a portion of the bus bandwidth for control transfers: 10 percent for low- and full-speed buses and 20 percent for high-speed buses. If the control transfers don't need this much time, bulk transfers may use what remains. If the bus has other unused bandwidth, control transfers may use more than the reserved amount.

The host attempts to parcel out the available time as fairly as possible to all devices. For each transfer, a single frame or microframe may contain multiple transactions, or the transactions may be in different (micro)frames.

There are two opinions on whether control transfers are appropriate for transferring data other than enumeration and configuration data. Some say that control transfers should be reserved as much as possible for servicing the standard USB requests and other performing other infrequent configuration tasks. This approach helps to ensure that the transfers complete quickly by keeping the bandwidth reserved for them as open as possible. But the USB specification doesn't forbid other uses for control transfers, and some believe that devices should be free to use control transfers for any purpose. Low-speed devices have no other choice except periodic interrupt transfers, which can waste bandwidth if data transfers are infrequent.

Control transfers aren't the most efficient way to transfer data. In addition to the data being transferred, each transfer with one data packet has an overhead of 63 bytes (low speed), 45 bytes (full speed), or 173 bytes (high speed). Each Data stage requires token and handshake packets, so stages with larger data packets are more efficient.

A single low-speed control transfer with 8 data bytes uses 29% of a frame's bandwidth, though the transfer's individual transactions may be spread among multiple frames. In a control transfer with multiple data packets in the Data stage, the data may travel in the same or different (micro)frames.

If the bus is very busy, all control transfers may have to share the reserved portion of the bandwidth. At low speed, one 8-byte transfer fits in the reserved portion of three frames. At full speed, one 64-byte transfer fits in the reserved portion of one frame (though again, any single transfer may be spread over multiple frames). At high speed, 512 transfers fit in the reserved portion of one frame.

Devices don't have to respond immediately to control-transfer requests. The USB specification includes timing limits that apply to most requests. A device class may require faster response to standard and class-specific requests. Where stricter timing isn't specified, in a transfer where the host requests data from the device, a device may delay as long as 500 milliseconds before making the data available to the host. To find out if data is available, the host sends a token packet requesting the data. If the data is ready, the device sends it immediately in that transaction's data packet. If not, the device returns a NAK to advise the host to retry later. The host keeps trying at intervals for up to 500 milliseconds. In a transfer where the host sends data to the device, the device can delay as long as 5 seconds before accepting all of the data and completing the Status stage (though the Status stage must complete within 50 milliseconds). The 5 seconds don't include any delays the host adds between packets. In a transfer with no Data stage, the device must complete the request and the Status stage within 50 milliseconds. The host and its drivers aren't required to enforce these limits.

Detecting and Handling Errors

If a device doesn't return an expected handshake packet during a control transfer, the host tries twice more. On receiving no response after a total of three tries, the host notifies the software that requested the transfer and stops communicating with the endpoint until the problem is corrected. The two retries include only those sent in response to no handshake at all. A NAK isn't an error.

Control transfers use data toggles to ensure that no data is lost. In the Data stage of a Control Read transfer, on receiving the data from the device, the host normally returns an ACK, then sends an OUT token packet to begin the Status stage. If the device for any reason doesn't see the ACK returned after the transfer's final data packet, the device must interpret a received OUT token packet as evidence that the handshake was returned and the Status stage can begin.

Devices must accept all Setup packets. If a new Setup packet arrives before a previous transfer completes, the device must abandon the previous transfer and start the new one.

Bulk Transfers

Bulk transfers are useful for transferring data when time isn't critical. A bulk transfer can send large amounts of data without clogging the bus because the transfers defer to the other transfer types and wait until time is available. Uses for bulk transfers include sending data from the host to a printer, sending data from a scanner to the host, and reading and writing to a disk. On an otherwise idle bus, bulk transfers are the fastest transfer type.

Availability

Only full- and high-speed devices can do bulk transfers. Devices aren't required to support bulk transfers, though a specific device class may require it. For example, a device in the mass-storage class must have a bulk endpoint in each direction.

Structure

A bulk transfer consists of one or more IN or OUT transactions (Figure 3-3). A bulk transfer is one-way: the transactions must all be IN transactions or all OUT transactions. Transferring data in both directions requires a separate pipe and transfer for each direction.

A bulk transfer ends in one of two ways: when the expected amount of data has transferred or when a transaction contains either zero data bytes or another number of bytes that is less than the endpoint's maximum packet size. The USB specification doesn't define a protocol for specifying the amount of data in a bulk transfer. When needed, the device and host can use a class-specific or vendor-specific protocol to pass this information. For example, a transfer can begin with a header that specifies the number of bytes to be transferred, or the device or host can use a class-specific or vendor-specific protocol to request a quantity of data.

To conserve bus time, the host may use the PING protocol in some high-speed bulk transfers. If a high-speed bulk OUT transfer has more than one data packet and the device returns NYET after receiving a packet, the host may use PING to find out when it's OK to begin the next data transaction. In a bulk transfer on a high-speed bus with a low- or full-speed device, the host uses split transactions for all of the transfer's transactions.

Data Size

A full-speed bulk transfer can have a maximum packet size of 8, 16, 32, or 64 bytes. For high speed, the maximum packet size must be 512 bytes. During enumeration, the host reads the maximum packet size for each bulk endpoint from the device's descriptors. The amount of data in a transfer may be less than, equal to, or greater than the maximum packet size. If the amount

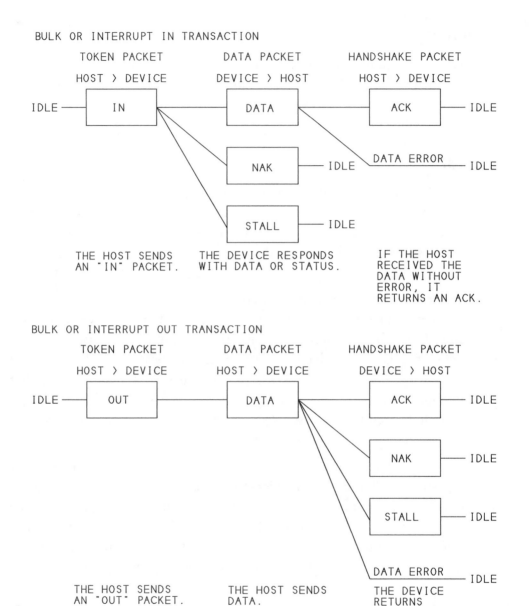

Figure 3-3: Bulk and interrupt transfers use IN and OUT transactions. Their structure is identical, but the host schedules them differently. Not shown are the PING protocol used in some high-speed bulk OUT transfers with multiple data packets or the split transactions used with low- and full-speed devices on a high-speed bus.

of data won't fit in a single packet, the host completes the transfer using multiple transactions.

Speed

The host controller guarantees that bulk transfers will complete eventually but doesn't reserve any bandwidth for the transfers. Control transfers are guaranteed to have 10 percent of the bandwidth at low and full speeds, and 20 percent at high speed. Interrupt and isochronous transfers may use the rest. So if a bus is very busy, a bulk transfer may take very long.

However, when the bus is otherwise idle, bulk transfers can use the most bandwidth of any type, and they have a low overhead, so they're the fastest of all. When an endpoint's maximum packet size is less than the maximum size allowed for the speed, some host controllers schedule no more than one packet per frame, even if more bandwidth is available. So it's best to specify the maximum allowed packet size for bulk endpoints if possible.

At full speed on an otherwise idle bus, up to nineteen 64-byte bulk transfers can transfer up to 1216 data bytes per frame, for a data rate of 1.216 Megabytes/sec. This leaves 18% of the bus bandwidth free for other uses. The protocol overhead for a bulk transfer with one data packet is 13 bytes at full speed and 55 bytes at high speed.

At high speed on an otherwise idle bus, up to thirteen 512-byte bulk transfers can transfer up to 6656 data bytes per microframe, for a data rate of 53.248 Megabytes/sec., using all but 2% of the bus bandwidth. The protocol overhead for a bulk transfer with one data packet is 55 bytes. Real-world performance varies with the host-controller hardware and driver and the host architecture, including latencies when accessing system memory. At this writing, some high-speed hosts can perform a single transfer at up to around 35 Megabytes/sec.

Detecting and Handling Errors

Bulk transfers use error detecting. If a device doesn't return an expected handshake packet, the host tries up to twice more. The host also retries on receiving NAK handshakes. The host's driver determines whether the host eventually gives up on receiving multiple NAKs. Bulk transfers use data toggles to ensure that no data is lost.

Interrupt Transfers

Interrupt transfers are useful when data has to transfer within a specific amount of time. Typical applications include keyboards, pointing devices, game controllers, and hub status reports. Users don't want a noticeable delay between pressing a key or moving a mouse and seeing the result on screen. A hub needs to report the attachment or removal of devices promptly. Low-speed devices, which support only control and interrupt transfers, are likely to use interrupt transfers for generic data.

At low and full speeds, the bandwidth available for an interrupt endpoint is limited, but high speed loosens the limits and enables an interrupt endpoint to transfer almost 400 times as much data as full speed per unit of time.

The name *interrupt transfer* suggests that a device might spontaneously send data that triggers a hardware interrupt on the host. But interrupt transfers, like all other USB transfers, occur only when the host polls a device. The transfers are interrupt-like, however, because they guarantee that the host requests or sends data with minimal delay.

Availability

All three speeds allow interrupt transfers. Devices aren't required to support interrupt transfers, but a device class may require it. For example, a HID-class device must support interrupt IN transfers for sending data to the host.

Structure

An interrupt transfer consists of one or more IN transactions or one or more OUT transactions. On the bus, interrupt transactions are identical to bulk transactions (Figure 3-3). The only difference is the scheduling. An interrupt transfer is one-way; the transactions must be all IN transactions, or all

OUT transactions. Transferring data in both directions requires a separate transfer and pipe for each direction.

An interrupt transfer ends in one of two ways: when the expected amount of data has transferred, or when a transaction contains either zero data bytes or another number of bytes that is less than the endpoint's maximum packet size. The USB specification doesn't define a protocol for specifying the amount of data in an interrupt transfer. When needed, the device and host can use a class-specific or vendor-specific protocol to pass this information. For example, a transfer can begin with a header that specifies the number of bytes to be transferred, or the device or host can use a class-specific or vendor-specific protocol to request a quantity of data.

In an interrupt transfer on a high-speed bus with a low- or full-speed device, the host uses the split transactions introduced in Chapter 2 for all of the transfer's transactions. Unlike high-speed bulk OUT transfers, high-speed interrupt OUT transfers can't use the PING protocol when a transfer has multiple transactions.

Data Size

For low-speed devices, the maximum packet size can be any value from 1 to 8 bytes. For full speed, the maximum packet size can range from 1 to 64 bytes. For high speed, the allowed range is 1 to 1024 bytes. In a device's default interface, interrupt endpoints must have a maximum packet size of 64 bytes or less. If the amount of data in a transfer won't fit in a single transaction, the host uses multiple transactions to complete the transfer.

Speed

An interrupt transfer guarantees a maximum latency, or time between transaction attempts. In other words, there is no guaranteed transfer rate, just the guarantee that there will be no more than the requested maximum latency period between transaction attempts.

High-speed interrupt transfers can be very fast. A high-speed endpoint can request up to three 1024-byte packets in each 125-microsecond microframe, which works out to 24.576 Megabytes/sec. An endpoint that requests more than 1024 bytes per microframe is called a high-bandwidth endpoint. Windows XP/Windows Server and earlier don't support high-bandwidth interrupt endpoints, however, so the achievable maximum for these operating systems is 8.192 Megabytes/sec. If the host's driver doesn't support alternate interfaces, the maximum is 64 kilobytes/sec. A full-speed endpoint can request up to 64 bytes in each 1-millisecond frame, or 64 kilobytes/sec. A low-speed endpoint can request up to 8 bytes every 10 milliseconds, or 800 bytes/sec.

The endpoint descriptor stored in the device specifies the maximum latency period. For low-speed devices, the maximum latency can be any value from 10 to 255 milliseconds. For full speed, the value can range from 1 to 255 milliseconds. For high speed, the range is 125 microseconds to 4 seconds, in increments of 125 microseconds. In addition, a high-speed interrupt endpoint with a maximum latency of 125 microseconds can request 1, 2, or 3 transactions per interval. The host controller ensures that transaction attempts occur within the specified period.

The host may begin each transaction at any time up to the specified maximum latency since the previous transaction began. So, for example, with a 10-millisecond maximum at full speed, five transfers could take as long as 50 milliseconds or as little as 5 milliseconds. OHCI host controllers use values that correspond to powers of 2, with a maximum of 32 milliseconds. So for a full-speed device that requests a maximum anywhere from 8 to 15 milliseconds, an OHCI host will begin a transaction every 8 milliseconds, and a maximum latency anywhere from 32 to 255 will cause a transaction attempt every 32 milliseconds. However, devices shouldn't rely on behavior that is specific to a type of host controller and should assume only that the host complies with the specification. (Chapter 8 has more about host-controller types.)

Because the host is free to transfer data more quickly than the requested rate, interrupt transfers don't guarantee a precise rate of delivery. The only exceptions are when the maximum latency equals the fastest possible rate. For example, with a 1.x host, a full-speed interrupt pipe configured for 1 transaction per millisecond will have bandwidth reserved for one transaction in each frame.

An otherwise idle bus can carry up to six low-speed, 8-byte transactions per frame. Note, however, that the maximum bandwidth that a single low-speed interrupt endpoint can request is 8 bytes every 10 milliseconds, and a low-speed device can have no more than two interrupt endpoints. Devices that need to transfer more than 800 bytes/sec. in each direction should be full or high speed. The reason for the limitation on low-speed endpoints is that low-speed traffic uses much more bandwidth compared to sending the same amount of data at full or high speed. Limiting the amount of bus time available to low-speed endpoints helps keep the bus available for other devices.

At full speed, nineteen 64-byte transactions can fit in a frame. Since the minimum time between transfers is one millisecond or more, each transaction in the frame would have to be for a different endpoint address. In reality, a host may not be able to schedule nineteen full-speed interrupt transactions in a single frame, so the practical maximum number of interrupt transactions per frame is likely to be less.

At high speed, the limit is two transfers per microframe, with each transfer consisting of three 1024-byte transactions.

The protocol overhead per transfer with one data packet is 19 bytes at low speed, 13 bytes at full speed, and 55 bytes at high speed. High-speed interrupt and isochronous transfers combined can use no more than 80 percent of a microframe. Full-speed isochronous transfers and low- and full-speed interrupt transfers combined can use no more than 90 percent of a frame. The section *More about Time-critical Transfers* later in this chapter has more about the capabilities and limits of interrupt transfers.

Detecting and Handling Errors

If a device doesn't return an expected handshake packet, host controllers in PCs will retry up to twice more. The host typically retries without limit on receiving NAKs. For example, a keyboard might sit idle for days before someone presses a key.

Interrupt transfers can use data toggles to ensure that all data is received without errors. A receiver that cares only about the most recent data can ignore the data toggle.

Isochronous Transfers

Isochronous transfers are streaming, real-time transfers that are useful when data must arrive at a constant rate, or by a specific time, and where occasional errors can be tolerated. At full speed, isochronous transfers can transfer more data per frame than interrupt transfers, but there is no provision for retransmitting data received with errors.

Examples of uses for isochronous transfers include encoded voice and music to be played in real time. But data that will eventually be consumed at a constant rate doesn't always require an isochronous transfer. For example, a host can use a bulk transfer to send a music file to a device. After receiving the file, the device can play the music at the appropriate rate.

Nor does the data in an isochronous transfer have to be consumed at a constant rate. An isochronous transfer is a way to ensure that a large block of data gets through quickly on a busy bus, even if the data doesn't need to transfer in real time. Unlike with bulk transfers, once an isochronous transfer begins, the host guarantees that the time will be available to send the data at a constant rate, so the completion time is predictable.

Availability

Only full- and high-speed devices can do isochronous transfers. Devices aren't required to support isochronous transfers but a device class may require it. For example, many audio- and video-class devices use isochronous endpoints.

Structure

Isochronous means that the data has a fixed transfer rate, with a defined number of bytes transferring in every frame or microframe. None of the other transfer types guarantee bandwidth for a specific number of bytes in each frame (except interrupt transfers with the shortest maximum latency).

A full-speed isochronous transfer consists of one IN or OUT transaction per frame in one or more frames at equal intervals. High-speed isochronous transfers are more flexible. They can request as many as three transactions per microframe or as little as one transaction every 32,768 microframes. Figure 3-4 shows the packets in full-speed isochronous IN and OUT transactions. An isochronous transfer is one-way. The transactions in a transfer must all be IN transactions or all OUT transactions. Transferring data in both directions requires a separate pipe and transfer for each direction.

The USB specification doesn't define a protocol for specifying the amount of data in an isochronous transfer. When needed, the device and host can use a class-specific or vendor-specific protocol to pass this information. For

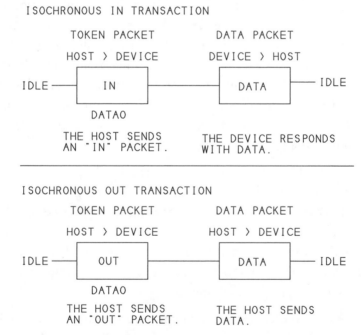

Figure 3-4: Isochronous transfers don't have handshake packets, so occasional errors must be acceptable. Not shown are the split transactions used with full-speed devices on a high-speed bus or the data PID sequencing in high-speed transfers with multiple data packets per microframe.

example, a transfer can begin with a header that specifies the number of bytes to be transferred, or the device or host can use a class-specific or vendor-specific protocol to request a quantity of data.

Before selecting a device configuration that consumes isochronous bandwidth, the host controller determines whether the requested bandwidth is available by comparing the available unreserved bus bandwidth with the maximum packet size and transfer rate of the configuration's isochronous endpoint(s). A full-speed transfer with the maximum 1023 bytes per frame uses 69 percent of the bus's bandwidth. If two full-speed devices want to transfer 1023 bytes per frame, a 1.x host will refuse to configure the second device because the data won't fit in the remaining bandwidth.

Every USB 2.0 device with isochronous endpoints must have an interface that requests no isochronous bandwidth so the host can configure the device even if there is no reservable bandwidth available. In addition to this interface and an interface that requests the optimum bandwidth for a device, a device can have alternate interfaces that have smaller isochronous data packets or use fewer isochronous packets per microframe. The device driver can then request to use an interface that transfers data at a lower rate when needed. Or the driver can try again later in the hope that the bandwidth will be available. After the host configures the device, the transfers are guaranteed to have the time they need.

Although isochronous transfers may send a fixed number of bytes per frame, the data doesn't transfer at a constant number of bits per second. Each transaction has overhead and must share the bus with other devices. So the data is actually a burst at 12 Megabits/sec. or 480 Megabits/sec. and may occur any time within the frame or microframe. To use the data at a constant rate, such as sending the data to a speaker, the receiver must convert the received bits to signals that span the interval.

Isochronous transfers may also synchronize to another data source or recipient, or to the bus's Start-of-Frame signals. For example, a microphone's input may synchronize to the output of speakers. The USB specification describes several methods of synchronizing to internal and external clocks. The descriptor for a USB 2.0 isochronous endpoint can specify a synchronization type and a usage value that indicates whether the endpoint is contains data or feedback information used to maintain synchronization.

If a host is performing an isochronous transfer on a high-speed bus with a full-speed device, the host uses the split transactions introduced in Chapter 2 for all of the transfer's transactions. Isochronous OUT transactions use start-split transactions, but not complete-splits because there is no status information to report back to the host. Isochronous transfers don't use the PING protocol.

Data Size

For full-speed endpoints, the maximum packet size can range from 0 to 1023 data bytes. High-speed endpoints can have a maximum packet size up to 1024 bytes. If the amount of data won't fit in a single packet, the host completes the transfer in multiple transactions.

Within a transfer, the amount of data in each frame doesn't have to be the same. For example, data at 44,100 samples per second could use a sequence of 9 frames containing 44 samples each, followed by 1 frame containing 45 samples.

Speed

A full-speed isochronous transaction can transfer up to 1023 bytes per frame, or up to 1.023 Megabytes/sec. This leaves 31% of the bus bandwidth free for other uses. The protocol overhead is 9 bytes per transfer for a transfer with one data packet, or less than 1% for a single 1023-byte transaction. The minimum requested bandwidth for a full-speed transfer is one byte per frame, which is 1 kilobyte per second.

A high-speed isochronous transaction can transfer up to 1024 bytes. An isochronous endpoint that requires more than 1024 bytes per microframe can request 2 or 3 transactions per microframe, for a maximum rate of 24.576 Megabytes/sec. An endpoint that requires multiple transactions per microframe is called a high-bandwidth endpoint. The protocol overhead is 38 bytes per transfer for a transfer with one data packet.

Because high-speed isochronous transfers don't have to do a transaction in every frame or microframe, they can request less bandwidth than full-speed transfers. The minimum requested bandwidth is one byte every 32,678 microframes, which works out to one byte every 4.096 seconds. However, any endpoint can transfer less data than the maximum reserved bandwidth by skipping available transactions or by transferring less than the maximum data per transfer.

On a high-speed bus, interrupt and isochronous transfers can use no more than 80 percent of a microframe. On a full-speed bus, isochronous transfers and low- and full-speed interrupt transfers combined can use no more than 90 percent of a frame. An otherwise idle high-speed bus can carry two isochronous transfers at the maximum rate.

The section *More about Time-critical Transfers* later in this chapter has more about the capabilities of isochronous transfers.

Detecting and Handling Errors

The price to pay for guaranteed on-time delivery of large blocks of data is no error correcting. Isochronous transfers are intended for uses where occasional, small errors are acceptable. For example, listeners may tolerate or not even notice a short dropout in voice or music. And in reality, under normal circumstances, a USB transfer should experience no more than a very occasional error due to line noise. Because isochronous transfers must keep to a schedule, the receiver can't request the sender to retransmit if the receiver is busy or detects an error. A receiver that suspects errors could ask the sender to resend the entire transfer, but this approach isn't very efficient.

More about Time-critical Transfers

Just because an endpoint is capable of a rate of data transfer doesn't mean that a particular device and host will be able to achieve the rate. Several things can limit an application's ability to send or receive data at the rate that a device requests. The limiting factors include bus bandwidth, the device's capabilities, the capabilities of the device driver and application software, and latencies in the host's hardware and software.

Bus Bandwidth

When a device requests more interrupt or isochronous bandwidth than is available, the host refuses to configure the device. Low- and full-speed interrupt transfers use little bandwidth, so the host isn't likely to deny a configuration due to their requirements. High-speed interrupt transfers are a different story. A high-speed endpoint can request up to three 1024-byte data packets in each microframe, using as much as 40 percent of the bus bandwidth. To help ensure that devices can enumerate without problems, the interrupt endpoints in a device's default interface must specify a maximum packet size no larger than 64 bytes. The device driver is then free to try to increase the endpoint's reserved bandwidth by requesting alternate interface settings or configurations.

Isochronous endpoints can also cause bandwidth problems. A frequent problem with isochronous endpoints on 1.x devices is that devices request more bandwidth than is available. The host properly refuses to configure the device and the user is left with a device that doesn't work without knowing why.

To help ensure that devices will enumerate without problems, the default interface setting of a 2.0-compliant device must request no isochronous bandwidth. In other words, the default interface can transfer no isochronous data at all. An obvious way to comply is to include no isochronous endpoints in the default interface. After enumeration, the device driver is free to attempt to request isochronous bandwidth by requesting an alternate interface or configuration with an isochronous endpoint. Note that even full-speed endpoints must meet this requirement to comply with USB 2.0.

Device Capabilities

If the host has promised that the requested USB bandwidth will be available, there's still no guarantee that the device will be ready to send or receive data when needed.

To use interrupt and isochronous transfers effectively, both the sender and receiver have to be capable of sending and receiving at the desired rate. A device that is sending data must write the data to send into the endpoint's transmit buffer in time to enable the controller to place the data on the bus on receiving an IN token packet. A device that is receiving data must read the previous data from the endpoint's buffer before the new data arrives. Otherwise either the old data will be overwritten or the device will NAK or drop the new data.

One way to help ensure that the device is always ready for a transfer is to use double (or quadruple) buffering, as described in Chapter 6. Multiple buffers give the firmware extra time to load the next data to transfer or to retrieve just-received data.

Host Capabilities

The capabilities of the device driver and application software on the host can also can affect whether all available transfers take place.

A device driver requests a transfer by submitting an I/O request packet (IRP) to a lower-level driver. For interrupt and isochronous transfers, if there is no outstanding IRP for an endpoint when its scheduled time comes up, the host controller skips the transaction attempt. To ensure that no transfer opportunities are missed, drivers typically submit a new IRP immediately on completing the previous one.

The application software that uses the data also has to be able to keep up with the transfers. For example, the driver for HID-class devices places report data received in interrupt transfers in a buffer, and applications use ReadFile to retrieve reports from the buffer. If the buffer is full when a new report arrives, the driver discards the oldest report and replaces it with the newest one. If the application can't keep up, some reports are lost. A solution is to increase the size of the buffer the driver uses to store received data or to read multiple reports at once.

One way to help ensure that an application sends or receives data with minimal delays is to place the code that communicates with the device driver in its own program thread. The thread should have few responsibilities other than managing these communications.

Doing fewer, larger transfers rather than multiple, small transfers can also help. An application can typically send or request a few large chunks of data more quickly than it can send or request many smaller chunks. When there are multiple transactions per transfer, the lower-level drivers take care of the scheduling.

Host Latencies

Another factor in the performance of time-critical USB transfers is the latencies due to how Windows handles multi-tasking. Windows was never designed as a real-time operating system that could guarantee a rate of data transfer with a peripheral.

Multi-tasking means that multiple program threads run at the same time. The operating system grants a portion of the available time to each thread. Different threads can have different priorities, but under Windows, no thread can be guaranteed CPU time at a defined, precise rate, such as once per millisecond.

Latencies under Windows are often well under 1 millisecond, but in some cases a thread can keep other code from executing for over 100 milliseconds. Newer Windows editions tend to have improved performance over older editions.

A USB device and its software have no control over what other tasks the host CPU is performing and how fast the CPU can perform them, so dealing with these latencies can be a challenge when timing is critical.

In general, it's best to let the device handle any required real-time processing and make the timing of the host communications as non-critical as possible. For example, imagine a full-speed device that reads a sensor once per millisecond. The device could attempt to send each reading to the host in a separate interrupt transfer, but if a transfer is skipped for any reason, the transfers will never catch up. If the device instead collects a series of readings and transfers them using less frequent, but larger transfers, the timing of the bus transfers is less critical. Data compression can also help by reducing the amount of data that must transfer.

4

Enumeration: How the Host Learns about Devices

Before applications can communicate with a device, the host needs to learn about the device and assign a device driver. Enumeration is the exchange of information that accomplishes these tasks. The process includes assigning an address to the device, reading descriptors from the device, assigning and loading a device driver, and selecting a configuration that specifies the device's power requirements, endpoints, and other features. The device is then ready to transfer data using any of the endpoints in its configuration.

This chapter describes the enumeration process, including the structure of the descriptors that the host reads from the device during enumeration. You don't need to know every detail about enumeration in order to design a USB peripheral, but understanding how enumeration works in general is essential in creating the descriptors that will reside in the device and in writing firmware that responds to enumeration requests.

The Process

One of the duties of a hub is to detect the attachment and removal of devices. Each hub has an interrupt IN endpoint for reporting these events to the host. On system boot-up, the host polls its root hub to learn if any devices are attached, including additional hubs and devices attached to those hubs. After boot-up, the host continues to poll periodically to learn of any newly attached or removed devices.

On learning of a new device, the host sends a series of requests to the device's hub, causing the hub to establish a communications path between the host and the device. The host then attempts to enumerate the device by sending control transfers containing standard USB requests to the device's Endpoint 0. All USB devices must support control transfers, the standard requests, and Endpoint 0. For a successful enumeration, the device must respond to each request by returning requested information and taking other requested actions.

From the user's perspective, enumeration is invisible and automatic except for possibly a message that announces the detection of a new device and whether the attempt to configure it succeeded. Sometimes on first use, the user needs to assist in selecting a driver or specifying where the host should look for driver files.

When enumeration is complete, Windows adds the new device to the Device Manager's display in the Control Panel. When a user removes a device from the bus, Windows removes the device from the Device Manager.

In a typical device, firmware contains the information the host will request, and a combination of hardware and firmware decodes and responds to requests for the information. Some controllers can manage the enumeration entirely in hardware, with no firmware support. On the host side, under

Windows there's no need to write code for enumerating because the operating system handles the process.

Enumeration Steps

The USB specification defines six device states. During enumeration, a device moves through four of the states: Powered, Default, Address, and Configured. (The other states are Attached and Suspend.) In each state, the device has defined capabilities and behavior.

The steps below are a *typical* sequence of events that occurs during enumeration under Windows. But device firmware *must not assume* that the enumeration requests and events will occur in a particular order. To function successfully, a device must detect and respond to any control request or other bus event at any time.

1. The user attaches a device to a USB port. Or the system powers up with a device already attached. The port may be on the root hub at the host or a hub that connects downstream from the host. The hub provides power to the port, and the device is in the Powered state.

2. The hub detects the device. The hub monitors the voltages on the signal lines of each of its ports. The hub has a pull-down resistor of 14.25 to 24.8 kilohms on each of the port's two signal lines (D+ and D-). A device has a pull-up resistor of 900 to 1575 ohms on either D+ for a full-speed device or D- for a low-speed device. High-speed-capable devices attach at full speed. When a device plugs into a port, the device's pull-up brings its line high, enabling the hub to detect that a device is attached. Chapter 15 has more on how hubs detect devices.

On detecting a device, the hub continues to provide power but doesn't yet transmit USB traffic to the device.

3. The host learns of the new device. Each hub uses its interrupt endpoint to report events at the hub. The report indicates only whether the hub or a port (and if so, which port) has experienced an event. On learning of an event, the host sends the hub a Get_Port_Status request to find out more. Get_Port_Status and the other requests described here are standard hub-class requests that all hubs support. The information returned tells the host when a device is newly attached.

4. The hub detects whether a device is low or full speed. Just before the hub resets the device, the hub determines whether the device is low or full speed by examining the voltages on the two signal lines. The hub detects the speed of a device by determining which line has the higher voltage when idle. The hub sends the information to the host in response to the next Get_Port_Status request. A 1.x hub may instead detect the device's speed just after a bus reset. USB 2.0 requires speed detection to occur before the reset so the hub knows whether to check for a high-speed-capable device during reset, as described below.

5. The hub resets the device. When a host learns of a new device, the host controller sends the hub a Set_Port_Feature request that asks the hub to reset the port. The hub places the device's USB data lines in the Reset condition for at least 10 milliseconds. Reset is a special condition where both D+ and D- are a logic low. (Normally, the lines have opposite logic states.) The hub sends the reset only to the new device. Other hubs and devices on the bus don't see the reset.

6. The host learns if a full-speed device supports high speed. Detecting whether a device supports high speed uses two special signal states. In the Chirp J state, only the D+ line is driven and in the Chirp K state, only the D- line is driven.

During the reset, a device that supports high speed sends a Chirp K. A high-speed-capable hub detects the chirp and responds with a series of alternating Chirp Ks and Chirp Js. On detecting the pattern KJKJKJ, the device removes its full-speed pull up and performs all further communications at high speed. If the hub doesn't respond to the device's Chirp K, the device knows it must continue to communicate at full speed. All high-speed devices must be capable of responding to enumeration requests at full speed.

7. The hub establishes a signal path between the device and the bus. The host verifies that the device has exited the reset state by sending a Get_Port_Status request. A bit in the returned data indicates whether the device is still in the reset state. If necessary, the host repeats the request until the device has exited the reset state.

When the hub removes the reset, the device is in the Default state. The device's USB registers are in their reset states and the device is ready to respond to control transfers at Endpoint 0. The device communicates with the host using the default address of 00h. The device can draw up to 100 milliamperes from the bus.

8. The host sends a Get_Descriptor request to learn the maximum packet size of the default pipe. The host sends the request to device address 0, Endpoint 0. Because the host enumerates only one device at a time, only one device will respond to communications addressed to device address 0, even if several devices attach at once.

The eighth byte of the device descriptor contains the maximum packet size supported by Endpoint 0. A Windows host requests 64 bytes, but after receiving just one packet (whether or not it has 64 bytes), the host begins the Status stage of the transfer. On completion of the Status stage, a Windows host requests the hub to reset the device, as in Step 5 above. The USB specification doesn't require a reset here. Resetting is a precaution that ensures that the device will be in a known state when the reset ends.

9. The host assigns an address. The host controller assigns a unique address to the device by sending a Set_Address request. The device completes the Status stage of the request using the default address and then implements the new address. The device is now in the Address state. All communications from this point on use the new address. The address is valid until the device is detached, the port is reset, or the system reboots. On the next enumeration, the host may assign a different address to the device.

10. The host learns about the device's abilities. The host sends a Get_Descriptor request to the new address to read the device descriptor. This time the host retrieves the entire descriptor. The descriptor is a data structure containing the maximum packet size for Endpoint 0, the number of configurations the device supports, and other basic information about the device. The host uses this information in the communications that follow.

The host continues to learn about the device by requesting the one or more configuration descriptors specified in the device descriptor. A request for a configuration descriptor is actually a request for the configuration descriptor followed by all of that descriptor's subordinate descriptors. A Windows host begins by requesting just the configuration descriptor's nine bytes. Included in these bytes is the total length of the configuration descriptor and its subordinate descriptors.

Windows then requests the configuration descriptor again, this time using the retrieved total length. The device responds by sending the configuration descriptor followed by the configuration's interface descriptor(s), with each interface descriptor followed by any endpoint descriptors for the interface. Some configurations also include class- or vendor-specific descriptors that extend or modify another descriptor. These descriptors follow the descriptor being extended or modified. Each descriptor begins with its length and type. The Descriptors section in this chapter has more on what each descriptor contains.

11. The host assigns and loads a device driver (except for composite devices). After learning about a device from its descriptors, the host looks for the best match in a device driver to manage communications with the device. In selecting a driver, Windows tries to match the information in the PC's INF files with the Vendor ID, Product ID, and (optional) release number retrieved from the device. If there is no match, Windows looks for a match with any class, subclass, and protocol values retrieved from the device. If the device has been enumerated previously, Windows can use information in the system registry instead of searching the INF files. After the operating system assigns and loads the driver, the driver may request the device to resend descriptors or send other class-specific descriptors.

An exception to this sequence is composite devices, which can have different drivers assigned to different interfaces in a configuration. The host can assign these drivers only after the interfaces are enabled, which requires the device to be configured (as described in the next step).

12. The host's device driver selects a configuration. After learning about a device from the descriptors, the device driver requests a configuration by sending a Set_Configuration request with the desired configuration number. Some devices support only one configuration. If a device supports multiple configurations, the driver can decide which configuration to request based on information the driver has about how the device will be used, or the driver can ask the user what to do or just select the first configuration. The device reads the request and enables the requested configuration. The device is now in the Configured state and the device's interface(s) are enabled.

For composite devices, the host assigns drivers at this point. As with other devices, the host uses the information retrieved from the device to find a matching driver for each active interface in the configuration. The device is now ready for use.

The other two device states are Attached and Suspend.

Attached state. If the hub isn't providing power to a device's VBUS line, the device is in the Attached state. The absence of power may occur if the hub has detected an over-current condition or if the host requests the hub to remove power from the port. With no power on VBUS, the host and device can't communicate, so from their perspective, the situation is the same as when the device isn't attached at all.

Suspend State. A device enters the Suspend state after detecting no bus activity, including Start-of-Frame markers, for at least 3 milliseconds. In the Suspend state, the device should limit its use of bus power. Both configured and unconfigured devices must support this state. Chapter 16 has more about the Suspend state.

Enumerating a Hub

Hubs are also USB devices, and the host enumerates a newly attached hub in exactly the same way as other devices. If the hub has devices attached, the host enumerates each of these after the hub informs the host of their presence.

Device Removal

When a user removes a device from the bus, the hub disables the device's port. The host learns that the removal occurred after polling the hub, learning that an event has occurred, and sending a Get_Port_Status request to find out what the event was. Windows removes the device from the Device Manager's display and the device's address becomes available to another newly attached device.

Tips for Successful Enumeration

Successful enumeration is essential. Without it, the device and host can't perform any additional communications. Most chip vendors provide example code to get you started. Even if your device uses a different class or has other differences, the example code can serve as a model. If your controller interfaces to an external CPU, you may have to adapt code written for another chip.

In general, a device should assume nothing about what requests or events the host will initiate and should just concentrate on responding to requests and events as they occur. The following tips have specific advice about how to avoid common problems.

Don't assume requests or events will occur in a specific order. The USB 2.0 specification says nothing about what order a host might choose in sending control requests during enumeration. A host might also choose to reset the bus at any time, and the device must detect the reset and respond appropriately.

Be ready to abandon a control transfer or end it early. On receiving a new Setup packet, a device must abandon any transfer in progress and begin the new one. On receiving an OUT token packet, the device must assume that the host is beginning the Status stage of the transfer even if the device hasn't sent all of the requested data in the Data stage.

Don't attempt to send more data than the host asks for. In the Data stage of a Control Read transfer, a device should send no more than the amount of data the host has asked for. If the host requests nine bytes, the device should send no more than nine bytes.

Send a zero-length data packet when required. If the device has less than the requested amount of data to return and if the amount of data is an exact multiple of the endpoint's maximum packet size, the device should indicate that there is no more data by returning a zero-length data packet in response to the next IN token packet.

Stall unsupported requests. A device shouldn't assume it knows every request the host might send. The device should return a STALL in response to any request the device doesn't recognize or support.

Don't set the address too soon. In a Set_Address request, the device should set its new address only after the Status stage of the request is complete.

Be ready to enter the Suspend state. A host can suspend the bus when the device is in any powered state, including before the device has been configured. When the bus is suspended, the device must reduce its use of bus power.

Test under different host-controller types. Some host controllers schedule multiple stages of a control transfer in a single frame, while others don't. Devices should be able to handle either way. Chapter 8 has more about host controllers.

Descriptors

USB descriptors are the data structures, or formatted blocks of information, that enable the host to learn about a device. Each descriptor contains information about the device as a whole or an element of the device.

All USB devices must respond to requests for the standard USB descriptors. The device must store the information in the descriptors and respond to requests for the descriptors.

Types of Descriptors

As described earlier in this chapter, during enumeration the host uses control transfers to request descriptors from the device. As enumeration progresses, the requested descriptors concern increasingly small elements of the device: first the entire device, then each configuration, each configuration's interface(s), and finally each interface's endpoint(s). Table 4-1 lists the descriptor types.

The higher-level descriptors inform the host of any additional, lower-level descriptors. Except for compound devices, each device has one and only one device descriptor that contains information about the device as a whole and specifies the number of configurations the device supports. Each device also has one or more configuration descriptors that contain information about the device's use of power and the number of interfaces supported by the configuration. Each interface descriptor specifies zero or more endpoint descriptors that contain the information needed to communicate with an endpoint. Each endpoint descriptor has information about how the endpoint transfers data. An interface with no endpoint descriptors must use the control endpoint for communications.

On receiving a request for a configuration descriptor, a device should return the configuration descriptor and all of the configuration's interface, endpoint, and other subordinate descriptors, up to the requested number of bytes. There is no request to retrieve, for example, only an endpoint descriptor. Devices that support both full and high speeds support two additional descriptor types: device_qualifier and other_speed_configuration. These and their subordinate descriptors contain information about the device's behavior when using the speed not currently selected.

A string descriptor can store text such as the vendor's or device's name. Other descriptors can contain index values that point to these string descriptors, and the host can read the string descriptors using Get_Descriptor requests.

In addition to the standard descriptors, a device may contain class- or vendor-specific descriptors. These descriptors offer a structured way for a device to provide more detailed information about itself. For example, an interface

Table 4-1: The bDescriptorType field in a descriptor contains a value that identifies the descriptor type.

bDescriptorType	Descriptor Type	Required?
01h	device	Yes.
02h	configuration	Yes.
03h	string	No. Optional descriptive text.
04h	interface	Yes.
05h	endpoint	No, if the device uses only Endpoint 0.
06h	device_qualifier	Yes, for devices that support both full and high speeds. Not allowed for other devices.
07h	other_speed_configuration	Yes, for devices that support both full and high speeds. Not allowed for other devices.
08h	interface_power	No. Supports interface-level power management.
09h	OTG	For On-The-Go devices only.
0Ah	debug	No.
0Bh	interface_association	For composite devices.

descriptor may specify that the interface belongs to the HID class and has a HID class descriptor.

Each descriptor contains a value that identifies the descriptor type. Table 4-1 shows the values for the standard descriptor types. In addition to these values, a class or vendor may define additional descriptors. Two examples of class codes are 29h for a hub descriptor and 21h for a HID descriptor. Within the HID class, 22h indicates a report descriptor and 23h indicates a physical descriptor.

In the descriptor's bDescriptorType value, bit 7 is always zero. Bits 6 and 5 identify the descriptor type: 00h=standard, 01h=class, 02h=vendor, 03h=reserved. Bits 4 through 0 identify the descriptor.

Each descriptor consists of a series of fields. Most of the field names use prefixes to indicate something about the format or contents of the data in that field: b = byte (8 bits), w = word (16 bits), bm = bit map, bcd = binary-coded decimal, i = index, id = identifier.

Device Descriptor

The device descriptor contains basic information about the device. This descriptor is the first one the host reads on device attachment and includes the information the host needs to retrieve additional information from the device. A host retrieves a device descriptor by sending a Get_Descriptor request with the high byte of the Setup transaction's wValue field equal to 1.

The descriptor has 14 fields. Table 4-2 lists the fields in the order they occur in the descriptor. The descriptor includes information about the descriptor itself, the device, its configurations, and any classes the device belongs to. The following descriptions group the information by function.

The Descriptor

bLength. The length in bytes of the descriptor.

bDescriptorType. The constant DEVICE (01h).

The Device

bcdUSB. The USB specification version that the device and its descriptors comply with in BCD (binary-coded decimal) format. If you think of the version's value as a decimal number, the upper byte represents the integer, the next four bits are tenths, and the final four bits are hundredths. So version 1.0 is 0100h; version 1.1 is 0110h, and version 2.0 is 0200h. Note that version 1.1 is *not* 0101h. Also remember that a 2.0 device does not have to be high speed. Any new low- or full-speed design should comply with the latest version of the specification.

idVendor. Members of the USB-IF and others who pay an administrative fee receive the rights to use a unique Vendor ID. The host may have an INF file that contains this value, and if so, Windows uses the value to help decide what driver to load for the device. Except for devices used only in-house where the user is responsible for preventing conflicts, every device descriptor must have a valid Vendor ID in this field.

idProduct. The owner of the Vendor ID assigns a Product ID to identify the device. Both the device descriptor and the device's INF file on the host may contain this value, and if so, Windows uses the value to help decide

Table 4-2: The device descriptor has 14 fields in 18 bytes.

Offset (decimal)	Field	Size (bytes)	Description
0	bLength	1	Descriptor size in bytes
1	bDescriptorType	1	The constant DEVICE (01h)
2	bcdUSB	2	USB specification release number (BCD)
4	bDeviceClass	1	Class code
5	bDeviceSubclass	1	Subclass code
6	bDeviceProtocol	1	Protocol Code
7	bMaxPacketSize0	1	Maximum packet size for Endpoint 0
8	idVendor	2	Vendor ID
10	idProduct	2	Product ID
12	bcdDevice	2	Device release number (BCD)
14	iManufacturer	1	Index of string descriptor for the manufacturer
15	iProduct	1	Index of string descriptor for the product
16	iSerialNumber	1	Index of string descriptor containing the serial number
17	bNumConfigurations	1	Number of possible configurations

what driver to load for the device. Each Product ID is specific to a Vendor ID, so multiple vendors can use the same Product ID without conflict.

bcdDevice. The device's release number in BCD format. The vendor assigns this value. The host may use this value in deciding which driver to load.

iManufacturer. An index that points to a string describing the manufacturer. This value is zero if there is no manufacturer descriptor.

iProduct. An index that points to a string describing the product. This value is zero if there is no string descriptor.

iSerialNumber. An index that points to a string containing the device's serial number. This value is zero if there is no serial number. Some device classes (such as mass storage) require serial numbers. Serial numbers are useful if users may have more than one identical device on the bus and the host needs to keep track of which is which even after rebooting. Serial numbers also enable a host to determine whether a peripheral is the same one used previously or a new installation of a peripheral with the same Vendor ID and Product ID. No devices with the same Vendor ID, Product ID, and device release number should have the same serial number.

The Configuration

bNumConfigurations. The number of configurations the device supports.

bMaxPacketSize0. The maximum packet size for Endpoint 0. The host uses this information in the requests that follow. For low-speed devices, this value must be 8. Full-speed devices may use 8, 16, 32, or 64. High-speed devices must use 64.

Classes

bDeviceClass. For devices whose function is defined at the device level, this field specifies the device's class. Values from 1 to FEh are reserved for USB's defined classes. Table 4-3 shows the defined codes. The value FFh means that the class is specific to the vendor and defined by the vendor. Many devices specify their class or classes in interface descriptors, and for these devices, the bDeviceClass field in the device descriptor is 00h (or EFh if the function uses an interface association descriptor).

bDeviceSubclass. This field can specify a subclass within a class. If bDeviceClass is 0, the bDeviceSubclass must be 0. If bDeviceClass is between 1 and FEh, bDeviceSubclass must be a code defined in a USB class specification. A value of FFh means that the subclass is specific to the vendor. A subclass can add support for additional features and abilities shared by a group of functions within a class.

bDeviceProtocol. This field can specify a protocol defined by the selected class or subclass. For example, a 2.0 hub uses this field to indicate whether the hub is currently supporting high speed and if so, if the hub supports one or multiple transaction translators. If bDeviceClass is between 01h and FEh, the protocol must be a code defined by a USB class specification.

Table 4-3: The bDeviceClass field in the device descriptor can name a class the device belongs to.

bDeviceClass	Description
00h	The interface descriptor names the class. (Use EFh if the function has an interface association descriptor.)
02h	Communications
09h	Hub
DCh	Diagnostic device (can also be declared at interface level) bDeviceSubClass = 1 for Reprogrammable Diagnostic Device with bDeviceProtocol = 1 for USB2 Compliance Device
E0h	Wireless Controller (can also be declared at interface level) bDeviceSubClass = 1 for RF Controller with bDeviceProtocol = 1 for Bluetooth Programming Interface
EFh	Miscellaneous Device bDeviceSubClass = 2 for Common Class with bDeviceProtocol = 1 for Interface Association Descriptor
FFh	Vendor-specific (can also be declared at interface level)

Device_qualifier Descriptor

Devices that support both full and high speeds must have a device_qualifier descriptor. When a device switches speeds, some fields in the device descriptor may change. The device_qualifier descriptor contains the values of these fields at the speed not currently in use. In other words, the contents of fields in the device and device_qualifier descriptors swap depending on which speed is being used. A host retrieves a device_qualifier descriptor by sending a Get_Descriptor request with the high byte of the Setup transaction's wValue field equal to 6.

The descriptor has nine fields. Table 4-4 lists the fields in the order they occur in the descriptor. The descriptor includes information about the descriptor itself, the device, its configurations, and its classes.

The Vendor ID, Product ID, device release number, manufacturer string, product string, and serial-number string don't change when the speed changes, so the device_qualifier descriptor doesn't include these values.

The host can use a Get_Descriptor request to retrieve the device_qualifier descriptor. The following descriptions group the information by function.

Table 4-4: The device_qualifier descriptor has nine fields.

Offset (decimal)	Field	Size (bytes)	Description
0	bLength	1	Descriptor size in bytes
1	bDescriptorType	1	The constant DEVICE_QUALIFIER (06h)
2	bcdUSB	2	USB specification release number (BCD)
4	bDeviceClass	1	Class code
5	bDeviceSubclass	1	Subclass code
6	bDeviceProtocol	1	Protocol Code
7	bMaxPacketSize0	1	Maximum packet size for Endpoint 0
8	bNumConfigurations	1	Number of possible configurations
9	Reserved	1	For future use

The Descriptor

bLength. The length in bytes of the descriptor.

bDescriptorType. The constant DEVICE_QUALIFIER (06h).

The Device

bcdUSB. The USB specification number that the device and its descriptors comply with. Must be at least 0200h (USB 2.0).

The Configuration

bNumConfigurations. The number of configurations the device supports.

bMaxPacketSize0. The maximum packet size for Endpoint 0.

Classes

bDeviceClass. For devices that belong to a class, this field can name the class.

bDeviceSubclass. For devices that belong to a class, this field can specify a subclass within the class.

bDeviceProtocol. This field can specify a protocol defined by the selected class or subclass. For example, a 2.0 hub must support both a low- and full-speed protocol and a high-speed protocol. The device descriptor contains the code for the currently active protocol, and the device_qualifier descriptor contains the code for the not-active protocol.

Reserved. For future use.

Configuration Descriptor

After retrieving the device descriptor, the host can retrieve the device's configuration, interface, and endpoint descriptors.

Each device has at least one configuration that specifies the device's features and abilities. Often a single configuration is enough, but a device with multiple uses or modes can support multiple configurations. Only one configuration is active at a time. Each configuration requires a descriptor. The configuration descriptor contains information about the device's use of power and the number of interfaces supported. Each configuration descriptor has subordinate descriptors, including one or more interface descriptors and optional endpoint descriptors. A host retrieves a configuration descriptor and its subordinate descriptors by sending a Get_Descriptor request with the high byte of the Setup transaction's wValue field equal to 2.

The host selects a configuration with the Set_Configuration request and reads the current configuration number with a Get_Configuration request.

The descriptor has eight fields. Table 4-5 lists the fields in the order they occur in the descriptor. The fields contain information about the descriptor itself, the configuration, and the device's use of power in that configuration. The following descriptions group the information by function.

The Descriptor

bLength. The length (in bytes) of the descriptor.

bDescriptorType. The constant CONFIGURATION (02h).

wTotalLength. The number of bytes in the configuration descriptor and all of its subordinate descriptors.

Table 4-5: The configuration descriptor has eight fields.

Offset (decimal)	Field	Size (bytes)	Description
0	bLength	1	Descriptor size in bytes
1	bDescriptorType	1	The constant Configuration (02h)
2	wTotalLength	2	The number of bytes in the configuration descriptor and all of its subordinate descriptors
4	bNumInterfaces	1	Number of interfaces in the configuration
5	bConfigurationValue	1	Identifier for Set_Configuration and Get_Configuration requests
6	iConfiguration	1	Index of string descriptor for the configuration
7	bmAttributes	1	Self/bus power and remote wakeup settings
8	bMaxPower	1	Bus power required, expressed as (maximum milliamperes/2)

The Configuration

bConfigurationValue. Identifies the configuration for Get_Configuration and Set_Configuration requests. Must be 1 or higher. A Set_Configuration request with a value of zero causes the device to enter the Not Configured state.

iConfiguration. Index to a string that describes the configuration. This value is zero if there is no string descriptor.

bNumInterfaces. The number of interfaces in the configuration. The minimum is 1.

Power Use

bmAttributes. Bit 6=1 if the device is self-powered or 0 if bus-powered. Bit 5=1 if the device supports the remote wakeup feature, which enables a suspended USB device to tell its host that the device wants to communicate. A USB device must enter the Suspend state if there has been no bus activity for 3 milliseconds. If an event at a suspended device requires action from the host, a device with remote wakeup enabled can request the host to resume communications.

The other bits in the field are unused. Bits 0 through 4 must be 0. Bit 7 must be 1. (In USB 1.0, bit 7 was set to 1 to indicate that the configuration was bus powered. In USB 1.1 and higher, setting bit 6 to 0 is enough to indicate that the configuration is bus powered.)

bMaxPower. Specifies how much bus current a device requires. The bMax-Power value equals *one half* the number of milliamperes required. If the device requires 200 milliamperes, bMaxPower=100. The maximum current a device can request is 500 milliamperes. Storing half the number of milli-amperes enables one byte to store values up to the maximum. If the requested current isn't available, the host will refuse to configure the device. A driver may then request an alternate configuration if available.

Other_speed_configuration Descriptor

The other descriptor unique to devices that support both full and high speeds is the other_speed_configuration descriptor. The structure of the descriptor is identical to that of the configuration descriptor. The only difference is that the other-speed_configuration_descriptor describes the configuration when the device is operating at the speed not currently active. The other_speed_configuration descriptor has subordinate descriptors just as the configuration descriptor does. A host retrieves an other_speed_configuration descriptor by sending a Get_Descriptor request with the high byte of the Setup transaction's wValue field = 7.

The descriptor has eight fields. Table 4-6 lists the fields in the order they occur in the descriptor.

Interface Association Descriptor

An interface association descriptor (IAD) identifies multiple interfaces that are associated with a function. In relation to a device and its descriptors, the term interface refers to a feature or function a device implements.

Most device classes specify their functions at the interface level rather than at the device level. Assigning functions to interfaces makes it possible for a single configuration to support multiple interfaces and thus multiple functions. As explained in Chapter 1, a device that has multiple interfaces that are

Table 4-6: The other_speed_configuration descriptor has the same eight fields as the configuration descriptor.

Offset (decimal)	Field	Size (bytes)	Description
0	bLength	1	Descriptor size in bytes
1	bDescriptorType	1	The constant OTHER_SPEED_CONFIGURATION (07h)
2	wTotalLength	2	The number of bytes in the configuration descriptor and all of its subordinate descriptors
4	bNumInterfaces	1	Number of interfaces in the configuration
5	bConfigurationValue	1	Identifier for Set_Configuration and Get_Configuration requests
6	iConfiguration	1	Index of string descriptor for the configuration
7	bmAttributes	1	Self/bus power and remote wakeup settings
8	MaxPower	1	Bus power required, expressed as (maximum milliamperes/2)

active at the same time is a composite device. Each interface has its own interface descriptor and an endpoint descriptor for each endpoint the interface uses. The host loads a driver for each interface.

When two or more interfaces in a configuration are associated with the same function, the interface association descriptor can tell the host which interfaces are associated with each other. For example, a video-camera function may use one interface to control the camera and another to carry the video data.

The USB Engineering Change Notice that defines the interface association descriptor says that the descriptor "must be supported by future implementations of devices that use multiple interfaces to manage a single device function." Devices that comply with the video-class specification must use an interface association descriptor. Class specifications that predate the descriptor of course don't require it. Hosts that don't support the descriptor ignore it. Support for the descriptor was added in Windows XP SP2.

To enable the host to identify devices that use the Interface Association descriptor, the device descriptor should contain the following values: bDeviceClass = EFh (miscellaneous device class), bDeviceSubClass = 02h (common class), and bDeviceProtocol = 01h (interface association descriptor). These codes are together referred to as the "Multi-interface Function Device Class Codes."

A host retrieves an interface association descriptor by requesting the configuration descriptor for the configuration the interface association belongs to.

An interface association descriptor has eight fields. Table 4-8 lists the fields in the order they occur in the descriptor. The following descriptions group the information by function.

The Descriptor

bLength. The number of bytes in the descriptor.

bDescriptorType. The constant INTERFACE ASSOCIATION (0Bh).

The Interfaces

bFirstInterface. Identifies the interface number of the first interface of multiple interfaces associated with a function. The interface number is the value of bInterfaceNumber in the interface descriptor. The interface numbers of associated interfaces must be contiguous.

bInterfaceCount. Gives the number of contiguous interfaces associated with the function.

The Function

bFunctionClass. A class code for the function shared by the associated interfaces. For classes that don't specify a value to use, the preferred value is the bInterfaceClass value from the descriptor of the first associated interface. Values from 01h to FEh are reserved for USB-defined classes. FFh indicates a vendor-defined class. Zero is not allowed.

bFunctionSubClass. A subclass code for the function shared by the associated interfaces. For classes that don't specify a value to use, the preferred value for existing device classes is the bInterfaceSubClass value from the descriptor of the first associated interface.

Table 4-7: The interface association descriptor has eight fields.

Offset (decimal)	Field	Size (bytes)	Description
0	bLength	1	Descriptor size in bytes
1	bDescriptorType	1	The constant Interface Association (0Bh)
2	bFirstInterface	1	Number identifying the first interface associated with the function
3	bInterfaceCount	1	The number of contiguous interfaces associated with the function
4	bFunctionClass	1	Class code
5	bFunctionSubClass	1	Subclass code
6	bFunctionProtocol	1	Protocol code
8	iFunction	1	Index of string descriptor for the function

bInterfaceProtocol. A protocol code for the function shared by the associated interfaces. For classes that don't specify a value to use, the preferred value for existing device classes is the bInterfaceProtocol value from the descriptor of the first associated interface.

iInterface. Index to a string that describes the function. This value is zero if there is no string descriptor.

Interface Descriptor

The interface descriptor provides information about a function or feature that a device implements. The descriptor contains class, subclass, and protocol information and the number of endpoints the interface uses.

A configuration can have multiple interfaces that are active at the same time. The interfaces may be associated with a single function or they may be unrelated. A configuration can also support alternate, mutually exclusive interfaces. The host can request an alternate interface with a Set_Interface request and read the current interface number with a Get_Interface request. Each interface has its own interface descriptor and subordinate descriptors. Devices that use isochronous transfers must have alternate interfaces because the default interface must request no isochronous bandwidth. Changing interfaces is simpler than changing configurations.

A host retrieves interface descriptors by requesting the configuration descriptor for the configuration the interface belongs to.

An interface descriptor has nine fields. Table 4-8 lists the fields in the order they occur in the descriptor. Many devices don't use the values in all of the fields, such as those that enable alternate settings and protocols. The following descriptions group the information by function.

The Descriptor

bLength. The number of bytes in the descriptor.

bDescriptorType. The constant INTERFACE (04h).

The Interface

iInterface. Index to a string that describes the interface. This value is zero if there is no string descriptor.

bInterfaceNumber. Identifies the interface. In a composite device, a configuration has multiple interfaces that are active at the same time. Each interface must have a descriptor with a unique value in this field. The default is zero.

bAlternateSetting. When a configuration supports multiple, mutually exclusive interfaces, each of the interfaces has a descriptor with the same value in bInterfaceNumber and a unique value in bAlternateSetting. The Get_Interface request retrieves the currently active setting. The Set_Interface request selects the setting to use. The default is zero.

bNumEndpoints. The number of endpoints the interface supports in addition to Endpoint 0. For a device that supports only Endpoint 0, NumEndpoints is zero.

bInterfaceClass. Similar to bDeviceClass in the device descriptor, but for devices with a class specified by the interface. Table 4-9 shows defined codes. Values from 01h to FEh are reserved for USB-defined classes. FFh indicates a vendor-defined class. Zero is reserved.

bInterfaceSubClass. Similar to bDeviceSubClass in the device descriptor, but for devices with a class defined by the interface. For interfaces that

Table 4-8: The interface descriptor has nine fields.

Offset (decimal)	Field	Size (bytes)	Description
0	bLength	1	Descriptor size in bytes
1	bDescriptorType	1	The constant Interface (04h)
2	bInterfaceNumber	1	Number identifying this interface
3	bAlternateSetting	1	Value used to select an alternate setting
4	bNumEndpoints	1	Number of endpoints supported, not counting Endpoint 0
5	bInterfaceClass	1	Class code
6	bInterfaceSubclass	1	Subclass code
7	bInterfaceProtocol	1	Protocol code
8	iInterface	1	Index of string descriptor for the interface

belong to a class, this field may specify a subclass within the class. If bInterfaceClass is zero, bInterfaceSubclass must be zero. If bInterfaceClass is between 01h and FEh, bInterfaceSubclass must zero or a code defined by a USB specification. A value of FFh means that the subclass is specific to the vendor. The diagnostic-device, wireless-controller, and application-specific classes have defined subclasses.

bInterfaceProtocol. Similar to bDeviceProtocol in the device descriptor, but for devices whose class is defined by the interface. May specify a protocol defined by the selected bInterfaceClass or bInterfaceSubClass. If bInterfaceClass is between 01h and FEh, bInterfaceProtocol must zero or a code defined by a USB specification.

Endpoint Descriptor

Each endpoint specified in an interface descriptor has an endpoint descriptor. Endpoint 0 never has a descriptor because every device must support Endpoint 0, the device descriptor contains the maximum packet size, and the USB specification defines everything else about the endpoint. A host retrieves endpoint descriptors by requesting the configuration descriptor for the configuration the endpoints belong to.

Table 4-9: The bInterfaceClass field in the interface descriptor can name a class the interface belongs to.

Class Code (hexadecimal)	Description
01	Audio
02	(Communication Device Class) Communication Interface
03	Human Interface Device
05	Physical
06	Image
07	Printer
08	Mass storage
09	Hub
0A	(Communication Device Class) Data Interface
0B	Smart Card
0D	Content Security
0E	Video
DC	Diagnostic device (can also be declared at the device level) bInterfaceSubClass = 1 for Reprogrammable Diagnostic Device with bInterfaceProtocol = 1 for USB2 Compliance Device
E0	Wireless controller (can also be declared at device level) bInterfaceSubClass = 1 for RF Controller with bInterfaceProtocol = 1 for Bluetooth Programming Interface
FE	Application specific bInterfaceSubClass = 1 for Device Firmware Update bInterfaceSubClass = 2 for IrDA Bridge bInterfaceSubClass = 3 for Test and Measurement
FF	Vendor specific (can also be declared at the device level)

Table 4-10 lists the endpoint descriptor's six fields in the order they occur in the descriptor. The following descriptions group the information by function.

The Descriptor

bLength. The number of bytes in the descriptor.

bDescriptorType. The constant ENDPOINT (05h).

Table 4-10: The endpoint descriptor has six fields.

Offset (decimal)	Field	Size (bytes)	Description
0	bLength	1	Descriptor size in bytes
1	bDescriptorType	1	The constant Endpoint (05h)
2	bEndpointAddress	1	Endpoint number and direction
3	bmAttributes	1	Transfer type supported
4	wMaxPacketSize	2	Maximum packet size supported
6	bInterval	1	Maximum latency/polling interval/NAK rate

The Endpoint

bEndpointAddress. Contains the endpoint number and direction. Bits 0 through 3 are the endpoint number. Low-speed devices can have a maximum of 3 endpoints (usually numbered 0 through 2), while full- and high-speed devices can have 16 (0 through 15). Bit 7 is the direction: Out = 0, In = 1, Bidirectional (for control transfers) = ignored. Bits 4, 5, and 6 are unused and must be zero.

bmAttributes. Bits 1 and 0 specify the type of transfer the endpoint supports. 00=Control, 01=Isochronous, 10=Bulk, 11=Interrupt. For Endpoint 0, Control is assumed.

In USB 1.1, bits 2 through 7 were reserved. USB 2.0 uses bits 2 through 5 for full- and high-speed isochronous endpoints. Bits 3 and 2 indicate a synchronization type: 00=no synchronization, 01=asynchronous, 10=adaptive, 11=synchronous. Bits 5 and 4 indicate a usage type: 00=data endpoint, 01=feedback endpoint, 10=implicit feedback data endpoint, 11=reserved. For non-isochronous endpoints, bits 2 through 5 must be zero. For all endpoints, bits 6 and 7 must be zero.

wMaxPacketSize. The maximum number of data bytes the endpoint can transfer in a transaction. The allowed values vary with the device speed and type of transfer.

Bits 10 through 0 are the maximum packet size, from 0 to 1024 (0 to 1023 in USB 1.x). In USB 2.0, bits 12 and 11 indicate how many additional transactions per microframe a high-speed endpoint supports: 00=no additional transactions (total of 1 transaction per microframe), 01=1 additional (total of 2 transactions per microframe), 10=2 additional (total of 3 transactions per microframe), 11=reserved. In USB 1.x, these bits were reserved and set to zero. Bits 13 through 15 are reserved and must be zero.

bInterval. Can indicate the maximum latency for polling interrupt endpoints, the interval for polling isochronous endpoints, or the maximum NAK rate for high-speed bulk OUT or control endpoints. The allowed range and how the value is used varies with the device speed, the transfer type, and whether or not the device complies with USB 2.0.

For low-speed interrupt endpoints, the maximum latency equals bInterval in milliseconds. The value may range from 10 to 255.

For all full-speed interrupt endpoints and for full-speed isochronous endpoints on 1.x devices, the interval equals bInterval in milliseconds. For interrupt endpoints, the value may range from 1 to 255. For isochronous endpoints in 1.x devices, the value must be 1. For isochronous endpoints in full-speed 2.0 devices, values from 1 to 16 are allowed, and the interval is calculated as $2^{\text{bInterval-1}}$, allowing a range from 1 millisecond to 32.768 seconds.

For full-speed bulk and control transfers, the value is ignored.

For high-speed endpoints, the value is in units of 125 microseconds, which is the width of a microframe. The value for interrupt and isochronous endpoints may range from 1 to 16, and the interval is calculated as $2^{\text{bInterval-1}}$ to allow a range from 125 microseconds to 4.096 seconds.

For high-speed bulk OUT and control endpoints, the value indicates the endpoint's maximum NAK rate. This value is relevant when the device has received data and returned ACK, and the host has more data to send in the transfer. By returning ACK, the device is saying that it expects to be able to accept the next transaction's data. (Otherwise the device would return NYET.) If the next data packet arrives and for some reason the device can't accept the packet, the endpoint returns NAK. The bInterval value says that the endpoint will return NAK no more than once in each period specified by bInterval. The value can range from 0 to 255 microframes. A value of zero means the endpoint will never NAK. The host isn't required to use the maximum-NAK-rate information.

String Descriptor

A string descriptor contains descriptive text. The USB 2.0 specification defines descriptors that can contain indexes to various strings, including strings that describe the manufacturer, product, serial number, configuration, and interface. Class- and vendor-specific descriptors can contain indexes to additional string descriptors. Support for string descriptors is optional, though a class may require them. A host retrieves a string descriptor by sending a Get_Descriptor request with the high byte of the Setup transaction's wValue field equal to 3. Table 4-11 shows the descriptor's fields and their purposes.

The Descriptor

bLength. The number of bytes in the descriptor.

bDescriptorType. The constant STRING (03h).

The String

When the host requests a String descriptor, the low byte of the wValue field is an index value. An index value of zero has the special function of requesting language IDs, while other index values request strings that may contain any text.

wLANGID[0...n]. Used in string descriptor 0 only. String descriptor 0 contains one or more 16-bit language ID codes that indicate the languages that the strings are available in. There are codes for several variants of English. U.S. English is 0409h. This is likely to be the only code supported by an operating system. The wLANGID value must be valid for any of the other strings to be valid. Devices that return no string descriptors must not return an array of language IDs. The USB-IF's web site has a list of defined USB language IDs.

bString. For values 1 and higher, the String field contains a Unicode string. Unicode uses 16 bits to represent each character. With a few exceptions,

Table 4-11: A string descriptor has three or more fields.

Offset (decimal)	Field	Size (bytes)	Description
0	bLength	1	Descriptor size in bytes
1	bDescriptorType	1	The constant String (03h)
2	bSTRING or wLANGID	varies	For string descriptor 0, an array of 1 or more Language Identifier codes. For other string descriptors, a Unicode string.

ANSI character codes 00h through 7Fh correspond to Unicode values 0000h through 007Fh. For example, a product string for a product called "Gizmo" would contain five 16-bit Unicode values that represent the characters in the product name: 0047 0069 007A 006D 006F. The strings are not null-terminated.

Other Standard Descriptors

The USB 2.0 specification lists three additional descriptor codes for interface_power, OTG, and debug descriptors.

The interface_power descriptor is defined in a proposed Interface Power Management specification to enable interfaces to manage their power consumption individually. The specification was proposed by Microsoft in 1998 but hasn't been approved or implemented. The document describing this descriptor's structure and use is *USB Feature Specification: Interface Power Management*.

The OTG descriptor is required for devices that support On-The-Go's Host Negotiation Protocol (HNP) or Session Request Protocol (SRP). The descriptor indicates the supported protocols. Chapter 20 has more about this descriptor.

The debug descriptor is defined in a proposed specification for USB2 Debug Devices. A debug device connects to the optional debug port defined in the EHCI specification for high-speed host controllers. The debug port and device are intended to replace the RS-232 port that PCs have long used for debugging purposes.

The Microsoft OS Descriptor

Microsoft has defined its own Microsoft OS descriptor for use with devices in vendor-defined classes. The descriptor is intended to assist in providing Windows-specific data such as icons and registry settings.

The descriptor consists of a special String descriptor and one or more Microsoft OS feature descriptors. The String descriptor must have an index of EEh and contains an embedded signature. Windows XP SP1 and later request this string descriptor on first attachment. A device that doesn't support this descriptor should return a STALL.

If a device contains a Microsoft OS String descriptor, Windows requests additional Microsoft-specific descriptors. Future editions of the Windows DDK will have more documentation about these descriptors.

Descriptors in 2.0-compliant Devices

If you're upgrading a 1.x-complaint device to 2.0, what changes are required in the descriptors? In a dual-speed device, can you detect whether a device is using full or high speed by reading its descriptors? This section answers these questions.

Making 1.x Descriptors 2.0-compliant

Table 4-12 lists the descriptor fields whose contents may require changes to enable a 1.x device to comply with the USB 2.0 specification. For all except some devices that have isochronous endpoints, the one and only required change is this: in the device descriptor, the bcdUSB field must be 0200h.

As Chapter 3 explained, a USB 2.0 device's default interface(s) must request no isochronous bandwidth. And because the default interface is of no use for transferring isochronous data, a device that wants to do isochronous transfers must support at least one alternate interface setting, and the alternate interface descriptor will have at least one subordinate endpoint descriptor. Some 1.x devices meet this requirement already.

Table 4-12: The descriptors in a 1.x-compliant device require very few changes to comply with USB 2.0.

Descriptor	Field	Change
Device	bcdUSB	Set to 0200h.
Endpoint	wMaxPacketSize	Isochronous only: must be 0 in the default configuration.

The USB 2.0 specification also adds two new descriptors and functions for bits in existing fields, but the new descriptors are used only in dual-speed devices and the other descriptors are backwards compatible with 1.x.

Full-speed isochronous endpoints have a few new, optional abilities. The endpoint descriptor can specify synchronization and usage types (bmAttributes field), and the interval can be greater than 1 millisecond (bInterval field). In 1.x descriptors, these bits default to 0 (no synchronization) and 1 (one millisecond).

When selecting bInterval values for interrupt and isochronous endpoints, don't forget that the relation between bInterval and the interval time will vary depending on the transfer type and speed. For low- and full-speed interrupt endpoints, the interval equals bInterval in milliseconds. For full-speed isochronous endpoints, the interval equals $2^{bInterval-1}$ in milliseconds. For high-speed interrupt and isochronous endpoints, the interval equals $2^{bInterval-1}$ in units of 125 microseconds. Note that if bInterval = 1, the full-speed interval is 1 millisecond in both USB 1.x and USB 2.0. So a 1.x isochronous endpoint, which must have bInterval = 1, requires no changes to comply with USB 2.0.

If you upgrade a full-speed device to support high speed as well, the device needs a device_qualifier descriptor, an other_speed_configuration descriptor, and a set of descriptors for the high-speed configuration. Any interrupt endpoints in the default interface must have a maximum packet size of 64 or less. A USB 2.0 device that supports only low speed or only full speed must return STALL in response to requests for the device_qualifier and other_speed_configuration descriptors.

Detecting the Speed of a Dual-Speed Device

A high-speed device must respond to enumeration requests at full speed, and the device may also be completely functional at full speed. As Chapter 1 explained, a high-speed-capable device must use full speed if it has a 1.x host or if there is a 1.x hub between the host and device. Applications and device drivers normally don't need to know which speed a dual-speed device is using because all of the speed-related details are handled at a lower level. Windows provides no straightforward way to learn a device's speed. But if a host application wants to know, there are a few techniques that can detect a the bus speed for many devices.

If a device has a bulk endpoint, you can learn the current speed by examining the endpoint descriptor in the active configuration. The wMaxPacketSize field must be 512 in a high-speed device and can't be 512 in a full-speed device. If there is no bulk endpoint, the wMaxPacketSize of an interrupt or isochronous endpoint provides speed information if the endpoint uses a maximum packet size available only at high speed. For an interrupt endpoint, a wMaxPacketSize greater than 64 indicates high speed. If the wMaxPacketSize is 64 or less, the device may be using full or high speed. For isochronous endpoints, a wMaxPacketSize of 1024 indicates high speed. If wMaxPacketSize is 1023 or less, the device may be using full or high speed.

If you're writing the device firmware, you can provide speed information in the optional strings indexed by the configuration and other_speed_configuration descriptors. For example, the string indexed by the configuration descriptor might contain the text "high speed," and the string indexed by the other_speed_configuration descriptor might contain the text "full speed." Applications can then read the configuration string to learn the current speed.

The USBView application in the Windows DDK shows how applications can read descriptors.

5

Control Transfers: Structured Requests for Critical Data

Of USB's four transfer types, control transfers have the most complex structure. They're also the only transfer type with functions defined by the USB specification. This chapter looks in greater detail at the structure of control transfers and the requests defined in the specification.

Elements of a Control Transfer

As Chapter 2 explained, control transfers enable the host and a device to exchange information about the device's capabilities. Control transfers also offer a way for devices to transfer other class-specific or vendor-specific information. As explained in Chapter 3, a control transfer has a defined format consisting of a Setup stage, a Data stage (optional for some transfers), and a Status stage. Each stage consists of one or more transactions that each contain a token phase, data phase, and handshake phase. Each phase transfers a token, data, or handshake packet.

As described in Chapter 2, low-speed transfers also use PRE packets, high-speed transfers use the PING protocol, and some low- and full-speed transfers use split transactions. Each packet also contains error-checking bits. Application programmers, device-driver writers, and firmware developers don't have to worry about PREs, PINGs, error-checking, or split transactions because the host controller, hubs, and device hardware handle these protocols.

Setup Stage

The Setup stage consists of a Setup transaction, which has two purposes: to identify the transfer as a control transfer and to transmit the request and other information that the device will need to complete the request.

Devices must accept and acknowledge every Setup transaction. A device that is in the middle of another control transfer must abandon that transfer and acknowledge the new Setup transaction. Here are more details about each of the packets in the Setup stage's transaction:

Token Packet

Purpose: identifies the receiver and identifies the transaction as a Setup transaction.

Sent by: the host.

PID: SETUP

Additional Contents: the device and endpoint addresses.

Data Packet

Purpose: transmits the request and related information.

Sent by: the host.

PID: DATA0

Additional Contents: eight bytes in five fields: bmRequestType, bRequest, wValue, wIndex, and wLength.

bmRequestType is a byte that specifies the direction of data flow, the type of request, and the recipient.

Bit 7 is a Direction bit that names the direction of data flow for data in the Data stage. Host to device (OUT) or no Data stage is 0; device to host (IN) is 1.

Bits 6 and 5 are Request Type bits that specify whether the request is one of USB's standard requests (00), a request defined for a specific USB class (01), or a request defined by a vendor-specific driver for use with a particular product or products (10).

Bits 4 through 0 are Recipient bits that define whether the request is directed to the device (00000) or to a specific interface (00001), endpoint (00010), or other element (00011) in the device.

bRequest is a byte that specifies the request. Every defined request has a unique bRequest value. When the Request Type bits in bmRequestType = 00, bRequest specifies one of the standard USB requests. When the Request Type bits = 01, bRequest specifies a request defined for the device's class. When the Request Type bits = 10, bRequest specifies a request defined by a vendor.

wValue is two bytes that the host may use to pass information to the device. Each request may define the meaning of these bytes in its own way. For example, in a Set_Address request, wValue contains the device address.

wIndex is two bytes that the host may use to pass information to the device. A typical use is to pass an index or offset such as an interface or endpoint number, but each request may define the meaning of these bytes in any way. When passing an endpoint index, bits 0-3 indicate the endpoint number, and bit 7 = 0 for a Control or OUT endpoint or 1 for an IN endpoint. When passing an interface index, bits 0–7 are the interface number. All unused bits are zero.

wLength is two bytes containing the number of data bytes in the Data stage that follows. For a host-to-device transfer, wLength is the exact number of bytes the host wants to transfer. For a device-to-host transfer, wLength is a maximum, and the device may return this number of bytes or fewer. If the wLength field is zero, there is no Data stage.

Handshake Packet

Purpose: transmits the device's acknowledgement.

Sent by: the device.

PID: ACK.

Additional Contents: none. The handshake packet consists of the PID alone.

Comments: If the device detects an error in the received Setup or Data packet, the device returns no handshake. The device's hardware typically handles the error checking and sending of the ACK, with no programming required.

Data Stage

When a control transfer contains a Data stage, the stage consists of one or more IN or OUT transactions. The device descriptor specifies the maximum number of data bytes in a transaction at Endpoint 0.

When the Data stage uses IN transactions, the device sends data to the host. An example is the Get_Descriptor request, where the device sends a requested descriptor to the host. When the Data stage uses OUT transactions, the host sends data to the device. An example is HID-class request Set_Report, where the host sends a report to a device. If the wLength field in the Setup transaction is zero, there is no Data stage. For example, in the Set_Configuration request, the host passes a configuration value to the peripheral in the wValue field of the Setup stage's data packet, so there's no need for a Data stage.

If all of the data can't fit in one packet, the stage uses multiple transactions. The number of transactions required to send all of the data for a transfer equals the value in the Setup transaction's wLength field divided by the wMaxPacketSize value in the endpoint's descriptor, rounded up. For example, in a Get_Descriptor request, if wLength is 18 and wMaxPacketSize is 8, the transfer requires 3 Data transactions. The transactions in the Data stage must all be in the same direction. When the Data stage is present but there is no data to transfer, the data phase consists of a zero-length data packet (the PID only).

The host uses split transactions in the Data stage when the device is low or full speed and an upstream hub connects to a high-speed bus. The host may use the PING protocol when the device is high speed, the Data stage uses OUT transactions, and there is more than one data transaction.

Each IN or OUT transaction in the Data stage contains token, data, and handshake packets. Here are more details about each of the packets in the Data stage's transaction(s):

Token Packet

Purpose: identifies the receiver and identifies the transaction as an IN or OUT transaction.

Sent by: the host.

PID: if the request requires the device to send data to the host, the PID is IN. If the request requires the host to send data to the device, the PID is OUT.

Additional Contents: the device and endpoint addresses.

Data Packet

Purpose: transfers all or a portion of the data specified in the wLength field of the Setup transaction's data packet.

Sent by: if the token packet's PID is IN, the device sends the data packet; if the token packet's PID is OUT, the host sends the data packet.

PID: The first packet is DATA1. Any additional packets in the Data stage alternate DATA0/DATA1.

Additional Contents: the data or a zero-length data packet.

Handshake Packet

Purpose: the data packet's receiver returns status information.

Sent by: the receiver of the Data stage's data packet. If the token packet's PID is IN, the host sends the handshake packet. If the token packet's PID is OUT, the device sends the handshake packet.

PID: Any device may return ACK (valid data was received), NAK (the endpoint is busy), or STALL (the request isn't supported or the endpoint is halted). A high-speed device that is receiving multiple data packets may return NYET (the current transaction's data was accepted but the endpoint isn't yet ready for another data packet). The host can return only ACK.

Additional Contents: None. The handshake packet consists of the PID alone.

Comments: If the receiver detected an error in the token or data packet, the receiver returns no handshake packet.

Status Stage

The Status stage is where the device reports the success or failure of the entire transfer. The purpose of the Status stage is similar to the purpose of a transaction's handshake packet, and in fact the status information sometimes travels in the handshake packet of the Status stage. But the Status stage reports the success or failure of the entire transfer, rather than of a single transaction.

In some cases (such as after receiving the first packet of a device descriptor during enumeration), the host may begin the Status stage before the Data stage has completed, and the device must detect the token packet of the Status stage, abandon the Data stage, and complete the Status stage.

Here are more details about each of the packets in the Status stage's transaction:

Token Packet

Purpose: identifies the receiver and indicates the direction of the Status stage's data packet.

Sent by: the host.

PID: the opposite of the direction of the previous transaction's data packet. If the Data stage's PID was OUT or if there was no Data stage, the Status stage's PID is IN. If the Data stage's PID was IN, the Status stage's PID is OUT.

Additional Contents: the device and endpoint addresses.

Data Packet

Purpose: enables the receiver of the Data stage's data to indicate the status of the transfer.

Sent by: if the Status stage's token packet's PID is IN, the device sends the data packet; if the Status stage's token packet's PID is OUT, the host sends the data packet.

PID type: DATA1

Additional Contents: The host sends a zero-length data packet. A device may send a zero-length data packet (success), NAK (busy), or STALL (endpoint halted).

Comments: For most requests, a zero-length data packet sent by the device indicates that the requested action (if any) has been taken. An exception is Set_Address, which the device implements after the Status stage has completed.

Handshake Packet

Purpose: the sender of the Data stage's data indicates the status of the transfer.

Sent by: the receiver of the Status stage's data packet. If the Status stage's token packet's PID is IN, the host sends the handshake packet; if the token packet's PID is OUT, the device sends the data packet.

PID type: the device's response may be ACK (success), NAK (busy), or STALL (the request isn't supported or the endpoint is halted). The host's response to a data packet received without error must be ACK.

Additional Contents: none. The handshake packet consists of the PID alone.

Comments: The Status stage's handshake packet is the final transmission in the transfer. If the receiver detected an error in the token or data packet, the receiver returns no handshake packet.

For any request that's expected to take many milliseconds to carry out, the protocol should define an alternate way to determine when the request has completed. Doing so ensures that the host doesn't waste a lot of time asking for an acknowledgement that will take a long time to appear. An example is the Set_Port_Feature(PORT_RESET) request sent to a hub. The reset signal lasts at least 10 milliseconds. Rather than forcing the host to wait this long for the device to complete the reset, the hub acknowledges receiving the request when the hub first places the port in the reset state. When the reset is complete, the hub sets a bit that the host can retrieve at its leisure, using a Get_Port_Status request.

Handling Errors

Devices don't always carry out every control-transfer request they receive. The device's firmware might not support a request. Or the device may be unable to respond because its firmware has crashed, or the endpoint is in the Halt condition, or the device is no longer attached to the bus. The host may also decide for any reason to end a transfer early, before all of the data has been sent.

An example of an unsupported request is one that uses a request code that the device's firmware doesn't know how to respond to. Or a device may support the request but other information in the Setup stage doesn't match what the device expects or supports. On these occasions, a Request Error condition exists and the device notifies the host by sending a STALL code in a handshake packet. Devices must respond to the Setup transaction with an ACK, so the STALL must transmit in a handshake packet in the Data or Status stage.

On failing to get an expected response or on detecting an error in received data or a Halt condition at the endpoint, the host abandons the transfer.

The host then tries to re-establish communications by sending the token packet for a new Setup transaction. If a device receives a token packet for a Setup transaction before completing a previous control transfer, the device must abandon the previous transfer and begin the new one. If the transfer is using the Default Control Pipe and a new token packet doesn't cause the device to recover, the host takes more drastic action, requesting the device's hub to reset the device's port.

The host may also end a transfer early by beginning the Status stage before completing all of the Data stage's transactions. In this case, the device must abandon the rest of the data and respond to the Status stage the same as if all of the data had transferred.

Device Firmware

The following descriptions are an overview of what typical device firmware must do to support control transfers.

Control Write Requests with a Data Stage

To complete a Control Write request where the host sends data to the device, the device must detect the request in the Setup stage, receive data in the Data stage, and return a handshake in the Status stage:

1. The hardware detects a Setup packet, stores the contents of the transaction's data packet, returns ACK, and triggers an interrupt.

2. The interrupt-service routine decodes the request and configures Endpoint 0 to accept data that arrives following an OUT token packet. The endpoint should also be able to handle the arrival of a new Setup packet, in case the host decides to abandon the transfer early.

3. The device returns to normal operation. The arrival of an OUT token packet at Endpoint 0 indicates that the host is sending data in the Data stage. The endpoint returns ACK in the handshake packet and the hardware triggers an interrupt.

4. The interrupt-service routine stores or uses the received data.

5. If more data packets are expected in the Data stage, steps 3 and 4 repeat for additional OUT transactions, up to the wLength value in the Setup transaction.

6. When all of the data has been received, the firmware configures Endpoint 0 to send a zero-length data packet in response to an IN token packet. The host returns ACK to complete the transfer.

Control Write Requests with No Data Stage

To complete a Control Write request when there is no Data stage, the device must detect the request in the Setup stage and send a handshake in the Status stage:

1. The hardware detects a Setup packet, stores the contents of the transaction's data packet, returns ACK, and triggers an interrupt.

2. The interrupt-service routine decodes the request, does what is needed to perform the requested action, and configures Endpoint 0 to respond to an IN token packet. The endpoint should also be able to handle the arrival of a new Setup packet in case the host decides to abandon the transfer early.

3. A received IN token packet begins the Status stage. The endpoint sends a zero-length data packet and the host returns ACK to complete the transfer.

Control Read Requests

To complete a Control Read request, where the host requests data from the device, the device must detect the request in the Setup stage, send data in the Data stage, and acknowledge a received handshake in the Status stage:

1. The hardware detects a Setup packet, stores the contents of the transaction's data packet, returns ACK, and triggers an interrupt.

2. The interrupt-service routine decodes the request and configures Endpoint 0 to send data on receiving an IN token packet. The endpoint should also be able to handle the arrival of a new Setup or OUT packet in case the host decides to abandon the transfer or begin the Status stage early.

3. The device returns to normal operation. The arrival of an IN token packet at Endpoint 0 indicates that the host is requesting data in the Data

stage. The device hardware sends the data, detects the received ACK from the host, and triggers an interrupt.

4. If there is more data to send, the interrupt service routine configures the endpoint to send the data on receiving another IN token packet and steps 3 and 4 repeat.

5. On receiving an OUT token packet followed by a zero-length data packet, the endpoint returns ACK to complete the transfer.

The Requests

Table 5-1 summarizes USB's eleven standard requests. Following the table is more information about each request. All devices must respond to these requests (though the response may be just a STALL). The values range from 00 to 0Ch, with some values unused.

Most of the requests are in pairs, with each Set request having a corresponding Get or Clear request. The exceptions are Set_Address, Synch_Frame, and Get_Status.

Table 5-1: The USB specification defines eleven standard requests for Control transfers.

Request Number	Request	Data source (Data stage)	Recipient	wValue	wIndex	Data Length (bytes) in Data stage (wLength)	Data (in Data stage)
00h	Get_Status	device	device, interface, endpoint	0	device, interface, or endpoint	2	status
01h	Clear_Feature	no Data stage	device, interface, endpoint	feature	device, interface, or endpoint	–	–
03h	Set_Feature	no Data stage	device, interface, endpoint	feature	device, interface, or endpoint	–	–
05h	Set_Address	no Data stage	device	device address	0	–	–
06h	Get_Descriptor	device	device	descriptor type and index	device or language ID	descriptor length	descriptor
07h	Set_Descriptor	host	device	descriptor type and index	device or language ID	descriptor length	descriptor
08h	Get_Configuration	device	device	0	device	1	configuration
09h	Set_Configuration	no Data stage	device	configuration	device	–	–
0Ah	Get_Interface	device	interface	0	interface	1	alternate setting
0Bh	Set_Interface	no Data stage	interface	interface	interface	–	–
0Ch	Synch_Frame	device	endpoint	0	endpoint	2	frame number

Get_Status

Purpose: The host requests the status of the features of a device, interface, or endpoint.

Request Number (bRequest): 00h

Source of Data: device

Data Length (wLength): 2

Contents of wValue field: 0

Contents of wIndex field: For a device, 0. For an interface, the interface number. For an endpoint, the endpoint number.

Contents of data packet in the Data stage: the device, interface, or endpoint status.

Supported states: Default: undefined. Address: OK for address 0, Endpoint 0. Otherwise the device returns a STALL. Configured: OK.

Behavior on error: The device returns a STALL if the interface or endpoint doesn't exist.

Comments: For requests directed to the device, two status bits are defined. Bit 0 is the Self-Powered field: 0=bus-powered, 1=self-powered. (The host can't change this value.) Bit 1 is the Remote Wakeup field. The default on reset is 0 (disabled). All other bits are reserved. For requests directed to an interface, all bits are reserved. For requests directed to an endpoint, only bit 0 is defined. Bit 0=1 indicates a Halt condition. See Set_Feature and Clear_Feature for more details on Remote Wakeup and Halt.

Clear_Feature

Purpose: The host requests to disable a feature on a device, interface, or endpoint.

Request Number (bRequest): 01h.

Source of Data: no Data stage

Data Length (wLength): none

Contents of wValue field: the feature to disable

Contents of wIndex field: For a device feature, 0. For an interface feature, the interface number. For an endpoint feature, the endpoint number.

Contents of data packet in the Data stage: none.

Supported states: Default: undefined. Address: OK for address 0, Endpoint 0. Otherwise the device returns a STALL. Configured: OK.

Behavior on error: If the feature, device, or endpoint specified doesn't exist, or if the feature can't be cleared, the device responds with a STALL. Behavior is undefined when wLength is greater than 0.

Comments: This request can clear the DEVICE_REMOTE_WAKEUP feature and the ENDPOINT_HALT feature, but not the TEST_MODE feature. Clear_Feature(ENDPOINT_HALT) resets the endpoint's data toggle to DATA0. See also Set_Feature and Get_Status.

Set_Feature

Purpose: The host requests to enable a feature on a device, interface, or endpoint.

Request Number (bRequest): 03h

Source of Data: no Data stage

Data Length (wLength): none

Contents of wValue field: the feature to enable

Contents of wIndex field: For a device, 0. For an interface, the interface number. For an endpoint, the endpoint number.

Contents of data packet in the Data stage: none.

Supported states: For features other than TEST_MODE: Default: undefined. Address: OK for address 0, Endpoint 0. Otherwise the device returns a STALL. Configured: OK. The TEST_MODE feature must be supported when using high speed in the Default, Address, and Configured states.

Behavior on error: If the endpoint or interface specified doesn't exist, the device responds with a STALL.

Comments: The USB 2.0 specification defines three features. ENDPOINT_HALT, with a value of 0, applies to endpoints. Bulk and interrupt endpoints must support the Halt condition. Two types of events may cause a Halt condition: a communications problem such as the device's not receiving a handshake packet or receiving more data than expected, or the device's receiving a Set_Feature request to halt the endpoint. DEVICE_REMOTE_WAKEUP, with a value of 1, applies to devices. When the host sets the DEVICE_REMOTE_WAKEUP feature, a device in the Suspend state can request the host to resume communications. TEST_MODE, with a value of 2, applies to devices. Setting this feature causes an the upstream-facing port to enter a test mode. Chapter 18 has more about test mode.

The Get_Status request tells the host what features, if any, are enabled. Also see Clear_Feature.

Set_Address

Purpose: The host specifies an address to use in future communications with the device.

Request Number (bRequest): 05h

Source of Data: no Data stage

Data Length (wLength): none

Contents of wValue field: new device address. Allowed values are 1 through 127. Each device on the bus, including the root hub, has a unique address.

Contents of wIndex field: 0

Contents of data packet in the Data stage: none

Supported States: Default, Address.

Behavior on error: not specified.

Comments: When a hub enables a port after power-up or attachment, the port uses the default address of 0 until completing a Set_Address request from the host.

This request is unlike most other requests because the device doesn't carry out the request until the device has completed the Status stage of the request by sending a zero-length data packet. The host sends the Status stage's token packet to the default address, so the device must detect and respond to this packet before changing its address.

After completing this request, all communications use the new address.

A device using the default address of zero is in the Default state. After completing a Set_ Address request to set an address other than zero, the device enters the Address state.

A device must send the handshake packet within 50 milliseconds after receiving the request and must implement the request within 2 milliseconds after completing the Status stage.

Get_Descriptor

Purpose: The host requests a specific descriptor.

Request Number (bRequest): 06h

Source of Data: device

Data Length (wLength): the number of bytes to return. If the descriptor is longer than wLength, the device returns up to wLength bytes. If the descriptor is shorter than wLength, the device returns the descriptor. If the descriptor is shorter than wLength and an even multiple of the endpoint's maximum packet size, the device follows the descriptor with a zero-length data packet. The host detects the end of the data on receipt of either the requested amount of data or a data packet containing less than the maximum packet size (including zero bytes).

Contents of wValue field: High byte: descriptor type. Low byte: descriptor index, to specify which descriptor to return when there are multiple descriptors of the same type.

Contents of wIndex field: for String descriptors, Language ID. Otherwise zero.

Contents of data packet in the Data stage: the requested descriptor.

Supported states: Default, Address, Configured.

Behavior on error: When a device receives a request that the device doesn't support, the device should return a STALL.

Comments: A host can request the following descriptor types: device, device_qualifier, configuration, other_speed configuration, and string. On receiving a request for a configuration or other_speed configuration descriptor, the device should return the requested descriptor followed by all of the configuration's subordinate descriptors up to the number of bytes requested. A class or vendor can also define descriptors that the host can request, such as the HID-class report descriptor. See also Set_Descriptor.

Set_Descriptor

Purpose: The host adds a descriptor or updates an existing descriptor.

Request Number (bRequest): 07h

Source of Data: host

Data Length (wLength): The number of bytes the host will transfer to the device.

Contents of wValue field: high byte: descriptor type. (See Get_Descriptor) Low byte: descriptor index to specify which descriptor is being sent when there are multiple descriptors of the same type.

Contents of wIndex field: For string descriptors, Language ID. Otherwise zero.

Contents of data packet in the Data stage: descriptor length.

Supported states: Address and Configured.

Behavior on error: When a device receives a request that the device doesn't support, the device should return a STALL.

Comments: This request makes it possible for the host to add new descriptors or change an existing descriptor. Many devices don't support this request because it allows errant software to place incorrect information in a descriptor. See also Get_Descriptor.

Get_Configuration

Purpose: The host requests the value of the current device configuration.

Request Number (bRequest): 08h

Source of Data: device

Data Length (wLength): 1

Contents of wValue field: 0

Contents of wIndex field: 0

Contents of data packet in the Data stage: Configuration value

Supported states: Address (returns zero), Configured

Behavior on error: not specified.

Comments: A device that isn't configured returns zero. See also Set_Configuration.

Set_Configuration

Purpose: The host requests the device to use the specified configuration.

Request Number (bRequest): 09h

Source of Data: no Data stage

Data Length (wLength): none

Contents of wValue field: The lower byte specifies a configuration. If the value matches a configuration supported by the device, the device implements the requested configuration. A value of zero indicates not configured. If the value is zero, the device enters the Address state and requires a new Set_Configuration request to be configured.

Contents of wIndex field: 0

Contents of data packet in the Data stage: none

Supported states: Address, Configured.

Behavior on error: If wValue isn't equal to zero or a configuration supported by the device, the device returns a STALL.

Comments: After completing a Set_Configuration request specifying a supported configuration, the device enters the Configured state. Many standard requests require the device to be in the Configured state. See also Get_Configuration. This request resets the endpoint's data toggle to DATA0.

Get_Interface

Purpose: For devices with interfaces that have multiple, mutually exclusive settings for an interface, the host requests the currently active interface setting.

Request Number (bRequest): 0Ah

Source of Data: device

Data Length (wLength): 1

Contents of wValue field: 0

Contents of wIndex field: interface number

Contents of data packet in the Data stage: the current setting

Supported states: Configured

Behavior on error: If the interface doesn't exist, the device returns a STALL.

Comments: The interface number in the wIndex field of this request refers to the bInterface field in an interface descriptor. This value distinguishes an interface from other interfaces that are active at the same time. The setting in the Data field in this request refers to the value in the bAlternateInterface field in the interface descriptor. This value identifies which of two or more alternate (mutually exclusive) settings an interface is currently using. Each setting has an interface descriptor and optional endpoint descriptors. Many devices support only one interface setting. See also Set_Interface.

Set_Interface

Purpose: For devices with interfaces that have alternate (mutually exclusive) settings, the host requests the device to use a specific interface setting.

Request Number (bRequest): 0Bh

Source of Data: no Data stage

Data Length (wLength): none

Contents of wValue field: alternate setting to select

Contents of wIndex field: interface number

Contents of data packet in the Data stage: none

Supported states: Configured

Behavior on error: If the device supports only a default interface, the device may return a STALL. If the requested interface or setting doesn't exist, the device returns a STALL.

Comments: This request resets the endpoint's data toggle to DATA0. See also Get_Interface

Synch_Frame

Purpose: The device sets and reports an endpoint's synchronization frame.

Request Number (bRequest): 0Ch

Source of Data: host

Data Length (wLength): 2

Contents of wValue field: 0

Contents of wIndex field: endpoint number

Contents of data packet in the Data stage: frame number

Supported states: Default: undefined. Address: The device returns STALL. Configured: OK.

Behavior on error: If the endpoint doesn't support the request, the endpoint should return STALL.

Comments: In isochronous transfers, a device endpoint may request data packets that vary in size, following a sequence. For example, an endpoint may send a repeating sequence of 8, 8, 8, 64 bytes. The Synch_Frame request enables the host and endpoint to agree on which frame will begin the sequence.

On receiving a Synch_Frame request, an endpoint returns the number of the frame that will precede the beginning of a new sequence

This request is rarely used because there is rarely a need for the information it provides.

Other Control Requests

In addition to the requests defined in the USB 2.0 specification, a device may respond to class-specific and vendor-specific control requests.

Class-specific Requests

A class may define requests for devices in its class. A class-specific request may be required or optional for devices in the class. Some requests are unrelated to the standard requests, while others build on the standard requests by defining class-specific fields in a request. An example of a request that's unrelated to the standard requests is the Get_Max_LUN request supported by some mass-storage devices. The host uses this request to find out the number of logical units the interface supports. An example of a request that builds on an existing request is the Get_Port_Status request that hubs must support. This request is structured like the standard Get_Status request. But Get_Port_Status has different values in two fields. In bmRequestType, bits 6 and 5 are 01 to indicate that the request is defined by a standard USB class, and bits 4 through 0 are 00011 to indicate that the request applies to a unit other than the device or an interface or endpoint. (The request applies to a port on a hub.) The wIndex field holds the port number.

Vendor-specific Requests

A vendor may define custom requests for control transfers with specific devices. Implementing a custom request in a control transfer requires all of the following:

- Vendor-defined fields as needed in the Setup and optional Data stages of the request. Bits 6 and 5 in the Setup stage's data packet are set to 10 to indicate a vendor-defined request.

- In the device, code that detects the request number in the Setup packet and knows how to respond.

- In the host, a vendor-specific device driver to initiate the request. Applications can't initiate vendor-specific requests on their own. The application must call a function exposed by a driver that defines the request.

6

Chip Choices

When you need to select a USB controller for a project, the good news is that there are plenty of chips to choose from. The down side is that deciding what controller to use in a project can be overwhelming at first.

As with any project involving embedded systems, the decision depends on what functions the chip has to perform, cost, availability, and ease of development. Ease of development depends on the availability and quality of development tools, device-driver software for the host, and sample code, plus your experience with and preferences for device architecture and language compilers.

This chapter is a guide to selecting a USB controller, including a tutorial about what you need to consider and descriptions of a sampling of chips with a range of abilities. The chips covered include inexpensive ones with simple architectures and basic USB support as well as more full-featured, high-end chips. Chapter 20 discusses controllers for use in USB On-The-Go devices.

Components of a USB Device

Every USB device must have the intelligence to implement the USB protocol. The device must detect and respond to requests and other events at its USB port. The device must be able to provide data to be sent on the bus and retrieve and use data received on the bus. A microcontroller or application-specific integrated circuit (ASIC) typically performs these functions in the device.

Controller chips vary in how much firmware support they require for USB communications. Some controllers require little more than accessing a series of registers to provide and retrieve USB data. Others require the device firmware to handle more of the protocol, including managing the sending of descriptors to the host, setting data-toggle values, and ensuring that the appropriate handshake packets are sent.

Some controllers have a general-purpose CPU on chip. Others must interface to an external CPU that handles the non-USB tasks and communicates with the USB controller as needed. These chips are sometimes called USB interface chips to distinguish them from microcontrollers with USB capabilities. All USB controllers have a USB port along with whatever buffers, registers, and other I/O capabilities the controller requires to accomplish its tasks. A controller chip with a general-purpose CPU has either program and data memory on-chip or an interface to these in external memory.

For high-volume applications that require fast performance, another option is to design and manufacture an ASIC. Several sources offer synthesizable VHDL and Verilog Source code for use in custom ASICs.

Not all controller chips support all four transfer types, and a controller may support one or more bus speeds. Many controllers support fewer than the maximum number of endpoint addresses (1 control endpoint and 30 other endpoint addresses) because few devices need the maximum number.

The USB Controller

A typical USB controller contains a USB transceiver, a serial interface engine, buffers to hold USB data, and registers to store configuration, status, and control information relating to USB communications.

The Transceiver

The USB transceiver provides a hardware interface between the device's USB connector and the circuits that control USB communications. The transceiver is typically on-chip, but some controllers allow interfacing to an external transceiver.

The Serial Interface Engine

The circuits that interface to the transceiver form a unit called the serial interface engine (SIE). The SIE typically handles the sending and receiving of data in transactions. The SIE doesn't interpret or use the data, but just sends the data that has been made available and stores any data received. A typical SIE does all of the following:

- Detect incoming packets.
- Send packets.
- Detect and generate Start-of-Packet, End-of-Packet, Reset, and Resume signaling.
- Encode and decode data in the format required on the bus (NRZI with bit stuffing).
- Check and generate CRC values.
- Check and generate Packet IDs.
- Convert between USB's serial data and parallel data in registers or memory.

Implementing these functions requires about 2500 gates.

Buffers

USB controllers use buffers to store recently received data and data that's ready to be sent on the bus. In some chips, such as PLX Technology's

NET2272, the CPU accesses the buffers by reading and writing to registers, while others, such as Cypress Semiconductor's EZ-USB, reserve a portion of data memory for the buffers.

Buffers that hold transmitted or received data are often structured as FIFO (first in, first out) buffers. Each read of a receive FIFO returns the byte that has been in the buffer the longest. Each write to a transmit FIFO stores a byte that will transmit after all of the bytes already in the buffer have transmitted. An internal pointer to the next location to be read or written to increments automatically as the firmware reads or writes to the FIFO.

In some chips, such as Cypress' enCoRe series, the USB buffers are in ordinary data memory and the firmware explicitly selects each location to read and write to. There is no pointer that increments automatically when the firmware reads or writes to the buffers. The bytes in the USB transmit buffer go out in order from the lowest address to the highest, and the bytes in a USB receive buffer are stored in the order they arrive, from lowest address to highest. These buffers technically aren't FIFOs, but are sometimes called that anyway.

To enable faster transfers, some chips have double buffers that can store two full sets of data in each direction. While one block is transmitting, the firmware can write the next block of data into the other buffer so the data will be ready to go as soon as the first block finishes transmitting. In the receive direction, the extra buffer enables a new transaction's data to arrive before the firmware has finished processing data from the previous transaction. The hardware automatically switches, or ping-pongs, between the two buffers. Some high-speed controllers, such as Cypress' EZ-USB FX2 series, support quadruple buffers.

Configuration, Status, and Control Information

USB controller chips typically have registers that hold information about what endpoints are enabled, the number of bytes received, the number of bytes ready to transmit, Suspend-state status, error-checking information, and other information about how the interface will be used and the current status of transmitted or received data. For example, setting a bit in a configuration register may enable an endpoint. The number of registers, their contents, and how to access them vary with the chip family. Because these details vary with the chip or chip family, the low-level device firmware for USB communications is specific to each chip or chip family.

Clock

USB communications require a timing source, typically provided by a crystal oscillator. Low-speed devices can sometimes use a less expensive ceramic resonator. Some controllers have on-chip clock circuits and don't require an external timing source.

Other Device Components

In addition to a USB interface, the circuits in a typical USB device include a CPU, program and data memory, other I/O interfaces, and additional features such as timers and counters. These circuits may be in the controller chip or in separate components.

CPU

A USB device's CPU controls the chip's actions by executing instructions in the firmware stored in the chip. If the USB controller has a CPU on-chip, the CPU may be based on a general-purpose microcontroller such as the 8051 or PICMicro, or the CPU may be an architecture developed specifically for USB applications. An interface-only USB controller can interface to any CPU with a compatible interface.

Program Memory

The program memory holds the code that the CPU executes. The program code assists in USB communications and carries out whatever other tasks the chip is responsible for. This memory may be in the microcontroller or in a separate chip.

The program storage may use any of a number of memory types: ROM, EPROM, EEPROM, Flash memory, or RAM. All except RAM (unless it's battery-backed) are nonvolatile; the memory retains its data after powering down. The amount of program memory may range from a couple of kilobytes on up. Chips that can access memory off-chip may support a Mega-byte or more of program memory.

Another name for the code stored in program memory is firmware, which indicates that the memory is non-volatile and not as easily changed as program code that can be loaded into RAM, edited, and re-saved on disk. In this book, I use the term firmware to refer to a controller's program code, with the understanding that the code may be stored in a variety of memory types, some more volatile than others.

ROM (read-only memory) must be mask-programmed at the factory and can't be erased. It's practical only for product runs in the thousands.

EPROM (erasable programmable ROM) is user-programmable. Many chips have inexpensive programming hardware and software available. To erase an EPROM, you insert the chip into an EPROM eraser, which exposes the circuits beneath the chip's quartz window to ultraviolet light. Data sheets rarely specify the number of erase/reprogram cycles that the chip can withstand, but it's typically at least 100.

OTP (one-time programmable) PROMs are a cheaper, non-erasable alternative to erasable EPROMs. Internally, they're identical to EPROMs, and you program them exactly like EPROMs. The difference is that the chips lack the window for erasing. The erasable varieties are useful for product development. Then to save cost, you can switch to OTP PROMs for the final product run. Many microcontrollers have both EPROM and OTP PROM variants.

Flash memory is another electrically-erasable memory technology that is popular because it doesn't need a quartz window and often doesn't need the special programming voltage required by other EPROMs. Current Flash-memory technology enables around 100,000 erase/reprogram cycles. Because Flash memory is easily reprogrammable, it's handy for making changes during project development and for programming the final firmware in low-volume projects

EEPROM (electrically erasable PROM) also doesn't need a window, nor does it need the special programming voltage required by other EPROMs. EEPROMs tend to have longer access times than Flash memory. EEPROMs are available both with the parallel interface used by EPROMs and Flash memory, and with a variety of synchronous serial interfaces: Microwire, I²C, and SPI. Serial EEPROMs are useful for storing small amounts of data that changes only occasionally, such as configuration data, including the Vendor ID and Product ID. Cypress' EZ-USB controllers can store their firmware in a serial EEPROM and load the firmware into RAM on powering up. Current EEPROM technology enables around 10 million erase/reprogram cycles.

RAM (random-access memory) can be erased and rewritten endlessly, but the stored data disappears when the chip powers down. It's possible to use RAM for program storage by using battery backup or by loading the code from a PC on each power-up. Any CPU with external program memory can use battery-backed RAM for program storage. Cypress Semiconductor's EZ-USB chips can use RAM for program storage, along with special hardware and driver code that loads code into the chip on power up or attachment. Host-loadable RAM has no limit on the number of erase/rewrite cycles. For battery-backed RAM, the limit is the battery life. Access times for RAM are fast.

Data Memory

Data memory provides temporary storage during program execution. The contents of data memory may include data received from the USB port, data to be sent to the USB port, values to be used in calculations, or anything else the chip needs to remember or keep track of. Data memory is usually RAM. Typical amounts of internal data memory are 128 to 1024 bytes.

Other I/O

Every USB controller has an interface to the world outside of itself in addition to the USB port. An interface-only chip must have a local bus or other interface to the device's CPU. (An exception is FTDI Chip's controllers used in Bit Bang mode to implement basic inputs and outputs.) Most chips also have a series of general-purpose input and output (I/O) pins that can connect to other circuits. A chip may have built-in support for other serial interfaces, such as an asynchronous interface for RS-232, or synchronous interfaces such as I²C, Microwire, and SPI. Some chips have special-purpose interfaces. For example, the Philips UDA1325 is a stereo USB codec for audio applications and contains an I²S (Inter-IC Sound) digital stereo playback input and output.

Other Features

A device controller chip may have additional features such as hardware timers, counters, analog-to-digital and digital-to-analog converters, and pulse-width-modulation (PWM) outputs. Just about anything that you might find in a general-purpose microcontroller is likely to be available in a USB device controller.

Simplifying Device Development

In selecting a chip for a project, an obvious consideration is finding a controller that meets the hardware requirements of the product being designed. In addition, project development will be easier and quicker if you select a controller chip with all of the following:

- A chip architecture and programming language that you're familiar with.
- Detailed and well-organized hardware documentation.
- Well-documented, bug-free example firmware for an application similar to yours.
- A development system that enables easy downloading and debugging of firmware.

In addition, your project will progress more quickly if the host system can use a class driver included with the operating system or a well-documented and bug-free driver provided by the chip vendor or another source and usable as-is or with minimal modifications.

These are not trivial considerations! The right choices will save you many hours and much aggravation.

Device Requirements

In selecting a device controller suitable for a project, these are some of the areas to consider:

How fast does the data need to transfer? A device's rate of data transfer depends on whether the device supports low, full, or high speed, the transfer type being used, and how busy the bus is. As a device designer, you don't control how busy a user's bus will be, but you can select a speed and transfer type that give the best possible performance for your application.

If a product requires no more than low-speed interrupt and control transfers, a low-speed chip may save money in circuit-board design, components, and cables. HID-class devices can use low-speed chips. But remember that low-speed devices can transfer only eight data bytes per transaction, and the USB specification limits the guaranteed bandwidth for an interrupt endpoint to 800 bytes/second, which is much less than the bus speed of 1.5 Megabits/second. Even if low speed is feasible, don't rule out full or high speed automatically. Implementing low speed's slower edge rates increases the manufacturing cost of low-speed controllers, so the controller chips themselves may not be cheaper. You may find a full-speed or even a high-speed chip that can do the job at the same or even a lower price.

Compared to low and full speed, circuit-board design for high-speed devices is more critical and can add to the cost of a product. In most cases, devices that support high speed should also support full speed to enable them to work with 1.x hosts and hubs.

How many and what type of endpoints? Each endpoint address is configured to support a transfer type and direction. A device that does only control transfers needs just the default endpoint. Interrupt, bulk, or isochronous transfers require additional endpoint addresses. Not all chips support all transfer types. Most support fewer than the maximum possible number of endpoints.

Must the firmware be easily upgradable? For program memory, some devices use windowed EPROM, OTP PROM, or other memory that isn't easily erased and re-written. To change the program, you need to insert a new chip or remove, erase, re-program, and replace the chip. Cypress' EZ-USB has an easier way, with the ability to load firmware from the host into RAM on each power up or attachment. Another option is to store the program code in electrically reprogrammable Flash memory or EEPROM. This memory can be in the device controller or in an external chip. The *Device Firmware Upgrade* class specification describes a mechanism for loading firmware from a host to a device. Chapter 7 has more about this class.

Does the device require a flexible cable? One reason why mice are almost certain to be low-speed devices is that the less stringent requirements for low-speed cables mean that the cable can be thinner and more flexible. However, USB 2.0-compliant low-speed cables have the same requirements as full and high speed except that the braided outer shield and twisted pair are recommended, but not required.

Does the device require a long cable? A cable that attaches to a low-speed device can be no longer than three meters, while full-speed cables can be five meters.

What other hardware features and abilities are needed? Other things to consider are the amount of general-purpose or specialized I/O, the size of program and data memory, on-chip timers, and other special features that a particular device might require.

Chip Documentation

Most vendors supplement their chips' data sheets with technical manuals, application notes, example code, and other documentation. The best way to get a head start on writing firmware is to begin with example code that's similar to your application. Working from an example is much easier than trying to put something together from scratch. Chip and tool vendors vary widely in the amount and quality of documentation and example code provided, so it's worth checking the manufacturers' Web sites to find out what's available before you commit to a chip. In some cases you can find code examples from other sources, especially via the Internet, from other users who are willing to share what they've written.

Driver Choices

The other side of programming a USB device is the driver and application software at the host. Here again, examples are useful.

If your device fits into a class supported by the operating systems the device will run under, you don't have to worry about writing or finding a device driver. For example, applications can access a HID-class device using standard API functions that communicate with the HID drivers included with Windows.

Some vendors provide a generic driver that you can use to exchange data with the device. An examples is Cypress' CyUsb driver, which is a general-purpose driver suitable for communicating with any device that contains a Cypress controller and doesn't belong to a standard class. Silicon Laboratories is another manufacturer that provides a general-purpose driver for use with the company's chips. Chapter 7 and Chapter 8 have more about classes and device drivers.

Debugging Tools

Ease of debugging also makes a big difference in how easy it is to get a project up and running. Products that can help include development boards and software offered by chip vendors and other sources. A protocol analyzer is also very useful during debugging. Chapter 17 has more about protocol analyzers.

Development Boards from Chip Vendors

Chip manufacturers offer development boards and debugging software to make it easier for developers to test and debug new designs. A development board enables you to load a program from a PC into the chip's program memory, or into circuits that emulate the chip's hardware.

Silicon Laboratories' C8051F32x controllers include a dedicated 2-wire debugging interface that uses no additional memory or port bits on the chip. These chips don't require using an emulator or assigning of chip resources to debugging.

The debugging software provided with a development board is typically a monitor program that runs on a PC and enables you to control program execution and watch the results. Standard features include the ability to step through a program line by line, set breakpoints, and view the contents of the chip's registers and memory. You can run the monitor program and a test application at the same time. You can see exactly what happens inside the chip when it communicates with your application.

If you have a development system for your favorite microcontroller family, you may be able to use the system for USB developing as well.

Boards from Other Sources

If you're on a strict budget, inexpensive printed-circuit boards from a variety of vendors can serve as an alternative to the development kits offered by chip manufacturers. You can also use these boards as the base for one-of-a-kind or small-scale projects, saving the time and expense of designing and making a board for the controller chip.

I/O Boards. A typical board contains a USB controller and connector along with a variety of I/O pins that you can connect to external circuits of your own design. The EZ-USB family is a natural choice for this type of board because its firmware is downloadable from the host, so you don't have to worry about programming hardware. Several sources offer boards with EZ-USB chips.

The USB I2C/IO board from DeVaSys Embedded Systems (Figure 6-1) contains an AN2131 EZ-USB chip, a connector with 20 bits of I/O, an I^2C interface for synchronous serial communications, and an asynchronous serial interface. The on-board 24LC128 is an I^2C EEPROM that can store 16 kilobytes of data, including a Vendor ID, Product ID, and firmware. The board can load its firmware from EEPROM or from the host on attachment or power-up.

DeVaSys provides the board's schematic and a free custom device driver and firmware that enable applications to open communications and read and write to ports, including the I^2C port. If you prefer, you can load your own

Figure 6-1: The USB I2C/IO board from DeVaSys contains an EZ-USB and a variety of options for I/O.

firmware into the device and use your own driver or a driver provided by Windows.

Other sources offer similar boards using the EZ-USB and other controllers.

Emulating a Device with a PC. Another option that can be useful in the early stages of developing is using a PC to emulate a device. You can use the compilers, debuggers, and other software tools you're familiar with on your PC and compile, run, and debug the device code on the PC.

PLX Technology's NET2272 PCI-RDK is a development kit that enables using a PC as a device when developing code using PLX Technology's NET2272 USB interface chip. The kit includes a PCI card with a header that attaches to a daughter card that contains a NET2272. You can install the PCI card in a PC and write applications that perform the role of device firmware that communicates with the interface chip. The application can run as a console application on the PC.

The USB connector on the PCI card can connect to any USB host. When development on the emulated device is complete, you can port the firmware to run on the CPU that the final design will use. If you want to use the development kit's circuits, you can remove the daughter board from the PCI card and wire the daughter board to your device's hardware.

Of course, there may be timing differences on the emulated device, and the PC won't have the same hardware architecture as the device, but the ease of developing on a PC can help in getting the code for enumerating and basic data transfers working quickly.

Controllers with Embedded CPUs

The following descriptions of USB controllers with embedded CPUs will give an idea of the range of chips available. The chips described are a sampling, and new chips are being released all the time, so any new project warrants checking the latest offerings.

If you have a favorite CPU family, the chances are good that a USB-capable variant is available. Controllers that are compatible with existing chip families have two advantages. Many developers are already familiar with the architecture and instruction set. And selecting a popular family means that programming and debugging tools are available, and example code and other advice is likely to be available from other users.

The family with the most sources for device controllers is the venerable 8051. Intel originated the 8051 family and was the first to release 8051-compatible USB controllers (the 8x930 and 8x931). Intel no longer offers USB-capable 8051s, but other manufacturers do. Controllers compatible with other families are available as well, including Atmel's AVR, Microchip's PICmicro, and Freescale Semiconductor's 68HC05 and 68HC08. Table 6-1 lists a variety of chips that are compatible with popular microcontroller families.

Some device controllers contain CPUs designed specifically for USB applications. Instead of adding USB capability to an existing architecture, the

Table 6-1: USB controller chips that are compatible with popular microcontroller families are available from many sources.

Compatibility	Manufacturer	Chips	Bus Speed
Atmel AVR	Atmel	AT43USB35x, AT76C713	Full
Freescale/Motorola 68HC05	Freescale Semiconductor	68HC05JB3/4	Low
Freescale/Motorola 68HC08	Freescale Semiconductor	68HC08JB8	Low
Freescale/Motorola PowerPC	Freescale Semiconductor	MCF5482	Full/High
Infineon C166	Infineon	C161U	Full
Intel 80C186	AMD	Am186CC	Full
Intel 8051	Atmel	AT89C513x	Full
	Cypress Semiconductor	EZ-USB, EZ-USB FX	Full
		EZ-USB FX2	Full/High
	Prolific Technology	PL-23xx	Full
		PL-25xx	Full/High
	Silicon Laboratories	C8051F32x	Full
	Standard Microsystems Corporation (SMSC)	USB97Cxxx, USB222x	Full, Full/High
	Texas Instruments	TUSB3210/3410	Full
		TUSB6250	Full/High
Microchip PIC16	Microchip Technology	PIC16C7x5	Low
Microchip PIC18	Microchip Technology	PIC18F2455/2550/ 4455/4550	Low/Full
STMicroelectronics ST7, ST9	STMicroelectronics	ST7265X, ST7263, ST92163	Low, Full

designs are optimized for USB from the start. Cypress Semiconductor's enCoRe family is an example.

For common applications such as keyboards, drives, and interface converters, there are application-specific controllers that include hardware to support a particular application. The vendor often provides example firmware and software drivers when needed as well. Chapter 7 has more about controllers for specific applications.

The chips described below each contain a CPU and a USB controller.

Microchip PIC18F4550

Microchip Technology's PICmicro microcontrollers have many fans because of the chips' low cost, wide availability, many variants, speed, and low power consumption. The PIC18F4550 is a PICmicro microcontroller with a USB controller that can function at low and full speeds. Microchip offers several other full-speed variants with different combinations of features.

Architecture

The chip is a member of Microchip's high-performance, low-cost PIC18 series. Program memory is Flash memory. The chip also has 256 bytes of EEPROM. A bootloader routine can upgrade firmware via the USB port.

The chip has 34 I/O pins that include a 10-bit analog-to-digital converter, a USART, a synchronous serial port that can be configured to use I^2C or SPI, enhanced PWM capabilities, and two analog comparators.

The USB module and CPU can use separate clock sources, enabling the CPU to use a slower, power-saving clock.

USB Controller

The USB controller supports all four transfer types and up to 30 endpoint addresses plus the default endpoint. The endpoints share 1 kilobyte of buffer memory, and transfers can use double buffering. For isochronous transfers, USB data can transfer directly to and from a streaming parallel port.

For each enabled endpoint address, the firmware must reserve memory for a buffer and a buffer descriptor. The buffer descriptor consists of four registers. The status register contains status information and the two highest bits of the endpoint's byte count. The byte count register plus the two bits in the status register contain the number of bytes to be transmitted or sent in an IN transaction or the number of bytes expected or received in an OUT transaction. The address low register and address high register contain the starting address for the endpoint's buffer in RAM.

The microcontroller's CPU and the USB SIE share access to the buffers and buffer descriptors. A UOWN bit in the buffer descriptor's status register determines whether the CPU or SIE owns a buffer and its buffer descriptor. The SIE has ownership when data is ready to transmit or when waiting to receive data on the bus. When the SIE has ownership, the CPU should not attempt to access the buffer or buffer descriptor, except to read the UOWN bit. When readying an endpoint to perform a transfer, the last operation the firmware should perform is updating the status register to set UOWN to pass ownership to the SIE. When a transaction completes, the SIE clears the UOWN bit, passing ownership back to the CPU.

Each endpoint number also has a control register that can enable either a control endpoint, an IN endpoint, an OUT endpoint, or a pair of IN and OUT endpoints with the same endpoint number. Other bits in the register can stall the endpoint and disable handshaking (for isochronous transactions).

Additional registers store the device's address on the bus and contain status and control information for USB communications and interrupts.

Microchip provides USB Firmware Framework code and example applications for USB communications. The firmware is written for Microchip's C18 C compiler. The Framework code is structured to make it as easy as possible to develop firmware for devices in different classes and vendor-specific devices. Chapter 11 has more about using this chip.

Two other USB-capable microcontrollers from Microchip are the PIC16C745 and PIC16C765. These are less flexible because they support low speed only and their program memory is EPROM instead of Flash memory.

Cypress EZ-USB

Cypress Semiconductor's EZ-USB family includes full-speed and full/high speed controllers. The chips support a variety of options for storing firmware, including loading firmware from the host on each power-up or attachment.

The EZ-USB family originated with Anchor Chips, which Cypress acquired in 1999. You may see the name *Anchor* in older documentation.

Architecture

The EZ-USB's architecture is similar to Maxim Integrated Products/Dallas Semiconductor's DS80C320, which is an 8051 whose core has been redesigned for enhanced performance. The chip uses four clock cycles per instruction cycle, compared to the original 8051's twelve. Each instruction takes between one and five instruction cycles. On average, an EZ-USB is 2.5 times as fast as an 8051 with the same clock speed.

The instruction set is compatible with the 8051's. All of the combined code and data memory is RAM. There is no non-volatile memory on-chip. However, the chips support non-volatile storage in I²C serial EEPROM and in external parallel memory.

The EZ-USB family includes three series: the basic EZ-USB (AN21XX), the FX (CY7C646XX), and the FX2 (CY7C68013). Within each series are chips that vary in features such as the number of I/O pins or availability of an external data bus. Table 6-2 summarizes the features of each series. The FX series adds faster I/O and a general programmable interface that supports configurable, automated handshaking. The FX2 series adds support for high speed.

Keil Software has a C compiler for the EZ-USB family, or you can use assembly code. The compiler has a limited but free evaluation version. Cypress provides Frameworks firmware in C to handle much of the work of USB communications.

USB Controller

Some of the EZ-USB chips support the maximum number of endpoints and all four transfer types. Chips with fewer endpoints are also available. The EZ-USB's many options for storing firmware make its architecture

Table 6-2: Cypress Semiconductor's EZ-USB family is compatible with the 8051 microcontroller.

Feature	AN21xx (EZ-USB)	CY7C646xx (EZ-USB-FX)	CY7C68013 (EZ-USB-FX2)
Speed	Full	Full	Full/High
Number of endpoints	13, 16, 31	31	11
Compatibility	80C320, 8051	80C320, 8051	80C320, 8051
RAM (bytes)	256 + 4-8K combined data and program memory	256 + 4-8K combined data and program memory	256 + 8K combined data and program memory
Program memory type	RAM, serial EEPROM, external parallel	RAM, serial EEPROM, external parallel	RAM, serial EEPROM, external parallel
Internal program memory (bytes)	4–8K combined data and program memory	4–8K combined data and program memory	8K combined data and program memory
External memory bus (bytes)	64K	64K	one or two 64K buses
General-purpose I/O pins	16–24	16–40	16–40
Other I/O	2 UARTs, I^2C	2 UARTs, I^2C	2 UARTs, I^2C
Power Supply Voltage	3–3.6	3–3.6	3–3.6
Number of Pins	44, 48, 80	52, 80, 128	56, 100, 128

more complicated compared to other chips. The options are useful because they make the chip very flexible, so I'll describe them in some detail.

When an EZ-USB wants to use firmware stored in the host, the device enumerates twice. On boot up or device attachment, the host attempts to enumerate the device. But how can the host enumerate a device with no stored firmware? Every EZ-USB contains a core that knows how to respond to enumeration requests and can control communications when the device first attaches to the bus. The EZ-USB core is independent from the 8051 core that normally controls the chip after enumeration. The EZ-USB core communicates with the host while holding the 8051 core in the reset state.

The EZ-USB core also responds to vendor-specific requests that enable the chip to receive, store, and run firmware received from the host. For basic testing, the core circuits also enable the device to transfer data using all four transfer types without any firmware programming.

A ReNum register bit determines whether the EZ-USB or 8051 core responds to requests at Endpoint 0. On power-up, ReNum is zero and the EZ-USB core controls Endpoint 0. When ReNum is set to one, the 8051 core controls Endpoint 0.

The source of an EZ-USB's firmware depends on two things: the contents of the initial bytes in an external EEPROM and the state of the chip's EA input. On power-up and before enumeration, the EZ-USB core attempts to read bytes from a serial EEPROM on the chip's I²C interface. The result, along with the state of the chip's EA input, tell the core what to do next: use the default mode, load firmware from the host, load firmware from EEPROM, or boot from code memory on the external parallel data bus (Table 6-3). Chips in all three EZ-USB series can use the methods described below. The values in the first EEPROM locations vary depending on whether the chip is an EZ-USB, EZ-USB-FX or EZ-USB-FX2. The description below uses the values for the basic EZ-USB. Table 6-3 has the values for the other series.

Default Mode. The default mode is the most basic mode of operation and doesn't use the serial EEPROM or other external memory. The EZ-USB core uses this mode if EA is logic low and either the core detects no EEPROM or the first byte read from EEPROM is not B0h or B2h.

When the host enumerates the device, the EZ-USB core responds to requests. During this time, the 8051 core is in the reset state. This reset state is controlled by a register bit in the chip. The host can request to write to this bit to place the chip in and out of reset. This reset affects the 8051 core only and is unrelated to USB's Reset signaling.

The descriptors retrieved by the host identify the device as a Default USB Device. The host matches the retrieved Vendor ID and Product ID with values in a Cypress-provided INF file that instructs the host to load one of Cypress' general purpose drivers (either the CyUsb driver or the older General Purpose Driver) to communicate with the chip. The ReNum bit remains at zero.

Table 6-3: An EZ-USB can run firmware from four sources.

Firmware Source	State of EA pin	First Byte in Serial EEPROM
Load from host on re-enumerating	Don't care	EZ-USB: B0h EZ-USB-FX: B4h EZ-USB-FX2: C0h
Load from serial EEPROM	Don't care	EZ-USB: B2h EZ-USB-FX: B6h EZ-USB-FX2: C2h
Default USB Device	L	No EEPROM present or EZ-USB: not B0h or B2h, EZ-USB-FX: not B4h or B6h, EZ-USB-FX2: not C0h or C2h,
External parallel memory	H	No EEPROM present or EZ-USB: not B0h or B2h, EZ-USB-FX: not B4h or B6h, EZ-USB-FX2: not C0h or C2h

This default mode is intended for use in debugging. You can use this mode to get the USB interface up and transferring data. In addition to supporting transfers over Endpoint 0, the Default USB Device can use the other three transfer types on other endpoints. All of this is possible without having to write any firmware or device drivers.

Load Firmware from the Host. The core can also read identifying bytes from the EEPROM on power up and provide this information to the host during enumeration. If the first value read from the EEPROM is B0h, the core reads EEPROM bytes containing the chip's Vendor ID, Product ID, and release number. On device attachment or system boot up, the host uses these bytes to find a matching INF file that identifies a driver for the device. The driver contains firmware to download to the device before re-enumerating. Cypress provides instructions for building a driver with this ability.

The driver uses the vendor-specific Firmware Load request to download the firmware to the device. The firmware contains a new set of descriptors and the code the device will run. For example, a HID-class device will have report descriptors and code for transferring HID report data.

On completing the download, the driver causes the chip to exit the reset state and run the firmware. By writing to a register that controls the chip's

DISCON# pin, the firmware causes the device to electrically emulate removal from, then reattachment to the bus. The pin either pulls up or floats one end of a resistor whose opposite end connects to D+. The pin indicates device attachment when pulled up and device removal when floating. The firmware also sets ReNum to 1 to cause the 8051 core, instead of the EZ-USB core, to respond to requests at Endpoint 0.

On detecting the emulated re-attachment, the host enumerates the device again, this time retrieving the newly stored descriptors and using the information in them to select a device driver to load.

The obvious advantage to storing the firmware on the host is easy updates. To update the firmware, you just store the new version on the host and the driver sends the firmware to the device on the next power up or attachment. There's no need to replace the chip or use special programming hardware or software. The disadvantages are increased complexity of the device driver, the need to have the firmware available on the host, and longer enumeration time.

Load Firmware from EEPROM. A third mode of operation provides a way for the chip to store its firmware in an external serial EEPROM. If the first byte read from the EEPROM is B2h, the core loads the EEPROM's entire contents into RAM on power-up. The EEPROM must contain the Vendor ID, Product ID, and release number as well as all descriptors required for enumeration and whatever other firmware and data the device requires. On exiting the reset state, the device has everything it needs for USB communications. The core sets the ReNum bit to 1 on completing the loading of the code. When enumerating the device, the host reads the stored descriptors and loads the appropriate driver. There is no re-enumeration.

Run Code from External Parallel Memory. If no EEPROM is detected, or if the first byte isn't B0h or B2h, and if EA is a logic high, the chip boots from code memory on the external parallel data bus. This memory can be EPROM, EEPROM, Flash memory, or battery-backed RAM. The memory contains the descriptors and other firmware. ReNum is set to 1. The host enumerates the device and loads a driver, and there is no re-enumeration.

Cypress enCoRe II

The chips in Cypress Semiconductor's enCoRe II series (yes, that odd capitalization is how Cypress has trademarked the name) are inexpensive, low-speed controllers with an instruction set optimized for USB communications.

CPU Architecture

The enCoRe II series is the latest in Cypress' offerings of low-speed controllers. The chips are similar to the original enCoRe controllers except that the program memory is Flash memory instead of OTP EPROM. The architecture is unique to Cypress, so to program in assembly code, you'll need to learn a new instruction set. However, the instruction set is small and learning the syntax should be fairly painless if you have experience with assembly-code programming. A C compiler is also available.

The series includes chips with varying amounts of program memory, number of I/O pins, and packaging. The options include up to 256 bytes of RAM, 8 kilobytes of Flash memory, and 36 I/O pins, with two of the pins serving as the USB interface.

The chips contain internal oscillators that eliminate the need to add external crystals or resonators. The USB port can be configured for PS/2 (synchronous serial) communications to enable a pointing device to support both interfaces. When USB mode is disabled, the two USB pins can serve as a serial-programming-mode interface for Flash programming.

USB Controller

The enCoRe II controllers have three endpoints, the required Endpoint 0 plus endpoints 1 and 2 for interrupt transfers. The chip can support one interrupt IN endpoint and one interrupt OUT endpoint, or two interrupt endpoints in the same direction. Each endpoint has an 8-byte buffer in RAM. USB communications require a fair amount of firmware support, so example code is helpful.

Freescale MC68HC908JB16

Freescale Semiconductor's MC68HC08 family of 8-bit microcontrollers includes chips with Flash memory and support for low-speed USB. The MC68HC908JB16 is an example. Freescale Semiconductor was created in 2004 when Motorola, Inc., spun off its Semiconductor Products sector.

Architecture

The MC68HC08 family is an upgrade to Freescale's popular MC68HC05 family. The 'HC08 chips are faster and more efficient, and the object code is upward compatible with 'HC05 code.

The 'HC908JB16 contains 16 kilobytes of Flash memory and 21 I/O pins. Two of the I/O pins are the USB interface. Some of the other I/O pins have hardware support for synchronous serial communications and a keyboard interface. A monitor ROM enables Flash-memory programming and debugging over an asynchronous serial interface using a single pin on the chip.

USB Controller

The USB controller is low speed and supports Endpoint 0, one interrupt IN endpoint, and one endpoint that can be configured as interrupt IN or interrupt OUT.

Freescale MCF5482 ColdFire

An example of a high-end controller with USB capability is Freescale Semiconductor's MCF5482 ColdFire microprocessor. The chip contains a 32-bit CPU and a full/high-speed USB device controller plus an Ethernet controller and plenty of other I/O. A request processor automatically processes many standard USB requests. For example, on receiving a Get_Descriptor request, the request processor retrieves the requested descriptor from RAM and returns the descriptor to the host. The chip supports Endpoint 0 and seven additional endpoint addresses.

Controllers that Interface to External CPUs

A controller that interfaces to an external CPU enables you to add USB to just about any microcontroller circuit. A disadvantage is the need to use two chips, while other controllers combine the CPU and USB controller on one chip. Also, example circuits and code for USB communications using your CPU may not be available.

Controllers that interface to an external CPU may support a command set for USB-related communications, or the controller may just use a series of registers to store USB data and configuration, status, and control information.

Most interface chips have a local data bus that uses a parallel interface to communicate with the CPU. For fast transfers with external memory, many chips support direct memory access (DMA). In a device with a DMA controller, the CPU can set up a transfer that reads or writes a block of data into or from data memory without CPU intervention. For CPUs that don't have external parallel buses, a few controllers can use a synchronous or asynchronous serial interface. An interrupt pin can signal the CPU when the controller has received USB data or needs new data to send.

Table 6-4 compares a selection of interface chips. The following descriptions will give an idea of the range of chips available. New chips are being released all the time, so any new project warrants checking the latest offerings.

National Semiconductor USBN9603

National Semiconductor's USBN9603 can interface to any CPU with a parallel data bus, a Microwire interface, or even just four spare I/O pins controlled entirely in firmware to support Microwire communications.

Architecture

The '9603 has a serial interface engine for handling USB communications, USB endpoint buffers, and status and control registers. A CPU can access

Table 6-4: A Selection of USB Controllers that Interface to an external CPU.

Company	Chips	CPU Interface	Bus Speed
Agere Systems	USS-820D	Parallel	Full
FTDI Chip	FT232BM	Asynchronous serial	Full
	FT245BM	Parallel	Full
National Semiconductor	USBN9603/4	Parallel, Microwire	Full
Philips Semiconductors	PDIUSBD12, ISP1181/83	Parallel	Full
	ISP1581	Parallel	Full/High
PLX Technology	NET22272	Parallel	Full/High

the endpoint buffers and status and control registers at addresses 00h through 3Fh via an external, local bus.

The chip offers three options for accessing the local data bus: non-multiplexed parallel, multiplexed parallel, and Microwire synchronous serial.

Most CPUs with external data buses can use one of the parallel interfaces with little or no additional logic. For faster transfers of blocks of data, the chip supports a burst mode where the CPU writes a starting address to the controller chip, then transmits or receives multiple bytes at consecutive addresses. The external CPU must also support this mode. The parallel interfaces also support DMA transfers.

For microcontrollers that don't have an external parallel data bus, the '9603 offers a solution in its Microwire interface. Microwire requires just four lines and can interface to just about any microcontroller with four spare I/O pins. The interface uses data lines serial in (SIN) and serial out (SOUT), a chip select (CS), and a clock line (SYNC). Command/address and data bytes shift in and out, bit by bit, using transitions on the SYNC line as a timing reference. The external CPU controls SYNC. There is no minimum SYNC frequency, and the signal doesn't have to have a constant frequency; the CPU can toggle the line as needed. The interface just has to be fast enough to keep up with the USB traffic. If the USB port transfers only small, occasional blocks of data, you can program Microwire communications in firmware. Some microcontrollers, such as National Semiconductor's COP888, have support for Microwire built in.

USB Controller

The '9603 supports seven endpoint addresses: Endpoint 0 for control transfers, three IN endpoints, and three OUT endpoints. Endpoint 0's buffer is 8 bytes; the others are 64 bytes. An endpoint can receive a packet larger than the buffer size if the firmware reads incoming data fast enough to prevent the buffer from overflowing. In a similar way, an endpoint can send a packet larger than the buffer size if the firmware writes to the buffer fast enough to prevent the buffer from emptying. The USBN9604 is an identical chip except that its chip reset also resets the chip's clock-generation circuit. The '9604 is recommended for use in bus-powered devices.

Philips Semiconductors ISP1181B

The ISP1181B from Philips Semiconductors is a full-speed chip that interfaces to an external CPU over a parallel interface.

Architecture

The chip has a serial interface engine for handling USB traffic, a configurable 8- or 16-bit data bus, and a 2-bit address bus. The controller communicates with a CPU via a command set. When address bit A0 = 1, the controller interprets the lower byte on the data bus as a command. For commands that are followed by data, the CPU sets address bit A0 = 0 and transfers data to or from a register or endpoint buffer.

The chip supports multiplexed and non-multiplexed address buses and DMA transfers.

The ISP1183 is a low-power version with an 8-bit data bus and 32 pins, compared to 48 pins on the '1181. An earlier Philips chip, the PDIUSBD12, has a similar architecture but is less capable, with a slower data bus and fewer USB endpoints.

USB Controller

The '1181B's USB controller supports Endpoint 0 plus up to 14 additional endpoint addresses. All enabled endpoints share 2462 bytes of buffer memory. The control endpoint has 64-byte buffers. The amount of memory allocated to each of the other endpoint addresses is configurable. Isochronous and bulk endpoints are double buffered.

Firmware controls when the chip attaches to the bus. The chip appears detached from the bus until the external CPU sends a command to switch an internal pull-up resistor onto the bus's D+ line. The firmware-controlled connection can give the chip time to initialize on power up before being enumerated by the host.

A status output can connect to an LED that lights when a USB connection has been established and blinks on data transfers.

Philips Semiconductors ISP1581

The ISP1581 from Philips Semiconductors is a full/high-speed controller that interfaces to an external CPU over a parallel interface.

Architecture

The chip has a serial interface engine for handling USB traffic, a 16-bit data bus, and an 8-bit address bus. An external CPU can communicate with the controller by accessing a series of registers. The controller supports multiplexed and non-multiplexed address buses and DMA transfers.

USB Controller

The USB controller supports full and high speeds. In addition to Endpoint 0, the chip can support up to seven IN endpoint addresses and seven OUT endpoint addresses. All enabled endpoints share 8 kilobytes of buffer memory. The control endpoint has 64-byte buffers. The amount of memory allocated to each of the other endpoint addresses is configurable, and any of these endpoint addresses can use double buffering.

Firmware controls when the chip attaches to the bus. An external pull-up resistor connects to the chip's RPU pin and to a pull-up voltage. After a hardware reset, the chip appears detached from the bus until the external CPU sets a register bit that causes the chip to switch the pull-up onto the bus's D+ line. This firmware-controlled connection can give the chip time to initialize on power up before being enumerated by the host.

PLX Technology NET2272

PLX Technology, Inc.'s NET2272 is a full/high-speed chip that interfaces to an external CPU over a parallel interface. PLX Technology acquired Netchip Technology, Inc. and its USB controllers in 2004.

Architecture

A series of registers hold configuration data and other information. Packet buffers hold USB data that has been received and data that is ready to transmit. The parallel interface has 5 address bits and 16 data bits. Transfers to and from the packet buffers can be 8 or 16 bits.

The registers store status and control information and the data received in the last Setup transaction. The CPU also uses registers to read and write endpoint data from and to the packet buffers.

The '2272 supports three modes for accessing its registers. In direct address mode, the five address bits specify a register to read or write to. In multiplexed address mode, the CPU places the register address on the data bits and the '2272 reads the address on the falling edge of the ALE control signal. In indirect address mode, the CPU uses the lowest address bit to distinguish between a register address pointer (0) and data (1). The CPU writes a register address pointer to specify a configuration register and then reads or writes data at the address pointed to. Direct and multiplexed address modes can access only the registers from 00h to 1Fh, which typically contain the information accessed most frequently. Indirect address mode can access all registers. The controller also supports DMA transfers. A CPU can write to the '2272 at up to 60 Megabytes/sec. and can read from the '2272 at up to 57 Megabytes/sec (in DMA mode).

To access endpoint data in the packet buffers, the CPU selects an endpoint by writing to the Endpoint Page Select register or the DMA Endpoint Select register and then accesses the data by reading or writing to the Endpoint Data register.

USB Controller

The '2272's USB controller supports full and high speeds and all four transfer types. The controller has three physical endpoints in addition to Endpoint 0. A device that needs more endpoints can use virtual endpoints, where one or more logical endpoints share a physical endpoint's resources. The device firmware must switch resources between the logical and physical endpoints as needed.

Endpoint 0 has a 128-byte buffer, and the other endpoints share 3 kilobytes of packet buffers. Two of the endpoints can use double buffers. On receiving a Setup packet, the device firmware must read the request and provide any data to return to the host. After a failed IN or OUT transaction, an endpoint automatically recovers and waits for the host to retry.

FTDI Chip FT232BM and FT245BM

Future Technology Devices International (FTDI) Chip offers controllers that take a different approach to USB design. The FT232BM USB UART and FT245BM USB FIFO are interface chips that manage enumeration and other bus communications completely in hardware. The chips are designed for use with host drivers provided by FTDI Chip. The controllers require no USB-specific firmware at all, though you can use an EEPROM to store values for some items in the descriptors. The device firmware only needs to provide data for the controller to send and retrieve received data. Because the USB communications are handled entirely in hardware and use FTDI Chip's driver, you can even use FTDI Chips' Vendor ID in devices you develop and market.

These controllers can be a good solution if your device doesn't require a standard class driver and you need no more than one bulk or isochronous port in each direction

Architecture

Both chips are full speed. The FT245BM has a parallel interface and the FT232BM has an asynchronous serial interface.

Table 6-5 shows the functions of the pins on the '245BM. The parallel interface has 8 data lines and four handshaking signals. The names of the handshaking signals are from the perspective of the external CPU that interfaces to the chip. The RXF# output is low when the CPU can read a byte received from the host. The CPU strobes RD# to read the byte. In the other direction, the TXE# output goes low when the CPU can write a byte to send to the USB host, and the CPU strobes WR to write the byte into the '245BM's buffer. The external CPU can use a data bus or any spare port pins to access the '245BM.

The '232BM converts between USB and an asynchronous serial interface. Table 6-6 shows the functions of the pins. The serial interface includes a TXD data output, an RXD data input, and pins for standard RS-232 handshaking signals (RTS, CTS, DTR, DSR, DCD, and RI). A TXDEN output is high when data is transmitting on TXD. This output can interface directly to the transmit-enable input of an RS-485 transceiver, eliminating the need to enable the transmitter using firmware and additional hardware. The '232BM functions as a DTE as defined by the EIA/TIA-232 standard. (The RS-232 ports on PCs are also DTEs.) On a DTE, the TXD, RTS#, and DTR signals are outputs, and the RXD, CTS#, and DSR signals are inputs. A device that functions as a DCE has complimentary signals. (For example, TXD is an input and RXD is an output.) To connect two DTEs to each other, use a null-modem cable that swaps the signal pairs so each output connects to its corresponding input.

To create a USB/RS-232 converter, use a Maxim MAX3245 or similar chip to convert between the '232BM's 5V logic signals and RS-232 voltages. In a similar way, you can interface the '232BM to an RS-485 transceiver. Chapter 7 has more about using the '232BM to convert devices to USB from these legacy interfaces.

Both chips also support a Bit Bang mode, where the chip operates as a very basic controller without requiring a connection to an external CPU. On the

Table 6-5: Pinout of the FT245BM USB FIFO.

Pin	Name	I/O	Description
1	EESK	Output	EEPROM clock
2	EEDATA	Output	EEPROM data
3	VCC	Power	+4.35 to 5.25V
4	RESET#	Input	Reset the chip
5	RSTOUT#	Output	Output of the Reset Generator
6	3V3OUT	Output	Regulated +3.3V output
7	USBDP	I/O	D+ USB data
8	USBDM	I/O	D- USB data
9	GND	Power	Ground
10	PWREN#	Output	Goes low when device is configured, goes high in Suspend state
11	SI/WU	IN	Send USB data on next bulk IN/request remote wakeup
12	RXF#	Output	Goes low when the FIFO contains data that the CPU can read
13	VCCIO	Power	+3.0 to 5.25V
14	TXE#	Output	Goes low when the CPU can write data into the FIFO
15	WR	Input	On H > L transition, writes D0–D7 to the transmit FIFO buffer
16	RD#	Input	On H > L transition, places a byte from the receive FIFO buffer on D0–D7 for the CPU to read
17	GND	Power	Ground
18	D7	I/O	Data bit 7
19	D6	I/O	Data bit 6
20	D5	I/O	Data bit 5
21	D4	I/O	Data bit 4
22	D3	I/O	Data bit 3
23	D2	I/O	Data bit 2
24	D1	I/O	Data bit 1
25	D0	I/O	Data bit 0
26	VCC	Power	+4.35 to 5.25V
27	XTIN	Input	Crystal oscillator cell input
28	XTOUT	Output	Crystal Oscillator cell output
29	AGND	Power	Analog ground
30	AVCC	Power	Analog power supply
31	TEST	Input	Bring high to enable Test mode
32	EECS	I/O	EEPROM Chip Select

USB Complete

Table 6-6: Pinout of the FT232BM USB UART.

Pin	Name	I/O	Description
1	EESK	Output	EEPROM clock
2	EEDATA	Output	EEPROM data
3	VCC	Power	+4.35 to 5.25V
4	RESET#	Input	Reset the chip
5	RSTOUT#	Output	Output of the Reset Generator
6	3V3OUT	Output	Regulated +3.3V output
7	USBDP	I/O	D+ USB data
8	USBDM	I/O	D- USB data
9	GND	Power	Ground
10	SLEEP#	Output	Goes low in Suspend state
11	RXLED#	Output	Receive LED driver, open-collector
12	TXLED#	Output	Transmit LED driver, open-collector
13	VCCIO	Power	+3.0 to 5.25V
14	PWRCTL	Input	Tie low for bus power, high for self power
15	PWREN#	Output	Goes low when device is configured, goes high in Suspend state
16	TXDEN	Output	Transmit enable for RS-485
17	GND	Power	Ground
18	RI#	Input	Ring Indicator
19	DCD	Output	Data Carrier Detect
20	DSR#	Input	Data Set Ready
21	DTR#	Output	Data Terminal Ready
22	CTS#	Input	Clear To Send
23	RTS#	Output	Request To Send
24	RXD	Input	Receive Data
25	TXD	Output	Transmit Data
26	VCC	Power	+4.35 to 5.25V
27	XTIN	Input	Crystal oscillator cell input
28	XTOUT	Output	Crystal Oscillator cell output
29	AGND	Power	Analog ground
30	AVCC	Power	Analog power supply
31	TEST	Input	Bring high to enable Test mode
32	EECS	I/O	EEPROM Chip Select

'245BM, the data-bus pins function as an 8-bit I/O port. On the '232BM, the data and handshaking pins are the I/O port. You can use FTDI Chip's driver to configure the pins as inputs or outputs in any combination. The outputs can control LEDs, relays, or other circuits. The inputs can interface to switches and logic-gate outputs. Host applications can read and write to the I/O pins over the USB connection.

USB Controller

Unlike other device controllers, the '232BM and '245BM aren't designed as general-purpose devices that can be programmed to use any host driver. Instead, FTDI Chip offers two driver options, a Virtual COM Port Driver and a D2XX Direct Driver.

With the Virtual COM Port driver, the device appears to the host as if the device were connected to a COM (RS-232) port. In most cases, an RS-232 device converted to USB with a '232BM requires no changes to application software that accesses the device. Under Windows, applications can access a device with a '232BM using standard API functions (ReadFile, WriteFile) or other classes, libraries, or toolkits for COM-port communications. The '245BM can use the Virtual COM Port driver as well.

If you don't want to use COM-port programming, need faster performance, or want to use Bit Bang mode, FTDI Chip provides the D2XX Direct Driver, which provides a series of vendor-specific functions that applications can use to communicate with the device.

The chips support a Microwire interface to an EEPROM that can store vendor-specific values for items such as a Vendor ID, Product ID, strings that contain a serial number, manufacturer, and product description, and specifying whether the device is bus- or self-powered. If there is no EEPROM data for an item, the controller uses a default value. FTDI Chip provides a utility that programs the information into an EEPROM connected to a '232BM or '245BM.

With no EEPROM, the chips use FTDI Chips' Vendor ID and Product ID. On request, FTDI Chip will also grant the right for your device to use their Vendor ID and a Product ID that FTDI Chip assigns to you. Eliminating

Figure 6-2: For easy prototyping with FTDI Chips' controllers, use DLP Design's DLP-USB232M and DLP-USBS245M modules.

the need to buy a Vendor ID is a huge advantage for developers of inexpensive products that sell in small quantities.

Both chips have a 384-byte transmit buffer and a 128-byte receive buffer. The '245BM's data bus can transfer data at up to 1 Megabyte/sec. The '232BM's asynchronous serial port can transfer data at up to 3 Million baud, which works out to 300 kilobytes/sec. with one Start bit and one Stop bit per byte.

The chips use bulk transfers by default. A driver for isochronous transfers is also available.

Another controller from FTDI Chip is the FT2232C Dual USB UART/FIFO. The chip contains two controllers that each support several configurations. The options include the equivalent of a '232BM or '245BM interface, a synchronous serial interface, and an 8051-compatible parallel interface. A fast, optoisolated serial-interface mode enables creating an isolated synchronous interface using external optoisolators. A high-drive-level option enables the I/O pins to source and sink up to 6 milliamperes (at 3.2V minimum for source current and 0.6V maximum for sink current).

All of the chips are available in surface-mount packages only. For easy proto-typing, a variety of sources provide circuit boards that contain a controller chip, EEPROM, a USB connector, and headers for easy attachment to your CPU and other circuits. One source is DLP Design, whose DLP-USB232M and DLP-USBS245M modules are circuit boards mounted on 24-pin DIP sockets (Figure 6-2). The circuits on the boards are similar to those in FTDI Chip's example schematics.

Chapter 14 has more about designing devices using these chips, including example applications.

7

Device Classes

This chapter is an introduction to the defined USB classes including how to decide whether a new design will fit a defined class or will require a custom driver.

About Classes

Most USB devices have much in common with other devices that perform similar functions. All mice send information about mouse movements and button clicks. All drives transfer files. All printers receive data to print and send status information back to the host.

When a group of devices or interfaces share many attributes or provide or request similar services, it makes sense to define the attributes and services in a class specification. The specification can serve as a guide for developers who design and program devices in the class and for programmers who write device drivers for host systems that communicate with the devices. Operating systems can provide drivers for common classes, eliminating the need for device vendors to provide drivers for devices in those classes.

When a device in a supported class has unique features or abilities not included in a class's driver, a device vendor sometimes can provide a filter driver to support the added features and abilities, rather than writing a complete device driver. In other cases, a filter driver isn't feasible and the device requires a custom driver.

Even if a device's class isn't supported by the operating system, a class may be supported in a future edition of the operating system. Firmware that complies with a class specification is likely to be compatible with any driver added in future editions of the operating system.

Device Working Groups

The USB-IF releases class specifications developed by Device Working Groups, whose members have expertise and interest in a particular area. A special case is the hub class, which is defined in the main USB 2.0 specification rather than in a separate document. Every operating system must support the hub class because the host requires a root hub to do any communications.

The defined classes cover most common device functions. A specification with a version number of 1.0 or higher is an approved specification and is suitable for use as a reference in developing devices and drivers for commercial release. Table 7-1 lists the classes with approved specifications.

Windows includes drivers to support many of these classes. As Windows and the class specifications have evolved, the number of supported classes and the level of support for the classes have improved. For some of the more obscure classes, such as Device Firmware Upgrade, Windows doesn't provide a driver even though the specification was approved years ago. Chapter 4 listed the defined class codes devices may have in their device and interface descriptors. Table 7-2 shows the class drivers added in each edition of Windows.

Elements of a Class Specification

All USB class specifications are based on the Common Class specification, which describes what information a class specification should contain and

Table 7-1: These classes have approved class specifications.

Class	Descriptor Where Class Is Declared
Audio	Interface
Chip/Smart Card Interface	Interface
Communication	Device or Interface
Content Security	Interface
Device Firmware Upgrade	Interface (subclass of Application Specific Interface)
Human Interface (HID)	Interface
IrDA Bridge	Interface (subclass of Application Specific Interface)
Mass Storage	Interface
Printer	Interface
Still Image Capture	Interface
Test and Measurement	Interface (subclass of Application Specific Interface)
Video	Interface

how to organize a specification document. A class specification defines the number and type of required and optional endpoints devices in a class may have. A specification may also define or name formats for data to be transferred, including both application data (such as keypresses or video data) and status and control information relating to the device and its operation. Some class specifications define functions or capabilities that describe how the data being transferred will be used. For example, the HID class has Usage Tables that define how to interpret data sent by keyboards, mice, joysticks, and other HIDs. Some classes use USB to transfer data in a format defined by another specification. An example is the SCSI commands used by mass-storage devices.

A class specification may define values for items in standard descriptors as well as defining class-specific descriptors, interfaces, endpoint uses, and control requests. For example, the device descriptor for a hub includes a bDeviceClass value of 09h to indicate that the device belongs to the hub class. The hub must have a class-specific hub descriptor with a descriptor type of 29h. Hubs must also support class-specific requests. For example, when the host sends a Get_Port_Status request to a hub with a port number in the Index field, the hub responds with status information for the port. A

Table 7-2: Microsoft has added USB class support with each release of Windows. The releases are listed top to bottom from earliest to latest. Except as noted, each release also includes the drivers provided with earlier releases.

Windows Edition	USB Version Compliance	USB Drivers Added
Windows 98 Gold (original release)	1.0	Audio
		HID 1.0
		Video (USB camera minidriver library USBCAMD 1.0; not supported under Windows 2000)
Windows 98 SE	1.1	Communication device: modem
		HID 1.1 (adds the ability to do interrupt OUT transfers)
		Still image (first phase/preliminary)
Windows 2000	1.1 (2.0 support added in Service Pack 4 (SP4)	Mass storage. Support for multiple LUNs (partitions) added in Service Pack 3 (SP3).
		Printer
		Communication device: Remote NDIS (Network Device Interface Specification)
		Still image (much improved)
		Chip/Smart Card Interface (available from Windows update)
Windows Me	1.1	Audio: MIDI
		Video (USB camera minidriver library USBCAMD 2.0)
Windows XP	1.1; 2.0 support added in Service Pack 1 (SP1); interface association descriptor support added in Service Pack 2 (SP2).	Audio: MIDI, improved
		Video-class driver added in Service Pack 2 (SP2).

class may also require a device to support specific endpoints or comply with tighter timing for standard requests.

Defined Classes

The following sections introduce the defined classes. I don't attempt to repeat every detail in the specification documents. Instead, my goal is to give enough information to help you decide what class a new design might fit into, what resources a device requires to support a class's communications, examples of device controllers to use for devices in the class, and what level of support, if any, to expect for the class under Windows.

Audio

The audio class is for devices that send or receive audio data, which may contain encoded voice, music, or other sounds. Audio functions are often part of a device that also supports video, storage, or other functions. Audio devices can use isochronous transfers for audio streams or bulk transfers for data encoded using the MIDI (Musical Instrument Digital Interface) protocol.

This section describes version 1.0 of the audio specification. At this writing, version 2.0 is under development. Version 2.0 will not be backwards compatible with version 1.0. In other words, a 2.0 device won't work with a 1.0 host driver. The proposed changes in version 2.0 include complete support for high-speed operation, use of the interface association descriptor, and support for many new capabilities and controls.

Documentation

The audio specification has separate Device Class Definition documents for Audio Devices, Audio Data Formats, Terminal Types, and MIDI Devices. At this writing, the latest version of each of these is 1.0. The MIDI standard is available from the MIDI Manufacturers Association at *www.midi.org*.

Overview

Each audio function in a device has an Audio Interface Collection that consists of one or more interfaces. The interfaces include one AudioControl (AC) interface, zero or more AudioStreaming (AS) interfaces and zero or more MIDIStreaming (MS) interfaces (Figure 7-1). In other words, every

Audio Interface Collection has an AudioControl interface, while Audio-Streaming and MIDIStreaming interfaces are optional.

An AudioControl interface can enable accessing controls such as volume, mute, bass, and treble. An AudioStreaming interface transfers audio data in isochronous transfers. A MIDIStreaming interface transfers MIDI data. MIDI is a standard for controlling synthesizers, sound cards, and other electronic devices that generate music and other sounds. A MIDI representation of a sound includes values for pitch, length, volume, and other characteristics. A pure MIDI hardware interface carries asynchronous data at 31.25 kilobits/sec. A USB interface that carries MIDI data uses the MIDI data format but doesn't use MIDI's asynchronous interface. Instead, the MIDI data travels on the bus in bulk transfers.

A device can have multiple Audio Interface Collections that are active at the same time, with each collection controlling an independent audio function.

Descriptors

Each audio interface type uses standard and class-specific descriptors to enable the host to learn about the interface, its endpoints, and what kinds of data the endpoints expect to transfer.

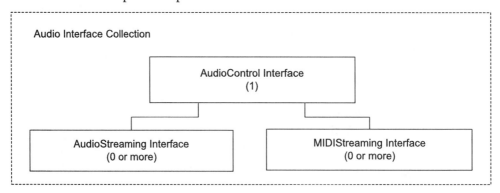

Figure 7-1: Each audio function has an Audio Interface Collection that contains one or more interfaces.

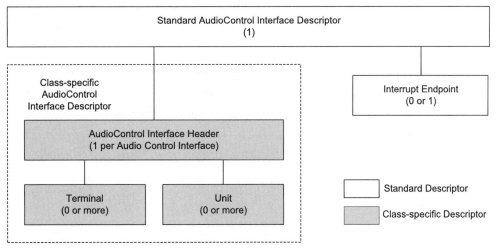

Figure 7-2: An AudioControl interface contains descriptors for audio Terminals and Units.

The AudioControl Interface. Figure 7-2 shows the descriptors in an AudioControl interface. In the AudioControl interface descriptor, bInterfaceClass = 01h to identify the interface as audio class and bInterfaceSubclass = 01h to identify the subclass as AudioControl.

Following the AudioControl interface descriptor is a Class-specific AC interface descriptor, which consists of a series of descriptors for the AudioControl interface. The Class-specific AC Interface Header descriptor contains the total length of itself and all of the Terminal and/or Unit descriptors in the interface.

A Terminal descriptor contains information about an addressable logical object that represents a USB endpoint or other interface to the outside world. Every IN or OUT isochronous endpoint in an audio interface must have an associated Output or Input Terminal with a Terminal descriptor. The audio function receives audio information from the host at an Input Terminal and transmits audio information to the host at an Output Terminal. Note that the terms Input Terminal and Output Terminal are from the perspective of the audio function, while USB endpoints are named from the perspective of the host. So an IN endpoint has an associated Output Terminal, while an OUT endpoint has an associated Input Terminal. Other Terminals in a function can represent interfaces to audio components such as microphones and speakers.

An audio function might receive a microphone's output at an Input Terminal and transmit the received audio data to the host at an Output Terminal that represents a USB IN endpoint. Or an audio function might receive audio data from the host at an Input Terminal that represents an OUT endpoint and send the received data to a speaker at an Output Terminal.

A Unit descriptor contains information about an addressable logical object that represents a subfunction within an audio function. Table 7-3 shows the Unit types defined in the specification.

If the AudioControl Interface has an interrupt endpoint, the interface includes an endpoint descriptor for the endpoint.

The AudioStreaming Interface. Following the AudioControl interface descriptor, an Audio Interface Collection may have one or more AudioStreaming interface descriptors with bInterfaceClass field = 01h to identify the interface as audio class and bInterfaceSubclass = 02h to identify the subclass as AudioStreaming. Figure 7-3 shows the descriptors.

Following each AudioStreaming interface descriptor is a class-specific AudioStreaming interface descriptor, which identifies the Terminal associated with the interface and contains information about the data format and any delay the function requires for internal processing. The *Audio Data Formats* specification lists the supported formats, which include Pulse Code Modulation (PCM), Digital Audio Compression (AC-3), and MPEG. A class-specific AS Format Type descriptor contains more information about the format. Some formats require an additional AS Format-specific Type descriptor.

Each AudioStreaming interface can have one isochronous endpoint. The endpoint has a standard endpoint descriptor and a class-specific AS Isochronous Audio Data endpoint descriptor. The class-specific descriptor indicates which audio controls the endpoint supports, specifies whether the endpoint requires all except zero-length data packets to contain wMaxPacketSize bytes, and can provide synchronizing information. Some endpoints also have a class-specific AS Isochronous Synch endpoint descriptor.

The MIDIStreaming Interface. To support MIDI data, an Audio Interface Collection can have one or more MIDIStreaming interfaces. Figure 7-4 shows the descriptors. In the MIDIStreaming interface descriptor, bInterfaceClass = 01h to identify the interface as audio class and bInterfaceSubclass = 03h to identify the subclass as MIDIStreaming.

Following this descriptor is a class-specific MIDIStreaming (MS) interface descriptor that consists of a series of descriptors for the interface. The first descriptor in the series is the class-specific MS Interface Header descriptor, which contains the total length of itself plus all of the Jack and/or Element descriptors that follow.

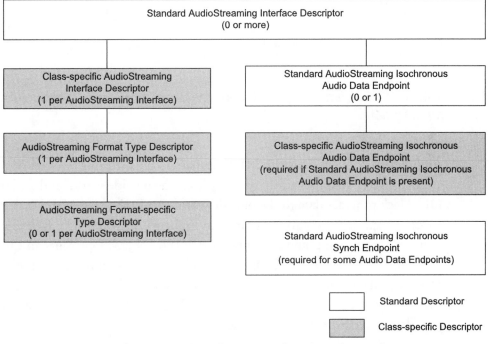

Figure 7-3: An AudioStreaming interface contains descriptors for an isochronous endpoint that carries audio data.

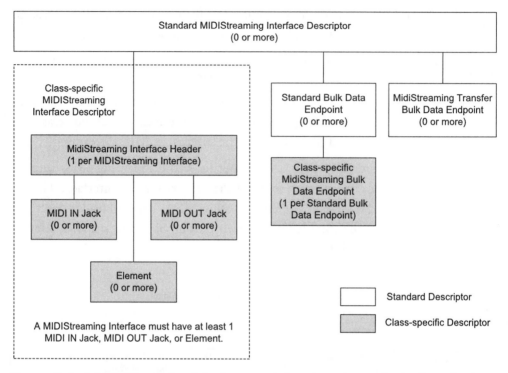

Figure 7-4: A MIDIStreaming interface contains descriptors for bulk endpoints that carry MIDI data.

An Element converts between MIDI and audio data streams or other MIDI streams. A MIDI IN Jack receives data from the outside world, and a MIDI OUT Jack provides data to the outside world. An Embedded MIDI Jack is a jack that represents a USB endpoint. An Embedded MIDI OUT Jack represents an IN endpoint, and an Embedded MIDI IN Jack represents an OUT endpoint. (The MIDI OUT and MIDI IN names are from the perspective of the MIDI function, while the IN endpoint and OUT endpoint names are from the perspective of the USB host.) An External MIDI Jack is a physical jack that connects to a MIDI device.

Every USB MIDI device contains a USB/MIDI converter that converts between USB data and the data at the Embedded MIDI Jack(s). Each USB endpoint can connect to up to 16 Embedded MIDI Jacks. Data travels in 32-bit USBMIDI Event Packets, with the first 4 bits designating a specific

Table 7-3: The specification for the audio class defines these Unit types.

Unit Type	Description
Mixer	Transforms a number of logical input channels into a number of logical output channels.
Selector	Selects from n audio channel clusters and routes them unaltered to a single output audio channel cluster
Feature	Provides controls such as volume, tone control, and mute
Processing	Transforms multiple logical input channels into a single audio channel cluster
Up/Down-mix Processing	Provides facilities to derive m output audio channels from n input audio channels.
Dolby Prologic Processing	Extracts additional audio data (a specialized derivative of the Up/Down-mix Processing Unit)
3D-Stereo Extender Processing	Processes an existing stereo sound track to add a spaciousness effect.
Reverberation Processing	Adds room-acoustics effects.
Chorus Processing	Adds chorus effects.
Dynamic Range Compressor	Intelligently limits the dynamic range.
Extension Unit	Enables adding vendor-specific building blocks.

Embedded MIDI Jack. Inside a device, External Jacks connect to Embedded MIDI Jacks, other External MIDI Jacks, or Elements. Multiple External MIDI OUT Jacks can implement MIDI PARALLEL OUT. Each Element, MIDI IN Jack, and MIDI OUT Jack has a class-specific descriptor.

A MIDIStreaming interface can have one or more Standard MS Bulk Data endpoints and one or more Class-specific MS Transfer Bulk Data endpoints. Many MIDI interfaces handle all traffic with one Standard Bulk Data IN endpoint and one Standard Bulk Data OUT endpoint. For audio streams that require more bandwidth, an interface can have one or more MS Transfer Bulk Data endpoints. A host can use the class-specific Set_Endpoint_Control request to dynamically allocate a Transfer Bulk Data endpoint to an Element. Typical applications for a Transfer Bulk Data endpoint are transferring DownLoadable Sounds (DLS) to a Synthesizer Element and transferring program code to a programmable Element.

Each endpoint of either type has a standard endpoint descriptor. Each Standard Bulk Data endpoint also has an MS Bulk Data endpoint descriptor that names the Embedded MIDI Jacks associated with the endpoint.

Class-specific Requests

The audio class defines optional class-specific requests for setting and getting the state of audio controls, accessing memory, and requesting status information.

Chips

USB-capable chips are available with built-in support for audio functions. The support includes codec (compressor/decompressor) functions, analog-to-digital converters (ADCs), digital-to-analog converters (DACs), and support for Sony/Philips Digital Interface (S/PDIF) encoding for transmitting audio data in digital format.

Texas Instruments' PCM2900 is a stereo audio codec with a full-speed USB port and 16-bit ADC and DAC. The chip has an AudioControl interface, an AudioStreaming interface for each direction, and a HID interface that reports the status of three pins on the chip. The chip requires no user programming but has the option to use a vendor-specific Vendor ID, Product ID, and strings. The PCM2902 adds support for S/PDIF encoding. Another option for a USB codec is Philips Semiconductors UDA1325.

Texas Instruments' PCM2702 is a 16-bit stereo DAC with a full-speed USB interface. The chip can accept data sampled at 48, 44.1, and 32 kilohertz using either 16-bit stereo or monaural audio data. The chip supports digital attenuation and soft-mute features.

Texas Instruments' TUSB3200A USB Streaming Controller contains an 8052-compatible microcontroller that supports up to seven IN endpoints and seven OUT endpoints. The audio support includes a codec port interface, a DMA controller with four channels for streaming isochronous data packets to and from the codec port, and a phase lock loop (PLL) and adaptive clock generator (ACG) to support synchronization modes.

Windows Support

Under Windows, the *usbaudio.sys* minidriver supports USB audio devices, including MIDI devices. In Windows editions up to and including Windows XP, the driver supports a subset of the features in the USB audio specification. Microsoft's Universal Audio Architecture (UAA) initiative promises an improved driver architecture for future Windows editions. *USB Audio Devices and Windows* is a white paper from Microsoft that details the abilities and limits of Windows XP's audio driver.

Applications can access USB audio devices using the DirectMusic and DirectSound components of Windows' DirectX technology or using Windows Multimedia audio functions.

Chip/Smart Card Interface

Smart cards are the familiar plastic cards used for phone calls, gift cards, keyless entry, access to toll roads and mass transit, storing medical and insurance data, enabling of satellite TV receivers, and other applications that require storing small-to-moderate quantities of information with easy and portable access.

Each card contains a module with memory and often a CPU. Many cards allow updating of their contents, to change a monetary value or an entry code, for example. Some cards have exposed electrical contacts, while others communicate via embedded antennas. Another term for smart card is chip card.

To access a smart card, you connect it to a Chip Card Interface Device (CCID), typically by inserting the card into a slot or waving a contactless card by a reader. A popular term for CCID is smart-card reader, though many CCIDs can also write to cards. USB enters the picture because some CCIDs have USB interfaces for communicating with USB hosts.

Documentation

The specification *USB Chip/Smart Card Interface Devices* defines a protocol for CCIDs with USB interfaces. The current version at this writing is 1.0. The ISO/IEC 7816 standard (available from *www.iso.ch*) defines the physical and electrical characteristics and commands for communicating with smart cards.

Overview

Every CCID must have a bulk endpoint in each direction. All readers with removable cards must also have an interrupt IN endpoint.

The host and device exchange messages on the bulk pipes. A CCID message consists of a 10-byte header followed by message-specific data. The specification defines 14 commands that the host can use to send data and status and control information in messages. Every command requires at least one response message from the CCID. A response contains a message code and status information and may contain additional requested data. The device uses the interrupt endpoint to report errors and the insertion or removal of a card.

Descriptors

A CCIS function is defined at the interface level. In the interface descriptor, bInterfaceClass = 0Bh to indicate the CCID class. Following the interface descriptor is a class-specific CCID Class descriptor with bDescriptorType = 21h. The class descriptor contains parameters such as the number of slots, slot voltages, supported protocols, supported clock frequencies and data rates, and maximum message length.

Class-specific Requests

There are three class-specific control requests:

Request	bRequest	Required?
Abort	01h	yes
Get_Clock_Frequencies	02h	yes, if the CCID doesn't support automatic selection of clock frequency (as specified in the CCID class descriptor, dwFeatures, bit 10h)
Get_Data_Rates	03h	yes, if the CCID doesn't support automatic selection of clock frequency (as specified in the CCID class descriptor, dwFeatures, bit 20h)

Chips

A CCID can use just about any full- or high-speed device controller. Some controllers have support for CCID functions built in. Alcor Micro Corporation has the AU9510 CCID chip with a USB interface. Winbond Electronics Corporation's W81E381D is an 8052-compatible microcontroller with USB and smart-card-reader interfaces.

Windows Support

A Windows USB driver for communicating with CCIDs wasn't included with Windows editions up to and including Windwos XP, but a driver is available for Windows 2000 and later via Windows update. Applications use DeviceIoControl API functions to communicate with CCIDs. The driver doesn't support PIN entry or multi-slot readers.

Communication Devices: Modems and Networks

The communication-device class encompasses two broad device types: telephones and "medium-speed" networking devices. Telephones include analog phones and modems, ISDN terminal adapters, and digital phones. Networking devices include ADSL modems, cable modems, and 10BASE-T Ethernet adapters and hubs. The USB interface in a communication device typically carries data that uses application-specific protocols such as V.250

for modem control or Ethernet for local-network traffic. The communication-device class is also an option for other devices accessed via COM-port functions on the host.

Documentation

The main documentation for communication devices is the specification for the communication-device class (CDC). Two subclasses have their own documents. The Wireless Mobile Communications (WMC) subclass includes terminal equipment for wireless devices that can perform multiple functions such as audio and data communications. The Ethernet Emulation Model (EEM) Devices subclass includes devices that send and receive Ethernat frames. At this writing, the latest specification versions are 1.1 for CDC and 1.0 for WMC and EEM. The V.250 standard (formerly known as V.25ter and encompassing the Hayes AT command set) is available from the International Telecommunication Union at *www.itu.int*. The Ethernet standard, IEEE 802.3, is available from *www.ieee.org*.

The Remote Network Driver Interface Specification (NDIS) defines a protocol for using USB and other buses to configure network interfaces and to send and receive Ethernet data. Remote NDIS is based on NDIS, which defines a protocol to manage communications with network adapters and higher-level drivers. NDIS and Remote NDIS are supported by Windows, but not by other operating systems. Documentation for NDIS and Remote NDIS are available from *www.microsoft.com*.

Overview

A communication device is responsible for the tasks of device management, call management (optional), and data transmission. Device management includes controlling and configuring a device and notifying the host of events. Call management involves establishing and terminating telephone calls or other connections. Not all devices require call management. Data transmission is the sending and receiving of application data such as phone conversations or files sent over a modem or network.

The communication device class supports three basic models for communicating. The POTS (Plain Old Telephone Service) model is for communica-

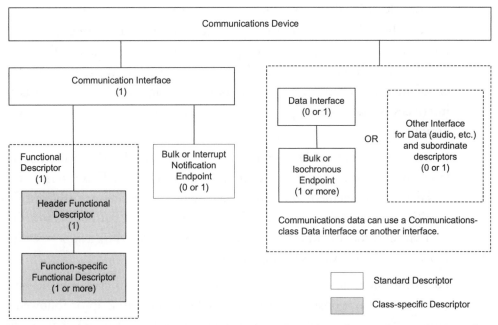

Figure 7-5: A communication-class interface has descriptors for endpoints that carry communication-device class data.

tions via ordinary phone lines. The ISDN model is for communications via phone lines with ISDN interfaces. The Networking model is for communications via Ethernet or ATM (Asynchronous Transfer Mode) networks. Some USB/Ethernet devices use the POTS model with a vendor-specific protocol.

Notifications, which announce events such as ring detect and network connect or disconnect, can travel to the host in an interrupt or bulk pipe. Most devices use interrupt pipes. Each notification consists of an 8-byte header followed by a variable-length data field.

Descriptors

A communication function can be defined at either the device or interface level. If defined at the device level, all of the device's interfaces belong to the communication function. In the device descriptor, bDeviceClass = 02h to indicate the communication-device class (Figure 7-5). If the communication function is defined at the interface level, an associated interface descriptor can specify which interfaces belong to the communication function, assuming that the operating system supports the associated interface descriptor. The 1.1 communication-device class specification doesn't mention the associated-interface descriptor by name but says that a method for associating interfaces is under development and that such a method would be a valid option.

Every communication device must have an interface descriptor with bInterfaceClass = 02h to indicate a Communication interface. This interface handles device management and call management. The bInterfaceSubClass field specifies a communication model. Table 7-4 shows defined values. The bInterfaceProtocol field can name a protocol supported by a subclass. Table 7-5 shows defined values for protocols.

Following the Communication interface descriptor is a class-specific Functional descriptor consisting of a Header Functional descriptor followed by one or more descriptors (also called Functional descriptors) that provide information about a specific communication function. Table 7-6 shows defined values for these descriptors.

One of these descriptors, the Union Functional descriptor, has the special function of defining a relationship among multiple interfaces that form a functional unit. The descriptor designates one interface as the master or controlling interface, which can send and receive certain messages that apply to the entire group. For example, a Communication interface can be a master interface for a group consisting of a Communication interface and a Data interface. The interfaces that make up a group can include communication-class interfaces as well as other related interfaces such as audio and HID.

If the Communication interface has a bulk or interrupt endpoint for event notifications, the endpoint has a standard endpoint descriptor.

A communication device may also have an interface descriptor with bInterfaceClass = 0Ah to indicate a Data interface. A Data interface can have bulk or isochronous endpoints for carrying application data. Each of these endpoints, when present, has a standard endpoint descriptor. Some devices use

Table 7-4: In the interface descriptor for a communication device, the bInterfaceSubClass field indicates the communication model the device supports.

Code	bInterfaceSubClass	Application
00h	RESERVED	–
01h	Direct Line Control Model	Telephone modem with the host providing any data compression and error correction. The device or host may provide modulation/demodulation of the modem data.
02h	Abstract Control Model	Telephone modem with the device providing any data compression, error correction, and modulation/demodulation of the modem data.
03h	Telephone Control Model	Telephone.
04h	Multi-Channel Control Model	ISDN device with multiple, multiplexed channels.
05h	CAPI Control Model	ISDN device with support for COMMON-ISDN-API (CAPI) commands and messages.
06h	Ethernet Networking Control Model	Device that exchanges Ethernet-framed data.
07h	ATM Networking Control Model	ATM device.
08h–0Bh	WMC models	Wireless mobile communications device.
0Ch	Ethernet Emulation Model (EEM)	Device that exchanges Ethernet frames.
0Dh–7Fh	Reserved	Future use.
80h–FEh	Reserved	Vendor specific.

other class or vendor-specific interfaces for data transmission. For example, a telephone might use an audio interface to send and receive voice data.

A USB/Ethernet converter that functions as a Remote NDIS device consists of a Communication interface and a Data interface. In the Communication interface, bInterfaceSubClass = 02h to specify the Abstract Control Model and bInterfaceProtocol = FFh to specify a vendor-specific protocol. (Remote NDIS devices don't use the communication class's Ethernet Control Model.) The Communication interface has an interrupt endpoint. The Data interface has two bulk endpoints. Each endpoint has an endpoint descriptor.

Table 7-5: In the interface descriptor for a communication device, the bInterfaceProtocol field can indicate a protocol the communications model supports.

Code	Description
00h	No class-specific protocol required
01h	AT commands (specified in ITU V.250)
02h–06h	AT commands for WMC devices
07h–FDh	Future use
FEh	External protocol for WMC devices
FFh	Vendor specific

The Ethernet Emulation Model Devices subclass defines an alternate way to use USB to send and receive Ethernet frames. The EEM subclass is intended to be less expensive and more efficient than the Ethernet Networking Control Module subclass defined in the communication-device class specification.

Class-specific Requests

The communication-device class has a variety of class-specific requests for getting and setting status and control information. Not every request is valid for every device. For example, Set_Hook_State requests to place a phone line on or off hook, and Set_Ethernet_Packet_Filter requests to filter Ethernet traffic according to specified settings.

Chips

For modems, Cypress Semiconductor provides several reference designs using EZ-USB controllers and modem components from partner companies.

For USB/Ethernet bridges, Asix Electronics Corporation has several chips, including the AX88172 controller, which converts between full- or high-speed USB and 10- or 100-Mbps Ethernet. The chip's Ethernet interface connects to an external Ethernet PHY. An external serial EEPROM can store the device's Ethernet hardware address, USB descriptors, and configuration data for the converter. The chip has two bulk endpoints for Ethernet

Table 7-6: A Functional descriptor consists of a Header functional descriptor followed by one or more function-specific descriptors.

bInterfaceSubClass	Functional Descriptor Type
00h	Header
01h	Call Management
02h	Abstract Control Management
03h	Direct Line Control Management
04h	Telephone Ringer
05h	Telephone Call and Line State Reporting Capabilities
06h	Union
07h	Country Selection
08h	Telephone Operational Modes
09h	USB Terminal
0Ah	Network Channel Terminal
0Bh	Protocol Unit
0Ch	Extension Unit
0Dh	Multi-channel Management
0Eh	CAPI Control Management
0Fh	Ethernet Networking
10h	ATM Networking
11h–18h	WMC Functional Descriptors
19h–FFh	Reserved

data and an interrupt endpoint for sending notifications. A series of vendor-specific requests enable configuring and reading status information from the chip and accessing three I/O bits.

Kawasaki Microelectronics has several chips that each contain Ethernet, USB, and serial-EEPROM interfaces and a 16-bit CPU. Freescale Semiconductor's 32-bit MCF5482 ColdFire microprocessor contains a full/high-speed USB device controller and an Ethernet controller.

Windows Support

The modem driver included with Windows 98 SE and later (*usbser.sys*) is compatible with modems that use the Abstract Control Model. A modem used by applications that use the Windows Telephony Application Programming Interface (TAPI) must have its own INF file. Microsoft provides a Modem Development Kit with tools, sample INF files, and information for creating and testing INF files for modems.

Devices other than modems can use the *usbser.sys* driver as well. To enable host applications to access a device using COM-port functions (a virtual COM port), bInterfaceSubClass must be set to the Abstract Control Model. For better performance, however, most device developers use a driver from another source.

Under Windows 2000 and later, the *usb8023.sys* driver maps Remote NDIS to USB.

Content Security

The Content Security class defines a way for content owners to control access to files, music, video, or other data transmitted on the bus. The control can use either of two defined Content Security Methods: Basic Authorization or Digital Transmission Content Protection (DTCP).

Documentation

In addition to the main Content Security specification, each content security method (CSM) has its own specification document. At this writing, the latest edition of the specifications is 1.0. The DTCP specification and license information are available from the Digital Transmission Licensing Administrator (*www.dtcp.com*).

Overview

The class defines a protocol for activating and deactivating a content security method and for associating a content security method to a channel. A channel represents a relationship between an interface or endpoint and one or more CSMs. Only one CSM can be active on a channel at a time.

Basic Authorization, also known as Content Security Method 1, or CSM-1, consists only of the class-specific request Get_Unique_ID, which enables a host to request an ID value from a device.

CSM-2 is DTCP, which was developed to prevent unauthorized copying of audio and video entertainment content via USB and other buses. A content owner can use DTCP to specify whether copying is allowed, identify authorized users, and specify an encryption method. A DTCP interface must have an interrupt endpoint in each direction for sending and receiving event notifications. A content provider who wants to use DTCP must sign a license agreement and pay an annual (not trivial) fee.

Two additional CSMs that don't have USB specifications at this writing are Open Copy Protection System (CSM-3) and Elliptic Curve Content Protection Protocol (CSM-4).

Descriptors

A Content Security function is defined at the interface level, with bInterfaceClass = 0Dh to indicate the Content Security class.

There are four class-specific descriptors:

Descriptor Name	Description	Use
CS_GENERAL	Identifies the Content Security Interface version number.	One per interface
Channel	Identifies one or more CSMs for a channel, which can be specified by interface number endpoint address.	One per channel
Content Security Method	Describes a CSM implemented on a device.	One per CSM
Content Security Method Variant	Describes a variant of the associated CSM.	Not used by CSM-1 or CSM-2

CSM-2 also defines a String descriptor for the string "Digital Transmission Content Protection Version 1.00".

Class-specific Requests

Two class-specific requests apply to all CSM interfaces. Get_Channel_Settings enables the host to learn what CSM is assigned to a channel. The Set_Channel_Settings request enables the host to assign a CSM to a channel or deactivate a previously assigned CSM.

CSM-2 has additional control requests to transfer Authentication and Key Exchange (AKE) commands and responses.

Chips

For a device using content security, the choice of a USB controller depends mainly on the capabilities needed to exchange the content being protected. Adding a Content-Security function requires only the occasional use of the control endpoint and for CSM-2, two interrupt endpoints.

Windows Support

Windows doesn't include a driver for the Content Security class, except for one function. Under Windows XP and later, if a device has a CSM-1 interface, an application can call the DeviceIoControl function with the dwIoControlCode parameter set to this value:

IOCTL_STORAGE_GET_MEDIA_SERIAL_NUMBER

The function requests the device's serial number from Windows' generic parent driver.

Device Firmware Upgrade

The Device Firmware Upgrade (DFU) class defines a protocol to enable a host to send firmware enhancements and patches to a device. After receiving the firmware upgrade, the device re-enumerates using its new firmware.

Documentation

The *Device Firmware Upgrade* specification defines the class. At this writing, the current version is 1.0.

Overview

To perform a firmware upgrade as described in the specification, a device must have two complete sets of descriptors: run-time and DFU-mode. The run-time descriptors are for normal operation and also include descriptors that inform the host that the device is capable of firmware upgrades. The DFU-mode descriptors are a separate set of descriptors for use when the device is upgrading its firmware. For example, a keyboard using its run-time descriptors enumerates as a HID-class device and sends keypress data to the host. During a firmware upgrade, the device suspends normal operations as a keyboard and uses the DFU-mode descriptors to communicate with the DFU driver on the host.

The upgrade process has four phases. In the first phase, device enumeration, the device sends its run-time descriptors to the host and operates normally. In the reconfiguration phase, the host sends a DFU_Upgrade request and then resets and re-enumerates the device, which returns its DFU-mode descriptors. In the transfer phase, the host transfers the firmware upgrade to the device. The manifestation phase begins when the device informs the host that the upgrade has been received. The host resets the bus, and the device enumerates using its upgraded firmware and resumes normal operation. During the upgrade process, the device transitions through defined states such as dfuIdle (waiting for DFU requests) or dfuError (an error has occurred).

An upgrade file stored on the host contains the firmware for the upgrade, followed by a DFU suffix that the host can use to help ensure that the firmware is valid and appropriate for a particular device. The suffix contains an error-checking value, a signature consisting of the ASCII codes for the text "DFU", and optional values for the Vendor ID, Product ID, and product release number the firmware is appropriate for. The suffix is for the host's use only; the host doesn't send the suffix to the device.

To ensure that the host will load a new driver for the firmware-upgrade process, the device should use different Product IDs in its run-time and DFU-mode device descriptors.

DFU communications use only the control endpoint.

Descriptors

The DFU function is defined at the interface subclass level. In a device that supports DFU, both the run-time and DFU-mode descriptors include a standard interface descriptor with bInterfaceClass = FEh to indicate an Application Specific class and bInterfaceSubClass = 01h to indicate the

Device Firmware Upgrade class. In DFU mode, the DFU interface must be the only active interface in the device.

Both descriptor sets include a Run-time DFU Functional descriptor that specifies whether the device can communicate on the bus immediately after the manifestation phase, how long to wait for a reset after receiving a DFU_Upgrade request, and the maximum number of bytes the device can accept in a control Write transfer during a firmware upgrade.

Class-specific Requests

There are seven class-specific requests:

Request	Description
DFU_Detach	If a bus reset occurs within the time period specified in the DFU Functional descriptor, enumerate using the DFU-mode descriptors.
DFU_Dnload	Accept new firmware in the request's Data stage. A request with wLength = 0 means that all of the firmware has been transferred.
DFU_Upload	Send firmware to the host in the request's Data stage.
DFU_GetStatus	Return status and error information. On error, enter the dfuError state.
DFU_ClrStatus	Clear the dfuError state reported in response to a DFU_GetStatus request and enter the dfuIdle state.
DFU_GetState	Same as DFU_GetStatus but with no change in state on error.
DFU_Abort	Return to the dfuIdle state.

Chips

The choice of USB controller depends mainly on the requirements of the device in run-time mode. The device must have enough memory and other resources to store and implement the upgraded firmware.

Windows Support

Windows doesn't provide a driver for this class. STMicroelectronics has a Windows driver and firmware examples for use with its ST7 microcontrollers with Flash memory.

Human Interface

The Human Interface Device (HID) class includes keyboards, pointing devices, and game controllers. With these devices, the host reads and acts on human input such as keypresses and mouse movements. Hosts must respond quickly enough so users don't notice a delay between an action and the expected response. Some devices that perform vendor-specific functions can also use the HID class.

All HID data travels in reports, which are structures with defined formats. Usage tags in a report tell the host or device how to use received data. For example, a Usage Page value of 09h indicates a button, and a Usage ID value tells which button, if any, was pressed.

Windows and other operating systems have included HID drivers beginning with the earliest editions with USB support. The availability of class drivers has helped to make the HID class popular for devices besides obvious human-interface applications. A HID can exchange any type of data, but can use only control and interrupt transfers. Chapter 11, Chapter 12, and Chapter 13 have more about using HIDs in custom devices.

Documentation

The HID specification is in several documents. At this writing, the current version of the HID specification is 1.11. The main change from version 1.0 is enabling the host to send reports in interrupt OUT transfers. In a HID 1.0 interface, the host must send all reports in control transfers.

Several documents define Usage-tag values for different device types. *HID Usage Tables* has values for keyboards, pointing devices, various game controllers, displays, telephone controls, and more. Four other device types have their own documents:

Class Definition for Physical Interface Devices (PID) defines values for force-feedback joysticks and other devices that require physical feedback in response to inputs.

The *Monitor Control* class specification defines values for user controls and power management for display monitors. (The HID interface controls the display's settings only. The image data uses a different hardware interface.)

Usage Tables for HID Power Devices defines values for Uninterruptible Power Supply (UPS) devices and other devices where the host monitors and controls batteries or other power components.

Point of Sale (POS) Usage Tables defines values for bar-code readers, weighing devices, and magnetic-stripe readers.

Overview

HIDs communicate by exchanging reports using control and interrupt transfers. Input and Output reports may use control or interrupt transfers. Feature reports use control transfers. A report descriptor defines the size of each report and Usage values for the report data.

Descriptors

A HID function is defined at the interface level. In the interface descriptor, bInterfaceClass = 03h to indicate the HID class. The bInterfaceSubClass field indicates whether the HID supports a boot protocol, which is a protocol that a host can use instead of the report protocol defined in the device's report descriptor. Mice and keyboards may support a boot protocol to enable using the devices before the full HID drivers are loaded.

Following the interface descriptor is a class-specific HID descriptor, which contains the size of the report descriptor. The report descriptor contains information about the data in the HID reports. An optional Physical Descriptor can describe the part(s) of the human body that activate a control.

Class-specific Requests

HIDs have six class-specific control requests to enable sending and receiving reports, setting and reading the Idle rate (how often the device sends a report if the data is unchanged), and setting or reading the currently active protocol (boot or report). To obtain a report descriptor or physical descriptor, the host sends a Get_Descriptor request to the interface with the high byte of wValue set to 01h to indicate a class-specific descriptor and the low byte of wValue set to 22h to request a report descriptor or 23h to request a physical descriptor.

Chips

For devices with a human interface, low speed is fast enough to enable acting on received user input with no detectable delay. Many HIDs use low speed because the device needs a more flexible and/or cheaper cable. A HID may use any speed, however.

A variety of controllers include additional support for keyboards, mice, and game controllers. Atmel Corporation's AT43USB325 contains an AVR microcontroller and a 5-port hub. One of the hub's ports connects to an embedded function with support for a 20 x 8 keyboard matrix. The controller supports low and full speeds. The AT43USB325 is similar but supports an 18 x 8 keyboard matrix. Other vendors with controllers designed for use in keyboards include Alcor Micro and Winbond Electronics Corporation. Some general-purpose controllers, such as Cypress' CY7C63743, support both USB and PS/2 interfaces to make it easy to design a dual-interface device.

Code Mercenaries offers programmed chips for use in pointing devices, keyboards, and joysticks. The MouseWarrior series has interfaces for sensors and buttons and supports four interfaces: USB, PS/2, asynchronous serial, and Apple Desktop Bus (ADB). The KeyWarrior series supports USB, PS/2, and ADB and has interfaces to keyboard matrixes and optional support for keyboard macros. The JoyWarrior series supports a variety of game-controller inputs.

Windows Support

Applications can communicate with HIDs using API functions. The API functions for exchanging reports include ReadFile and WriteFile as well as HID-specific APIs such HidD_SetFeature and HidD_GetFeature. Applications that access game controllers can use DirectX's DirectInput component for fast, more direct access.

Windows requests exclusive access to Input reports from system keyboards and pointing devices, so applications can't directly read the reports that describe keypresses, mouse movements, and mouse-button clicks. Instead, the operating system handles this data at a lower level. For example, a Visual-Basic application doesn't have to read mouse clicks to find out if a user has clicked on an option button because the button's click event executes automatically on a button click.

If a system has multiple keyboards or pointing devices, Windows treats them all as a single "virtual" keyboard or pointing device. If you want to limit the applications that can access a keyboard or pointing device, or if you want to determine which keyboard or pointing device is the source of input, you need to either provide a digitally signed filter driver or design a vendor-specific device that the host doesn't identify as a system mouse or keyboard.

IrDA Bridge

The IrDA (Infrared Data Association) interface defines hardware requirements and protocols for exchanging data over short distances via infrared energy. A USB IrDA bridge converts between USB and IrDA data and enables a host to use USB to monitor, control, and exchange data over an IrDA interface.

Documentation

The specification for USB IrDA bridges is *IrDA Bridge Device Definition*. The current version at this writing is 1.0. The IrDA specifications are available from *www.irda.org*.

Overview

The data in an IrDA link uses the Infrared Link Access Protocol (IrLAP), which defines the format of the IrDA frames that carry data, addresses, and status and control information. The IrLAP Payload consists of the address, control, and optional information (data) fields in an IrLAP frame. In addition to the IrLAP Payload, each frame contains an error-checking value and markers for the beginning and end of the frame.

A USB IrDA bridge uses bulk pipes to exchange data with the host. The host and bridge place status and control information in headers whose format is defined in the IrDA bridge specification On receiving data from the IrDA link, the IrDA bridge extracts the IrLAP Payload, adds a header, and passes the data and header to the host. The header can contain values for the IrDA link's Media_Busy and Link_Speed parameters. On receiving IrDA data from the host, the IrDA bridge removes the header added by the host. The header can specify new values for Link_Speed and the number of beginning-of-frame markers. The bridge then places the IrDA Payload in an IrDA frame for transmitting.

Descriptors

An IrDA-bridge function is defined at the interface subclass level. In the interface descriptor, bInterfaceClass = FEh to indicate an application-specific interface and bInterfaceSubclass 02h to indicate an IrDA Bridge Device. A class-specific descriptor contains IrDA-specific information such as the maximum number of bytes in an IrDA frame and supported Baud rates.

Class-specific Requests

There are five class-specific control requests:

Request	bRequest	Description
Receiving	1	Is the device currently receiving an IrLAP frame?
Check_Media_Busy	3	Is infrared traffic present?
Set_IrDA_Rate_Sniff	4	Accept frames at any speed or at a single speed.
Set_IrDA_Unicast_List	5	Accept frames from the named addresses only.
Get_Class_Specific_Descriptors	6	Return the class-specific descriptor.

Chips

SigmaTel, Inc.'s STIR4000 is an IrDA USB bridge chip that contains a full-speed USB transceiver and an interface to an IrDA transceiver. The host communicates with the chip by accessing a series of registers that enable configuring, obtaining status information, and exchanging data. The chip supports vendor-specific control requests for reading and writing to the registers. The STIR4200 is a high-speed version of the chip.

Another approach to adding IrDA to a USB host is to use a USB/asynchronous-serial converter with an IrDA interface. Texas Instruments' TUSB3410 is a USB/asynchronous-serial converter for use in wired and IrDA serial interfaces. For a wired link, the chip's internal UART interfaces to serial-data pins. For an IrDA link, the UART interfaces to an internal IrDA encoder/decoder, which in turn connects to an external IrDA transceiver.

Windows Support

Windows XP supports IrDA communications via two software profiles. The dial-up networking profile enables using IrDA to connect a PC and a mobile phone. The LAN access profile enables using the Point-to-Point Protocol (PPP), a direct peer-to-peer network connection, or a direct connection to a network access point. Windows XP doesn't include a generic driver for the USB-IrDA-bridge function, but SigmaTel provides a driver for use with their chips.

Mass Storage

The mass-storage class is for devices that transfer files in one or both directions. Typical devices are floppy, hard, CD, DVD, and Flash-memory drives. Cameras can use the mass-storage class to enable accessing picture files in a camera's memory. In Windows computers, devices that use the mass-storage driver appear as drives in My Computer and the file system enables users to copy, move, and delete files in the devices.

Documentation

The USB specification for mass storage devices is in four documents: an overview (version 1.2), specifications for the bulk-only transport protocol (version 1.0) and the control/bulk/interrupt (CBI) transport protocol (version 1.1) and commands for the Universal Floppy Interface (UFI) (version 1.0).

Each media type has an industry-standard command-block set to enable controlling devices and reading status information. These are specifications that define command-block sets for device types supported by the mass-storage class:

ATAPI CD/DVD devices use the *ATA/ATAPI* specification from *www.t13.org* and the *MultiMedia Command (MMC) Set* from *www.t10.org*. (An earlier version of the ATA/ATAPI specification was called *SFF 8020i*.)

ATAPI removable media uses *SFF-8070i: ATAPI Removable Rewritable Media Devices*, available from *www.sffcommittee.com*. This document is a supplement to the ATA/ATAPI specification. Floppy drives often belong to this subclass.

Generic SCSI media uses the mandatory commands from the *SCSI Primary Command (SPC) Set* and *SCSI Block Command (SBC) Set* from *www.t10.org*.

QIC-157 tape drives use the *Common SCSI/ATAPI Command Set for Streaming Tape*, available from *www.qic.org*.

UFI uses the *UFI Command Specification* from *www.usb.org*. The commands are based on the SCSI-2 and SFF-8070i command sets.

Overview

Mass-storage devices use bulk transfers to exchange data. Control transfers send class-specific requests and can clear Stall conditions on bulk endpoints. For exchanging other information, a device may use either of two transport protocols: bulk only or control/bulk/interrupt (CBI). CBI is approved for use only with full-speed floppy drives. Bulk-only is recommended for new devices of all types.

In the bulk-only protocol, a successful data transfer has three stages: command transport, data transport, and status transport. In the command-transport stage, the host sends a command in a structure called a Command Block Wrapper (CBW). In the data-transport stage, the host or device sends the requested data. In the status-transport stage, the device

Table 7-7: The CBW contains a command block and other information about the command.

Name	Bits	Description
dCBWSignature	32	The value 43425355h, which identifies the structure as a CBW.
dCBWTag	32	A tag that associates this CBW with the CSW the device will send in response.
dCBWDataTransferLength	32	The number of bytes the host expects to transfer in the data-transport stage.
bmCBWFlags	8	Specifies the direction of the data-transport stage. Bit 7 = 0 for an OUT (host-to-device) transfer. Bit 7 = 1 for an IN (device-to-host) transfer. All other bits are zero. If there is no data-transport stage, bit 7 is ignored.
Reserved	4	0
bCBWLUN	4	For devices with multiple LUNs, specifies the LUN the command block is directed to. Otherwise the value is zero.
Reserved	3	0
bCBWCBLength	5	The length of the command block in bytes (1–16)
CBWCB	128	The command block for the device to execute.

sends status information in a structure called a Command Status Wrapper (CSW). Some commands have no data-transport stage.

Table 7-7 shows the fields in the CBW, which is 31 bytes. The meaning of the command-block value in the CBWCB field varies with the command set specified by the interface descriptor's bInterfaceSubClass field.

On receiving a CBW, a device must check that the structure is valid and has meaningful content. A CBW is valid if it is received after a CSW or reset, is 31 bytes, and has the correct value in dCBWSignature. The contents are considered meaningful if no reserved bits are set, bCBWLUN contains a supported LUN value, and bCBWCBLength and CBWCB are valid for the interface's subclass.

Table 7-8 shows the fields in the CSW, which is 13 bytes. On receiving a CSW, the host must check that the structure is valid and has meaningful content. A CSW is valid if it has 13 bytes, has the correct value in

Table 7-8: The CSW contains status and related information about a command.

Name	Bits	Description
dCBWSignature	32	The value 53425355h, which identifies the structure as a CSW.
dCBWTag	32	The value of the dCBWTag in a CBW received from the host.
dCSWDataResidue	32	For OUT transfers, the difference between dCBWDataTransferLength and the number of bytes the device processed. For IN transfers, the difference between dCBWDataTransferLength and the number of bytes the device sent.
bCSWStatus	8	00h = command passed 01h = command failed 02h = phase error

dCSWSignature, and has a dCSWTag value that matches dCBWTag of a corresponding CBW. The contents are considered meaningful if bCSWStatus equals 02h or if bCSWStatus equals either 00h or 01h and dCSWDataResidue is less than or equal to dCBWDataTransferLength.

Descriptors

The mass-storage function is defined at the interface level. In the device's interface descriptor, bInterfaceClass = 08h to indicate that the interface belongs to the mass-storage class.

The bInterfaceSubClass field indicates the supported command-block set:

bInterfaceSubClass	Subclass Description
02h	ATAPI CD/DVD devices
03h	QIC-157 tape devices
04h	USB Floppy Interface (UFI)
05h	ATAPI removable media
06h	Generic SCSI media

The bInterfaceProtocol field indicates the supported transport protocol:

bInterfaceProtocol	Protocol Description
00h	CBI with command completion interrupt transfers
01h	CBI without command completion interrupt transfers
50h	bulk only

Every bulk-only mass-storage device must have a serial number of at least 12 characters using only the characters in the range 0–9 and A–F. The serial number enables the operating system to retain properties such as the drive letter and access policies after a user moves a device to another port or attaches multiple devices with the same Vendor ID and Product ID. The device descriptor's iSerialNumber field contains an index to the serial number, which is stored in a string descriptor. The value must be different from any serial number used by other devices with the same values in the idVendor, idProduct, and bcdDevice fields in the device descriptor.

A mass-storage device must have a bulk endpoint for each direction.

Class-specific Requests

The bulk-only protocol has two defined control requests: Bulk Only Mass Storage Reset (reset the device) and Get Max Lun (get the number of logical units, or partitions, that the device supports). All other commands and status information travel in bulk transfers.

The control/bulk/interrupt (CBI) protocol has one defined control request: Accept Device-Specific Command (ADSC). The Data stage of the request carries the command. A device can use an interrupt transfer to indicate that the device has completed a command's requested action.

Chips

A mass-storage device can use just about any full- or high-speed controller chip, but several manufacturers have controllers designed specifically for use in mass-storage devices. Prolific Technology and Standard Microsystems Corporation (SMSC) each have a variety of chips with interfaces to a variety of mass-storage device types. Controllers with direct interfaces to

ATA/ATAPI devices include Philips Semiconductor's ISP1183, Texas Instruments' TUSB6250, and Cypress Semiconductor's EZUSB AT2.

Windows Support

Windows 2000 and later include a driver that supports bulk-only and CBI devices. When a device's descriptors identify the device as mass-storage class, the operating system loads the USB storage port driver (*usbstor.sys*). This driver manages communications between the lower-level USB drivers and Windows' storage-class drivers. When the device is formatted using a supported file system, the operating system assigns a drive letter to the device and the device appears in My Computer.

The mass-storage driver in Windows XP supports bInterfaceSubClass codes 02h, 05h, and 06h. Support for drives with multiple Logical Unit Numbers (LUNs) was added in Windows 2000 SP3.

One point of confusion relating to the mass-storage support under Windows is the difference between removable devices and removable media. All USB drives are removable devices because they're easily attached and detached from the PC. A removable device may have removable or non-removable media. CD, DVD, and floppy drives have removable media. A hard disk is a non-removable medium because you can't easily remove the disk from the drive. Windows' Autorun capability (also called AutoPlay) applies to devices with removable media. Autorun enables the operating system to run a program, play a movie, or perform other actions when a disk or other removable media is inserted.

Printers

The printer class is for devices that convert received data into text and/or images on paper or other media. The most basic printers print lines of text in a single font. Most laser and inkjet printers understand one or more page description languages (PDLs) and can print text in any font and complex images.

Documentation

The USB Printing Devices specification is for printers of all types. At this writing, the current version of the specification is 1.1. The IEEE-1284 standard from *www.ieee.org* describes the interface used by parallel-port printers and includes information, such as the format for Device IDs, used by USB printers.

Overview

Printer data uses a bulk OUT pipe. The host obtains status information in control requests or an optional bulk IN pipe.

Descriptors

The printer function is defined at the interface level. In the interface descriptor, bInterfaceClass = 07h to specify the printer class.

The interface descriptor's bInterfaceProtocol field contains a value that names a type of printer interface:

bInterfaceProtocol	Type
01h	Unidirectional
02h	Bidirectional
03h	IEEE-1284.4-compatible Bidirectional

With all three interface protocols, the host uses the bulk OUT endpoint to send data to the printer. With the unidirectional protocol, the host retrieves status information by sending a class-specific Get_Port_Status request. With the bidirectional protocol, the host can retrieve status information using Get_Port_Status or the bulk IN pipe, which can provide more detailed information. The IEEE-1284.4-compatible bidirectional protocol is like the bidirectional protocol but with added support to enable communications with individual functions in a multifunction peripheral.

Class-specific Requests

The printer class has three class-specific requests:

Request	bRequest
Get_Device_ID	0
Get_Port_Status	1
Soft_Reset	2

In response to a GET_DEVICE_ID request, the device returns a Device ID in the format specified by the IEEE-1284 standard. The first two bytes of the Device ID are the length in bytes, most significant byte first. Following the length is a string containing a series of keys and their values in this format:

```
key: value {,value};
```

All Device IDs must contain the keys MANUFACTURER, COMMAND SET, and MODEL, or their abbreviated forms (MFG, CMD, and MDL). The COMMAND SET key names any PDLs the printer supports, such as Hewlett Packard's Printer Control Language (PCL) or Adobe Postscript. Additional keys, which may be vendor-defined, are optional.

Here is an example Device ID:

```
MFG:My Printer Company;
MDL:Model 5T;
CMD:MLC,PCL,PML;
DESCRIPTION:My Printer Company Laser Printer 5T;
CLASS:PRINTER;
REV:1.3.2;
```

In response to the GET_PORT_STATUS request, the device returns a byte that emulates the Status-port byte on a parallel printer port. Three bits in the byte contain status information:

Bit	Name	meaning when = 1	meaning when = 0
3	Not Error	no error	error
4	Select	printer selected	printer not selected
5	Paper Empty	out of paper	not out of paper

A printer that can't obtain the status information should respond with 18h to signify *no error, printer selected*, and *not out of paper*. Parallel-port printers have two additional status bits, Busy and Ack, which are used in handshaking and don't apply to USB printers.

On receiving a Soft_Reset request, a device should flush all buffers, reset the interface's bulk pipes to their default states, and clear all Stall conditions.

In a Soft_Reset request, the bmRequestType value in the Setup transaction should be 21h to signify a class-specific request that is directed to an interface and has no Data stage. However, version 1.0 of the printer-class specification incorrectly listed the bmRequestType for Soft_Reset as 23h. So to be on the safe side, devices should respond to hosts that use a bmRequestType of 23h with this request, and hosts should try the incorrect value on receiving a STALL in response to this request using the correct value.

Chips

Just about any full- or high-speed controller will have the one or two bulk endpoints for a printer function. For converting parallel-port printers to USB, Prolific Technology has the PL-2305 USB-to-IEEE-1284 Bridge Controller. The chip supports three endpoints: one bulk IN, one bulk OUT, and one interrupt IN. The chip's IEEE-1284 parallel port can interface to an existing parallel port on a printer or other peripheral.

Windows Support

Windows includes drivers that handle tasks common to both non-Postscript and Postscript printers. A printer manufacturer can customize a driver for a specific printer by providing a minidriver that consists of one or more text files with the customization information. The Windows DDK has information on how to create printer minidrivers.

When an application requests to print a file, the printer driver sends the printer data to the print spooler's print processor. If the printer has a USB interface, the print processor sends the data either directly to the *Usbmon* port driver or to a language monitor that modifies the data stream and passes it on to *Usbmon*. *Usbmon* in turn communicates with lower-level USB drivers that access the port.

Usbmon and the *Usbprint* driver provide a software interface that is similar to the interface for accessing parallel-port printers. In many cases, a printer can use the same printer driver and language monitor for both parallel-port and USB interfaces. If needed, a language monitor or other upper-level software can support USB-specific, vendor-specific requests.

Still Image Capture: Cameras and Scanners

The still-image class encompasses cameras that capture still images (in other words, not video) and scanners. The main job of a still-image device's USB interface is to transfer image data from the device to the host. Some devices can receive image data from the host as well. If all you need is a way to transfer image files from a camera, another option is to use the mass-storage driver.

Documentation

The USB class specification, *Still Image Capture Device Definition*, includes features and commands from *PIMA 15740: 2000 Picture Transfer Protocol*, which describes requirements for transferring files and controlling digital still cameras. At this writing, the current version of the still-image specification is 1.0. The PIMA document is available from the International Imaging Industry Association (I3A) at *www.i3a.org*.

Overview

A still-image device has one bulk IN endpoint and one bulk OUT endpoint for transferring both image data and non-image data. The specification also requires an interrupt IN endpoint for event data.

In the bulk and interrupt pipes, information travels in structures called containers. The four container types are the Command Block, Data Block, Response Block, and Event Block. The bulk OUT pipe carries Command and Data Blocks. The bulk IN pipe carries Data and Response Blocks. The interrupt IN pipe carries Event Blocks.

On the bulk pipes, the host communicates by using a protocol with three phases: Command, Data, and Response. A short packet indicates the end of a phase. In the Command phase, the host sends a Command Block that names an operation defined in PIMA 15740. The Command Block contains an operation code that determines if the operation requires a data transfer and if so, the direction of data transfer. If there is a data transfer, the data travels in a Data Block in the Data phase. The first four bytes of the Data Block are the length in bytes of the data being transferred. Some operations have no Data phase. The final phase is the Response phase, where the device sends a Response Block containing completion information.

On the interrupt pipe, an Event Block can contain up to three Event Codes with status information such as a low-battery warning or a notification that a memory card has been removed. The Check Device Condition Event Code requests the host to send a class-specific Get_Extended_Event_Data request for more information about an event.

A device using the bulk-only protocol cancels a transfer by stalling the bulk endpoints. The host then sends a class-specific Get_Device_Status request and uses the Clear_Feature request to clear the stalled endpoints. The host cancels a transfer by sending a class-specific Cancel_Request request. A device is ready to resume data transfers when it returns OK (PIMA 15740 Response Code 2001h) in response to a Get_Device_Status request.

Descriptors

A still-image function is defined at the interface level. In the interface descriptor, bInterfaceClass = 06h to indicate a still-image device, bInterfaceSubclass = 01h to indicate an image interface, and bInterfaceProtocol = 01h to indicate a still-image capture function. The interface must have descriptors for the bulk IN, bulk OUT, and interrupt IN endpoints.

Class-specific Requests

There are four class-specific control requests:

Request	bRequest	Required?
Cancel_Request	64h	yes
Get_Extended_Event_Data	65h	no
Device_Reset_Request	66h	yes
Get_Device_Status	67h	no

With Cancel_Request, the host requests to cancel the PIMA 15740 transaction named in the request. With Get_Extended_Event_Data, the host requests extended information regarding an event or vendor condition. With Device_Reset_Request, the host requests the device to return to the Idle state. The host can use this request after a bulk endpoint has returned a STALL or to clear a vendor-specific condition. With Get_Device_Status, the host requests information needed to clear halted endpoints. The host uses this request after a device has canceled a data transfer.

Chips

Just about any full- or high-speed USB controller will have the three endpoints required by the still-image class.

Windows Support

Recent Windows editions support the Windows Image Acquisition (WIA) API for communicating with devices in the still-image class. Applications communicate with devices by using ReadFile, WriteFile, and DeviceIoControl commands. The drivers that add USB support to WIA are *usbscan.sys* in Windows XP and later and *usbscn9x.sys* in Windows Me.

Under Windows XP, cameras that use the Picture Transfer Protocol (PTP) described in the PIMA 15740 standard require no vendor-provided driver components, though vendors can provide a minidriver to enhance the driver and support vendor-specific features and capabilities. For scanners, the vendor must provide a microdriver, which is a "helper DLL" that translates between the driver's communications and a language the scanner understands, or a minidriver to work with the provided drivers to enable communications with the device.

Windows 98 and Windows 2000 use an earlier Still Image architecture (STI). Product vendors must provide a user-mode driver to work with the provided STI driver.

Test and Measurement

The test-and-measurement class (USBTMC) is suited for instrumentation devices where the data doesn't need guaranteed timing. These devices typically contain components such as ADCs, DACs, sensors, and transducers. A device may be a stand-alone unit or a card in a larger computer.

Before USB, many test-and-measurement devices used the IEEE-488 parallel interface, also known as the General Purpose Interface Bus (GPIB). The USB488 subclass of the test-and-measurement class defines protocols for communicating using IEEE-488's data format and commands.

Documentation

The class's specifications include the main *Test and Measurement Class* specification and a separate document for the USB488 subclass. At this writing, the current version of both documents is 1.0. The IEEE-488 standards are available from *www.ieee.org*.

Overview

A test-and-measurement device requires a bulk OUT endpoint and a bulk IN endpoint. An interrupt IN endpoint is required for devices in the USB488 subclass and otherwise is optional for returning event and status information.

The bulk pipes exchange messages, with each message consisting of a header followed by data. The bulk OUT endpoint receives command messages, and the bulk IN endpoint sends response messages. The header for a command message contains a message ID, a bTag value that identifies the transfer, and message-specific information. The header for a response message contains the message ID and bTag values of the command that prompted the response, followed by message-specific information. The message ID specifies whether a command is device-dependent or vendor-specific and whether the host expects a response.

Descriptors

A test-and-measurement function is specified at the interface subclass level. In the interface descriptor, bInterfaceClass = FEh to indicate an application-specific interface and bInterfaceSubClass = 03h to indicate the test-and-measurement class. There are no class-specific descriptors.

Class-specific Requests

The class defines eight control requests for controlling and requesting the status of an interface or transfer and requesting information about the interface's attributes and capabilities.

Chips

Just about any full- or high-speed device will have the two or three endpoints this class requires.

Windows Support

Windows doesn't include a driver for this class. National Instruments provides a driver for use with its hardware. Other options for test-and-measurement devices that use bulk transfers include the mass-storage class or a vendor-specific driver. A HID-class device can also perform test and measurement functions. For an existing device with an IEEE-488 interface, the quick solution is to use a commercial IEEE-488/USB converter.

Video

The video class supports digital camcorders, webcams, and other devices that send, receive, or manipulate transient or moving images. The class also supports transferring still images from video devices. Because transmitting high-quality video requires a lot of bandwidth, using USB for video has become a more attractive option since high-speed hosts and devices have become available.

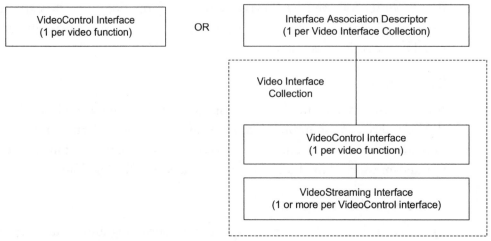

Figure 7-6: A video interface consists of a VideoControl interface and zero or more VideoStreaming interfaces.

Documentation

A variety of documents make up the video specification. The *Video Class Definition* defines standard and class-specific descriptors and class-specific control requests for video devices. The *Media Transport Terminal* specification defines descriptors and requests for devices such as video cameras and digital VCRs, which stream data stored in sequential media and may require functions such as play, record, rewind, and eject. Separate payload specifications contain format-specific information for a variety of video formats such as MJPEG, MPEG2-TS, DV, and uncompressed video. Version 1.1 of the video class specification (under development at this writing) will retire some additional 1.0 formats and add generic frame-based and generic stream-based formats. Other specification documents include a video camera example, an FAQ, and an Identifiers document that gathers together identifier values defined in the other video-class specifications. At this writing, the current version of all of these specifications is 1.0.

Overview

Figure 7-6 shows the elements that make up a video function in a USB device. Every function must have a VideoControl interface, which provides information about inputs, outputs, and other components of the function. Most functions also have one or more VideoStreaming interfaces that enable transferring video data. A Video Interface Collection consists of a Video-Control interface and its associated VideoStreaming interfaces. (A function with only a VideoControl interface isn't part of a Video Interface Collection.) A device can have multiple, independent VideoControl interfaces and Video Interface Collections.

The VideoControl interface uses the control endpoint and may use an interrupt IN endpoint. Each VideoStreaming interface has one isochronous or bulk endpoint for video data and an optional bulk endpoint for still-image data.

Descriptors

The video class defines an extensive set of descriptors that enable devices to provide detailed information about the device's abilities. Each Video Interface Collection must have an interface association descriptor that specifies the interface number of the first VideoControl interface and the number of VideoStreaming interfaces associated with the function.

The VideoControl Interface. The VideoControl interface (Figure 7-7) has a standard interface descriptor with bInterfaceClass = 0Eh to indicate the video class, plus a class-specific VideoControl interface descriptor, which consists of a VideoControl interface header descriptor followed by one or more Terminal and/or Unit descriptors. A Terminal is the starting or ending point for information that flows into or out of a function. A Terminal may represent a USB endpoint or another component such as a CCD sensor, display module, or composite-video input or output. A Terminal descriptor can describe an Input Terminal or Output Terminal. The descriptor's wTerminalType field names the function of the terminal the descriptor is associated with, such as camera, media transport input, or media transport output. A Unit transforms data flowing through a function. There are three types of Unit descriptors: Selector Unit for routing a data stream to an output, Processing Unit for controlling video attributes, and Extension Unit for vendor-defined functions.

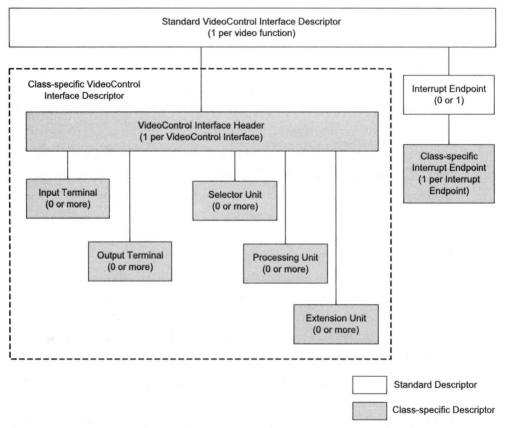

Figure 7-7: The VideoControl interface provides information about inputs, outputs, and other components of a video function.

If the interface has an interrupt endpoint, the endpoint has a standard endpoint descriptor followed by a class-specific endpoint descriptor.

The VideoStreaming Interface. Each VideoStreaming interface (Figure 7-8) has a standard interface descriptor. Following the standard interface descriptor, an interface with an IN endpoint has a class-specific Video-Streaming Input Header descriptor, and an interface with an OUT endpoint has a class-specific VideoStreaming Output Header descriptor.

Following the Header descriptor is a Payload Format descriptor for each supported video format. For frame-based formats, the Payload Format descriptor is followed by one or more Frame descriptors that describe the

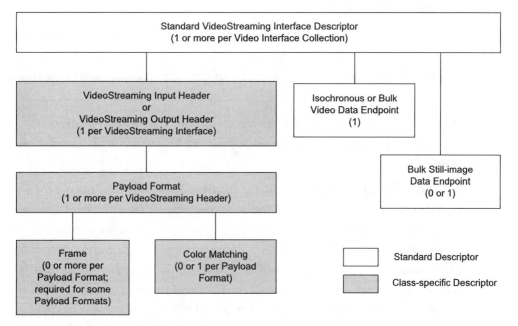

Figure 7-8: A VideoStreaming interface has an endpoint for video data and an optional endpoint for still-image data.

dimensions of the video frames and other characteristics specific to a format. A Payload Format can also have a Color Matching descriptor to describe a color profile. Each VideoStreaming interface has one isochronous or bulk endpoint descriptor for video data and an optional bulk endpoint descriptor for still-image data.

Class-specific Requests

Class-specific control requests enable setting and reading the states of controls in VideoControl and VideoStreaming interfaces.

Chips

Vista Imaging's ViCAM-III chip contains a programmable digital imaging engine with extensive support for video functions and a USB controller. Cypress Semiconductor has partnered with several companies to offer reference designs that use EZ-USB controllers in various video applications.

Windows Support

A driver compatible with the video class (*usbvideo.sys*) was released in Windows XP SP2. Vendors of video-class devices that use the driver don't need to provide any driver software but can provide a Control or Streaming extension to support vendor-specific functions or features.

Applications can access video devices using the DirectShow component of DirectX. The *usbvideo.sys* driver is supported beginning with DirectX version 9.2.

For earlier Windows editions, manufacturers of video devices must provide a minidriver to specify a format for streaming video, implement device-specific functions and properties, and perform bulk transfers if required for video data. Windows' USBCAMD driver manages isochronous data transfers, including synchronizing, starting, and stopping communications and recovering from errors. The driver communicates with Windows' stream-class driver and with the lower-level USB drivers.

Implementing Non-standard Functions

Some devices don't have an obvious match to a defined class. Examples include some data-acquisition devices and controllers for motors, relays, or other circuits. Another common application that doesn't fit into an obvious class is linking two hosts. Before USB, these types of applications used the legacy serial and parallel ports. USB is flexible enough to accommodate these and other vendor-specific applications.

Standard or Custom Driver?

When possible, it's almost always preferable to use a class that has drivers provided by the operating systems the device will operate under. Using a provided driver saves much time and effort.

Some devices with vendor-specific functions can be designed as HIDs. A HID doesn't have to be a standard device type and doesn't even need a human interface. The only requirements are that the descriptors must meet the class's requirements, and the device must transfer data using only interrupt or control transfers as defined in the HID specification.

The mass-storage class is another option for devices that exchange data in files and support a file system the host understands.

Some devices need to provide their own drivers. Using a driver provided by a chip manufacturer is one option. This approach saves you from having to develop a driver but leaves you dependent on the chip vendor to fix bugs and keep up with new operating-system editions. Chapter 8 has more about creating custom drivers.

Converting from RS-232

The RS-232 serial port has been with the PC since its beginning. The port has been used in thousands of peripherals. Just about any device that uses RS-232 can be implemented with USB. There are several approaches to making the switch.

First determine if the device fits into a defined class. Modems should use the communication-device class. Pointing devices, uninterruptible power supplies, and point-of-sale devices should be designed as HIDs.

For many other devices, FTDI Chip's FT232BM USB UART introduced in Chapter 6 provides a quick way to upgrade a design to USB. The chip can convert an existing RS-232 device to USB with minimal design changes and in most cases no changes to host software.

Figure 7-9 shows an example. A typical device with an RS-232 interface contains a UART that converts between the serial data used in RS-232 communications and the parallel data the CPU uses. The signals on the line side of the UART connect to converters that translate between RS-232 voltages and the 5V logic used by the UART. The line side of the converter connects to a cable to the remote computer with an RS-232 interface. To convert from RS-232 to USB, you replace the RS-232 converter with a '232BM. On the host computer, FTDI Chip's Virtual COM port driver enables applications to access the device using the same functions used for RS-232 communications.

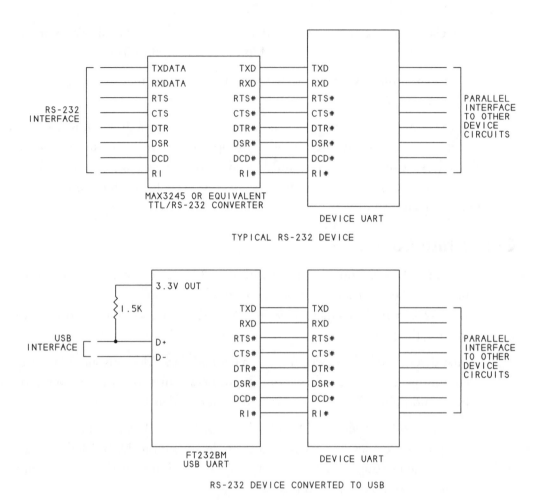

Figure 7-9: FTDI's USB UART can convert devices with RS-232 interfaces to USB. A driver provided by FTDI causes the device to appear like a conventional COM-port device to host applications.

An even easier solution is to use an RS-232/USB converter module. These typically contain little more than an FT232BM or similar chip, an RS-232 interface chip, an RS-232 connector, and a USB connector. Users then have a choice of using the original interface or adding the converter and using USB.

When using a USB/RS-232 converter, devices that use the status and control signals in unconventional ways and with critical timing requirements may require modifications to device hardware or firmware or application software.

Converting from the Parallel Port

Another port that all PCs had from the beginning was the parallel port. The port was originally intended for connecting printers, but many other device types took advantage of the port as well. The parallel interface is faster than RS-232 and thus became a favored connection for scanners and external drives. Scanners, drives, and printers can now use USB and the standard classes for these device types.

For other devices, there are several options for converting to USB. A peripheral-side parallel-port interface has 8 bidirectional data pins, 5 status outputs, and 4 control inputs. A USB controller with 17 or more I/O bits can emulate a parallel port. Prolific Technology's PL-2305 has a USB interface and a complete PC-side IEEE-1284 parallel port that can interface directly to existing parallel-port devices.

For the firmware and driver, devices that can function using only control and interrupt transfers may be able to use the HID class. The device will need new application software to communicate with the HID drivers in place of the driver that accessed the parallel port. If you want to make minimal changes to the application software, you can provide a custom driver that provides functions that emulate the functions called by the original application.

PC-to-PC Communications

Every USB communication must be between a host and a device. USB doesn't allow hosts to exchange data with each other directly. Yet because every PC has a USB port, it's natural to want to use the interface to connect PCs to each other, especially when the PCs don't have Ethernet ports.

USB On-The-Go enables a device to also function as a host. Most PCs don't contain On-The-Go host controllers, however. Another solution is to use a

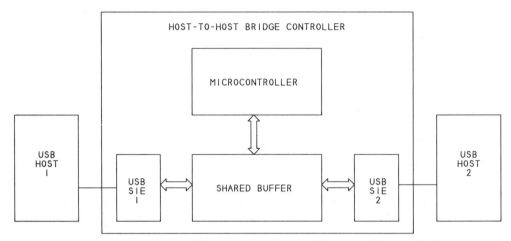

Figure 7-10: To enable two USB hosts to communicate with each other, two USB serial interface engines can share a buffer. Each SIE copies received USB data into the shared buffer, and the other device retrieves the data from the buffer and sends the data to the other host.

host-to-host bridge cable that contains two serial interface engines. Each PC has a USB connection to one of the SIEs, and the two devices communicate with each other via a shared buffer (Figure 7-10). Data sent by a PC travels to one of the SIEs, through the shared buffer, and out the other SIE to the remote PC.

Prolific Technology's PL-2501 Hi-Speed USB Host to Host Bridge Controller is a single chip designed for this type of host-to-host application. The chip contains an 8032 microcontroller and two USB SIEs that can access a common buffer. The PL-2301 is a full-speed version. Many commercial "data-link file-transfer cables" contain one of these chips. Typically, the drivers enable each PC to see the other as a network-connected computer.

An alternate approach is to use two FTDI Chip USB UARTs and cross-connect the asynchronous interfaces in a "null modem" configuration. The PCs then see each other as COM-port devices. Yet another option is to establish a network connection by attaching a USB/Ethernet converter to each PC and connecting each converter to a local network.

Using a Generic Driver

For devices that don't fit into a standard class, a generic driver can be a solution. Generic drivers typically enable applications to request control, interrupt, bulk, and isochronous transfers using a driver-specific API. Two such options are the DriverX USB toolkit from Tetradyne Software, Inc. and the USBIO Development Kit from Thesycon Systemsoftware & Consulting GmbH. (Yes, that spelling is correct.)

The DriverX USB toolkit includes a generic driver, header and library files for use with Visual C++ and Borland C++ Builder, and additional support for Delphi and Visual Basic.

To communicate with the driver included with the USBIO Development Kit, applications can use standard Windows API functions (ReadFile, WriteFile, DeviceIoControl), a C++ class library, native Delphi and Java interfaces, or a USBIO COM interface based on Microsoft's Component Object Model (COM) technology.

Chapter 7

8

How the Host Communicates

Under Windows, an application that wants to access a USB peripheral must communicate with a device driver that knows how to manage communications with the system's USB drivers. This chapter explains how Windows manages USB communications and explores the options for device drivers.

Device Driver Basics

A device driver is a software component that enables applications to access a hardware device. The hardware device may be a printer, modem, keyboard, video display, data-acquisition unit, or just about anything controlled by circuits that the CPU can access. Some devices, such as internal disk drives, are inside the box with the CPU. Others, including just about all USB devices, are external devices that connect to the system via cables (or wireless links). As Chapter 7 explained, some device drivers are class drivers that handle communications with a variety of devices that perform similar functions.

Insulating Applications from the Details

Applications are the programs that users run, including everything from word processors and databases to special-purpose applications that access custom hardware. A device driver insulates applications from having to know details about the physical connections, signals, and protocols required to communicate with a device.

A device driver can enable application code to access a peripheral when the application knows only the peripheral's name (such as HP LaserJet 2300) or the device's function (joystick, drive, scanner). The application doesn't have to know the physical address of the port the peripheral attaches to or monitor and control handshaking signals. Applications don't even have to know whether a device uses USB or another interface. The application code can be the same for devices that perform similar functions but have different interfaces, with the hardware-specific details handled at a lower level.

The device driver translates between application-level and hardware-specific code. Applications communicate with device drivers using functions supported by the operating system. The hardware-specific code handles the protocols needed to access the peripheral's circuits, including detecting the states of status signals and toggling control signals at appropriate times.

The Windows drivers for USB devices use a layered driver model where each driver in a series performs a portion of the communication. The top layer contains a client device driver (or client driver for short) that manages communications between applications and lower-level bus drivers. Another term for client driver is function driver. The bottom layer contains bus drivers that manage communications between the client driver and the hardware. One or more filter drivers may supplement the client and bus drivers.

The layered driver model simplifies the job of writing drivers. Devices can share code for tasks they have in common. The drivers that handle communications with the system's USB hardware are included with Windows, so writers of client drivers don't have to handle these details. Note also that the layered driver model means that applications *can't* access USB ports directly. Windows doesn't allow it. All application communications must be with a driver assigned to a device.

Options for USB Devices

There are several approaches to obtaining a driver for a USB device that you're developing. Many devices can use a driver that's included with Windows or provided by a chip vendor or other source. Other devices may require custom drivers. When a custom driver is necessary, toolkits are available to simplify and speed up the task of driver writing. Sometimes more than one way will work, and the choice depends on what's easier, cheaper, or offers better performance.

As Chapter 7 showed, many peripherals fit into standard classes such as disk drives, printers, modems, keyboards, and mice. Each of these devices is available with a choice of interfaces, including USB. For example, a disk drive may use ATA/ATAPI, SCSI, IEEE-1394, or USB. When the devices in a class may have any of multiple hardware interfaces, supplemental drivers can support different interfaces. If a device has features or capabilities beyond what a class driver supports, a device-specific filter driver may be able to support these as needed.

User and Kernel Modes

To understand what the device driver has to do, you need to understand where the driver fits in the communications path of a data transfer. Even if you don't need to write a driver for your device, understanding the driver's role will help in understanding the application-level code that you do write.

In the most general sense, a device driver is any code that handles communication details for a hardware device that interfaces to a CPU. Even a short subroutine in an application can be considered a device driver. Under Windows, the code for most drivers, including USB drivers, differs from application code because the operating system allows the driver code a greater level of privilege than applications are allowed.

Program code in a Windows system runs in one of two modes: user or kernel. Each allows a different level of privilege in accessing memory and other system resources. Applications must run in user mode. Most drivers, including all USB drivers, run in kernel mode, though a driver for a USB device

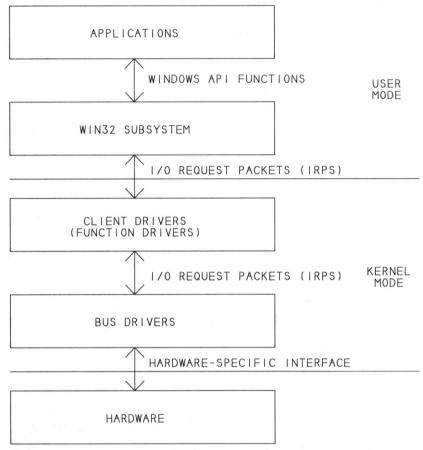

Figure 8-1: USB uses a layered driver model under Windows, with separate drivers for devices and the buses they connect to.

may have a supplementary user-mode driver. Figure 8-1 shows the major components of user and kernel modes in a USB communication.

In user mode, Windows limits access to memory and other system resources. Windows doesn't allow an application to access memory that the operating system has designated as protected. Managing memory in this way enables a PC to run multiple applications at the same time. If an application crashes, other applications shouldn't be affected. On x86 processors, user mode corresponds to the CPU's Ring 3 mode.

In kernel mode, the code has unrestricted access to system resources, including the ability to execute memory-management instructions and control access to I/O ports. A kernel-mode driver can permit or deny an application access to a device. For example, a joystick driver can allow any application to use a device, or the driver can allow an application to reserve the device for exclusive use. Other abilities that Windows reserves for kernel-mode drivers include DMA transfers and responding to hardware interrupts. On x86 processors, kernel mode corresponds to the CPU's Ring 0 mode.

Applications communicate with client drivers using Windows API functions or other components that call API functions internally but shield application programmers from the details. The Windows WIN32 subsystem manages communications between applications and client drivers. To communicate with a USB device, an application typically doesn't have to know anything about the USB protocol, or even if a device uses USB at all.

Drivers communicate with each other using structures called I/O request packets (IRPs). Windows defines a set of IRPs that drivers can use. Each IRP requests a single input or output action. A client driver for a USB device uses IRPs to communicate with the bus drivers that handle USB communications. The bus drivers are included with Windows and require no programming by applications programmers or device-driver writers.

WDM Drivers

USB device drivers for Windows are kernel-mode drivers that must conform to the Windows Driver Model defined by Microsoft for use under Windows 98 and later. These drivers are known as WDM drivers and have the extension *.sys*. (Other driver types may also use the *.sys* extension.)

Application programmers have a choice of programming languages, including Visual Basic, Delphi, and C and its derivatives. But to write a driver for a USB device, you need a tool that is capable of compiling a WDM driver. The Windows DDK includes a C compiler for this purpose. An exception is driver toolkits that provide a generic driver and either require no programming at all or permit you to use other compilers to customize a generic driver with a user-mode component.

Layered Drivers

In the layered driver model used in USB communications, each layer handles a piece of the communication process. Dividing communications into layers is efficient because devices that have tasks in common can use the same driver for those tasks. For example, all kinds of devices may use USB, so it makes sense to have one set of drivers to handle the USB-specific tasks that are common to all. Including these drivers with Windows means that device vendors don't have to provide drivers. The alternative would be to have each device driver handle communicating directly with the USB hardware, with much duplication of effort.

Figure 8-2 shows the layers involved with USB communications under Windows XP.

Client Drivers

A client driver can consist of one or more files. The main client driver can be a class driver provided with Windows or a vendor-provided driver. The client driver manages communications that are specific to a device or a class of devices. A class driver may also communicate with a miniclass driver that manages communications with a subset of devices in a class. For example, the HID USB miniclass driver manages USB-specific communications with HID-class devices that have USB interfaces. Other HID miniclass drivers could manage bus-specific communications with HIDs that have other hardware interfaces.

A client driver or miniclass driver may also have one or more upper and lower filter drivers (Figure 8-3). An upper-level filter driver can monitor and modify communications between applications and a client driver. A lower-level filter driver can monitor and modify communications between a client driver and the bus drivers.

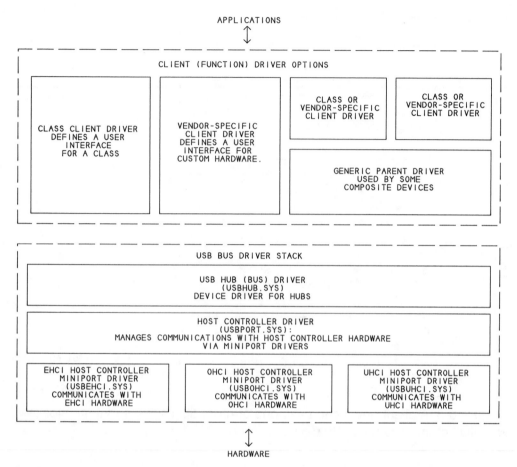

Figure 8-2: USB communications under Windows XP involve the USB bus driver stack and one or more client drivers.

For some composite devices, Windows XP loads a USB common-class generic parent driver between the bus drivers and the client drivers for the device's interfaces. The generic parent driver handles synchronization, Plug-and-Play, and power-management functions for the device as a whole and manages communications between the bus drivers and the client drivers for the composite device's interfaces.

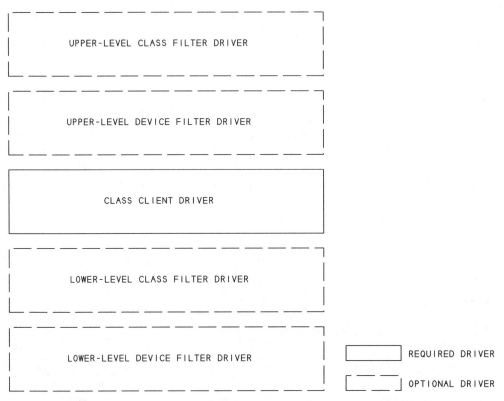

Figure 8-3: A client driver can have one or more filter drivers that monitor or modify communications with devices.

USB Drivers

Under Windows XP, the USB bus drivers consist of the host-controller driver, one or more miniport drivers, and the hub driver. The host-controller driver, sometimes called the port driver, manages tasks that are common to all host controllers. The host controller driver consists of a port driver (*usbport.sys*) and one or more miniport drivers that each manage communications with one of the three host-controller types. The hub driver manages communications with the system's hubs. In Windows XP, the hub driver is *usbhub.sys*.

The bus drivers are included with Windows, and application and device-driver writers don't have to know the details about how they work.

Perhaps because of this, Microsoft provides little documentation for these drivers. If you want to know more about how low-level communications work, one source of information is the source code and other documentation from the Linux USB Project.

Host Controller Types

There are three types of host controllers. Two support low- and full-speed communications and one supports high-speed communications. The low- and full-speed controller types are the Open Host Controller Interface (OHCI) and the Universal Host Controller Interface (UHCI). High-speed host controllers implement the Enhanced Host Controller Interface (EHCI). The USB-IF's Web site has links to the specifications.

Windows' Device Manager enables you to view information about the host controllers in a PC. To view the driver type, right-click the host controller name, select Properties, then Driver and Driver Details. One of the drivers should have *ohci*, *uhci*, or *ehci* in the name. Chapter 9 has more about using the Device Manager.

OHCI and UHCI Differences

In Windows XP, controllers that conform to the OHCI standard use the driver *usbohci.sys*, and controllers that conform to the UHCI standard use the driver *usbuhci.sys*. In other Windows editions, the driver names can vary but will contain *ohci* or *uhci*. Both drivers provide a way for the USB hardware to communicate with the bus-class driver. The two drivers take different approaches to implementing the host-controller's functions. UHCI places more of the communications burden on software and allows using of simpler, cheaper hardware. OHCI places more of the burden on the hardware and allows simpler software control. UHCI was developed by Intel and OHCI was developed by Compaq, Microsoft, and National Semiconductor.

The differences should be transparent to driver developers and application programmers. Both controllers comply fully with the USB specification. Their performance can differ, however. Developers shouldn't assume their device works fine based on tests with one host-controller type.

An OHCI controller is capable of scheduling more than one stage of a control transfer in a single frame, while a UHCI controller always schedules each stage in a different frame. For bulk endpoints with a maximum packet size less than 64 bytes, a UHCI driver attempts no more than one transaction per frame, while an OHCI driver may schedule additional transactions in a frame. An OHCI controller will poll an interrupt endpoint at least once every 32 milliseconds, even if the endpoint descriptor requests a maximum latency of 255 milliseconds, while UHCI controllers can, but don't have to, support less-frequent polling.

Developers who use UHCI hosts are sometimes surprised when their devices fail when connected to an OHCI host, usually because the device isn't expecting to see multiple transaction attempts per frame for a single transfer. Every device should work with both controller types. Test your device on both!

Supporting All Speeds

An EHCI controller handles high-speed communications only. The EHCI specification says that a host that supports EHCI must also support low and full speeds except for the unusual situation where every port has a permanently attached high-speed device. To support low and full speeds, the host must have a companion OHCI or UHCI host controller or a USB 2.0-compliant hub, which performs the function of a host controller for low- and full-speed devices. Just about every PC with an EHCI controller has a companion OHCI or UHCI controller. An EHCI controller and a companion OHCI or UHCI controller can share a bus.

Users and application programmers don't have to know or care which host controller is communicating with a device, though Windows will warn if the system has high-speed-capable ports and a user attaches a high-speed-capable device to a 1.x hub. The driver for EHCI controllers is *usbechi.sys*.

Communication Flow

One way to better understand what happens during a USB transfer is to look at an example. The following are the steps in a USB transfer with a data-acquisition device that uses a vendor-specific client device driver.

Preliminary Requirements

Before an application can communicate with the device, several things must happen. When a device is attached, Windows manages enumeration, as described in Chapter 4. To identify which driver to use on first enumeration, Windows compares the retrieved descriptors with the information in the system's INF files. Chapter 9 has more about INF files. When a device supports multiple configurations, the driver selects a configuration. The application that will access the device can then obtain a handle that identifies the device and enables communications with it.

Initiating Data Transfers

To read data from a data-acquisition device, a user might click a button in a data-acquisition application. Or a user might select an option that causes the application to request a reading once per minute. Or periodic data acquisitions might start automatically when the device's driver is loaded or when the user runs the application.

The Application's Role

Windows includes API functions that enable applications to communicate with client drivers. Applications written in Visual Basic, C/C++/C#, Delphi, and other languages can call API functions. The available functions vary with the driver, but applications typically can open communications with CreateFile, exchange data using a combination of ReadFile/ReadFileEx, WriteFile/WriteFileEx, and DeviceIoControl, and close communications with CloseHandle.

To make programming simpler and safer, many languages support alternate ways to access devices of various types. Microsoft's .NET platform includes classes and methods that eliminate the need to call many API functions directly. Instead, applications communicate via intermediate layers with a

Common Language Runtime (CLR) component that in turn calls the API functions. For example, in Visual Basic .NET, the PrintDocument class includes methods that enable applications to send text and images to a printer.

Communications with any device may require calling API functions at times, however. For example, .NET doesn't provide methods for detecting device attachment and removal via WM_DEVICECHANGE messages.

Each call to an API function includes the request, other required information such as the data to write or amount of data to read, and a handle for accessing the device. Microsoft's Platform Software Development Kit (SDK) documents the functions.

Although the names suggest that the functions are used only with files, ReadFile and WriteFile (as well as ReadFileEx and WriteFileEx) can transfer data to and from any driver that supports handle-based operations. The data being read or data to be written is stored in a buffer specified by the function call. A call to ReadFile doesn't always cause the driver to retrieve data from a device. The function may instead return data that a driver has already requested and stored in a buffer. The details vary with the driver.

DeviceIoControl is another way to transfer data to and from buffers. Included in each DeviceIoControl request is a control code that identifies a specific request. Unlike ReadFile and WriteFile, a single DeviceIoControl call can transfer data in both directions. The driver specifies what data, if any, to pass in each direction for each control code. Some control codes are commands that don't need to pass additional data.

Windows drivers define control codes used by drives and other common devices. For example, IOCTL_STORAGE_CHECK_VERIFY determines if media is present and readable on removable media and IOCTL_STORAGE_GET_MEDIA_TYPES returns the types of media supported by a drive.

A vendor-specific driver can also define control codes. Because the codes are sent only to a specific driver, it doesn't matter if other drivers use the same codes. For example, Cypress Semiconductor's general-purpose driver

CyUsb.sys defines a series of DeviceIoControl codes for transferring data, configuring a device, and requesting status and configuration information.

A driver may also define additional functions that applications can use. For example, the HID driver defines the functions Hid_GetFeature and HidD_SetFeature for retrieving and sending Feature reports. These functions use DeviceIoControl internally, but expose driver-specific functions for application programmers.

The Client Driver's Role

When an application calls an API function that reads or writes to a USB device, Windows passes the call to the appropriate client driver. The driver passes the request on in a format the USB bus-class driver can understand.

As mentioned earlier, drivers communicate with each other using IRPs. For USB communications, the IRPs contain structures called USB Request Blocks (URBs), which enable a driver to configure devices and transfer data. For example, a driver requests a descriptor by submitting an IRP that contains this URB:

```
URB_FUNCTION_GET_DESCRIPTOR_FROM_DEVICE
```

The Windows DDK documents the URBs.

A client driver requests a transfer by creating an URB and submitting it in an IRP to a lower-level driver. The bus and host-controller drivers handle the details of scheduling transactions on the bus. For interrupt and isochronous transfers, if there is no outstanding IRP for an endpoint when its scheduled time comes up, the host controller skips the transaction.

For transfers that require multiple transactions, the client driver submits a single IRP for the entire transfer. All of the transfer's transactions are then scheduled without requiring further communications with the client driver.

If you're using an existing client driver (rather than writing your own), you need to understand how to access the driver's application-level interface, but you don't have to concern yourself with IRPs and URBs. If you're writing a client driver, you need to provide the IRPs that communicate with the system's USB drivers.

The Hub Driver's Role

The USB hub driver, also called the bus driver, is the device driver for the hubs on the bus. The bus driver requires no programming by device developers.

The Host-controller Driver's Role

The host-controller driver passes data provided by the client driver to the host-controller hardware, which in turn connects to the bus. The host-controller driver requires no programming by device developers.

The Device's Role

Data that leaves the host's port may pass through additional hubs. Eventually the data reaches the hub that connects to the device, and the hub passes the data on to the device. The device recognizes its address, reads the incoming data, and takes appropriate action.

The Response

Most communications require a response, which may include data sent in response to the request or a packet with a status code. This information travels back to the host in reverse order: through the device's hub, onto the bus, and to the PC's hardware and software. A client driver may pass a response on to an application, which may display the result or take other action.

Ending Communications

When communications are complete, an application can use the API function CloseHandle to free system resources.

More Examples

Communications with other USB devices follow a similar path, but there can be differences in how the transfer initiates and in how the client driver handles communications.

Other examples of a user initiating a transfer are clicking on a USB drive's icon to view a disk's folders or clicking Print in an application to send a file to a USB printer. In each of these cases, no data transfers until the application requests a communication and the device driver fills a buffer with data to send or makes a buffer available for received data.

A driver can also cause the host to continuously request data from a device whether or not an application has requested it. For example, a keyboard driver causes the host to request keypress data at frequent intervals because there is no way to predict when a user will press a key.

The host also sends requests to enumerate devices on system power-up or device attachment. The device's hub causes the host to initiate these requests when the hub notifies the host of the presence of a device. A suspended device can use USB's remote-wakeup feature to initiate a transfer by signaling its hub, and in turn the host, to request resuming communications.

Creating a Custom Driver

Creating a WDM driver is not a trivial task. Writing a driver requires expertise in C programming and a fair amount of knowledge about how Windows communicates with hardware and applications. However, several products can help to simplify and speed up the process.

Writing a Driver from Scratch

The minimum requirement for writing a device driver from scratch is the Windows Driver Development Kit (DDK), which includes what you need to create a driver: a C compiler, a linker, build utilities, and documentation. Also included is example source code for filter drivers and drivers that request bulk and isochronous transfers. The example drivers are a useful starting point for developing a custom driver.

How to write a USB driver from the ground up is a much bigger topic than this book has room for. An excellent book in this topic is *Programming the Microsoft Windows Driver Model* by Walter Oney.

Using a Driver Toolkit

A driver toolkit provides a way to jump start driver development by doing as much of the work for you as possible. Toolkits that support creating USB drivers are available from Jungo Ltd. and Compuware NuMega.

There are two general categories of toolkits. One provides a generic driver that handles USB communications and generates a device-specific user-mode driver and INF file for use with the driver. This approach is very fast and requires no programming at all to create the driver but can't handle every situation. Other toolkits provide libraries and other tools that assist in writing a custom driver for a device. This approach is more flexible but requires programming expertise.

Automated Driver Generation

All USB communications follow the protocols defined in the USB specification, so it makes sense that a single generic driver should be able to communicate with just about any device. A full-featured generic USB driver should support all four transfer types, including vendor-defined control requests. The driver should also support the power-management and Plug-and-Play capabilities required of all WDM drivers. Additional functions such as the ability to retrieve descriptors or select a configuration or interface are useful as well.

Jungo's WinDriver USB Device toolkit requires no driver programming at all. A DriverWizard generates files that you can compile to create a custom user-mode driver in an *.exe* file. The user-mode driver communicates with the provided kernel-mode driver. You can compile the files generated by the Wizard using Visual C++, C++ Builder, or Delphi. The DriverWizard also creates an INF file for the device.

From the DriverWizard, you can select your device from the detected devices and test communications by reading and writing to the device's endpoints. You can then request the DriverWizard to create the driver files. When the driver has been installed, applications can communicate with the device using device-specific functions such as MyDevice_Open and MyDevice_GetDeviceInfo.

For faster performance, you can move portions of your code from the user-mode driver to a kernel-mode driver called a Kernel PlugIn, which you compile with Visual C++. For debugging, the included Debug Monitor application enables you to monitor communications handled by the driver. Different editions of WinDriver USB support Windows, Windows CE .NET, and Linux.

Toolkits that Provide Libraries for Creating Custom Drivers

The completely automated toolkits aren't suitable for every device. They can't create filter drivers, and you may want a completely custom driver for the best possible performance. Two products for creating custom drivers are CompuWare's DriverWorks in the DriverStudio suite and Jungo's Kernel-Driver USB.

Each of these products has Wizards and code libraries that do much of the work for you. You need to fill in the provided skeleton code and compile the driver. The driver's performance can be as fast as if you had written the driver from scratch. DriverWorks is capable of generating driver code for devices that use other buses besides USB. Jungo has a separate KernelDriver product for non-USB devices.

Using GUIDs

A Globally Unique Identifier (GUID) is a 128-bit value that uniquely identifies a class or other entity. Windows uses GUIDs in identifying two types of device classes: device setup classes and device interface classes. A device setup GUID identifies a device setup class, which encompasses devices that Windows installs in the same way. A device interface GUID identifies a device interface class. The device interface GUID provides a mechanism for applications to communicate with a driver assigned to devices in the class. In many cases, devices that belong to a particular device setup class also belong to the same device interface class. Some SetupDi_ API functions accept either type of GUID. But each type of GUIDs provides access to different types of information used for different purposes.

The conventional format for expressing GUIDs divides the GUID into five sets of hex characters, with the sets separated by hyphens.

This is the GUID for the HIDCLASS device setup class:

745a17a0-74d3-11d0-b6fe-00a0c90f57da

This is the GUID for the HID device interface class:

4d1e55b2-f16f-11cf-88cb-001111000030

Driver writers who need to provide a custom GUID can generate one using the *guidgen* utility included with Visual C++. The utility uses an algorithm that makes it extremely unlikely that someone else will create an identical GUID.

Device Setup GUIDs

A device setup GUID identifies devices that Windows sets up and configures in the same way, using the same class installer and co-installers. The system file *devguid.h* defines device setup GUIDs for a variety of classes. The file is included in the Windows DDK.

Table 8-1 shows some device setup classes that might apply to USB devices. Most peripherals should use a device setup class that corresponds to the device's function, such as printer or disk drive. Several of the class names describe functions that obviously match one of the defined USB classes. A single device can belong to multiple setup classes, such as HID and Mouse. The USB class is appropriate for USB hosts and hubs, as well as any device that has unique installation and configuration requirements or capabilities that don't fit another class. A vendor-specific class is another option for such devices, but Microsoft discourages adding vendor-specific classes.

Each device setup GUID corresponds to a Class key in the system registry. Each Class key has a subkey for each instance of a device in the class. Chapter 9 has more about Class keys.

Applications can use device setup GUIDs to retrieve information and perform various installation functions on devices. The *devcon* example in the Windows DDK shows how to use device setup GUIDs in detecting and

Table 8-1: A selection of the device setup classes supported by Windows and the USB device classes that encompass devices in the setup class.

Device Setup Class	USB Class
Battery Devices	HID
CD-ROM Drives	Mass storage
Disk Drives	Mass storage
Human Interface Devices (HID)	HID
Imaging Device (still image)	Still image capture
Keyboard	HID
Modem	Communications
Mouse	HID
Printers	Printer
Smart Card Readers	Chip/smart card interface
Tape Drives	Mass storage
USB	Host controllers and hubs, vendor-specific functions

retrieving information about devices and performing functions such as enabling, disabling, restarting, updating drivers for, and removing devices. Users can perform these same functions via Windows' Device Manager.

Device Interface GUIDs

A class or device driver can register one or more device interface classes to enable applications to learn about and communicate with devices that use the driver. Each device interface class has a device interface GUID.

Using a device interface GUID and SetupDi_ functions, an application can find all attached devices in a device interface class. On detecting a device, the application can obtain a device path name to pass to the CreateFile function. CreateFile returns a handle that the application can use to read and write to the device. Applications can also use device interface GUIDs to request to be notified when a device is attached or removed. Chapter 10 has more about using GUIDs for this purpose.

Unlike the device setup GUIDs, device interface GUIDs aren't stored in one file. A driver package may include a C header file or Visual-Basic declaration that contains a device interface GUID. For the HID class, applications can retrieve the GUID with the function HidD_GetHidGuid.

Not all devices require using device interface GUIDs. For example, applications can use Windows' file system to access files on mass-storage devices and printing functions to access printers. A custom driver can define its own API to enable applications to access devices without having to provide a GUID.

Some older drivers define a symbolic link for each device they control. For example, the first device attached might be \\.*mydevice0*, followed by \\.*mydevice1,* \\.*mydevice2*, and so on up as needed. Applications access these devices using the symbolic links instead of device interface GUIDs.

9

Matching a Driver to a Device

On detecting a newly attached USB device, the operating system needs to decide what driver to assign to the device. This chapter shows how Windows uses INF files to select a driver. I also show how the Windows Device Manager and the system registry store information about devices and their drivers.

Using the Device Manager

Windows' Device Manager displays information about all installed devices and presents a user interface for enabling, disabling, and uninstalling devices and updating or changing a device's assigned driver. For developers, the Device Manager is useful for showing whether the correct driver is assigned and successfully installed and for providing a way to force Windows to forget what it knows about a device and start fresh.

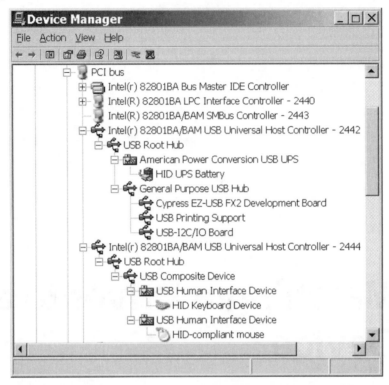

Figure 9-1: Device Manager's option to view devices by connection quickly shows which devices connect to which hubs and host controllers.

Viewing Devices

To view the Device Manager, in Windows XP, right-click on My Computer, click Manage, and in the Computer Management pane, select Device Manager. Or click Start and select Settings > Control Panel > System > Hardware > Device Manager. Or save some clicks by creating a shortcut to the file *devmgmt.msc* in *Windows\System32*.

The Device Manager's View menu offers four ways to view information: as devices by type and by connection and as resources by type and by connection. Viewing devices by connection (Figure 9-1) shows the physical connections from each host controller and root hub, through any additional hubs, to the attached devices. To view information about a device, including

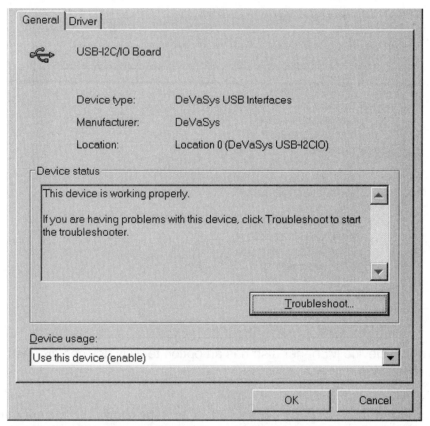

Figure 9-2: Device Manager's Properties screens provide more information about a device, including what driver the operating system has assigned to the device.

its driver(s) and any problem the operating system has detected with the device, right-click the device's listing and select Properties (Figure 9-2).

Viewing devices by type (Figure 9-3) groups devices according to their functions, with little regard to hardware interface. The Class key(s) in the registry determine what category or categories a device appears in. Many devices fit into standard categories such as Disk Drives, Keyboards, and Modems. Some devices are in multiple categories. For example, a keyboard may appear under both Human Interface Devices and Keyboards. The USB category lists host controllers, hubs, and some other devices. A device with a vendor-specific driver can have its own category or use the USB category.

Figure 9-3: Device Manager also has an option to view devices grouped by type, or function.

Viewing resources by connection or by type shows the memory and I/O addresses and interrupt request (IRQ) lines assigned to each host controller. It's unlikely you'll need this information when developing USB devices, drivers, or applications.

An exclamation point over a device's icon means that the host had a problem communicating with the device or finding a driver. An X over an icon means that the device is present but disabled, possibly by the user.

By default, the Device Manager shows only attached USB devices. To view devices that have been removed but whose drivers are still installed, set the following system environment variable:

```
DEVMGR_SHOW_NONPRESENT_DEVICES=1
```

To set the variable, in Windows' Control Panel, click System > Advanced > Environment Variables, enter the variable's name, and set its value. Then in

Device Manager, click View and check the option to Show Hidden Devices. You may need to reboot after setting the environment variable.

Property Pages

Each listing in the Device Manager has Property Pages that provide additional information about a device and the ability to control the device and its driver. To view the Property Pages, double-click the device's listing. You can request to enable or disable the device or view, update, roll back, or uninstall the device's driver. A Details page provides additional information, including various system IDs, any filter drivers or coinstallers the device uses, and power capabilities.

Device Information in the Registry

The system registry is a database that Windows maintains for storing critical information about the hardware and software installed on a system. The registry stores information about all devices that have been installed, whether or not they're currently attached. When a new device is enumerated, Windows stores information about the device in the registry.

Some of the information about USB devices in the registry comes from the bus drivers, which obtain the information from the devices. Other information is from the INF file that the operating system selects when assigning a driver to a device.

You can view the registry's contents using Windows' *regedit* utility. (From the Start menu, select Run and enter *regedit*.) You can also use regedit to edit the registry's contents, but making registry changes this way isn't recommended and is seldom necessary. The Windows Platform SDK documents API functions that enable applications to read and write to the registry. Typically, device installation is the only time it's necessary to change device information in the registry. A request to uninstall a device via the Device Manager or another application also results in changes to the registry.

The system registry is a vital and essential component of Windows. It's so important that Windows maintains multiple backup copies in case the cur-

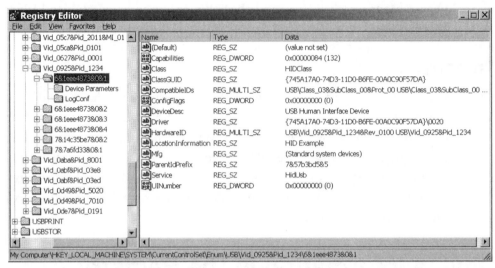

Figure 9-4: A hardware key contains information about an instance of a device with a specific Vendor ID and Product ID.

rent copy becomes unusable. Be extremely careful about making changes to the registry. Windows' System Restore utility can restore the registry to an earlier state. Just viewing the registry is safe, however.

The registry's data has a tree structure. Each node on the tree is a registry *key*. Each key can have entries with assigned values and subkeys that in turn may have entries and subkeys. Information about the system's hardware and installed software is under the HKEY_LOCAL_MACHINE key, with information about USB devices under several subkeys: the hardware key, the class key, the driver key, and the service key.

The Hardware Key

The hardware key, also called the instance key or device key, stores information about an instance of a specific device. Hardware keys are under the enumerator (Enum) key:

```
HKEY_LOCAL_MACHINE\System\CurrentControlSet\Enum
```

Under the Enum key is a USB key. Each subkey of the USB key contains the Vendor ID and Product ID of a USB device. Figure 9-4 shows the entry for a device with a Vendor ID of 0925h and Product ID or 1234h. Under each of these keys may be one or more hardware keys, with each hardware key identifying an instance of the device. Table 9-1 lists some of the entries under the hardware key.

A device without a USB serial number gets a new hardware key every time the device attaches to a port the device hasn't been attached to previously. If you physically remove the device and attach a different device with identical descriptors to the same port, the operating system doesn't know the difference so there is no new hardware key. Devices with USB serial numbers have one hardware key per physical device, without regard to what port the device is attached to.

A USB device may also have one or more keys for additional enumerators such as HID, USBPRINT, and USBSTOR. For example, a UPS back-up device with a HID interface can have a key in the Enum\USB branch to name the HidUsb service and a key in the Enum\HID branch to name the HidBatt service.

The Class Key

The class key stores information about device setup class and the devices that belong to it. The class keys are under this registry key:

```
HKEY_LOCAL_MACHINE\System\CurrentControlSet\Control\
Class
```

The name of a class key is the device setup GUID for the class. This is the same as the value stored in the hardware key for devices in the class, under ClassGUID. Figure 9-5 shows the class key for the HID class. The class key contains a friendly name for the setup class, the class name from the header file that defines the GUID, and an index value that specifies the icon to use in Device Manager and other windows that display setup information. Applications can retrieve the index of the mini-icon for a class by calling SetupDiGetClassBitmapIndex. A vendor-specific class installer or co-installer can provide a vendor-specific icon.

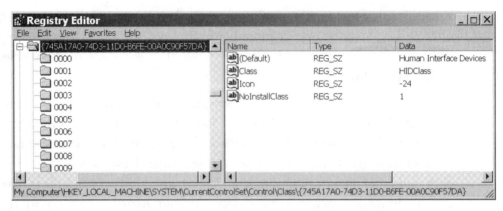

Figure 9-5: The class key for the HID class includes a friendly name for the class and an index to an icon.

Optional entries in the class key can affect what users see on device installation. If NoInstallClass is present and not equal to zero, users will never need to manually install devices in the class. If SilentInstall is present and not equal to zero, the Plug and Play manager will install devices in the class without displaying dialog boxes or requiring user interaction. If NoDisplayClass is present and not equal to zero, the Device Manager doesn't display devices of the class.

UpperFilters and LowerFilters entries can specify upper filter and lower filter drivers that apply to all devices in the class.

The Driver Key

Under the class key, each device in a class has a driver key, also called a software key. In the hardware key for a device instance, the Driver entry names a device setup GUID that matches a class key and a device instance number that matches a driver subkey under the class key. Figure 9-6 shows the key for a generic HID-class device. Table 9-2 lists some of the entries for a driver key.

The driver key contains the name of the INF file that in turn names the driver files for the device.

Table 9-1: These are some of the entries in a USB device's hardware key.

Key	Description	Source of Information
Class	Name of the device's setup class	INF file (from *devguid.h*)
ClassGUID	GUID of the device's setup class	INF file (from *devguid.h*)
DeviceDesc	Device Description	INF file, Models section, device description entry
HardwareID	ID string containing the device's Vendor ID and Product ID	Device descriptor
CompatibleIDs	ID string(s) containing the device's class and (optional) subclass and protocol	Device and interface descriptors
Mfg	Device manufacturer	INF file, Manufacturer section, manufacturer name entry
Driver	Name of the device's driver key	System registry, under CurrentControlSet\Control\Class
Location Information	"USB Device" or iProduct string	Bus driver or string descriptor
Service	Name of the device's Service key	System registry, under HKLM\System\ CurrentControlSet\Services

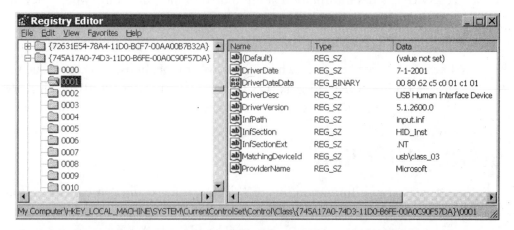

Figure 9-6: The driver keys under each class key have information about the drivers assigned to instances of devices in the class.

Table 9-2: The driver key contains information about the driver assigned to a device.

Key	Description	Source of Information
DriverDate	Date of the driver file	INF file, Version section, DriverVer directive
DriverDesc	Driver description	INF file
DriverVer	Driver version	INF file, Version section, DriverVer directive
InfPath	Name of INF file	INF file name
InfSection	Name of the driver's DDInstall section	INF file
InfSectionExt	"Decorated" extension used in INF file (.NT, etc.)	INF file
MatchingDeviceID	The hardware or compatible ID used to assign the driver	Device descriptor and INF file
ProviderName	The provider of the driver	INF file, Provider string

The Service Key

A service key has information about a driver's files, including where they are stored and how to load them. Service keys are in this branch:

```
HKEY_LOCAL_MACHINE\System\CurrentControlSet\Services
```

There are service keys for each host controller type, hubs, and classes such as storage (USBSTOR), printers (USBPRINT), and HIDs (HidBatt, HidServ, HidUsb). Figure 9-7 shows the Service key for HidUsb.

Inside INF Files

A device setup information file, or INF file, is a text file that contains information about one or more devices in a device setup class. The devices may be from one or more manufacturers. The file tells Windows what driver or drivers to use and contains information to store in the registry. Windows includes INF files for the drivers provided with the operating system. The files are in the *%SystemRoot%\inf* folder. Any new INF files for added devices are copied to this folder as well. By default, the folder is hidden. If you don't see it in Windows Explorer, select Tools > Folder Options > View,

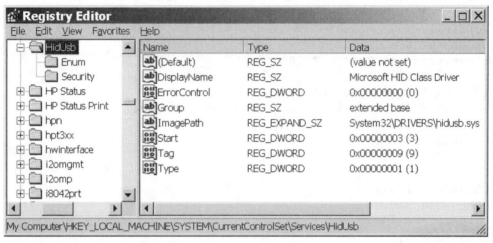

Figure 9-7: The service key names a driver's file.

then under Hidden Files, select *Show hidden files and folders*. Do not select *Hide file extensions for known file types*.

On first attachment, after retrieving descriptors from a USB device, Windows looks for a match between the information in the descriptors and the information in the system's INF files.

This section doesn't attempt to document every nuance of INF-file creation. Instead, I use an example INF file to show the kinds of information an INF file can contain. The Windows DDK documentation has more details. Examining the INF files included with Windows is another way to learn about the kinds of things contained in the files and how the information is structured.

Listing 9-1 shows an INF file for the Ellisys USB Explorer protocol analyzer, which uses a vendor-specific driver. (The analyzer has a USB interface that communicates with the PC running the analyzer software.) This INF file is suitable for use under Windows 98, Windows Me, Windows 2000, and Windows XP.

```
; Copyright (C) 1999-2004 Ellisys. All rights reserved.

[Version]
Signature="$CHICAGO$"
DriverVer=01/29/2004,2.0.1600.0
Provider=%Provider%
Class=EllisysProtocolAnalyzers
ClassGUID={D8854594-A4EF-480e-B8D8-CBDDADB4F3B4}

[ClassInstall]
AddReg=ClassAddReg

[ClassInstall32]
AddReg=ClassAddReg

[ClassAddReg]
HKR,,,,"%ClassName%"
HKR,,Icon,,-20

[Manufacturer]
%Manufacturer%=Models

[DestinationDirs]
DefaultDestDir=10,System32\Drivers

[SourceDisksNames]
1=%SourceDisk%,,,.

[SourceDisksFiles]
ellex200.sys=1

[Models]
%DeviceDesc%=Install,USB\VID_0ABA&PID_8002

[Install]
CopyFiles=Install.CopyFiles
AddReg=Install.AddReg

[Install.CopyFiles]
ellex200.sys,,,2
```

Listing 9-1: The INF file for the Ellisys USB Explorer 200 protocol analyzer
(Sheet 1 of 2).

```
[Install.AddReg]
HKR,,DevLoader,,*ntkern
HKR,,NTMPDriver,,ellex200.sys

[Install.NT]
CopyFiles=Install.CopyFiles

[Install.NT.Services]
AddService=ellex200,2,Install.NT.AddService

[Install.NT.AddService]
DisplayName=%SvcDesc%
ServiceType=1
StartType=3
ErrorControl=1
ServiceBinary=%10%\system32\drivers\ellex200.sys

[Strings]
ClassName="Ellisys protocol analyzers"
Provider="Ellisys "
Manufacturer="Ellisys"
SourceDisk="USB Explorer 200 Installation Disk"
DeviceDesc="USB Explorer 200"
SvcDesc="USB Explorer 200 Driver (ellex200.sys)"
```

Listing 9-1: The INF file for the Ellisys USB Explorer 200 protocol analyzer (Sheet 2 of 2).

Syntax

The contents of an INF file must follow a few syntax rules.

- The information is arranged in sections, with each section containing one or more items. The section name is in square brackets [ ]. Some of the sections (Version, Manufacturer) are standard sections that every INF file has. Other sections match values specified in other sections. For example, if the Manufacturer section designates the manufacturer as Lakeview, the INF file will also have a [Lakeview] section. The sections can be in any order, but the order of the items within a section can be critical.

- A semicolon (;) indicates a comment.
- A backslash (\) at the end of a line acts as a line continuator, unless it's enclosed in quotes ("\").
- Text enclosed in percent symbols (%sampletext%) refers to a string. For example, you might have the following item:

```
Provider=%Provider%
```

with an item in the Strings section that defines the provider string:

```
Provider="Ellisys"
```

- Some items set the value of an entry. For example, this item specifies a device's class:

```
Class=EllisysProtocolAnalyzers
```

- Some items provide information to store in the system registry. This item stores the name of a device's driver:

```
HKR,,NTMPDriver,,ellex200.sys
```

Sections

Each section of an INF file has a role in helping Windows find a file that matches a device, load the appropriate drivers, and store information about the device in the registry. The discussion that follows explains the purpose of each section in the example INF file with the aim of showing the types of information an INF file can provide.

Copyright Comment

To pass the tests in the Chkinf utility (described later in this chapter), an INF file must have a comment that contains the word *copyright*:

```
; Copyright (C) 1999-2004 Ellisys. All rights
reserved.
```

Version

The Version section is the file's header. Every INF file must have this section. The Version section in the example has these items:

```
[Version]
Signature="$CHICAGO$"
DriverVer=01/29/2004,2.0.1600.0
Provider=%Provider%
Class=EllisysProtocolAnalyzers
ClassGUID={D8854594-A4EF-480e-B8D8-CBDDADB4F3B4}
```

The Signature directive specifies what operating systems the INF file is intended for. For devices that use WDM drivers, the value can be $Windows 95$, $Windows NT$, or $Chicago$, no matter which operating system the PC is using. Chicago was a name used when Windows 95 was under development and its use is still valid under later editions of Windows. The value is case-insensitive.

The DriverVer directive gives the date and version number for the driver(s) named in the INF file. In selecting a driver, all else being equal, Windows will select the more recent driver. A DriverVer directive can also appear in a DDInstall section to provide information that applies only to the driver(s) in that section. Windows 2000 and Windows XP must have a DriverVer directive in the Version section and may have DriverVer directives in DDInstall sections. Windows 98 and Windows Me don't recognize DriverVer directives in the Version section, so any DriverVer directives for these Windows editions must be in the DDInstall sections.

The Provider directive names the creator of the INF file. In the example, %Provider% is a string defined later in the file.

The Class directive specifies the class for devices installed with the INF file. The example specifies the vendor-specific class EllisysProtocolAnalyzers.

The ClassGUID directive is the device setup GUID to store in the device's Class key in the registry. A vendor-specific driver can use the GUID for USB devices or a vendor-specific GUID. The example uses a vendor-specific GUID.

ClassInstall32

The ClassInstall32 section installs a new class in the Class section of the registry. This section is processed only if a device's class hasn't been installed previously. This section should exist only in INF files for devices in vendor-specific device setup classes.

The example ClassInstall32 section has one item:

```
[ClassInstall32]
Addreg=Class.AddReg
```

The Addreg directive adds a class description to the registry. In the example, the directive's value refers to the Class.Addreg section. This section provides a class description in the %ClassName% string and an index value for an icon to display in Device Manager:

```
[ClassAddReg]
HKR,,,,"%ClassName%"
HKR,,Icon,,-20
```

A negative Icon value refers to an icon defined in Windows' *setupapi.dll*. A positive Icon value refers to an icon to be extracted from a class installer DLL or property page DLL.

HKR stands for HKEY_ROOT, which is the base registry key for the section that AddReg appears in. In this example, the information is stored under the device's Class key.

The example also has a section titled [ClassInstall] for Windows 98 systems.

Manufacturer

The Manufacturer section identifies one or more groups of devices and an Install section for each group. Every INF file must have this section.

In the example, %Manufacturer% is a string defined later in the file, and Models is the name of a section that identifies the manufacturer's devices. Models is the generic name for the section. The name can be more specific, such as *CypressMice* or *PhilipsAudio*, and an INF file with multiple Models sections must of course use a different name for each section.

```
[Manufacturer]
%Manufacturer%=Models
```

DestinationDirs

The DestinationDirs section names the folder or folders that any CopyFiles, RenFiles, and DelFiles items in the INF file will use. A *dirid* value of 10 specifies the Windows folder. The Windows DDK documentation lists other dirid values. Windows 98 documentation uses the term LDID (logical disk identifier) instead of dirid.

```
[DestinationDirs]
DefaultDestDir=10,System32\Drivers
```

SourceDisksNames

The SourceDisksNames section provides a text description for the installation disk(s). In the entry below, there is one source disk whose name is the %SourceDisk% string defined later in the file. An entry can also specify a volume label and serial number for the disk.

```
[SourceDisksNames]
1=%SourceDisk%,,,.
```

SourceDisksFiles

The SourceDisksFiles section names any file(s) to install from the installation disk. If a file isn't in the disk's root directory, the entry can specify a subdirectory.

```
[SourceDisksFiles]
ellex200.sys=1
```

Models

The Manufacturer section names one or more Models sections. Each Models section contains one or more entries that match a device description to a DDInstall section and hardware ID.

In the example, the device description is the %DeviceDesc% string defined later in the file. Install is the name of the INF file's DDInstall section, which has installation instructions for the device and can add device information to the registry. USB\VID_0ABA&PID_8001 is the hardware ID that identifies the device by its Vendor ID and Product ID. Following the hardware ID, an entry can provide one or more compatible IDs that provide alternate, typically more general, ways to identify devices that use the same driver. The section *Using Device Identification Strings* later in the chapter has more about hardware and compatible IDs.

```
[Models]
%DeviceDesc%=Install,USB\VID_0ABA&PID_8001
```

The example INF file has two sets of Install sections. One set (Install, Install.CopyFiles, and Install.AddReg) is for Windows 98 and Windows Me. The other set (Install.NT, Install.CopyFiles, Install.NT.Services, and Install.NT.AddService) is for Windows 2000 and Windows XP. Both sets use the same Install.CopyFiles section. The section names that contain *.NT* are known as *decorated* sections:

```
[Install]
CopyFiles=Install.CopyFiles
AddReg=Install.AddReg

[Install.CopyFiles]
ellex200.sys,,,2

[Install.AddReg]
HKR,,DevLoader,,*ntkern
HKR,,NTMPDriver,,ellex200.sys

[Install.NT]
CopyFiles=Install.CopyFiles

[Install.NT.Services]
AddService=ellex200,2,Install.NT.AddService

[Install.NT.AddService]
DisplayName=%SvcDesc%
ServiceType=1
StartType=3
ErrorControl=1
ServiceBinary=%10%\system32\drivers\ellex200.sys
```

In the example's Install section, the CopyFiles directive names the Install.CopyFiles section, which specifies the driver file to copy (*ellex200.sys*). A flag value of 2 tells Windows not to allow the user to skip copying the file. The AddReg directive names the Install.AddReg section, which provides information to add to the registry. In the Install.AddReg section, DevLoader names the device loader associated with the device and NTMPDriver names the driver.

The DDInstall section for Windows 2000 and Windows XP is Install.NT. The CopyFiles directive names the same Install.CopyFiles section used for Windows 98 and Windows Me. These Windows editions don't require the DevLoader and NTMPDriver entries, so there is no AddReg section.

Windows 2000 and Windows XP require two additional sections: Install.NT.Services and Install.NT.AddService. The Services section specifies a ServiceName for the driver (*ellex200*), assigns the service as the Plug-and-Play function driver for the device (flags = 2), and names an AddService section that specifies how and when the driver's services are loaded (Install.NT.AddService).

The AddService section in the example has five entries. DisplayName specifies a friendly name for the service. ServiceType = 1 indicates that the entry is for a kernel-mode device driver. StartType = 3 to start the driver on enumeration. ErrorControl = 1 to display a warning and proceed if there is an error when loading or initializing the device. ServiceBinary specifies the location of the driver named in the CopyFiles section. This section can have many additional directives that are optional or required only for some device and drivers.

Strings

The Strings section defines all of the strings that other sections refer to.

```
[Strings]
ClassName="Ellisys protocol analyzers"
Provider="Ellisys "
Manufacturer="Ellisys"
SourceDisk="USB Explorer 200 Installation Disk"
DeviceDesc="USB Explorer 200"
SvcDesc="USB Explorer 200 Driver (ellex200.sys)"
```

Using Device Identification Strings

To identify possible drivers for a device, Windows searches the system's INF files for a device identification string that matches a string created from information in the device's descriptors. There are three categories of device identification strings: device IDs, hardware IDs, and compatible IDs.

Identification Strings Obtained from a Device

Every USB device has at least one device ID, which the hub driver creates from the Vendor ID, Product ID, and revision number in the device descriptor. A device ID for a USB device has one of these forms:

```
USB\VID_xxxx&PID_yyyy&REV_zzzz
USB\VID_xxxx&PID_yyyy
```

The values in xxxx, yyyy, and zzzz are four characters each: xxxx is the idVendor value, yyyy is the idProduct value, and zzzz is the bcdDevice value. The idVendor and idProduct values are hexadecimal values, except for Windows Me, which uses decimal, and bcdDevice is in BCD format.

For example, a device with VID = 0925h, PID = 1234h, and bcdDevice = 0310 has this device ID:

```
USB\VID_0925&PID_1234&REV_0310
```

Devices with multiple interfaces can specify a driver for each interface. In this case, the device has multiple device IDs, one for each interface. A device ID for an interface has one of these forms:

```
USB\VID_xxxx&PID_yyyy&REV_zzzz&MI_ww
USB\VID_xxxx&PID_yyyy&MI_ww
```

The values in xxxx, yyyy, and zzzz are the same as in the previous device IDs. The 2-character value in ww equals bInterfaceNumber in the interface descriptor for one of the device's interfaces. For example, a composite device that functions as a mouse and keyboard might have entries in two Models sections, one for the keyboard (interface 00) and one for the mouse (interface 01):

```
[LAKEVIEW_KEYBOARD]
%USB\VID_0925&PID_0801&MI_00.DeviceDesc%=
HID_Inst,, USB\VID_0925&PID_0801&MI_00
```

```
[LAKEVIEW_MOUSE]
%USB\VID_0925&PID_0801&MI_01.DeviceDesc%=
HID_Inst,, USB\VID_0925&PID_0801&MI_01
```

A HID-class device whose report descriptor contains more than one top-level collection can have a device ID for each collection. A device ID for a collection can have any of these forms, where bb indicates the collection number:

```
USB\VID_xxxx&PID_yyyy&REV_zzzz&Colbb
USB\VID_xxxx&PID_yyyy&Colbb
USB\VID_xxxx&PID_yyyy&REV_zzzz&MI_ww&Colbb
USB\VID_xxxx&PID_yyyy&MI_ww&Colbb
```

In addition to a device ID, some drivers create one or more compatible ID strings for a device. A compatible ID can identify a device by its class code and any subclass and protocol codes in the device descriptor. A compatible ID uses one of the following forms:

```
USB\CLASS_aa&SUBCLASS_bb&PROT_cc
USB\CLASS_aa&SUBCLASS_bb
USB\CLASS_aa
```

The values aa, bb, and cc match values in the device descriptor and are two characters each: aa is the bDeviceClass value, bb is the bDeviceSubclass value, and cc is the bDeviceProtocol value. The values are expressed in hexadecimal, except for Windows Me, which uses decimal.

For example, the class code for HIDs is 03h, so HID-class devices have the following compatible ID:

```
USB\Class_03
```

For some compatible IDs, Windows defines descriptive names such as USBSTOR_BULK or GENERIC_USB_PRINTER.

A compatible ID in an INF file indicates a less desirable but acceptable match. Compatible IDs enable Windows to find and load a driver if the INF files don't contain a matching device ID. A vendor's INF file should not contain a compatible ID.

Obtaining Identification Strings from an INF File

In an INF file, each entry in a Models section has one hardware ID and zero or more compatible IDs. The hardware ID is listed first, followed by any compatible IDs, with commas separating the IDs.

A hardware ID can have any of several forms. It can have one of the forms described above for a device ID for a device, interface, or HID collection. INF files provided with Windows may contain hardware IDs that use the compatible-ID formats described above to identify a device by class or descriptive name.

Finding a Match

In looking for the best match between the information retrieved from a device and the information in INF files, Windows assigns a rank to every match found, with a lower rank indicating a better match (Table 9-3). NT-based operating systems, which include Windows 2000 and Windows XP, give a much lower rank to "trusted" drivers. These are drivers whose catalog (*.cat*) file has a digital signature that indicates that the driver has passed Windows Hardware Quality Labs (WHQL) testing. Chapter 17 has more about WHQL testing. A trusted driver is also called a signed driver. Windows 98 doesn't check for trusted drivers.

In an NT-based operating system, the best match is a device ID that matches a hardware ID in a trusted INF file. The second-best match is a device ID that matches a compatible ID in a trusted INF file. Next is a match between a compatible ID from the device and a hardware ID in a trusted INF file, followed by a match of compatible IDs from the device and a trusted INF file. Only if there are no matches at all with a trusted INF file will an NT-based operating system consider an ID from an untrusted INF file.

If Windows can't find a match, it starts the Found New Hardware wizard and gives the user a chance to specify a location (such as a CD drive) to look for the INF file.

Composite devices, which have multiple interfaces, are a special case. Because each interface may require a different driver, selecting a driver using

Table 9-3: Windows assigns a rank to each INF file that matches a device ID or compatible ID from the device.

Rank (Hex)	ID from Descriptors	ID from INF file	Trusted Driver?	"Decorated" INF section?
0000–0FFF	Device	Hardware	yes	Yes. (All trusted drivers have decorated INF sections for NT-based OS's.)
1000–1FFF	Device	Compatible	yes	
2000–2FFF	Compatible	Hardware	yes	
3000–3FFF	Compatible	Compatible	yes	
8000–8FFF	Device	Hardware	no	yes*
9000–BFFF	Compatible	Compatible	no	yes*
C000–CFFF	Device	Hardware	no	no
D000–FFFE	Compatible	Compatible	no	no
FFFF	Worst-case match. Used by components such as co-installers			
*Considered only by NT-based operating systems (Windows 2000, Windows XP).				

only the Vendor ID and Product ID isn't always sufficient. If there is no better match, Windows XP uses the compatible ID USB\COMPOSITE, which results in loading the USB common class generic parent driver. This driver creates a set of device and compatible IDs for each interface, and Windows can then assign a driver to each interface. In earlier Windows editions, the bus or hub driver handles this task.

Windows comes with hundreds of INF files, and a new device may come with its own INF file. To speed up searching, during device installation, Windows creates a PNF (precompiled INF) file and stores it in the same folder as the device's INF file. The PNF file contains much of the same information as the INF file but in a format that enables quicker searching.

Do You Need to Provide an INF File?

Not every device requires its own INF file. Many devices that use only the system's class drivers can use the INF file that Windows provides for the class. These are some INF files for USB classes in Windows XP:

Class	INF File
Audio	wdmaudio.inf
Human Interface Device (HID)	input.inf (hiddev.inf in Windows 98)
Hub	usb.inf
Mass Storage	usbstor.inf
Printer	usbprint.inf
Smart Card	smartcrd.inf
Still Image	sti.inf

Because Windows XP and later prefer trusted drivers, if you provide an untrusted driver for a device in a supported class, Windows XP and later won't use your driver and instead will select a compatible ID from the class's INF file. An INF file is considered part of the driver package, so if you attempt to provide an untrusted INF file that assigns a trusted driver to your device, Windows XP and later will prefer a system-provided INF file over your INF file. Any change to the contents of a trusted INF file causes an INF file to become untrusted, so you can't add your device to an existing INF file without causing the INF file to become untrusted.

When the best match is an unsigned driver, operating-system settings control whether Windows blocks installation, installs the driver with a warning, or installs with no warning. To change the setting, in Windows Control Panel, click System > Hardware > Driver Signing.

A device that uses a class driver can have a custom INF file with vendor-specific strings that display in the Device Manager. For example, the entry for a HID can be a vendor-specific string such as "My Marvelous HID" instead of the default "USB Human Interface Device." But using a custom INF file under Windows XP and later requires the device and INF file to pass WHQL tests.

The INF files provided with Windows typically contain sections with manufacturer-specific information. When a device passes the WHQL tests, Microsoft often adds the device's sections to an existing INF file or adds a manufacturer-specific INF file to the files distributed with Windows.

Some devices, such as modems, must provide their own INF files. The Windows DDK has examples. A device with a vendor-specific driver must also have its own INF file.

Tools and Diagnostic Aids

Microsoft provides several tools to help in creating and testing INF files: *GenInf* for creating files, *ChkInf* for testing a file's structure and syntax, and a log file of events that occur during device installation.

GenInf is a wizard that asks questions about your device and uses the information to create an INF file. The documentation warns that the created file is a skeleton that may not be fully valid and is likely to need additions or revisions. In particular, the generated INF files do not support older Windows editions or create multi-platform INF files.

ChkINF is a Perl script that requires a Perl interpreter, which you can download free from *www.activeware.com* and other sources. The script runs from a command prompt and creates an HTML page that annotates an INF file with errors and warnings.

When a device is detected, Windows uses Setup and device-installation functions to select a matching INF file and install the device's drivers. The functions also log events and errors in a text file stored in *%SystemRoot%\setupapi.log*. The log can be useful when debugging problems with device installations. The Windows DDK documentation has more about how to use the logging capability.

Tips for Using INF Files

Here are some tips for using and experimenting with INF files:

Use a Valid Vendor ID

Firmware that you make available outside of a controlled environment must use a Vendor ID assigned by the USB-IF. My example code uses the Vendor ID of 0925h, which is assigned to my company, Lakeview Research. The owner of the Vendor ID is responsible for ensuring that each product and version has a unique Vendor ID/Product ID pair. Borrowing someone else's Vendor ID can lead to conflicts if the owner of the ID uses the same values for a different device.

Finding INF Files

On installing a device with a new INF file, Windows copies the INF file to *%SystemRoot%\inf* and may rename the file *oem*.inf* and create a .PNF file named *oem*pnf*, where *** is a number. To find INF files that contain a specific Vendor ID and Product ID, search from Windows' Start menu > Search > For Files or Folders. Browse to the *%SystemRoot%\inf* folder and search for the text *VID_xxxx&PID_yyyy*, where *xxxx* is the device's vendor ID and *yyyy* is the product ID.

Removing Device Information

When experimenting with different settings in an INF file, you may find that at times Windows is using information stored in the system registry from a previous version of the INF file. If you want Windows to use a different or changed INF file for a device (because you want to change the driver or device description, for example), you may need to tell Windows to forget what it knows about the device. With the device installed, right-click its listing in the Device Manager, and select Uninstall. Delete any unwanted INF and PNF files that contain your device's Vendor ID and Product ID. You can then remove the device and reattach it, and Windows will start fresh in searching for a driver. (If this approach fails, you may need to delete the unwanted INF and PNF files and registry keys manually.)

To cause Windows 98 to forget what it knows about a device, you may need to rebuild the driver information database. In the *%SystemRoot%\inf* folder, rename *drvdata.bin* to *drvdata.xxx* and rename *drvidx.bin* to *drvidx.xxx*. By renaming the files rather than deleting them, you can restore them if necessary.

INF File Names

The INF files that ship with Windows all have file names with no more than eight characters plus the 3-character extension. Microsoft says that this is due to "technical issues with the product install," but that INF files added after Windows is installed may use longer file names.

What the User Sees

What the user sees on the screen after attaching a USB device can vary depending on the Windows edition, the contents of the device's INF file, the driver's location, whether the driver has a co-installer and is digitally signed, and whether the device has been attached and enumerated previously and has a serial number.

Device and Class Installers

Device and class installers provide functions relating to device installation. The installers are DLLs (dynamic link libraries). Windows provides default installers for devices in supported device setup classes. A device vendor can provide a co-installer that works along with a class installer to support operations that are specific to one or more devices in a class. A co-installer can add information to the registry, request additional configuration information from the user, provide device-specific Properties pages for the Device Manager to display, and perform other tasks relating to device installation. A vendor-defined device setup class can have its own class installer. The Windows DDK documentation has information about writing installers and co-installers.

Searching for a Driver

On boot up or device attachment, after retrieving a device's descriptors, the operating system searches for a matching hardware key. If a key exists, the operating system has what it needs to assign a driver to the device. The hardware key's Driver entry points to the driver key, which names the INF file.

The hardware key's Service entry points to the service key, which has information about the driver files.

On first attachment, there is no matching hardware key and Windows searches its INF files for a match. If the device uses a vendor-specific driver, Windows won't find an INF file and will start the New Device Wizard. The user can let Windows search for a driver or specify what disk and/or folder to search. If your driver is signed and you want to eliminate the need for users to specify the driver's location, you can provide an installation program that uses the API function SetupCopyOEMInf to copy your INF file to the INF folder on the user's system.

On finding a matching INF file, Windows copies the file to *%System-Root%\inf* (if the file isn't already there), loads the driver(s) specified in the file if necessary, adds the appropriate keys to the system registry (which also adds the device to the Device Manager), and may display a message to inform the user that the device has been installed.

After installing a device, when installing additional devices that are identical except for the serial number, Windows behaves differently depending on whether the driver is digitally signed. When the driver is signed, Windows uses administrative privileges to install the driver for additional devices after the first, even if the current user doesn't have these privileges. If the driver is unsigned, Windows uses the privileges of the current user in deciding whether to install the driver for additional devices.

When re-attaching a previously attached device, whether Windows finds a driver key can depend on whether the device's descriptors include a USB serial number string. If the device doesn't have a serial number, the hardware key will be found only if the device is re-attached to a port where the device was attached previously. If the device has a serial number, the hardware key will be found no matter which port the device attaches to.

10

Detecting Devices

This chapter shows how applications can obtain information about attached devices, request a handle for communicating with a device, and detect when a device is attached or removed. Each of these tasks involve using Windows API functions and the device interface GUIDs introduced in Chapter 8. As an aid to those with limited experience with API functions, the chapter begins with a short tutorial on the topic.

A Brief Guide to Calling API Functions

You can do a lot of programming without ever calling an API function. Microsoft's .NET Framework provides classes that support common tasks such as creating user interfaces, accessing files, manipulating text and graphics, accessing common peripheral types, networking, security functions, and exception handling. Internally, the classes' methods are likely to call API functions, but the classes offer a safer, more secure, and more modular, object-oriented way to accomplish the tasks. Languages that support using the .NET Framework include Visual Basic .NET, Visual C# .NET, and Visual C++ .NET.

But the .NET Framework doesn't handle every task. Applications still need to call API functions for some things. A .NET application can use the .NET Framework where possible and API calls when needed. Applications in languages that predate the .NET platform, such as Visual Basic 6, sometimes need to call API functions as well. The examples in this chapter are written for Visual Basic .NET and Visual C++. NET.

Because calling API functions can be an obscure art at times, this section includes an introduction to some things that are useful to know when using the Windows API.

Managed and Unmanaged Code

Understanding how to call API functions in Visual Basic .NET applications requires understanding the difference between managed and unmanaged code. Windows API functions use unmanaged code. Their DLLs contain compiled machine code that executes directly on the target CPU. In Visual Basic .NET and Visual C# .NET, all program code is managed code that compiles to the Microsoft Intermediate Language (MSIL). The .NET platform's common language runtime (CLR) environment executes the MSIL code.

Managed code has advantages. Because all .NET languages use the same CLR, components written in different .NET languages can easily interoperate. For example, a Visual Basic .NET application can call a function written in Visual C# .NET without worrying about differences in calling conventions. The CLR also simplifies programming by using garbage collection to manage memory.

A .NET application can call functions that use unmanaged code, including Windows API functions. But Visual Basic .NET and Visual C# .NET applications must take special care to ensure that any data being passed survives the trip from managed to unmanaged code, and back if necessary.

To use data returned by an API function, a Visual Basic .NET or Visual C# .NET application often must *marshal* the data to make it available to the managed code. Marshaling means doing whatever is needed to make the data available and typically involves copying data into managed memory and/or converting data from one type or format to another.

The .NET Framework's Marshal class provides methods for allocating memory that unmanaged code will use, for copying blocks of unmanaged memory to managed memory, and for converting between managed and unmanaged data types. For example, the PtrToStringAuto method accepts a pointer to a string in unmanaged memory and returns the string being pointed to. This Visual-Basic code retrieves a string from a pointer (IntPtr pdevicePathName) returned by an API function:

```
Dim DevicePathName as String
DevicePathName = _
    Marshal.PtrToStringAuto(pdevicePathName)
```

Arrays that will contain data copied from unmanaged code must use the MarshalAs attribute to define the size of the array. This Visual-Basic code declares a 16-byte array that will hold a GUID copied from a structure returned by an API call:

```
<MarshalAs(UnmanagedType.ByValArray, _
    ArraySubType:=UnmanagedType.U1, SizeConst:=16)> _
    Public dbcc_classguid() _
    As Byte
```

The GUID is marshaled into the byte array as an UnmanagedType.ByValArray. The ArraySubType field defines the array's elements as unsigned, 1-byte (U1) values and the SizeConst field sets the array's size as 16 bytes.

What about Visual C++ .NET? A Visual C++ .NET application can compile to managed code, unmanaged code, or even some of each. The language also incorporates the "It Just Works" technology, which enables managed code to call API functions in exactly the same way that unmanaged code does, without the marshaling required by other .NET languages. This versatility means that Visual C++ .NET code that calls API functions can often be simpler and more concise than equivalent code in Visual Basic .NET or Visual C# .NET.

Documentation

The Windows API functions are in various DLLs and libraries whose documentation is spread among several areas in the Windows DDK and Platform SDK. Functions related to detecting devices are in *setupapi.dll* and are documented in the Windows DDK under Device Installation and also in the Platform SDK under Base Services > Device Management. Functions relating to opening communications with devices are in *kernel32.dll* and are documented in the Platform SDK under Base Services in Storage > File Management and in Device Input and Output Control. Functions relating to device notifications are in *user32.dll* and are documented in the Platform SDK under Base Services > Device Management.

The header files for the DLLs often have useful comments as well. A function's documentation typically names the header file. If not, a quick way to find it is to use Windows' *Search > For Files or Folders* utility available from the Start menu. In the text box for file names, enter **.h*, and in the text box for words or phrases, enter the name of the function whose declaration you want to find. Be sure that *Include Subfolders* is checked, and let Windows go to work finding the file for you.

Using Visual C++ .NET

To use an API function, a Visual C++ application needs three things: the ability to locate the file containing the function's compiled code, a function declaration, and a call that causes the function to execute.

Each DLL has two or more companion files, a library file (*setupapi.lib, kernel32.lib, user32.lib*) and one or more header files (*setupapi.h, kernel32.h, user32.h*). The library file eliminates the need for the application to get a pointer to the function in the DLL. The header file contains the prototypes, structures, and symbols for the functions that applications may call.

A DLL contains compiled code for the functions the DLL exports, or makes available to applications. For each exported function, the DLL's library file contains a stub function whose name and arguments match the name and arguments of one of the DLL's functions. The stub function calls its corresponding function in the DLL. During the compile process, the linker incorporates the code in the library file into the application's executable file. When the application calls a function in the library file, the function of the same name in the DLL executes.

The DLLs included with Windows are typically stored in the *%SystemRoot%\system32* folder. Windows searches this folder when an application calls a DLL function. The library and header files for Windows API functions are included in the Windows DDK.

To include a API function in an application, you need to do the following:

1. Add the library files to the project. In Visual Studio, click Project > Properties > Linker > Input. In the *Additional Dependencies* box enter the names of the *.lib* files. If needed, you can enter a path for the library files in the Linker > General window under *Additional Library Directories*.

2. Include the header files in one of the application's files. Here is an example:

```
extern "C" {
#include "hidsdi.h"
#include <setupapi.h>
}
```

The `#include` directive causes the contents of the named file to be included in the file, the same as if they were copied and pasted into the file. The `extern "C"` modifier enables a C++ module to include header files that use C naming conventions. The difference is that C++ uses name decoration, also called name mangling, on external symbols.

To add a path to an include directory, in Visual Studio, click Project > Properties > Resources > General. In the *Additional Include Directories* box enter the path(s) to your *.h* files. (On a command line, these paths are in the compiler's */I* option.)

The punctuation around the file name determines where the compiler will search for the file, and in what order. This is relevant if you have different versions of a file in multiple locations! Enclosing the file name in brackets

(`<setupapi.h>`) causes the compiler to search for the file first in the path specified by the compiler's *∕I* option, then in the paths specified by the Include environment variable. Enclosing the file name in quotes (`"hidsdi.h"`) causes the compiler to search for the file first in the same directory as the file containing the `#include` directive, then in the directories of any files that contain `#include` directives for that file, then in the path specified by the compiler's *∕I* option, and finally in the paths specified by the Include environment variable.

The header files for many functions are included automatically when you create a project. For example, *afxwin.h* adds headers for common Windows and MFC functions.

3. Call the function. Here is code that declares the variable `HidGuid` and passes a pointer to it in the function `HidD_GetHidGuid` in *hid.dll*:

```
GUID    HidGuid;
HidD_GetHidGuid(&HidGuid);
```

Using Visual Basic .NET

To use an API function in a Visual Basic .NET program, you need three things: the DLL containing the function, a declaration that enables the application to find the function, and a call that causes the function to execute.

Compared to Visual C++, Visual Basic .NET has additional considerations when calling API functions. The information in the C include files must be translated to Visual-Basic syntax and data types, and the managed .NET code often requires marshaling to enable accessing the unmanaged data returned by an API function.

Instead of a C include file, a Visual Basic .NET application must have Visual-Basic declarations for a DLL's functions and structures. Visual Basic requires references only to the DLLs, not to the library files.

The code to call an API function (or any function in a DLL) follows the same syntax rules as the code to call other Visual-Basic functions. But instead of placing the function's executable code in a routine within the application, the application requires only a declaration that enables Windows to find the DLL containing the function's code.

Microsoft's documentation for API functions uses C syntax to show how to declare and call the functions. To use an API function in Visual Basic, you need to translate the declaration and function call from C to Visual Basic. The process is more complicated than simple syntax changes, mainly because many of the variable and structure types don't have exact equivalents in Visual Basic.

The Declaration

This is a Visual-Basic declaration for the API function RegisterDeviceNotification, which applications can use to request to be informed when a device is attached or removed:

```
<DllImport("user32.dll", CharSet:=CharSet.Auto)> _
Function RegisterDeviceNotification _
  (ByVal hRecipient As IntPtr, _
  ByVal NotificationFilter As IntPtr, _
  ByVal Flags As Int32) _
  As IntPtr
End Function
```

The declaration contains this information:

- A DllImport attribute that names the file that contains the function's executable code (*user32.dll*). The optional CharSet field is set to CharSet.Auto to cause the operating system to select ANSI (8-bit) or Unicode (16-bit) characters according to the target platform. ANSI is the default for Windows 98 and Windows Me. Unicode is the default for Windows 2000 and Windows XP.
- The function's name (RegisterDeviceNotification).
- The parameters the function will pass to the operating system (hRecipient, NotificationFilter, Flags).
- The data types of the values passed (IntPtr, Int32).
- Whether the parameters will be passed by value (ByVal) or by reference (ByRef). All three parameters in this declaration are passed ByVal.

- The data type of the value returned for the function (IntPtr). A few API calls have no return value and may be declared as subroutines rather than functions.

The declaration must be in the Declarations section of a module.

Providing the DLL's Name

Each declaration must name the file that contains the function's executable code. The file is a DLL. When the application runs, Windows loads the named DLLs into memory (unless they're already loaded).

In most cases, the declaration only has to provide the file name and not the location. The DLLs containing Windows API functions are stored in standard locations (such as *%SytemRoot%\system32*) that Windows searches automatically. For some system files, such as *kernel32.dll*, the *.dll* extension is optional in the declaration.

Data Types

A Visual Basic .NET application can use Visual Basic's data types or their equivalent data types in the .NET Framework. For example, Visual Basic's Integer type is equivalent to a System.Int32 in the .NET Framework.

The C header files for API calls often use additional data types defined in the Platform SDK but not explicitly defined by Visual Basic. So creating a Visual-Basic declaration often requires additional translating. To specify a variable type for an API call, in many cases all you need to do is determine the variable's length, then use a Visual-Basic type that matches. For example, a DWORD is a 32-bit integer, so a Visual-Basic .NET application can declare a DWORD as an Integer. An LPDWORD is a pointer to a DWORD, and can be declared as an Integer passed by reference. A parameter defined in C as a HANDLE can use the System.IntPtr type, which is an Integer with a platform-specific size. A GUID translates to the System.Guid type.

ByRef and ByVal

In calling a function, you can pass the arguments, or parameters, by reference (ByRef) or by value (ByVal). Often either will work. But the concept is important to understand when calling API functions, because many of the functions have variables that must be passed a specific way.

ByRef and ByVal determine what information the call passes to enable the function to access the variable. Every variable has an address in memory where the variable's value is stored. When passing a variable to a function, an application can pass the variable's address or the value itself. The information is passed by placing it on the stack (a temporary storage location).

Passing a variable ByRef means that the function call places the address of the variable on the stack. If the function changes the value by writing a new value to the address, the new value will be available to the calling application because the value will be stored at the address where the application expects to find the variable. The address passed is called a pointer, because it points to, or indicates, the address where the value is stored.

Passing a variable ByVal means that the function call places the value of the variable on the stack. The value at the variable's original address in memory is unchanged. If the function changes the value, the calling application won't know about the change because the function has no way to pass the new value back to the application.

Passing ByVal is the default under Visual Basic .NET. If you want to pass a parameter ByRef, you must specify it in the declaration. (Passing ByRef is the default in Visual Basic 6.)

Except for strings, you must pass a variable ByRef if the called function changes the value and the calling application needs to use the new value. Passing ByRef enables the calling application to access the new value.

Strings are a special case and should be passed ByVal to API functions. If you pass a string ByVal to an API function, Visual Basic actually passes a pointer to the string, as if the string had been declared ByRef. If the function will change the contents of the string, the application should initialize the string to be at least as long as the longest expected returned string.

Passing Structures

Some API functions pass and return structures, which contain multiple items that may be of different types. The documentation for the API functions also documents the structures that the functions pass. The header files contain declarations for the structures in C syntax.

A Visual Basic .NET application can usually declare an equivalent structure in a structure or a class. To ensure that the managed and unmanaged code agree on the layout and alignment of the structure's members, a structure's declaration or class definition can set the StructLayout attribute to Layout-Kind.Sequential:

```
<StructLayout(LayoutKind.Sequential)>
```

As with function declarations, the CharSet attribute can determine whether strings are converted to ANSI or Unicode before passing the strings to unmanaged code:

```
<(CharSet:=CharSet.Auto)>
```

A structure can be passed to an API function ByVal, or the application can pass a pointer to the structure using ByRef.

Some structures are difficult or impractical to duplicate in Visual Basic. A solution is to use a generic buffer of the expected size. The application can fill the buffer before passing it and extract returned data from the buffer as needed.

Calling a Function

After declaring a function and any structures or classes to be passed, an application can call the function. This is a call to the RegisterDeviceNotification function declared earlier:

```
Public Const DEVICE_NOTIFY_WINDOW_HANDLE As Integer _
  = 0

deviceNotificationHandle = _
  RegisterDeviceNotification _
  (formHandle, _
  DevBroadcastDeviceInterfaceBuffer, _
  DEVICE_NOTIFY_WINDOW_HANDLE)
```

The DEVICE_NOTIFY_WINDOW_HANDLE constant is defined in *dbt.h*. The formHandle and DevBroadcastDeviceInterfaceBuffer parameters are IntPtr variables. The function returns an IntPtr in deviceNotification-Handle.

Finding Your Device

The Windows API provides a series of SetupDi_ API functions that enable applications to find all devices in a device interface class and to obtain a device path name for each device. The CreateFile function can use the device path name to obtain a handle for accessing the device.

Obtaining a device path name requires these steps:

1. Obtain the device interface GUID.

2. Request a pointer to a device information set with information about all installed and present devices in the device interface class.

3. Request a pointer to a structure that contains information about a device interface in the device information set.

4. Request a structure containing a device interface's device path name.

5. Extract the device path name from the structure.

The application can then use the device path name to open a handle for communicating with the device.

Table 10-1 lists the API functions that applications can use to perform these actions. The functions can be useful for finding devices that use some vendor-specific drivers and HID-class devices that perform vendor-specific functions. For many devices that perform standard functions, applications have other ways to find and gain access to devices. For example, to access a drive, the .NET Framework's Directory class includes a GetLogicalDrives method that enables applications to find all of the logical drives on a system (whether or not they use USB). You can then use methods of the Directory and File classes to access files on the drives.

Table 10-1: Applications use these functions to find devices and obtain device path names to enable accessing devices.

API Function	DLL	Purpose
HidD_GetHidGuid	hid	Retrieve the device interface GUID for the HID class
SetupDiDestroyDeviceInfoList	setupapi	Free resources used by SetupDiGetClassDevs.
SetupDiGetClassDevs	setupapi	Retrieve a device information set for the devices in a specified class.
SetupDiGetDeviceInterfaceDetail	setupapi	Retrieve a device path name.
SetupDiEnumDeviceInterfaces	setupapi	Retrieve information about a device in a device information set.

The following code shows how to use API functions to find a device and obtain its device path name. For complete Visual C++ .NET and Visual Basic .NET applications that demonstrate how to use these functions, go to *www.Lvr.com*.

Obtaining the Device Interface GUID

As Chapter 8 explained, for many drivers, applications can obtain a device interface GUID from a C header file or Visual-Basic declaration provided with the driver. For the HID class, Windows provides an API function to obtain the GUID, which is also defined in *hidclass.h*.

Visual C++

This is the function's declaration:

```
VOID
  HidD_GetHidGuid(
    OUT LPGUID HidGuid
    );
```

This is the code to call the function:

```
HidD_GetHidGuid(&HidGuid);
```

Visual Basic

The function has no return value, so it's declared as a Sub:

```
<DllImport("hid.dll")>
Sub HidD_GetHidGuid _
    (ByRef HidGuid As System.Guid)
End Sub
```

This is the code to call the function:

```
Dim HidGuid As System.Guid
HidD_GetHidGuid(HidGuid)
```

Requesting a Pointer to a Device Information Set

The SetupDiGetClassDevs function can return a pointer to an array of structures containing information about all devices in the device interface class specified by a GUID.

Visual C++

This is the function's declaration:

```
HDEVINFO
  SetupDiGetClassDevs(
    IN LPGUID  ClassGuid,   OPTIONAL
    IN PCTSTR  Enumerator,  OPTIONAL
    IN HWND  hwndParent,  OPTIONAL
    IN DWORD  Flags
    );
```

This is the code to call the function:

```
HANDLE DeviceInfoSet;

DeviceInfoSet = SetupDiGetClassDevs
  (&HidGuid,
  NULL,
  NULL,
  DIGCF_PRESENT|DIGCF_INTERFACEDEVICE);
```

Visual Basic

This is the function's declaration:

```
<DllImport("setupapi.dll", CharSet:=CharSet.Auto)> _
Function SetupDiGetClassDevs _
    (ByRef ClassGuid As System.Guid, _
    ByVal Enumerator As String, _
    ByVal hwndParent As Integer, _
    ByVal Flags As Integer) _
    As IntPtr
End Function
```

This is the code to call the function:

```
Public Const DIGCF_PRESENT As Short = &H2S
Public Const DIGCF_DEVICEINTERFACE As Short = &H10S

Dim DeviceInfoSet As IntPtr

DeviceInfoSet = SetupDiGetClassDevs _
    (HidGuid, _
    vbNullString, _
    0, _
    DIGCF_PRESENT Or DIGCF_DEVICEINTERFACE)
```

Details

For HID-class devices, the ClassGuid parameter is the HidGuid value returned by HidD_GetHidGuid. For other drivers, the application can pass a reference to the appropriate GUID. The Enumerator and hwndParent parameters are unused in this example. The Flags parameter consists of system constants defined in *setupapi.h*. The flags in this example tell the function to look only for device interfaces that are currently present (attached and enumerated) and that are members of the device interface class identified by the ClassGuid parameter.

The value returned, DeviceInfoSet, is a pointer to a device information set that contains information about all attached and enumerated devices in the specified device interface class. The device information set contains a device information element for each device in the set. Each device information element contains a handle to a device's devnode (a structure that represents the device) and a linked list of device interfaces associated with the device.

When finished using the device information set, the application should free the resources used by calling SetupDiDestroyDeviceInfoList, as described later in this chapter.

Identifying a Device Interface

A call to SetupDiEnumDeviceInterfaces retrieves a pointer to a structure that identifies a specific device interface in the previously retrieved Device-InfoSet array. The call specifies a device interface by passing an array index. To retrieve information about all of the device interfaces, an application can loop through the array, incrementing the array index until the function returns zero, indicating that there are no more interfaces. The GetLastError API function then returns *No more data is available*.

How do you know if a device interface is the one you're looking for? The application may need to request more information before deciding to use a device interface. On detecting multiple interfaces, the application can investigate each in turn until finding the desired device or determining that the device isn't present.

Visual C++

This is the declaration for DeviceInterfaceData's type:

```
typedef struct _SP_DEVICE_INTERFACE_DATA {
    DWORD cbSize;
    GUID InterfaceClassGuid;
    DWORD Flags;
    ULONG_PTR Reserved;
} SP_DEVICE_INTERFACE_DATA,
*PSP_DEVICE_INTERFACE_DATA;
```

This is the function's declaration:

```
BOOLEAN
  SetupDiEnumDeviceInterfaces(
    IN HDEVINFO  DeviceInfoSet,
    IN PSP_DEVINFO_DATA  DeviceInfoData,  OPTIONAL
    IN LPGUID  InterfaceClassGuid,
    IN DWORD  MemberIndex,
    OUT PSP_DEVICE_INTERFACE_DATA  DeviceInterfaceData
    );
```

And this is the code to call the function:

```
BOOLEAN Result;
SP_DEVICE_INTERFACE_DATA MyDeviceInterfaceData;

MyDeviceInterfaceData.cbSize =
  sizeof(MyDeviceInterfaceData);
MemberIndex = 0;

Result=SetupDiEnumDeviceInterfaces
  (DeviceInfoSet,
  0,
  &HidGuid,
  MemberIndex,
  &MyDeviceInterfaceData);
```

Visual Basic

This is the declaration for the DeviceInterfaceData structure:

```
<StructLayout(LayoutKind.Sequential)> _
Public Structure SP_DEVICE_INTERFACE_DATA
    Dim cbSize As Integer
    Dim InterfaceClassGuid As System.Guid
    Dim Flags As Integer
    Dim Reserved As Integer
End Structure
```

This is the function's declaration:

```
<DllImport("setupapi.dll")> _
Function SetupDiEnumDeviceInterfaces _
    (ByVal DeviceInfoSet As IntPtr, _
    ByVal DeviceInfoData As Integer, _
    ByRef InterfaceClassGuid As System.Guid, _
    ByVal MemberIndex As Integer, _
    ByRef DeviceInterfaceData As _
        SP_DEVICE_INTERFACE_DATA) _
    As Boolean
End Function
```

This is the code to call the function:

```
Dim MemberIndex As Integer
Dim MyDeviceInterfaceData As SP_DEVICE_INTERFACE_DATA
Dim Result As Boolean

myDeviceInterfaceData.cbSize = _
    Marshal.SizeOf(myDeviceInterfaceData)
MemberIndex = 0

Result = SetupDiEnumDeviceInterfaces _
    (DeviceInfoSet, _
    0, _
    HidGuid, _
    MemberIndex, _
    MyDeviceInterfaceData)
```

Details

In the SP_DEVICE_INTERFACE_DATA structure, the parameter cbSize is the size of the structure in bytes. Before calling SetupDiEnumDevice-Interfaces, the size must be stored in the structure that the function will pass. The sizeof operator in Visual C++ or the Marshal.SizeOf method in Visual Basic retrieves the size. The other values in the structure should be zero.

The HidGuid and DeviceInfoSet parameters are values retrieved previously. DeviceInfoData is an optional pointer to an SP_DEVINFO_DATA structure that limits the search to a particular device instance. MemberIndex is an index to a structure in the DeviceInfoSet array. MyDeviceInterfaceData is the returned SP_DEVICE_INTERFACE_DATA structure that identifies a device interface of the requested type.

Requesting a Structure Containing the Device Path Name

The SetupDiGetDeviceInterfaceDetail function returns a structure that contains a device path name for a device interface identified in an SP_DEVICE_INTERFACE_DATA structure.

Before calling this function for the first time, there's no way to know the value of the DeviceInterfaceDetailDataSize parameter, which must contain the size in bytes of the DeviceInterfaceDetailData structure. Yet the function won't return the structure unless the function call contains this information. The solution is to call the function twice. The first time, GetLastError returns the error *The data area passed to a system call is too small,* but the RequiredSize parameter contains the correct value for DeviceInterfaceDetailDataSize. The second time, you pass the returned size value and the function returns the structure.

Visual C++

This is the declaration for DeviceInterfaceDetailData's structure:

```
typedef struct _SP_DEVICE_INTERFACE_DETAIL_DATA {
    DWORD cbSize;
    TCHAR DevicePath[ANYSIZE_ARRAY];
} SP_DEVICE_INTERFACE_DETAIL_DATA,
*PSP_DEVICE_INTERFACE_DETAIL_DATA;
```

This is the function's declaration:

```
BOOLEAN
  SetupDiGetDeviceInterfaceDetail(
    IN HDEVINFO  DeviceInfoSet,
    IN PSP_DEVICE_INTERFACE_DATA  DeviceInterfaceData,
    OUT PSP_DEVICE_INTERFACE_DETAIL_DATA
      DeviceInterfaceDetailData,  OPTIONAL
    IN DWORD  DeviceInterfaceDetailDataSize,
    OUT PDWORD  RequiredSize,  OPTIONAL
    OUT PSP_DEVINFO_DATA  DeviceInfoData  OPTIONAL
    );
```

This is the code to call the function the first time:

```
BOOLEAN Result;
PSP_DEVICE_INTERFACE_DETAIL_DATA DetailData;
ULONG Length;

Result = SetupDiGetDeviceInterfaceDetail
  (DeviceInfoSet,
  &MyDeviceInterfaceData,
  NULL,
  0,
  &Length,
  NULL);
```

The code then allocates memory for the DetailData structure, sets the cbSize property of DetailData, and calls the function again, passing the returned buffer size in Length:

```
DetailData =
  (PSP_DEVICE_INTERFACE_DETAIL_DATA)malloc(Length);

DetailData -> cbSize =
  sizeof(SP_DEVICE_INTERFACE_DETAIL_DATA);

Result = SetupDiGetDeviceInterfaceDetail
  (DeviceInfoSet,
  &MyDeviceInterfaceData,
  DetailData,
  Length,
  &Length,
  NULL);
```

Visual Basic

The Visual-Basic code doesn't explicitly declare an SP_DEVICE_INTERFACE_DETAIL_DATA structure for the Device-InterfaceDetailData parameter. Instead, the code reserves a generic buffer, passes a pointer to the buffer, and extracts the device path name directly from the buffer. So the application doesn't use the following declaration, but I've included it to show what the returned buffer will contain:

```
<StructLayout(LayoutKind.Sequential)> _
Public Structure SP_DEVICE_INTERFACE_DETAIL_DATA
    Dim cbSize As Integer
    Dim DevicePath As String
End Structure
```

This is the function's declaration:

```
<DllImport("setupapi.dll", CharSet:=CharSet.Auto)> _
Function SetupDiGetDeviceInterfaceDetail _
    (ByVal DeviceInfoSet As IntPtr, _
    ByRef DeviceInterfaceData _
        As  SP_DEVICE_INTERFACE_DATA, _
    ByVal DeviceInterfaceDetailData As IntPtr, _
    ByVal DeviceInterfaceDetailDataSize As Integer, _
    ByRef RequiredSize As Integer, _
    ByVal DeviceInfoData As IntPtr) _
    As Boolean
End Function
```

This is the code for the first call:

```
Dim BufferSize As Integer
Dim Success As Boolean

Success = SetupDiGetDeviceInterfaceDetail _
    (DeviceInfoSet, _
    MyDeviceInterfaceData, _
    IntPtr.Zero, _
    0, _
    BufferSize, _
    IntPtr.Zero)
```

After calling SetupDiGetDeviceInterfaceDetail, BufferSize contains the value to pass in the DeviceInterfaceDetailDataSizebuffer parameter in the next call. But before calling the function again, we need to take care of a few things.

The function will return a pointer (DetailDataBuffer) to an SP_DEVICE_INTERFACE_DETAIL_DATA structure in unmanaged memory. The Marshal.AllocGlocal method uses the returned BufferSize value to reserve memory for the structure:

```
Dim DetailDataBuffer As IntPtr
DetailDataBuffer = Marshal.AllocHGlobal(BufferSize)
```

The cbSize member of the structure passed in DetailDataBuffer equals four bytes for the cbSize integer plus the length of one character for the device path name (which is empty when passed to the function). The Marshal.WriteInt32 method copies the cbSize value into the first member of DetailDataBuffer:

```
Marshal.WriteInt32 _
    (DetailDataBuffer, _
    4 + Marshal.SystemDefaultCharSize)
```

The second call to SetupDiGetDeviceInterfaceDetail passes the Detail-DataBuffer pointer and sets the DeviceInterfaceDetailDataSize parameter equal to the BufferSize value returned previously in RequiredSize:

```
Success = SetupDiGetDeviceInterfaceDetail _
    (deviceInfoSet, _
    MyDeviceInterfaceData, _
    DetailDataBuffer, _
    BufferSize, _
    BufferSize, _
    IntPtr.Zero)
```

When the function returns, DetailDataBuffer points to a structure containing a device path name.

Extracting the Device Path Name

The device path name is in the DevicePath member of the SP_DEVICE_INTERFACE_DETAIL_DATA structure returned by Setup-DiGetDeviceInterfaceDetail.

Visual C++

The device path name is in DetailData -> DevicePath.

Visual Basic

The string containing the device path name is stored beginning at byte 5 in DetailDataBuffer. (The first four bytes are the cbSize member.) The pDevicePathName variable points to this location:

```
Dim DevicePathName(127) As String

Dim pDevicePathName As IntPtr = _
    New IntPtr(DetailDataBuffer.ToInt32 + 4)
```

The Marshal.PtrToString method retrieves the string from the buffer:

```
DevicePathName = _
    Marshal.PtrToStringAuto(pDevicePathName)
```

We're finished with DetailDataBuffer, so we should free the memory previously allocated for it:

```
Marshal.FreeHGlobal(DetailDataBuffer)
```

Closing Communications

When finished using the DeviceInfoSet returned by SetupDiGetClassDevs, the application should call SetupDiDestroyDeviceInfoList.

Visual C++

This is the function's declaration:

```
BOOL SetupDiDestroyDeviceInfoList(
   HDEVINFO DeviceInfoSet);
```

This is the code to call the function:

```
SetupDiDestroyDeviceInfoList(DeviceInfoSet);
```

Visual Basic

This is the function's declaration:

```
<DllImport("setupapi.dll")> Function
SetupDiDestroyDeviceInfoList _
        (ByVal DeviceInfoSet As IntPtr) _
        As Integer
    End Function
```

This is the code to call the function:

```
SetupDiDestroyDeviceInfoList (deviceInfoSet)
```

Obtaining a Handle

An application can use a retrieved device path name to obtain a handle that enables communicating with the device. Table 10-2 shows the API functions related to requesting a handle.

Requesting a Communications Handle

After retrieving a device path name, an application is ready to open communications with the device. The CreateFile function requests a handle to an object, which can be a file or another resource managed by a driver that supports handle-based operations. For example, applications can request a handle to use in exchanging reports with HID-class devices.

Visual C++

This is the function's declaration:

```
HANDLE CreateFile(
  LPCTSTR lpFileName,
  DWORD dwDesiredAccess,
  DWORD dwShareMode,
  LPSECURITY_ATTRIBUTES lpSecurityAttributes,
  DWORD dwCreationDisposition,
  DWORD dwFlagsAndAttributes,
  HANDLE hTemplateFile
);
```

Table 10-2: Applications can use CreateFile to request a handle to a device and CloseHandle to free the resources used by a handle.

API Function	DLL	Purpose
CloseHandle	kernel32	Free resources used by CreateFile.
CreateFile	kernel32	Retrieve a handle for communicating with a device.

This is the code to call the function:

```
HANDLE DeviceHandle;

DeviceHandle=CreateFile
   (DetailData->DevicePath,
   GENERIC_READ|GENERIC_WRITE,
   FILE_SHARE_READ|FILE_SHARE_WRITE,
   (LPSECURITY_ATTRIBUTES)NULL,
   OPEN_EXISTING,
   0,
   NULL);
```

Visual Basic

This is a declaration for the the SECURITY_ATTRIBUTES structure:

```
<StructLayout(LayoutKind.Sequential)> _
Public Structure SECURITY_ATTRIBUTES
    Dim nLength As Integer
    Dim lpSecurityDescriptor As Integer
    Dim bInheritHandle As Integer
End Structure
```

This is the function's declaration:

```
<DllImport("kernel32.dll", CharSet:=CharSet.Auto)>
Function CreateFile _
    (ByVal lpFileName As String, _
    ByVal dwDesiredAccess As Integer, _
    ByVal dwShareMode As Integer, _
    ByRef lpSecurityAttributes As _
        SECURITY_ATTRIBUTES, _
    ByVal dwCreationDisposition As Integer, _
    ByVal dwFlagsAndAttributes As Integer, _
    ByVal hTemplateFile As Integer) _
    As Integer
End Function
```

This is the code to call the function:

```
Public Const GENERIC_READ = &H80000000
Public Const GENERIC_WRITE = &H40000000
Public Const FILE_SHARE_READ = &H1
Public Const FILE_SHARE_WRITE = &H2
Public Const OPEN_EXISTING = 3
Dim DeviceHandle As Integer
Dim Security As SECURITY_ATTRIBUTES

Security.lpSecurityDescriptor = 0
Security.bInheritHandle = CInt(True)
Security.nLength = Len(Security)

DeviceHandle = CreateFile _
    (DevicePathName, _
    GENERIC_READ Or GENERIC_WRITE, _
    FILE_SHARE_READ Or FILE_SHARE_WRITE, _
    Security, _
    OPEN_EXISTING, _
    0, _
    0)
```

Details

The function passes a pointer to the device-path-name string returned by SetupDiGetDeviceInterfaceDetail. The dwDesiredAccess parameter requests read/write access to the device. The dwShareMode parameter allows other processes to access the device while the handle is open. The lpSecurityAttributes parameter is a pointer to a SECURITY_ATTRIBUTES structure. The dwCreationDisposition parameter must be OPEN_EXISTING for devices. The final two parameters are unused in this example.

Closing the Handle

Chapter 13 shows how to use a handle to exchange information with a HID-class device. For other device classes, the details will vary with the driver. When finished communicating with a device, the application should call CloseHandle to free the resources used by CreateFile.

Visual C++

This is the function's declaration:

```
BOOL CloseHandle(
   HANDLE hObject);
```

This is the code to call the function:

```
CloseHandle(DeviceHandle);
```

Visual Basic

This is the function's declaration:

```
<DllImport("kernel32.dll")> Function CloseHandle _
   (ByVal hObject As Integer) _
   As Integer
End Function
```

This is the code to call the function:

```
CloseHandle(DeviceHandle)
```

Detecting Attachment and Removal

Many applications find it useful to know when a device has been attached or removed. An application that detects when a device has been attached can begin communicating automatically on attachment. An application that detects when a device has been removed can stop attempting to communicate, notify the user, and wait for reattachment. Windows provides device-notification functions for this purpose.

About Device Notifications

To request to be informed when a device is attached or removed, an application's form can register to receive notification messages for devices in a device interface class. The messages are WM_DEVICECHANGE messages that the operating system passes to the form's WindowProc (WndProc in Visual Basic) method. An application can override the WindowProc method in a form's base class with a method that processes the messages and then passes them to the base class's WindowProc method. Each notification contains a device path name that the application can use to identify the device the notification applies to. Table 10-3 lists the API functions used in registering for device notifications. The example that follows shows how to use the functions.

Registering for Device Notifications

Applications use the RegisterDeviceNotification function to request to receive notification messages. The function requires a pointer to a handle for the window or service that will receive the notifications, a pointer to a DEV_BROADCAST_DEVICEINTERFACE structure that holds information about the request, and flags to indicate whether the handle is for a window or service status.

In the DEV_BROADCAST_DEVICEINTERFACE structure passed to RegisterDeviceNotification, the dbcc_devicetype member is set to DBT_DEVTYP_DEVICEINTERFACE to specify that the application wants to receive notifications about a device interface class, and classguid is the GUID of the device interface class (HidGuid in the examples).

When the WM_DEVICECHANGE messages are no longer of interest, the application should call UnregisterDeviceNotification, as described later in this chapter.

Table 10-3: These functions enable an application to request to receive or stop receiving notifications about device attachment and removal.

API Function	DLL	Purpose
RegisterDeviceNotification	user32	Request to receive device notifications
UnregisterDeviceNotification	user32	Request to stop receiving device notifications

Visual C++

The declaration for the DEV_BROADCAST_DEVICEINTERFACE structure is this:

```
typedef struct _DEV_BROADCAST_DEVICEINTERFACE {
    DWORD dbcc_size;
    DWORD dbcc_devicetype;
    DWORD dbcc_reserved;
    GUID dbcc_classguid;
    TCHAR dbcc_name[1];
} DEV_BROADCAST_DEVICEINTERFACE
*PDEV_BROADCAST_DEVICEINTERFACE;
```

This is the function's declaration:

```
HDEVNOTIFY RegisterDeviceNotification(
    HANDLE hRecipient,
    LPVOID NotificationFilter,
    DWORD Flags
);
```

This is the code to call the function:

```
HDEVNOTIFY DeviceNotificationHandle;

DEV_BROADCAST_DEVICEINTERFACE
    DevBroadcastDeviceInterface;

DevBroadcastDeviceInterface.dbcc_size =
    sizeof(DevBroadcastDeviceInterface);

DevBroadcastDeviceInterface.dbcc_devicetype =
    DBT_DEVTYP_DEVICEINTERFACE;

DevBroadcastDeviceInterface.dbcc_classguid = HidGuid;
```

```
DeviceNotificationHandle = RegisterDeviceNotification
  (m_hWnd,
  &DevBroadcastDeviceInterface,
  DEVICE_NOTIFY_WINDOW_HANDLE);
```

Visual Basic

The device-notification functions use several constants defined in header files. These are from *dbt.h*:

```
Public Const DBT_DEVTYP_DEVICEINTERFACE As Integer = 5
Public Const DEVICE_NOTIFY_WINDOW_HANDLE As Integer _
  = 0
Public Const WM_DEVICECHANGE As Integer = &H219
```

These are from *setupapi.h*:

```
Public Const DIGCF_PRESENT As Short = &H2S
Public Const DIGCF_DEVICEINTERFACE As Short = &H10S
```

The DEV_BROADCAST_DEVICEINTERFACE structure has this declaration:

```
<StructLayout(LayoutKind.Sequential)> _
Public Class DEV_BROADCAST_DEVICEINTERFACE
    Public dbcc_size As Integer
    Public dbcc_devicetype As Integer
    Public dbcc_reserved As Integer
    Public dbcc_classguid As Guid
    Public dbcc_name As Short
End Class
```

This is the declaration for RegisterDeviceNotification:

```
<DllImport("user32.dll", CharSet:=CharSet.Auto)> _
Function RegisterDeviceNotification _
    (ByVal hRecipient As IntPtr, _
    ByVal NotificationFilter As IntPtr, _
    ByVal Flags As Int32) _
    As IntPtr
End Function
```

This is the code to call the function:

```
Dim DevBroadcastDeviceInterface _
    As DEV_BROADCAST_DEVICEINTERFACE = _
        New DEV_BROADCAST_DEVICEINTERFACE()
Dim DevBroadcastDeviceInterfaceBuffer As IntPtr
Dim DeviceNotificationHandle As IntPtr
Dim Size As Integer
Friend frmMy As frmMain
```

The Marshal.SizeOf method retrieves the size of the DEV_BROADCAST_DEVICEINTERFACE structure, which is then stored in the structure's dbcc_size member:

```
Size = Marshal.SizeOf(DevBroadcastDeviceInterface)

DevBroadcastDeviceInterface.dbcc_size = Size
DevBroadcastDeviceInterface.dbcc_devicetype = _
    DBT_DEVTYP_DEVICEINTERFACE
DevBroadcastDeviceInterface.dbcc_reserved = 0
DevBroadcastDeviceInterface.dbcc_classguid = _
    HidGuid
```

Marshal.AllocGlobal reserves memory for a buffer that will hold the DEV_BROADCAST_DEVICEINTERFACE structure. The Marshal.StructureToPointer method copies the structure into the buffer. The application is then ready to call RegisterDeviceNotification:

```
DevBroadcastDeviceInterfaceBuffer = _
    Marshal.AllocHGlobal(Size)

Marshal.StructureToPtr _
    (DevBroadcastDeviceInterface, _
    DevBroadcastDeviceInterfaceBuffer, _
    True)

DeviceNotificationHandle = _
    RegisterDeviceNotification _
    (frmMy.Handle, _
    DevBroadcastDeviceInterfaceBuffer, _
    DEVICE_NOTIFY_WINDOW_HANDLE)
```

When finished using DevBroadcastDeviceInterfaceBuffer, the application should free the memory allocated for it by AllocHGlobal:

```
Marshal.FreeHGlobal _
    (DevBroadcastDeviceInterfaceBuffer)
```

Capturing Device Change Messages

The WindowProc function processes messages received by a form, dialog box, or other window.

Visual C++

To receive WM_DEVICECHANGE messages, a dialog box's message map must contain the line ON_WM_DEVICECHANGE():

```
BEGIN_MESSAGE_MAP(MyApplicationDlg, CDialog)
    //{{AFX_MSG_MAP(MyApplicationDlg)
    .
    .
    .
    //}}AFX_MSG_MAP
    ON_WM_DEVICECHANGE()
END_MESSAGE_MAP()
```

Visual Basic

This is the code for a WndProc routine that overrides the base form's default WndProc routine:

```
Protected Overrides Sub WndProc(ByRef m As Message)

    If m.Msg = WM_DEVICECHANGE Then
        OnDeviceChange(m)
    End If

    MyBase.WndProc(m)

End Sub
```

On receiving a WM_DEVICECHANGE message, the method calls the OnDeviceChange method and then passes the message to the WndProc method in the form's base class.

Reading Device Change Messages

On receiving a WM_DEVICECHANGE message, a window's OnDevice-Change method executes. The method can examine the message's contents and take any needed action. The message contains two pointers: lParam and wParam.

The wParam property is a code that indicates device arrival, removal, or another event.

The lParam property is a device management structure. There are several types of device-management structures, but all begin with the same header, which has three members. The header is a DEV_BROADCAST_HDR structure whose dbch_devicetype member indicates the type of device-management structure that lParam points to.

If dbch_devicetype = DBT_DEVTYP_DEVICEINTERFACE, the structure is a DEV_BROADCAST_INTERFACE and the application can retrieve the complete structure, read the device path name in the dbcc_name member, and compare the name to the device path name of the device of interest.

Visual C++

This is the declaration for the DEV_BROADCAST_HDR structure:

```
typedef struct _DEV_BROADCAST_HDR {
    DWORD dbch_size;
    DWORD dbch_devicetype;
    DWORD dbch_reserved;
} DEV_BROADCAST_HDR, *PDEV_BROADCAST_HDR;
```

This is the code for the OnDeviceChange function:

```
BOOL CUsbhidiocDlg::OnDeviceChange
  (WPARAM wParam,
  LPARAM lParam)
{
  switch(wParam)
  {
    case DBT_DEVICEARRIVAL:
      // Find out if the device path name matches
      // wParam.
      // If yes, perform any tasks required
      // on device attachment.

        return TRUE;

    case DBT_DEVICEREMOVECOMPLETE:

      // Find out if the device path name matches
      // wParam.
      // If yes, perform any tasks required
      // on device removal.

      return TRUE;

    default:
      return TRUE;
  }
}
```

Visual Basic

These constants are from dbt.h:

```
Public Const DBT_DEVICEARRIVAL As Integer = &H8000
Public Const DBT_DEVICEREMOVECOMPLETE As Integer _
  = &H8004
```

This is the declaration for the DEV_BROADCAST_HDR structure:

```
<StructLayout(LayoutKind.Sequential)> _
Public Class DEV_BROADCAST_HDR
    Public dbch_size As Integer
    Public dbch_devicetype As Integer
    Public dbch_reserved As Integer
End Class
```

This is code to check for device arrival and removal messages:

```
Friend Sub OnDeviceChange(ByVal m as Message)

    If (m.WParam.ToInt32 = DBT_DEVICEARRIVAL) Then

        ' Find out if the device path name matches
        ' wParam.
        ' If yes, perform any tasks required
        ' on device removal.

    ElseIf (m.WParam.ToInt32 = _
        DBT_DEVICEREMOVECOMPLETE) Then

        ' Find out if the device path name matches
        ' wParam.
        ' If yes, perform any tasks required
        ' on device removal.

    End If

End Sub
```

Retrieving the Device Path Name in the Message

If the message indicates a device arrival or removal (or another event of interest), the application can investigate further.

In the structure that lParam points to, if dbch_devicetype contains DBT_DEVTYP_DEVICEINTERFACE, the event relates to a device interface. The structure in lParam is a DEV_BROADCAST_INTERFACE structure, which begins with a DEV_BROADCAST_HDR structure. The dbcc_name member contains the device path name of the device the message applies to.

The application can compare this device path name with the device path name of the device of interest. On a match, the application can take any desired actions.

Visual C++

This is the code to retrieve the device path name and look for a match:

```
PDEV_BROADCAST_HDR lpdb = (PDEV_BROADCAST_HDR)lParam;

if (lpdb->dbch_devicetype ==
  DBT_DEVTYP_DEVICEINTERFACE)
{
  PDEV_BROADCAST_DEVICEINTERFACE lpdbi =
    (PDEV_BROADCAST_DEVICEINTERFACE)lParam;

  CString DeviceNameString;

  DeviceNameString = lpdbi->dbcc_name;

  if
    ((DeviceNameString.CompareNoCase
        (DetailData>DevicePath)) == 0)
  {
    // The names match.
  }
  else
  {
    // It's a different device.
  }
}
```

Visual Basic

The application uses two declarations for the DEV_BROADCAST_DEVICEINTERFACE structure. The first declaration, presented earlier, is used when calling RegisterDeviceNotification. The second declaration, DEV_BROADCAST_DEVICEINTERFACE_1, enables marshaling the data in dbcc_name and classguid:

```
<StructLayout _
    (LayoutKind.Sequential, _
    CharSet:=CharSet.Unicode)> _
Public Class DEV_BROADCAST_DEVICEINTERFACE_1
    Public dbcc_size As Integer
    Public dbcc_devicetype As Integer
    Public dbcc_reserved As Integer
    <MarshalAs _
        (UnmanagedType.ByValArray, _
        ArraySubType:=UnmanagedType.U1, _
        SizeConst:=16)> _
        Public dbcc_classguid() As Byte
    <MarshalAs _
        (UnmanagedType.ByValArray, sizeconst:=255)> _
        Public dbcc_name() As Char
    End Class
```

This is the code to retrieve the device path name and look for a match:

```
Dim DevBroadcastDeviceInterface As _
    New DEV_BROADCAST_DEVICEINTERFACE_1()
Dim DevBroadcastHeader As New DEV_BROADCAST_HDR()

Marshal.PtrToStructure(m.LParam, DevBroadcastHeader)

If (DevBroadcastHeader.dbch_devicetype = _
    DBT_DEVTYP_DEVICEINTERFACE) Then
    Dim StringSize As Integer = _
        CInt((DevBroadcastHeader.dbch_size - 32) / 2)
    ReDim DevBroadcastDeviceInterface.dbcc_name _
            (StringSize)

    Marshal.PtrToStructure _
        (m.LParam, DevBroadcastDeviceInterface)
```

```
Dim DeviceNameString As New String _
    (DevBroadcastDeviceInterface.dbcc_name, _
    0, _
    StringSize)

If (String.Compare _
    (DeviceNameString, _
    DevicePathName, _
    True) = 0) Then
        'The name matches.
Else
        'It's a different device.
End If
End If
```

MarshalPtrToStructure copies the message's lParam property into a DEV_BROADCAST_HDR structure. If lParam indicates that the message relates to a device interface, the application retrieves the device path name.

The name is in a Char array in unmanaged memory. The application needs to retrieve the Char array and convert it to a String.

The dbch_size member of DEV_BROADCAST_HDR contains the number of bytes in the complete DEV_BROADCAST_INTERFACE structure. To obtain the number of characters in the device path name stored in dbch_name, subtract the 32 bytes in the structure that are not part of the name and divide by 2 because there are 2 bytes per character.

DevBroadcastDeviceInterface is a DEV_BROADCAST_INTERFACE_1 structure that marshals the data in the classguid and dbcc_name members. A ReDim statement trims dbcc_name to match the size of the device path name. Marshal.PtrToStructure copies the data from the unmanaged block in lParam to the DevBroadcastDeviceInterface structure. The Char array containing the device path name is then stored as a String in Device-NameString, and the String.Compare method looks for a match.

Stopping Device Notifications

To stop receiving device notifications, an application calls UnregisterDeviceNotification. The application should call the function before closing.

Visual C++

This is the function's declaration:

```
BOOL UnregisterDeviceNotification(
  HDEVNOTIFY Handle
);
```

This is the code to call the function:

```
UnregisterDeviceNotification(
  DeviceNotificationHandle);
```

Visual Basic

This is the function's declaration:

```
<DllImport("user32.dll")> Function
UnregisterDeviceNotification _
    (ByVal Handle As IntPtr) _
    As Boolean
    End Function
```

This is the code to call the function:

```
UnregisterDeviceNotification _
    (DeviceNotificationHandle)
```

11

Human Interface Devices: Using Control and Interrupt Transfers

The human interface device (HID) class was one of the first USB classes supported under Windows. On PCs running Windows 98 or later, applications can communicate with HIDs using the drivers built into the operating system. For this reason, many vendor-specific USB devices use the HID class.

Chapter 7 introduced the class. This chapter shows how to determine whether a specific device can fit into the human-interface class, details the firmware requirements that define a device as a HID and enable it to exchange data with its host, introduces the six HID-specific control requests, and presents an example of HID firmware. Chapter 12 describes the reports that HIDs use to exchange information and Chapter 13 shows how to access HIDs from applications.

What is a HID?

The *human interface* in the name suggests that HIDs interact directly with people, and many HIDs do. A mouse may detect when someone presses a key or moves the mouse, or the host may send a message that translates to a joystick effect that the user experiences. Besides keyboards, mice, and joysticks, the HID class encompasses front panels with knobs, switches, buttons, and sliders; remote controls; telephone keypads; and game controls such as data gloves and steering wheels.

But a HID doesn't have to have a human interface. The device just needs to be able to function within the limits of the HID class specification. These are the major abilities and limitations of HID-class devices:

- All data exchanged resides in structures called reports. The host sends and receives data by sending and requesting reports in control or interrupt transfers. The report format is flexible and can handle just about any type of data, but each defined report has a fixed size.

- A HID interface must have an interrupt IN endpoint for sending Input reports.

- A HID interface can have at most one interrupt IN endpoint and one interrupt OUT endpoint. If you need more interrupt endpoints, you can create a composite device that contains multiple HIDs. An application must obtain a separate handle for each HID in the composite device.

- The interrupt IN endpoint enables the HID to send information to the host at unpredictable times. For example, there's no way for the computer to know when a user will press a key on the keyboard, so the host's driver uses interrupt transactions to poll the device periodically to obtain new data.

- The rate of data exchange is limited, especially at low and full speeds. As Chapter 3 explained, a host can guarantee a low-speed interrupt endpoint no more than 800 bytes/sec. For full-speed endpoints, the maximum is 64 kilobytes/sec., and for high-speed endpoints, the maximum is about 24 Megabytes/sec. if the host supports high-bandwidth endpoints and about 8 Megabytes/sec. if not. Control transfers have no guaranteed bandwidth except for the bandwidth reserved for all control transfers on the bus.

• Windows 98 Gold (original edition) supports USB 1.0, so interrupt OUT transfers aren't supported and all host-to-device reports must use control transfers.

Any device that can live within the class's limits is a candidate to be a HID. The HID specification mentions bar-code readers, thermometers, and voltmeters as examples of HIDs that might not have a conventional human interface. Each of these sends data to the computer and may also receive requests that configure the device. Examples of devices that mostly receive data are remote displays, control panels for remote devices, robots, and devices of any kind that receive occasional or periodic commands from the host.

A HID interface may be just one of multiple USB interfaces supported by a device. For example, a USB speaker that uses isochronous transfers for audio may also have a HID interface for controlling volume, balance, treble, and bass. A HID interface is often cheaper than traditional physical controls on a device.

Hardware Requirements

To comply with the HID specification, the interface's endpoints and descriptors must meet several requirements.

Endpoints

All HID transfers use either the control endpoint or an interrupt endpoint. Every HID must have an interrupt IN endpoint for sending data to the host. An interrupt OUT endpoint is optional. Table 11-1 shows the transfer types and their typical uses in HIDs.

Table 11-1: The transfer type used in a HID transfer depends on the chip's abilities and the requirements of the data being sent.

Transfer Type	Source of Data	Typical Data	Required Pipe?	WIndows Support
Control	Device (IN transfer)	Data that doesn't have critical timing requirements.	yes	Windows 98 and later
	Host (OUT transfer)	Data that doesn't have critical timing requirements, or any data if there is no OUT interrupt pipe.		
Interrupt	Device (IN transfer)	Periodic or low-latency data.	yes	
	Host (OUT transfer)	Periodic or low-latency data.	no	Windows 98 SE and later

Reports

The requirement for an interrupt IN endpoint suggests that every HID must have at least one Input report defined in the HID's report descriptor. Output and Feature reports are optional.

Control Transfers

The HID specification defines six class-specific requests. Two requests, Set_Report and Get_Report, provide a way for the host and device to transfer reports to and from the device using control transfers. The host uses Set_Report to send reports and Get_Report to receive reports. The other four requests relate to configuring the device. The Set_Idle and Get_Idle requests set and read the Idle rate, which determines whether or not a device resends data that hasn't changed since the last poll. The Set_Protocol and Get_Protocol requests set and read a protocol value, which can enable a device to function with a simplified protocol when the full HID drivers aren't loaded on the host, such as during boot up.

Interrupt Transfers

Interrupt endpoints provide an alternate way of exchanging data, especially when the receiver must get the data quickly or periodically. Control transfers can be delayed if the bus is very busy, while the bandwidth for interrupt transfers is guaranteed to be available when the device is configured.

The ability to do Interrupt OUT transfers was added in version 1.1 of the USB specification, and the option to use an interrupt OUT pipe was added to version 1.1 of the HID specification. Windows 98 SE was the first Windows edition to support USB 1.1 and HID 1.1.

Firmware Requirements

The device's firmware must also meet class requirements. The device's descriptors must include an interface descriptor that specifies the HID class, a HID descriptor, and an interrupt IN endpoint descriptor. An interrupt OUT endpoint descriptor is optional. The firmware must also contain a report descriptor that contains information about the contents of a HID's reports.

A HID can support one or more reports. The report descriptor specifies the size and contents of the data in a device's reports and may also include information about how the receiver of the data should use the data. Values in the descriptor define each report as an Input, Output, or Feature report. The host receives data in Input reports and sends data in Output reports. A Feature report can travel in either direction.

Every device should support at least one Input report that the host can retrieve using interrupt transfers or control requests. Output reports are optional. To be compatible with Windows 98 Gold, devices that use Output reports should support sending the reports using control transfers. Using interrupt transfers for Output reports is optional. Feature reports always use control transfers and are optional.

Identifying a Device as a HID

As with any USB device, a HID's descriptors tell the host what it needs to know to communicate with the device. Listing 11-1 shows example device, configuration, interface, class, and endpoint descriptors for a vendor-specific HID. The host learns about the HID interface during enumeration by send-

```
{
// Device Descriptor

0x12,          // Descriptor size in bytes
0x01,          // Descriptor type (Device)
0x0200,        // USB Specification release number (BCD) (2.00)
0x00,          // Class Code
0x00,          // Subclass code
0x00,          // Protocol code
0x08,          // Endpoint 0 maximum packet size
0x0925,        // Vendor ID (Lakeview Research)
0x1234,        // Product ID
0x0100,        // Device release number (BCD)
0x01,          // Manufacturer string index
0x02,          // Product string index
0x00,          // Device serial number string index
0x01           // Number of configurations

// Configuration Descriptor

0x09,          // Descriptor size in bytes
0x02,          // Descriptor type (Configuration)
0x0029,        // Total length of this and subordinate descriptors
0x01,          // Number of interfaces in this configuration
0x01,          // Index of this configuration
0x00,          // Configuration string index
0xA0,          // Attributes (bus powered, remote wakeup supported)
0x32,          // Maximum power consumption (100 mA)

// Interface Descriptor

0x09,          // Descriptor size in bytes
0x04,          // Descriptor type (Interface)
0x00,          // Interface Number
0x00,          // Alternate Setting Number
0x02,          // Number of endpoints in this interface
0x03,          // Interface class (HID)
0x00,          // Interface subclass
0x00,          // Interface protocol
0x00,          // Interface string index
```

Listing 11-1: Descriptors for a vendor-specific HID (Sheet 1 of 2)

```
// HID Descriptor

0x09,          // Descriptor size in bytes
0x21,          // Descriptor type (HID)
0x0110,        // HID Spec. release number (BCD) (1.1)
0x00,          // Country code
0x01,          // Number of subordinate class descriptors
0x22,          // Descriptor type (report)
002F,          // Report descriptor size in bytes

// IN Interrupt Endpoint Descriptor

0x07,          // Descriptor size in bytes
0x05,          // Descriptor type (Endpoint)
0x81,          // Endpoint number and direction (1 IN)
0x03,          // Transfer type (interrupt)
0x40,          // Maximum packet size
0x0A,          // Polling interval (milliseconds)

// OUT Interrupt Endpoint Descriptor

0x07,          // Descriptor size in bytes
0x05,          // Descriptor type (Endpoint)
0x01,          // Endpoint number and direction (1 OUT)
0x03,          // Transfer type (interrupt)
0x40,          // Maximum packet size
0x0A           // Polling interval (milliseconds)
}
```

Listing 11-1: Descriptors for a vendor-specific HID (Sheet 2 of 2)

ing a Get_Descriptor request for the configuration containing the HID interface. The configuration's interface descriptor identifies the interface as HID-class. The HID class descriptor specifies the number of report descriptors supported by the interface. During enumeration, the HID driver requests the report descriptor and any physical descriptors.

The HID Interface

In the interface descriptor, bInterfaceclass = 3 to identify the interface as a HID. Other fields that contain HID-specific information in the interface descriptor are the subclass and protocol fields, which can specify a boot interface.

If bInterfaceSubclass = 1, the device supports a boot interface. A HID with a boot interface is usable when the host's HID drivers aren't loaded. This situation might occur when the computer boots directly to DOS, or when viewing the system setup screens that you can access on bootup, or when using Windows' Safe mode for system troubleshooting. A keyboard or mouse with a boot interface can use a simplified protocol supported by the BIOS of many hosts. The BIOS loads from ROM or other non-volatile memory on bootup and is available in any operating-system mode. The HID specification defines boot-interface protocols for keyboards and mice. If a device has a boot interface, the bInterfaceProtocol field indicates if the device supports the keyboard (1) or mouse (2) interface.

The HID Usage Tables document defines the report format for keyboards and mice that use the boot protocol. The BIOS knows what the boot protocol is and assumes that a boot device will support this protocol, so there's no need to read a report descriptor from the device. Before sending or requesting reports, the BIOS sends the HID-specific Set_Report request to request to use the boot protocol. When the full HID drivers have been loaded, the driver can use Set_Protocol to cause the device to switch from the boot protocol to the report protocol, which uses the report formats defined in the report descriptor

The bInterfaceSubclass field should equal zero if the HID doesn't support a boot protocol.

HID Class Descriptor

The HID class descriptor identifies additional descriptors for HID communications. The class descriptor has seven or more fields depending on the number of additional descriptors. Table 11-2 shows the fields. Note that the

Table 11-2: The HID class descriptor has 7 or more fields in 9 or more bytes.

Offset (decimal)	Field	Size (bytes)	Description
0	bLength	1	Descriptor size in bytes.
1	bDescriptorType	1	This descriptor's type: 21h to indicate the HID class.
2	bcdHID	2	HID specification release number (BCD).
4	bCountryCode	1	Numeric expression identifying the country for localized hardware (BCD).
5	bNumDescriptors	1	Number of subordinate report and physical descriptors.
6	bDescriptorType	1	The type of a class-specific descriptor that follows. (A report descriptor (required) is type 22h.)
7	wDescriptorLength	2	Total length of the descriptor identified above.
9	bDescriptorType	1	Optional. The type of a class-specific descriptor that follows. A physical descriptor is type 23h.
10	wDescriptorLength	2	Total length of the descriptor identified above. Present only if bDescriptorType is present immediately above. May be followed by additional wDescriptorType and wDescriptorLength fields to identify additional physical descriptors.

descriptor has two or more bDescriptorType fields. One identifies the HID descriptor and the other(s) identify the type of a subordinate descriptor.

The Descriptor

bLength. The length in bytes of the descriptor.

bDescriptorType. The value 21h indicates a HID descriptor.

The Class

bcdHID. The HID specification number that the interface complies with. In BCD format. Version 1.0 is 0100h; Version 1.1 is 0110h.

bCountryCode. If the hardware is localized for a specific country, this field is a code identifying the country. The HID specification lists the codes. If the hardware isn't localized, this field is 00h.

bNumDescriptors. The number of class descriptors that are subordinate to this descriptor.

bDescriptorType. The type of a descriptor that is subordinate to the HID class descriptor. Every HID must contain a report descriptor. One or more physical descriptors are optional.

wDescriptorLength. The length of the descriptor described in the previous field.

Additional bDescriptorType, wDescriptorLength (optional). If there are physical descriptors, the descriptor type and length for each follow in sequence.

Report Descriptors

A report descriptor defines the format and use of the data in the HID's reports. If the device is a mouse, the data reports mouse movements and button clicks. If the device is a relay controller, the data specifies which relays to open and close.

A report descriptor needs to be flexible enough to handle devices with different purposes. The data should use a concise format to keep from wasting storage space in the device or bus time when the data transmits. HID report descriptors achieve both goals by using a format that's more complex and less readable than a more verbose format might be.

A report descriptor is a class-specific descriptor. The host retrieves the descriptor by sending a Get_Descriptor request with the wValue field containing 22h in the high byte.

Listing 11-2 is a bare-bones report descriptor that describes an Input report, an Output report, and a Feature report. The device sends two bytes of data in the Input report. The host sends two bytes of data in the Output report. The Feature report is two bytes that the host can send to the device or request from the device.

Each item in the report descriptor consists of a byte that identifies the item and one or more bytes containing the item's data. The HID class specifica-

```
0x06    0xFFA0                Usage Page (vendor-defined)
0x09    0x01                  Usage (vendor-defined)
0xA1    0x01                  Collection (Application)

0x09    0x03                  Usage (vendor-defined)
0x15    0x00                  Logical Minimum (0)
0x26    0x00FF                Logical Maximum (255)
0x95    0x02                  Report Count (2)
0x75    0x08                  Report Size (8 bits)
0x81    0x02                  Input (Data, Variable, Absolute)

0x09    0x04                  Usage (vendor-defined)
0x15    0x00                  Logical Minimum (0)
0x26    0x00FF                Logical Maximum (255)
0x75    0x08                  Report Count (2)
0x95    0x02                  Report Size (8 bits)
0x91    0x02                  Output (Data, Variable, Absolute)

0x09    0x05                  Usage (vendor-defined)
0x15    0x00                  Logical Minimum (0)
0x26    0x00FF                Logical Maximum (255)
0x75    0x08                  Report Size (8 bits)
0x95    0x02                  Report Count (2)
0xB1    0x02                  Feature (Data, Variable, Absolute)

0xC0                          End Collection
```

Listing 11-2: This report descriptor defines an Input report, an Output report, and a Feature report. Each report transfers two vendor-defined bytes.

tion defines items that a report can contain. Here is what each item in the example descriptor specifies:

The **Usage Page** item is identified by the value 06h and specifies the general function of the device, such as generic desktop control, game control, or alphanumeric display. In the example descriptor, the Usage Page is the vendor-defined value FFA0h. The HID specification lists values for different Usage Pages and values reserved for vendor-defined Usage Pages.

The **Usage** item is identified by the value 09h and specifies the function of an individual report in a Usage Page. For example, Usages available for generic desktop controls include mouse, joystick, and keyboard. Because the example's Usage Page is vendor-defined, all of the Usages in the Usage Page are vendor-defined also. In the example, the Usage is 01h.

The **Collection (Application)** item begins a group of items that together perform a single function, such as keyboard or mouse. Each report descriptor must have an application collection.

The Collection contains three reports. Each report has these items:

A vendor-defined Usage applies to the data in the report.

A Logical Minimum and Logical Maximum specify the range of values that the report can contain.

The Report Count item indicates how many data items the report contains. In the example, each report contains two data items.

The Report Size item indicates how many bits are in each reported data item. In the example, each data item is eight bits.

The final item specifies whether the report is an Input report (81h), Output report (91h), or Feature report (B1h). The bits provided with the item contain additional information about the report data.

The End Collection item closes the Application Collection.

Chapter 12 has more about report formats.

HID-specific Requests

The HID specification defines six HID-specific requests. Table 11-3 lists the requests, and the following pages describe each request in more detail. All HIDs must support Get_Report, and boot devices must support Get_Protocol and Set_Protocol. The other requests (Set_Report, Get_Idle, and Set_Idle) are optional except that a keyboard using the boot protocol must support Set_Idle. If a HID doesn't have an Interrupt OUT endpoint or if the HID is communicating with a 1.0 host such as Windows 98 Gold, a HID that wants to receive reports from the host must support Set_Report.

Table 11-3: The HID class defines six HID-specific requests.

Request Number	Request	Data Source (Data stage)	wValue (high byte, low byte)	wIndex	Data Length (bytes) (wLength)	Data Stage Contents	Required?
01h	Get_ Report	device	report type, report ID	interface	report length	report	yes
02h	Get_ Idle	device	0, report ID	interface	1	idle duration	no
03h	Get_ Protocol	device	0	interface	1	protocol	required for HIDs that support a boot protocol
09h	Set_ Report	host	report type, report ID	interface	report length	report	no
0Ah	Set_ Idle	no Data stage	idle duration, report ID	interface	–	–	no, except for keyboards using the boot protocol
0Bh	Set_ Protocol	no Data stage	0, protocol	interface	–	–	required for HIDs that support a boot protocol

Get_Report

Purpose: The host requests an Input or Feature report from a HID using a control transfer.

Request Number (bRequest): 01h

Source of Data: device

Data Length (wLength): length of the report

Contents of wValue field: The high byte contains the report type (1=Input, 3=Feature), and the low byte contains the report ID. The default report ID is zero.

Contents of wIndex field: the number of the interface the request is directed to.

Contents of data packet in the Data stage: the report

Comments: All HIDs must support this request. See also Set_Report

Get_Idle

Purpose: The host reads the current Idle rate from a HID.

Request Number (bRequest): 02h

Source of Data: device

Data Length (wLength): 1

Contents of wValue field: The high byte is zero. The low byte indicates the report ID that the request applies to. If the low byte is zero, the request applies to all of the HID's Input reports.

Contents of wIndex field: the number of the interface that supports this request.

Contents of data packet in the Data stage: the Idle rate, expressed in units of 4 milliseconds.

Comments: See Set_Idle for more details. HIDs aren't required to support this request.

Get_Protocol

Purpose: The host learns whether the boot or report protocol is currently active in the HID.

Request Number (bRequest): 03h

Source of Data: device

Data Length (wLength): 1

Contents of wValue field: 0

Contents of wIndex field: the number of the interface that supports this request.

Contents of data packet in the Data stage: The protocol (0 = boot protocol, 1 = report protocol).

Comments: Boot devices must support this request. See also Set_Protocol.

Set_Report

Purpose: The host sends an Output or Feature report to a HID using a control transfer.

Request Number (bRequest): 09h

Source of Data: host

Data Length (wLength): length of the report

Contents of wValue field: The high byte contains the report type (2=Output, 3=Feature), and the low byte contains the report ID. The default report ID is zero.

Contents of wIndex field: the number of the interface the request is directed to.

Contents of data packet in the Data stage: the report

Comments: If a HID interface doesn't have an Interrupt OUT endpoint or if the host complies only with version 1.0 of the HID specification, this request is the only way the host can send data to the HID. HIDs aren't required to support this request. See also Get_Report.

Set_Idle

Purpose: Saves bandwidth by limiting the reporting frequency of an interrupt IN endpoint when the data hasn't changed since the last report.

Request Number (bRequest): 0Ah

Source of Data: no Data stage

Data Length (wLength): no Data stage

Contents of wValue field: The high byte sets the duration, or the maximum amount of time between reports. A value of zero means that the HID will send a report only when the report data has changed. The low byte indicates the report ID that the request applies to. If the low byte is zero, the request applies to all of the HID's Input reports.

Contents of wIndex field: the number of the interface that supports this request.

Contents of data packet in the Data stage: no Data stage.

Comments: The duration is in units of 4 milliseconds, which gives a range of 4 to 1,020 milliseconds. No matter what the duration value is, if the report data has changed since the last Input report sent, on receiving an interrupt IN token packet, the HID sends a report. If the data hasn't changed and the duration time hasn't elapsed since the last report, the HID returns NAK. If the data hasn't changed and the duration time has elapsed since the last report, the HID sends a report. A duration value of zero indicates an infinite duration: the HID sends a report only if the report data has changed and responds to all other interrupt IN requests with NAK.

If the HID returns a STALL in response to this request, the HID can send reports whether or not the data has changed. On enumerating a HID, the Windows HID driver attempts to set the idle rate to zero. The HID should Stall this request if an infinite Idle duration isn't wanted! HIDs aren't required to support this request except for keyboards using the boot protocol.

See also Get_Idle.

Set_Protocol

Purpose: The host specifies whether the HID should use the boot or report protocol.

Request Number (bRequest): 0Bh

Source of Data: no Data stage

Data Length (wLength): no Data stage

Contents of wValue field: the protocol (0 = boot protocol, 1 = report protocol).

Contents of wIndex field: the number of the interface that supports this request.

Contents of data packet in the Data stage: no Data stage

Comments: Boot devices must support this request. See also Get_Protocol

Transferring Data

When enumeration is complete, the host has identified the device interface as a HID and has established pipes with the interface's endpoints and learned what report formats to use to send and receive data.

The host can then request reports using either interrupt IN transfers and/or control transfers with Get_Report requests. The device also has the option to support receiving reports using interrupt OUT transfers and/or control transfers with Set_Report requests.

If you don't have example firmware for Get_Report and Set_Report, enumeration code can serve as a model. Get_Report is a control Read transfer that behaves in a similar way to Get_Descriptor except that the device returns a report instead of a descriptor. Set_Report is a control Write transfer. Unfortunately, the only standard USB request with a host-to-device Data stage is the rarely supported Set_Descriptor, so example code for control Write transfers is harder to find.

About the Example Code

The example code in this chapter is written for the Microchip PIC18F4550 introduced in Chapter 6. The code is based on Microchip's USB Firmware Framework. The Framework code is for the PIC18 family of microcontrollers but can give an idea of how to structure code for other CPUs. My code is adapted from Microchip's mouse code and implements a generic HID device that exchanges reports in both directions.

Portions of the code can be useful even if your device isn't a HID. The control-transfer examples can serve as models for responding to other class-specific and vendor-specific requests. From the firmware's point of view, bulk and interrupt transfers are identical, so the interrupt-transfer code can serve as a model for any firmware that uses bulk or interrupt transfers.

In the Framework code, a group of system files handles general USB tasks and class-specific tasks. These files typically require no changes or only minor changes and additions for specific applications. The system files include these:

usbmmap.c allocates memory for variables, endpoints, and other buffers used in USB communications.

usbdrv.c contains functions to detect device attachment and removal, check and respond to USB hardware interrupts, enter and exit the Suspend state, and respond to bus resets.

usbctrltrf.c contains functions for handling transactions in control transfers. The functions decode received Setup packets, manage the sending and receiving of data in the Data stage, and manage the sending and receiving of status information in the Status stage.

usb9.c contains functions that manage responding to the requests defined in Chapter 9 of the USB specification. The functions decode received requests, provide pointers to descriptors and other requested data to return, and take requested actions such as selecting a configuration or setting an address.

hid.c contains functions that manage tasks that are specific to the HID class. The functions decode received Setup data directed to the HID interface, define pointers to data to be sent and locations to store received data in control and interrupt transfers, and respond to other HID-specific requests such as Get_Idle and Set_Idle.

Additional files handle other tasks:

usbdesc.c contains structures that hold the device's descriptors, including the device descriptor, configuration and subordinate descriptors, string descriptors, and report descriptor. This information will of course differ for every device.

user_generic_hid.c contains most of the code that is specific to the generic HID application. The functions obtain the data that the device will send in reports and use the data received in reports.

main.c initializes the system and executes a loop that checks the bus status and calls functions in the *user_generic_hid* file to carry out the device's purpose.

The sections that follow contain excerpts from this code. The excerpts concentrate on the application-specific code used to send and receive reports.

The complete device firmware and host applications to communicate with the device are available from *www.Lvr.com*.

See Chapter 6 for an introduction to the '18F4550's architecture.

Sending Reports via Interrupt Transfers

When the HID driver is loaded on the host, the host controller begins sending periodic IN token packets to the HID's interrupt IN endpoint. The endpoint should NAK these packets until the HID has an Input report to send. To send data in an interrupt transfer, device firmware typically places the data in the endpoint's buffer and configures the endpoint to send the data to the host on receiving an IN token packet.

The code below executes after the host has configured the HID. The *usbmmap.c* file declares hid_report_in as a char array whose length equals the endpoint's wMaxPacketSize:

```
extern volatile far unsigned char
   hid_report_in[HID_INT_IN_EP_SIZE];
```

The code initializes the interrupt IN endpoint by setting values in the endpoint's buffer descriptor (HID_BD_IN):

```
// Set the endpoint's address register to the address
// of the hid_report_in buffer.

HID_BD_IN.ADR = (byte*)&hid_report_in;

// Set the status register bits:
// _UCPU = the CPU owns the buffer.
// _DAT1 = a DATA1 data toggle is expected next.
// (Before sending data, call the mUSBBufferReady
// macro to toggle the data toggle.)

HID_BD_IN.Stat._byte = _UCPU|_DAT1;
```

Listing 11-3 is a function that accepts a pointer to a buffer containing report data (*buffer) and the number of bytes to send (len) and makes the data available in the endpoint's buffer.

```
void HIDTxReport(char *buffer, byte len)
{
    byte i;

    // len can be no larger than the endpoint's wMaxPacketSize
    // (HID_INT_IN_EP_SIZE). Trim len if necessary

    if(len > HID_INT_IN_EP_SIZE)
        len = HID_INT_IN_EP_SIZE;

    // Copy data from the passed buffer to the endpoint's buffer.

    for (i = 0; i < len; i++)
        hid_report_in[i] = buffer[i];

    // To send len bytes, set the buffer descriptor's count
    // register to len.

    HID_BD_IN.Cnt = len;

    // Toggle the data toggle and transfer ownership of the
    // buffer to the SIE, which will send the data on receiving
    // an interrupt IN token packet.

    mUSBBufferReady(HID_BD_IN);

}//end HIDTxReport
```

Listing 11-3: The HIDTxReport function provides data to send in an Input report at the HID's interrupt IN endpoint and prepares the endpoint to send the report.

This code calls the function:

```
char transmit_buffer[2];

// Place report data in transmit_buffer:

transmit_buffer[0] = 104;
transmit_buffer[1] = 105;

// If necessary, wait until the CPU owns the interrupt
// IN endpoint's buffer.

while(mHIDTxIsBusy())
{
    // Service USB interrupts.

    USBDriverService();
}

// Make the report data available to send in the next
// interrupt IN transaction.

HIDTxReport(transmit_buffer, 2);
```

Before calling the function, the firmware places the report data in a char array (transmit_buffer) and waits if necessary for the mHIDTxIsBusy macro to return false, indicating that the CPU owns the HID's interrupt IN endpoint buffer. While waiting, the loop calls the USBDriverService function to service any USB interrupts that occur.

In the HIDTxReport function, if the len value passed to the function is greater than the endpoint's wMaxPacketSize value, len is trimmed to wMaxPacketSize. The function copies the report data from the passed buffer to the endpoint's buffer (hid_report_in).

The endpoint's byte-count register (HID_BD_IN.Cnt) holds the number of bytes to send. The macro mUSBBufferReady toggles the data-toggle bit and transfers ownership of the endpoint buffer to the SIE. On receiving an interrupt IN token packet, the SIE sends the packet and returns ownership of the buffer to the CPU.

Receiving Reports via Interrupt Transfers

If the HID interface has an interrupt OUT endpoint and the operating system supports USB 1.1 or later, the host can send Output reports to the device using interrupt transfers.

To receive data in an interrupt transfer, device firmware typically configures the endpoint to receive data from the host on receiving an OUT token packet, and an interrupt or polled register announces that data has been received.

The code below executes after the host has configured the HID. The *usbmmap.c* file declares hid_report_out as a char array whose length equals the endpoint's wMaxPacketSize:

```
extern volatile far unsigned char
    hid_report_out[HID_INT_OUT_EP_SIZE];
```

The code initializes the interrupt OUT endpoint by setting values in the endpoint's buffer descriptor (HID_BD_OUT):

```
// Set the endpoint's byte-count register to the
// length of the output report expected.

HID_BD_OUT.Cnt = sizeof(hid_report_out);

// Set the endpoint's address register to the address
// of the hid_report_out buffer.

HID_BD_OUT.ADR = (byte*)&hid_report_out;

// Set the status register bits:

// _USIE =  The SIE owns the buffer.
// _DATA0 = a DATA0 data toggle is expected next.
// _DTSEN = Enable data-toggle synchronization.

HID_BD_OUT.Stat._byte = _USIE|_DAT0|_DTSEN;
```

The endpoint is then ready to receive a report. Listing 11-4 is a function that retrieves data that has arrived at an interrupt OUT endpoint. The function accepts a pointer to a buffer to copy the report data to (*buffer) and the

```
byte HIDRxReport(char *buffer, byte len)
{
    // hid_rpt_rx_len is a byte variable declared in hid.c
    hid_rpt_rx_len = 0;

    if(!mHIDRxIsBusy())
    {
        // If necessary, trim len to equal
        // the actual number of bytes received.

        if(len > HID_BD_OUT.Cnt)
            len = HID_BD_OUT.Cnt;

        // The report data is in hid_report_out.
        // Copy the data to the user's buffer (buffer).

        for(hid_rpt_rx_len = 0;
            hid_rpt_rx_len < len;
            hid_rpt_rx_len++)

            buffer[hid_rpt_rx_len] =
                hid_report_out[hid_rpt_rx_len];

        // Prepare the endpoint buffer for next OUT transaction.

        // Set the endpoint's count register to the length of
        // the report buffer.

        HID_BD_OUT.Cnt = sizeof(hid_report_out);

        // The mUSBBufferReady macro toggles the data toggle
        // and transfers ownership of the buffer to the SIE.

        mUSBBufferReady(HID_BD_OUT);

    }//end if

        return hid_rpt_rx_len;

}//end HIDRxReport
```

Listing 11-4: The HIDRxReport function retrieves data received in an Output report at the HID's interrupt OUT endpoint.

number of bytes expected (len). The function returns the number of bytes copied or zero if no data is available.

This code calls the function:

```
byte number_of_bytes_read;
char receive_buffer[2];

number_of_bytes_read =
    HIDRxReport(receive_buffer, 2);
```

In the HIDRxReport function, the mHIDRxIsBusy macro checks to see if the CPU has ownership of the buffer. If not, the function returns zero. Otherwise, if necessary, the function trims the expected number of bytes (len) to match the number of bytes received as reported in the endpoint's byte-count register (HID_BD_OUT.Cnt). The received report is in the buffer hid_report_out. The function copies the received bytes from hid_report_out to the buffer that was passed to the function (receive_buffer). To prepare for a new transaction, the function sets the endpoint's byte-count register to the size of the hid_report_out buffer and calls the mUSBBufferReady macro, which toggles the data toggle and transfers ownership of the buffer to the SIE. The endpoint can then receive new data. When the function returns, the report data is available in receive_buffer. The hid_rpt_rx_len variable contains the number of bytes received (zero if no bytes were received).

Sending Reports via Control Transfers

To send an Input or Feature report using a control transfer, device firmware must detect the Get_Report code in the bRequest field of the Setup stage of a control request directed to the HID interface. The firmware then configures Endpoint 0 to send the report in the Data stage and receive the host's response in the Status stage.

Microchip's Framework HID example includes code that detects the request and calls the HIDGetReportHandler function in Listing 11-5.

The function examines the high byte of the wValue field of the Setup stage's data packet (MSB(SetupPkt.W_Value)) to determine if the host is request-

```
void HIDGetReportHandler(void)
{
    // The report type is in the high byte of the setup packet's
    // wValue field. 1 = Input; 3 = Feature.

    switch(MSB(SetupPkt.W_Value))
    {
        byte count;

        case 1: // Input report

            // Find out which report ID was specified.
            // The report ID is in the low byte (LSB) of the
            // wValue field. This example supports Report ID 0.
            switch(LSB(SetupPkt.W_Value))
            {
                case 0: // Report ID 0

                // The HID class code will handle the request.
                ctrl_trf_session_owner = MUID_HID;

                // Provide the data to send.
                GetInputReport0();

                break;

                case 1: // Report ID 1
                  // Add code to handle Report ID 1 here.
                break;

            } // end switch(LSB(SetupPkt.W_Value))

            break;

        case 3: // Feature report

            // Add code to handle Feature reports here.

    } // end switch(MSB(SetupPkt.W_Value))
}//end HIDGetReportHandler
```

Listing 11-5: The HIDGetReportHandler function is called on receiving a Get_Report request.

ing an Input or Feature report. The low byte of the wValue field (LSB(Set-upPkt.W_Value)) is the report ID that names the specific report requested.

If the code supports the requested report, the ctrl_trf_session_owner variable is set to MUID_HID. The firmware handling other stages of the transfer can use this variable to detect who is handling the request.

To send Input report 0, the function calls the GetInputReport0 function (Listing 11-6). This function sets pSrc.bRam, a pointer to data in RAM, to the location of the report's data (hid_report_in).

The Framework firmware prepares Endpoint 0 to send the data that pSrc.bRam points to on receiving an IN token packet and accepts the host's zero-length packet in the Status stage of the transfer.

The code for sending other reports, including Input reports with other report IDs and Feature reports, is much the same except that the source of the report's contents will change depending on the report.

Receiving Reports via Control Transfers

To receive an Output or Feature report in a control transfer, the firmware must detect the Set_Report request in the bRequest field of a request directed to the HID interface. The device must also receive the report data in the Data stage and return a handshake in the Status stage. Microchip's Framework HID example includes code that detects the request and calls the HIDSetReportHandler function in Listing 11-7.

The function examines the high byte of the wValue field of the Setup stage's data packet (MSB(SetupPkt.W_Value)) to determine if the host is sending an Output or Feature report. The low byte of the wValue field (LSB(Setup-Pkt.W_Value)) is the report ID that names the specific report being sent.

If the code supports the requested report, the ctrl_trf_session_owner variable is set to MUID_HID so the firmware that handles other stages of the transfer can detect who is handling the request.

The Framework firmware prepares Endpoint 0 to receive the report data on receiving an OUT token packet.

```
void GetInputReport0(void)
{
    byte count;

    // Set pSrc.bRam to point to the report.

    pSrc.bRam = (byte*)&hid_report_in;
}
```

Listing 11-6: The GetInputReport0 function handles report-specific tasks.

When Output report 0 arrives in the Data stage of the transfer, the Framework firmware makes the data available at the RAM location pointed to by pDst.bRam and manages the sending of a zero-length packet in the transfer's Status stage. In this example, pDst.bRam has been set to point to the char array hid_report_out. The firmware can call a function that uses the report data:

```
if (ctrl_trf_session_owner == MUID_HID)
{
    // Call a function that uses the report data.

    HandleControlOutReport();
}
```

The code for receiving other reports, including Output reports with other report IDs and Feature reports, is much the same except that the firmware's use of the report's contents will change depending on the report.

```
void HIDSetReportHandler(void)
{
    // The report type is in the high byte of the Setup packet's
    // wValue field. 2 = Output; 3 = Feature.

    switch(MSB(SetupPkt.W_Value))
    {
        case 2: // Output report

            // The report ID is in the low byte of the Setup
            // packet's wValue field.
            // This example supports Report ID 0.

            switch(LSB(SetupPkt.W_Value))
            {
                case 0: // Report ID 0

                    // The HID-class code will handle the request.
                    ctrl_trf_session_owner = MUID_HID;

                    // When the report arrives in the Data stage,
                    // the report data will be available in
                    // hid_report_out.
                    pDst.bRam = (byte*)&hid_report_out;
                    break;

                case 1: // Report ID 1
                // Place code to handle Report ID 1 here.

            } // end switch(LSB(SetupPkt.W_Value))

            break;

        case 3: // Feature report

            // Place code to handle Feature reports here.

    } // end switch(MSB(SetupPkt.W_Value))

} //end HIDSetReportHandler
```

Listing 11-7: The HIDSetReportHandler function prepares to receive an Output or Feature report from the host.

12

Human Interface Devices: Reports

Chapter 11 introduced the reports that HIDs use to exchange data. A report can be a basic buffer of bytes or a complex assortment of items, each with assigned functions and units. This chapter shows how to design a report to fit a specific application.

Report Structure

A report descriptor may contain any of dozens of items arranged in various combinations. The advantage of a more complex descriptor is that the device can provide detailed information about the data it sends and expects to receive. The descriptor can specify the values' uses and what units to apply to the raw data. From a report descriptor, an application can learn whether a device supports a particular feature, such as force feedback on a joystick.

But just because the specification defines an item that could apply to a device's data doesn't mean that the report descriptor has to use that item. For vendor-specific devices that are intended for use with a single application, the application often knows in advance the type, size, and order of the data in a report, so there's no need to obtain this information from the device. For example, when the vendor of a data-acquisition unit creates an application for use with the unit, the vendor already knows the data format the device uses in its reports. At most, the application might check the product ID and release number from the device descriptor to learn whether the application can request a particular setting or action.

Some of the details about report structures can get tedious, and it's rarely necessary to understand every nuance about every item type. So feel free to skim through the details in this chapter and come back to them later if you need to.

A report descriptor contains one or more controls and data items that describe values to be transferred in one or more reports. A control is a button, switch, or other physical entity that operates or regulates an aspect of a device. Data items describe any other data the report transfers. Each control or data item has a defined scope. Some items can apply to multiple values, eliminating the need for repetition.

Using the HID Descriptor Tool

The HID Descriptor Tool (Figure 12-1) is a free utility available from the USB-IF. The tool helps in creating report descriptors, and will also check your descriptor's structure and report errors. Instead of having to look up the values that correspond to each item in your report, you can select the item from a list and enter the value you want to assign to it, and the tool adds the item to the descriptor. You can also add items manually. The Parse Descriptor function displays the raw and interpreted values in your descriptor and comments on any errors found. When you have a descriptor with no errors, you can convert it to the syntax required by your firmware. The tool has limited support for vendor-specific items, however, and may flag these as errors.

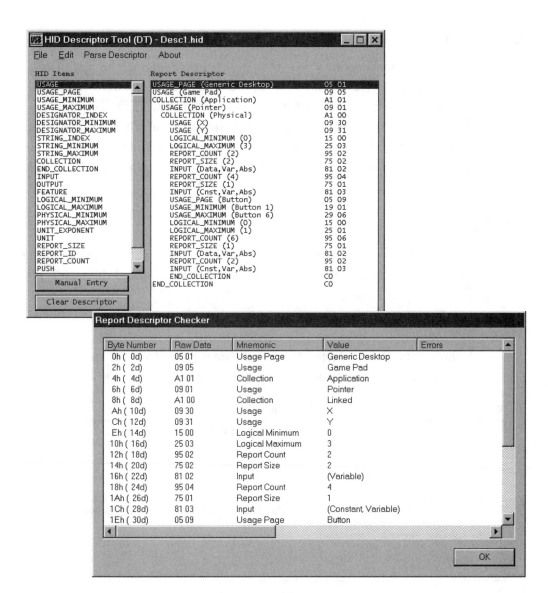

Figure 12-1: The HID Descriptor Tool helps in creating and testing HID report descriptors.

Control and Data Item Values

Several documents define values that reports may contain. The first place to look is the *HID Usage Tables* document, which defines values for generic desktop controls, simulation controls, game controls, LEDs, buttons, telephone devices, and more. The document also tells you where to find values defined elsewhere. Some are in the HID specification, while others are in the class specifications for specific device functions such as monitor, power, and point-of-sale devices.

Item Types

The HID specification defines two report item types: short items and long items. As of HID 1.1, there are no defined Long items, and the type is just reserved for future use.

Short Items

A Short item's 1-byte prefix specifies the item type, item tag, and item size. These are the elements that make up the prefix byte:

Bit Number	Contents	Description
0	Item Size	Number of bytes in the item
1		
2	Item Type	Item scope: Main, Global, or Local
3		
4	Item Tag	Numeric value that indicates the item's function
5		
6		
7		

The item size (bits 1 and 0) indicates how many data bytes the item contains. Note that an item size of 3 (11 in binary) corresponds to 4 data bytes:

Item Size (binary)	Number of Data Bytes
00	0
01	1
10	2
11	4

The item type (bits 3 and 2) describes the scope of the item: Main (00), Global (01), or Local (10). Main items define or group data fields in the descriptor. Global items describe data. Local items define characteristics of individual controls or data. (This chapter has more information about these item types.)

The item tag (bits 4-7) indicates the item's function.

Long Items

A Long item uses multiple bytes to store the same information as the Short item's 1-byte prefix stores. A Long item's 1-byte prefix (FEh) identifies the item as a Long item. In addition, the item has a byte that specifies the number of data bytes, a byte containing the item tag, and up to 255 bytes of data.

The Main Item Type

A Main item defines or groups data items within a report descriptor. There are five Main item types. Input, Output, and Feature items each define fields in a type of report. Collection and End Collection items group related items within a report. The default value for all Main items is zero.

Input, Output, and Feature Items

Table 12-1 shows supported values for the Input, Output, and Feature items, including the item prefix and the meanings of the bits in the data that follows the prefix.

An Input item applies to data a device sends to the host. An Input report contains one or more Input items. The host uses interrupt IN transfers or Get_Report requests to request Input reports.

An Output item applies to information that the host sends to the device. An Output report contains one or more Output items. Output reports contain data that reports the states of controls, such as whether to open or close a switch or the intensity to apply to an effect. As explained earlier, if the HID has an interrupt OUT endpoint, a HID 1.1-compliant host can use interrupt OUT transfers to send Output reports. All hosts can also use Set_Report requests to send Output reports.

A Feature item typically applies to information that the host sends to the device. However, it's also possible for the host to read Feature items from a device. A Feature report contains one or more Feature items. Feature reports often contain configuration settings that affect the overall behavior of the device or one of its components. The reports often control settings that you might otherwise adjust in a physical control panel. For example, the host may have a virtual (on-screen) control panel to enable users to select and control a device's capabilities and settings. The host uses control transfers with Set_Report and Get_Report requests to send and receive Feature reports.

Following each Input, Output, or Feature item prefix are up to 9 bits that describe the item's data. (An additional 23 bits are reserved.) For example, an Input item prefix followed by 9 bits of data has the value 82h. The prefix's high four bits equal 08h to indicate an Input item, and the low four bits equal 02h to indicate that the data's 9 bits require 2 bytes. An Input item prefix followed by 8 bits of data has the value 81h. The prefix's high four bits equal 08h to indicate an Input item, and the low four bits equal 01h to because the data's 8 bits fit in 1 byte. The device firmware and host software may use or ignore the information in these items.

Table 12-1: The bits that follow Input, Output, and Feature Item prefixes describe the data in report items.

Main Item Prefix	Bit Number	Meaning if bit = 0	Meaning if bit = 1
Input (100000nn, where nn=the number of bytes in the data following the prefix) Use 81h for 1 byte of item data or use 82h for 2 bytes of item data.	0	Data	Constant
	1	Array	Variable
	2	Absolute	Relative
	3	No wrap	Wrap
	4	Linear	Non-linear
	5	Preferred state	No preferred state
	6	No null position	Null state
	7	Reserved	
	8	Bit field	Buffered bytes
	9-31	Reserved	
Output (100100nn, where nn=the number of bytes in the data following the prefix) Use 91h for 1 byte of item data or use 92h for 2 bytes of item data.	0	Data	Constant
	1	Array	Variable
	2	Absolute	Relative
	3	No wrap	Wrap
	4	Linear	Non-linear
	5	Preferred state	No preferred state
	6	No null position	Null state
	7	Non-volatile	Volatile
	8	Bit field	Buffered bytes
	9-31	Reserved	
Feature (101100nn, where nn=the number of bytes in the data following the prefix) Use B1h for 1 byte of item data or use B2h for 2 bytes of item data.	0	Data	Constant
	1	Array	Variable
	2	Absolute	Relative
	3	No wrap	Wrap
	4	Linear	Non-linear
	5	Preferred state	No preferred state
	6	No null position	Null state
	7	Non-volatile	Volatile
	8	Bit field	Buffered bytes
	9-31	Reserved	

The bit functions are the same for Input, Output, and Feature items, except that Input items don't support the volatile/non-volatile bit. These are the uses for each bit:

Data | Constant. Data means that the contents of the item are modifiable (read/write). Constant means the contents are not modifiable (read-only).

Array | Variable. This bit specifies whether the data reports the state of every control (Variable) or just reports the states of controls that are asserted, or active (Array). Reporting only the asserted controls results in a more compact report for devices such as keyboards, where there are many controls (keys) but only one or a few are asserted at the same time.

For example, if a keypad has eight keys, setting this bit to Variable would mean that the keypad's report would contain a bit for each key. In the report descriptor, the report size would be one bit, the report count would be eight, and the total amount of data sent would be eight bits. Setting the bit to Array would mean that each key has an assigned index, and the keypad's report would contain only the indexes of keys that are pressed. With eight keys, the report size would be three bits, which can report a key number from 0 through 7. The report count would equal the maximum number of simultaneous keypresses that could be reported. If the user can press only one key at a time, the report count would be 1 and the total amount of data sent would be just 3 bits. If the user can press all of the keys at once, the report count would be 8 and the total amount of data sent would be 24 bits.

An out-of-range value reported for an Array item indicates that no controls are asserted.

Absolute | Relative. Absolute means that the value is based on a fixed origin. Relative means that the data indicates the change from the last reading. A joystick normally reports absolute data (the joystick's current position), while a mouse reports relative data (how far the mouse has moved since the last report).

No Wrap | Wrap. Wrap indicates that the value rolls over to the minimum if the value continues to increment after reaching its maximum and that the value rolls over to the maximum if the value continues to decrement after reaching its minimum. An item specified as No Wrap that exceeds the specified limits may report a value outside the limits. This bit doesn't apply to Array data.

Linear | Non-linear. Linear indicates that the measured data and the reported value have a linear relationship. In other words, a graph of the reported data and the property being measured forms a straight line. In non-linear data, a graph of the reported data and the property being measured forms a curve. This bit doesn't apply to Array data.

Preferred State | No Preferred State. Preferred state indicates that the control will return to a particular state when the user isn't interacting with it. A momentary pushbutton has a preferred state (out) when no one is pressing the button. A toggle switch has no preferred state and remains in the last state selected by a user. This bit doesn't apply to Array data.

No Null Position | Null State. Null state indicates that the control supports a state where the control isn't sending meaningful data. A control indicates that it's in the null state by sending a value outside the range defined by its Logical Minimum and Logical Maximum. No Null Position indicates that any data sent by the control is meaningful data. A hat switch on a joystick is in a null position when it isn't being pressed. This bit doesn't apply to Array data.

Non-volatile | Volatile. The Volatile bit applies only to Output and Feature report data. Volatile means that the device can change the value on its own, without host interaction, as well as when the host sends a report requesting the device to change the value. For example, a control panel may have a control that users can set in two ways. A user may use a mouse to click a button on the screen to cause the host to send a report to the device, or a user may press a physical button on the device. Non-volatile means that the device changes the value only when the host requests a new value in a report.

When the host is sending a report and doesn't want to change a volatile item, the value to assign to the item depends on whether the data is defined as relative or absolute. If a volatile item is defined as relative, a report that assigns a value of 0 should result in no change. If a volatile item is defined as absolute, a report that assigns an out-of-range value should result in no change.

This bit doesn't apply to Array data.

Bit Field | Buffered Bytes. Bit Field means that each bit or a group of bits in a byte can represent a separate piece of data and the byte doesn't represent a single quantity. The application interprets the contents of the field. Buffered Bytes means that the data consists of one or more bytes. The report size for Buffered Byte items must be eight. This bit doesn't apply to Array data. Note that this bit is bit 8 in the item's data so using this bit requires two data bytes in the item.

Collection and End Collection Items

All of the report types can use Collection and End Collection items to group related items.

The three defined types of collections are application, physical, and logical. Vendors can also define collection types. Collections can be nested. Table 12-2 shows the values of the Collection and End Collection tags and the defined values for the different collection types.

An application collection contains items that have a common purpose or that together carry out a single function. For example, the boot descriptor for a keyboard groups the keypress and LED data in an application collection. All report items must be in an application collection.

A physical collection contains items that represent data at a single geometric point. A device that collects a variety of sensor readings from multiple locations might group the data for each location in a physical collection. The boot descriptor for a mouse groups the button and position indicators in a physical collection.

A logical collection forms a data structure consisting of items of different types that are linked by the collection. An example is the contents of a data buffer and a count of the number of bytes in the buffer.

Each collection begins with a Collection item and ends with an End Collection item. All Main items between the Collection and End Collection items are part of the collection. Each collection must have a Usage tag (described below).

Table 12-2: Data values for the Collection and End Collection Main Item Tags.

Main Item Type	Value	Description
Collection (A1h)	00h	Physical
	01h	Application
	02h	Logical
	03h-7Fh	Reserved
	80h-FFh	Vendor-defined
End Collection (C0h)	None	Closes a collection

A top-level collection is a collection that isn't nested within another collection. A HID interface can have more than one top-level collection, with each top-level collection representing a different HID. For example, a keyboard with an embedded pointing device can have a HID interface with two top-level collections, one for the pointing-device's reports and one for the keyboard's reports. Unlike HIDs in separate interfaces, these HIDs share interrupt endpoints.

If a report contains an unknown vendor-defined collection type, the host should ignore all Main items in the collection. If a known collection type has an unknown Usage, the host should ignore all items in the collection.

The Global Item Type

Global items identify reports and describe the data in them, including characteristics such as the data's function, maximum and minimum allowed values, and the size and number of report items. A Global item tag applies to every item that follows until the next Global tag. To save storage space in the device, the report descriptor doesn't have to repeat values that don't change from one item to the next. There are 12 defined Global items, shown in Table 12-3. The following sections describe the items in more detail.

Identifying the Report

Report ID. This value can identify a specific report. A HID can support multiple reports of the same type, with each report having its own report

Table 12-3: There are twelve defined Global items.

Global Item Type	Value (nn indicates the number of bytes that follow)	Description
Usage Page	000001nn	Specifies the data's usage or function.
Logical Minimum	000101nn	Smallest value that an item will report.
Logical Maximum	001001nn	Largest value that an item will report.
Physical Minimum	001101nn	The logical minimum expressed in physical units.
Physical Maximum	010001nn	The logical maximum expressed in physical units.
Unit exponent	010101nn	Base 10 exponent of units.
Unit	011001nn	Unit values.
Report Size	011101nn	Size of an item's fields in bits.
Report ID	100001nn	Prefix that identifies a report.
Report Count	100101nn	The number of data fields for an item.
Push	101001nn	Places a copy of the global item state table on the stack.
Pop	101101nn	Replaces the item state table with the last structure pushed onto the stack.
Reserved	110001nn to 111101nn	For future use.

ID, contents, and format. This way, a transfer doesn't have to include every piece of data every time. Often, however, the simplicity of having a single report is more important than the need to reduce the bandwidth used by longer reports.

In a report descriptor, a Report ID item applies to all items that follow until the next Report ID. If there is no Report ID item, the default ID of zero is assumed. A descriptor should not declare a Report ID of zero. The Report IDs are specific to each report type, so a HID can have one report of each type with the default ID. However, if at least one report type uses multiple report IDs, every report in the HID must have a declared ID. For example, if an interface supports Report ID 1 and Report ID 2 for Feature reports, any Input or Output reports must also have a Report ID greater than zero.

In a transfer that uses a Set_Report or Get_Report request, the host specifies a report ID in the Setup transaction, in the low byte of the wValue field. In an interrupt transfer, if the interface supports more than one report ID, the report ID precedes the report data on the bus. If the interface supports only the default report ID of zero, the report ID isn't sent with the report when using interrupt transfers.

Under Windows, the report buffer provided to an API call must be large enough to hold the report plus one byte for the report ID. When a HID supports multiple report IDs for Input reports of different sizes, the Windows HID driver requires applications to use a buffer large enough to hold the longest report. When the HID supports multiple reports of the same type and different sizes and the HID is sending a report whose data is a multiple of the endpoint's maximum packet size, the HID indicates the end of the report data by sending a zero-length data packet

For Input reports when there are multiple Input Report IDs, the host's driver has no way to request a specific report from the HID. On receiving the IN token packet, the device returns whatever report is in its buffer. In other words, the device firmware decides which report to send. At the host, the HID driver stores the received report and its report ID in a buffer.

Describing the Data's Use

The Global items that describe the data and how it will be used are Usage Page, Logical and Physical Maximums and Minimums, Unit, and Unit Exponent. Each of these items helps the receiver of the report interpret the report's data. All but the Usage Page are involved with converting raw report data to values with units attached. The items make it possible for a report to contain data in a compact form, with the receiver of the data responsible for converting the data to meaningful values. However, the sender of the report data may instead choose to do some or all of the converting.

Usage Page. An item's Usage is a 32-bit value that identifies a function that a device performs. A Usage contains two values: the upper 16 bits are a Global Usage Page item and the lower 16 bits are a Local Usage item. The value in the Local Usage item is a Usage ID. The term *Usage* can refer to either the 32-bit value or the 16-bit Local value. To prevent confusion, some sources use the term Extended Usage to refer to the 32-bit value. In Microsoft's documentation, the USAGE type is a 16-bit value that can contain a Usage Page or a Usage ID.

Multiple items can share a Usage Page while having different Usage IDs. After a Usage Page appears in a report, all Usage IDs that follow use that Usage Page until a new Usage Page is declared.

The HID Usage Tables document lists the defined Usage Pages and their values and also names the section or other document that describes each page and its indexes. There are Usage Pages for many common device types, including generic desktop controls (mouse, keyboard, joystick), digitizer, bar-code scanner, camera control, and various game controls. In specialized devices that don't have a defined Usage Page, a vendor can define the Usage Page using values from FF00h to FFFFh.

Logical Minimum and Logical Maximum. The Logical Minimum and Logical Maximum define the limits for reported values. The limits are expressed in "logical units," which means that they use the same units as the values they describe. For example, if a device reports readings of up to 500 milliamperes in units of 2 milliamperes, the Logical Maximum is 250.

If the most significant bit of the highest byte is 1, the value is negative, expressed as a two's complement. (To find the negative value represented by a two's complement, complement each bit and add 1 to the result.) Using 1-byte values, 00h to 7Fh are the positive decimal values 0 through 127, and FFh to 80h are the negative decimal values -1 through -128.

The HID specification says that if both the Logical Minimum and Logical Maximum are considered positive, there's no need for a sign bit. But the report-descriptor test in the USB-IF Compliance Tool assumes that if the most-significant bit is 1, the value is negative. These values will fail the compliance test because the Logical Minimum (0) is greater than the Logical Maximum (-1):

```
0x15 0x00    // Logical Minimum
0x25 0xFF    // Logical Maximum WRONG!
```

If the desired result is a minimum of zero and a maximum of 255, the solution is to use a 2-byte value for the maximum:

```
0x15 0x00      // Logical Minimum
0x26 0x00FF    // Logical Maximum
```

Note that the Logical Maximum item tag is now 26h to indicate that the data that follows the tag is two bytes. Because the most-significant bit of the Logical Maximum is zero, the value is assumed to be positive and the compliance test accepts the values as valid.

Converting Units

The Physical Minimum, Physical Maximum, Unit Exponent, and Unit items define how to convert reported values into more meaningful units.

Physical Minimum and Physical Maximum. The Physical Minimum and Physical Maximum define the limits for a value when expressed in the units defined by the Units tag. In the earlier example of values of 0 through 250 in units of 2 milliamperes, the Physical Minimum is 0 and the Physical Maximum is 500. The receiving device uses the logical and physical limit values to obtain the value in the desired units. In the example, reporting the data in units of 2 milliamperes means that the value can transfer in a single byte, with the receiver of the data using the Physical Minimum and Maximum values to translate to milliamperes. The price is a loss in resolution, compared to reporting 1 bit per milliampere. If the report doesn't specify the values, they default to the same as the Logical Minimum and Logical Maximum.

Unit Exponent. The Unit Exponent specifies what power of 10 to apply to the value obtained after using the logical and physical limits to convert the value into the desired units. The exponent can range from -8 to +7. A value of 0 causes the value to be multiplied by 10^0, or 1, which is the same as applying no exponent. These are the codes:

Exponent	0	1	2	3	4	5	6	7	-8	-7	-6	-5	-4	-3	-2	-1
Code	00h	01h	02h	03h	04h	05h	06h	07h	08h	09h	0Ah	0Bh	0Ch	0Dh	0Eh	0Fh

For example, if the value obtained is 1234 and the Unit Exponent is 0Eh, the final value is 12.34.

Unit. The Unit tag specifies what units to apply to the report data after the value is converted using the Physical and Unit Exponent items. The HID specification defines codes for the basic units of length, mass, time, temperature, current, and luminous intensity. Most other units can be derived from these.

Specifying a Unit value can be more complicated than you might expect. Table 12-4 shows values you can work from. The value can be as long as four bytes, with each nibble having a defined function. Nibble 0 (the least significant nibble) specifies the measurement system, either English or SI (International System of Units) and whether the measurement is in linear or angular units. Each of the nibbles that follow represents a quality to be measured, with the value of the nibble representing the exponent to apply to the value. For example, a nibble with a value of 2 means that the corresponding value is in units squared. A nibble with a value of Dh, which represents -3, means that the units are expressed as $1/units^3$. These exponents are separate from the Unit Exponent value, which is a power of ten applied to the data, rather than an exponent applied to the units.

Converting Raw Data

To convert raw data to values with units attached, three things must occur. The firmware's report descriptor must contain the information needed for the conversion. The sender of the data must send data that matches the specification in the descriptor. And the receiver of the data must apply the conversions specified in the descriptor.

Below are examples of descriptors and raw and converted data. Remember that just because a tag exists in the HID specification doesn't mean you have to use it. If the application knows what format and units to use for the values it's going to send or receive, the firmware doesn't have to specify these items.

To specify time in seconds, up to a minute, the report descriptor might include this information:

> Logical Minimum: 0
> Logical Maximum: 60

Table 12-4: The units to apply to a reported value are a function of the measuring system and exponent values specified in the Unit item

Nibble Number	Quality Measured	Measuring System (Nibble 0 value)				
		None (0)	SI Linear (1)	SI Rotation (2)	English Linear (3)	English Rotation (4)
1	Length	None	Centimeters	Radians	Inches	Degrees
2	Mass	None	Grams		Slugs	
3	Time	None	Seconds			
4	Temperature	None	Kelvin		Fahrenheit	
5	Current	None	Amperes			
6	Luminous Intensity	None	Candelas			
7	Reserved	None				

Physical Minimum: 0

Physical Maximum: 60

Unit: 1003h. Nibble 0 = 3 to select the English Linear measuring system (though in this case, any value from 1 to 4 would work). Nibble 3 = 1 to select time in seconds.

Unit Exponent: 0

With this information, the receiver knows that the value sent equals a number of seconds.

Now, what if instead you want to specify time in tenths of seconds, again up to a minute? You would need to increase the Logical and Physical Maximums and change the Unit Exponent:

Logical Minimum: 0

Logical Maximum: 600

Physical Minimum: 0

Physical Maximum: 600

Unit: 1003h. Nibble 0 = 3 to select the English Linear measuring system. Nibble 3 = 1 to select time in seconds.

Unit Exponent: 0Fh. This represents an exponent of -1, to indicate that the value is expressed in tenths of seconds rather than seconds.

Sending values as large as 600 will require 3 bytes, which the firmware specifies in the Report Size tag.

To send a temperature value using one byte to represent temperatures from -20 to 110 degrees Fahrenheit, the report descriptor might contain the following:

> Logical Minimum: -128 (80h when expressed in hexadecimal as a two's complement)
>
> Logical Maximum: 127 (7Fh)
>
> Physical Minimum: -20 (ECh when expressed in hexadecimal as a two's complement)
>
> Physical Maximum: 110 (6Eh)
>
> Unit: 10003h. Nibble 0 is 3 to select the English Linear measuring system, though in this case, any value from 1 to 4 is OK. Nibble 4 is 3 to select degrees Fahrenheit.
>
> Unit Exponent: 0

These values ensure the highest possible resolution for a single-byte report item, because the transmitted values can span the full range from 0 to 255.

In this case the logical and physical limits differ, so converting is required. This Visual-Basic code finds the resolution, or number of bits per unit:

```
Resolution = _
    (Logical_Maximum - Logical_Minimum) / _
    ((Physical_Maximum - Physical_Minimum) * _
    (10 ^ Unit_Exponent))
```

With the example values, the resolution is 1.96 bits per degree, or 0.51 degree per bit.

This Visual-Basic code converts a value to the specified units:

```
Value = _
    Value_In_Logical_Units * _
    ((Physical_Maximum - Physical_Minimum) * _
    (10 ^ Unit_Exponent )) / _
    (Logical_Maximum - Logical_Minimum)
```

If the value in logical units (the raw data) is 63, the converted value in the specified units is 32 degrees Fahrenheit.

As another example, specifying velocity in centimeters per second requires a Unit value that contains units of both centimeters and seconds. From Table 12-4, the Unit value to use is 1011h. Nibble 0 = 1 to select the SI measuring system, nibble 1 = 1 to select length in centimeters, and nibble 3 = 1 to select time in seconds.

To show how complicated it can get, the Unit value for volts is F0D121h, which indicates the SI Linear measuring system in units of $(cm^2)(gm)/(sec^{-3})(amp^{-1})$. However, remember that the Unit value only specifies the units. All the receiver has to do is identify the Units value and assign the units to received data; there's no need to do the calculations implied in the Units value.

Describing the Data's Size and Format

Two Global items describe the size and format of the report data.

Report Size specifies the size in bits of a field in an Input, Output, or Feature item. Each field contains one piece of data.

Report Count specifies how many fields an Input, Output, or Feature item contains.

For example, if a report has two 8-bit fields, Report Size is 8 and Report Count is 2. If a report has one 16-bit field, Report Size is 16 and Report Count is 1.

A single Input, Output, or Feature report can have multiple items, each with its own Report Size and Report Count.

Saving and Restoring Global Items

The final two Global items enable saving and restoring sets of Global items. These items allow flexibility in the report formats while using minimum storage space in the device.

Push places a copy of the Global-item state table on the CPU's stack. The Global-item state table contains the current settings for all previously defined Global items.

Pop is the complement to Push. It restores the saved states of the previously pushed Global item states.

The Local Item Type

Local items specify qualities of the controls and data items in a report. A Local item's value applies to all items that follow within a Main item until a new value is assigned. Local items don't carry over to the next Main item; each Main item begins fresh, with no Local items defined.

Local items relate to general usages, body-part designators, and strings. A Delimiter item enables grouping sets of Local items. Table 12-5 shows the values and meaning of each of the items.

Usage. The Local Usage item is the Usage ID that works together with the Global Usage Page to describe the function of a control, data, or collection.

As with the Usage Page item, the HID Usage Tables document lists many Usage IDs. For example, the Buttons Usage Page uses Local Usage IDs from 1 to FFFFh to identify which buttons in a set is pressed, with a value of 0 meaning no button pressed.

A report may assign one Usage to multiple items. If a report item is preceded by a single Usage, that Usage applies to all of the item's data. If a report item is preceded by more than one Usage and the number of controls or data items equals the number of Usages, each Usage applies to one control or data item, with the Usages and controls/data items pairing up in sequence. In the following example, the report contains two bytes. The first byte's Usage is X, and the second byte's Usage is Y.

```
Usage (X),
Usage (Y),
Report Count (2),
Report Size (8),
Input (Data, Variable, Absolute),
```

If a report item is preceded by more than one Usage and the number of controls or data items is greater than the number of Usages, each Usage pairs up with one control or data item in sequence, and the final Usage applies to all

Table 12-5: There are ten defined Local items.

Local Item Type	Value (nn indicates the number of bytes that follow)	Description
Usage	000010nn	An index that describes the use for an item or collection.
Usage Minimum	000110nn	The starting Usage associated with the elements in an array or bitmap.
Usage Maximum	001010nn	The ending Usage associated with the elements in an array or bitmap.
Designator Index	001110nn	A Designator value in a physical descriptor. Indicates what body part applies to a control.
Designator Minimum	010010nn	The starting Designator associated with the elements in an array or bitmap.
Designator Maximum	010110nn	The ending Designator associated with the elements in an array or bitmap.
String Index	011110nn	Associates a string with an item or control.
String Minimum	100010nn	The first string index when assigning a group of sequential strings to controls in an array or bitmap.
String Maximum	100110nn	The last string index when assigning a group of sequential strings to controls in an array or bitmap.
Delimiter	101010nn	The beginning (1) or end (0) of a set of Local items.
Reserved	101011nn to 111110nn	For future use.

of the remaining controls/data items. In the following example, the report is 16 bytes. Usage X applies to the first byte, Usage Y applies to the second byte, and a vendor-defined Usage applies to the third through 16th bytes.

```
Usage (X)
Usage (Y)
Usage (vendor defined)
Report Count (16),
Report Size (8),
Input (Data, Variable, Absolute)
```

Usage Minimum and Maximum. The Usage Minimum and Usage Maximum can assign a series of Usage IDs to the elements in an array or bitmap. The following example describes a report that contains the state (0 or 1) of each of three buttons. The Usage Minimum and Usage Maximum specify that the first button has a Usage ID of 1, the second button has a Usage ID of 2, and the third button has a Usage ID of 3:

```
Usage Page (Button Page)
Logical Minimum (0)
Logical Maximum (1)
Usage Minimum (1)
Usage Maximum (3)
Report Count (3)
Report Size (1)
Input (Data, Variable, Absolute)
```

Designator Index. For items with a physical descriptor, the Designator Index specifies a Designator value in a physical descriptor. The Designator specifies what body part the control uses.

Designator Minimum and Designator Maximum. When a report contains multiple Designator Indexes that apply to the elements in a bitmap or array, a Designator Minimum and Designator Maximum can assign a sequential Designator Index to each bit or array item.

String Index. An item or control can include a String Index to associate a string with the item or control. The strings are stored in the same format described in Chapter 4 for product, manufacturer, and serial-number strings.

String Minimum and Maximum. When a report contains multiple string indexes that apply to the elements in a bitmap or array, a String Minimum and String Maximum can assign a sequential String Index to each bit or array item.

Delimiter. A Delimiter defines the beginning (1) or end (0) of a local item. A delimited local item may contain alternate usages for a control. Different applications can thus define a device's controls in different ways. For example, a button may have a generic use (Button1) and a specific use (Send, Quit, etc.).

Physical Descriptors

A physical descriptor specifies the part or parts of the body intended to activate a control. For example, each finger might have its own assigned control. Similar physical descriptors are grouped into a physical descriptor set. A set consists of a header, followed by the physical descriptors.

A physical descriptor is a HID-specific descriptor. The host can retrieve a physical descriptor set by sending a Get_Descriptor request with 23h in the high byte of the wValue field and the number of the descriptor set in the low byte of the wValue field.

Physical descriptors are optional. For most devices, these descriptors either don't apply at all or the information they could provide has no practical use. The HID specification has more information on how to use physical descriptors, for those devices that need them.

Padding

To pad a descriptor so it contains a multiple of eight bits, a descriptor can include a Main item with no assigned Usage. The following excerpt from a keyboard's report descriptor specifies an Output report that transfers five bits of data and three bits of padding:

```
Usage Page (LEDs)
Usage Minimum (1)
Usage Maximum (5)
Output (Data, Variable, Absolute) (5 1-bit LEDs)

Report Count (1)
Report Size (3)
Output (Constant) (3 bits of padding)
```

13

Human Interface Devices: Host Application

Chapter 10 showed how to obtain a handle to communicate with a device. This chapter shows how Visual Basic .NET and Visual C++ .NET applications can use the handle to communicate with a HID-class device.

HID API Functions

The Windows API includes functions that applications can use to learn about a HID's reports and to send and receive report data. The Windows DDK documents the functions.

The HID API considers each report item to be either a button or value. As defined by the HID API, a button is a control or data item that has a discrete, binary value, such as ON (1) or OFF (0). Buttons include items represented by unique Usage IDs in the Buttons, Keyboard, and LED Usage pages. A value usage, or value, can have any of a range of values. Any report item that isn't a button is a value.

Windows 98 Gold was the first to include the HID API. Windows 98 SE, Windows 2000, and Windows Me support additional HID functions. The API was expanded again for Windows XP. The tables in this chapter note the functions that aren't available in all Windows editions.

Requesting Information about the HID

Table 13-1 lists API functions that request information about a HID and its reports. HidD_GetPreparsedData retrieves a pointer to a buffer that contains information about the HID's reports. HidP_GetCaps uses the pointer to retrieve a HIDP_CAPS structure that specifies what report types a device supports and provides information about the type of information in the reports. For example, the structure includes the number of HIDP_BUTTON_CAPS structures that have information about a button or set of buttons. The application can then use the HidP_GetButtonCaps function to retrieve these structures

The API also includes several functions for retrieving strings. Table 13-2 lists these.

Sending and Receiving Reports

Table 13-3 lists functions that applications can use to send and receive reports.

Windows' HID driver causes the host controller to request Input reports periodically. The driver stores received reports in a buffer. ReadFile retrieves one or more reports from the buffer. If the buffer is empty, ReadFile waits for a report to arrive. ReadFile thus does not cause the device to send a report but just reads reports that the driver has requested.

WriteFile sends an Output report to the HID. WriteFile uses an interrupt transfer if the HID has an interrupt OUT endpoint and the operating system is later than Windows 98 Gold. Otherwise, WriteFile uses a control

Table 13-1: Applications can use these API functions to obtain information about a HID and its reports.

API Function	Purpose
HidD_FreePreparsedData	Free resources used by HidD_GetPreparsedData.
HidD_GetPhysicalDescriptor[1]	Retrieve a physical descriptor.
HidD_GetPreparsedData	Return a handle to a buffer with information about the HID's reports.
HidP_GetButtonCaps	Retrieve an array with information about the buttons in a top-level collection for a specified report type.
HidP_GetCaps	Retrieve a structure describing a HID's reports.
HidP_GetExtendedAttributes[1]	Retrieve a structure with information about Global items the HID parser didn't recognize.
HidP_GetLinkCollectionNodes	Retrieve a structure with information about collections within a top-level collection.
HidP_GetSpecificButtonCaps	Like HidP_GetButtonCaps but can specify a Usage Page, Usage ID, and link collection.
HidP_GetSpecificValueCaps	Like HidP_GetValueCaps but can specify a Usage Page, Usage ID, and link collection.
HidP_GetValueCaps	Retrieve an array with information about the values in a top-level collection for a specified report type.
HidP_IsSameUsageAndPage	Determine if two Usages (Usage Page and Usage ID) are equal.
HidP_MaxDataListLength	Retrieve the maximum number of HIDP_DATA structures that HidP_GetData can return for a HID report type and top-level collection.
HidP_MaxUsageListLength	Retrieve the maximum number of Usage IDs that HidP_GetUsages can return for a report type and top-level collection.
HidP_TranslateUsagesToI8042ScanCodes	Map Usages on the HID_USAGE_PAGE_KEYBOARD Usage Page to PS/2 scan codes.
HidP_UsageAndPageListDifference	Retrieve the differences between two arrays of Usages (Usage Page and Usage ID).
HidP_UsageListDifference	Retrieve the differences between two arrays of Usage IDs.

[1]Not supported under Windows 98 Gold.

Table 13-2: Applications can use these API functions to retrieve strings from a HID.

API Function	Purpose
HidD_GetIndexedString[1]	Retrieve a specified string.
HidD_GetManufacturerString[1]	Retrieve a manufacturer string
HidD_GetProductString[1]	Retrieve a product string.
HidD_GetSerialNumberString[1]	Retrieve a serial-number string.
[1]Not supported under Windows 98 Gold.	

transfer with a Set_Report request. If using interrupt transfers, WriteFile will wait if the device NAKs. If using control transfers, WriteFile returns with an error code on failure or a timeout.

HidD_GetInputReport requests an Input report using a control transfer with a Get_Report request, bypassing the Input report buffer. HidD_SetOutputReport provides a way to send an Output report using a control transfer with a Set_Report request, even if the HID and operating system support using interrupt transfers.

For Feature reports, HidD_GetFeature retrieves a report using a control transfer and Get_Report request and HidD_SetFeature sends a report using a control transfer and Set_Report request. Note that HidD_SetFeature is not the same as the standard USB request Set_Feature!

All of the functions that use control transfers return with an error code on failure or a timeout.

Providing and Using Report Data

After retrieving a report, an application can use the raw data directly from the buffer or use API functions to extract button or value data. In a similar way, an application can write data to be sent directly into a report's buffer or use API functions to place the data into a buffer for sending.

Table 13-4 lists API functions that extract information in received reports and store information in reports to be sent. For example, an application can

Table 13-3: Applications can use these API functions to send and receive reports.

API Function	Purpose
HidD_GetFeature	Read a Feature report.
HidD_GetInputReport[1]	Read an Input report using a control transfer.
HidD_SetFeature	Send a Feature report.
HidD_SetOutputReport[1]	Send an Output report using a control transfer.
ReadFile	Read an Input report obtained via an interrupt transfer.
WriteFile	Send an Output report. Use an interrupt transfer if possible, otherwise use a control transfer.
[1]Requires Windows XP or later.	

find out what buttons have been pressed by calling HidP_GetButtons, which returns a buffer containing the Usage IDs of all buttons that belong to a specified Usage Page and are set to ON. An application can set and clear buttons in a report to be sent by calling HidP_SetButtons and HidP_UnsetButtons. In a similar way, applications can retrieve and set values in a report using HidP_GetUsageValue and Hid_Set_UsageValue.

Managing HID Communications

Table 13-5 lists API functions that applications can use in managing HID communications.

Chapter 10 showed how to use HidD_GetHidGuid to obtain the device interface GUID for the HID class. HidD_SetNumInputBuffers enables an application to change the size of the HID driver's buffer for Input reports. A larger buffer can be helpful if the application might be too busy at times to read reports before the buffer overflows. The value set is the number of reports the buffer will hold. HidD_FlushQueue deletes any Input reports in the buffer.

Identifying a Device

After obtaining a handle to a HID as described in Chapter 10, an application can use the HID API functions to find out whether the HID is one that

Table 13-4: Applications can use these API functions to extract information in retrieved reports and store information in reports to be sent.

API Function	Purpose
HidP_GetButtons	Same as HidP_GetUsages.
HidP_GetButtonsEx	Same as HidP_GetUsagesEx.
HidP_GetData	Retrieve an array of structures, with each structure identifying either the data index and state of a button control that is set to ON (1) or the data index and data for a value control.
HidP_GetScaledUsageValue	Retrieve a signed and scaled value from a report.
HidP_GetUsages	Retrieve a list of all of the buttons that are on a specified Usage Page and are set to ON (1).
HidP_GetUsagesEx	Retrieve a list of all of the buttons that are set to ON (1).
HidP_GetUsageValue	Retrieve the data for a specified value.
HidP_GetUsageValueArray	Retrieve data for an array of values with the same Usage ID.
HidP_InitializeReportForID[1]	Set all buttons to OFF (0) and set all values to their null values if defined and otherwise to zero.
HidP_SetButtons	Same as HidP_SetUsages.
HidP_SetData	Sets the states of buttons and data in values in a report.
HidP_SetScaledUsageValue	Convert a signed and scaled physical number to a Usage's logical value and set the value in a report.
HidP_SetUsages	Set one or more buttons in a report to ON (1).
HidP_SetUsageValue	Set the data for a specified value.
HidP_SetUsageValueArray	Set the data for an array of values with the same Usage ID.
HidP_UnsetButtons	Same as HidP_UnsetUsages.
HidP_UnsetUsages	Set one or more buttons in a report to OFF (0).

[1]Not supported under Windows 98 Gold.

the application wants to communicate with. The application can identify a device by its Vendor ID and Product ID, or by searching for a device with a specific Usage, such as a game controller.

Reading the Vendor and Product IDs

For vendor-specific devices that don't have standard Usages, searching for a device with a specific Vendor ID and Product ID is often useful. The API

Table 13-5: Applications can use these API functions in managing HID communications.

API Function	Purpose
HidD_FlushQueue	Delete all Input reports in the buffer.
HidD_GetHidGuid	Retrieve the device interface GUID for HID-class devices.
HidD_GetNumInputBuffers[1]	Retrieve the number of reports the Input report buffer can hold.
HidD_SetNumInputBuffers[1]	Set the number of reports the Input report buffer can hold.
HidRegisterMinidriver	HID mini-drivers call this function during initialization to register with the HID class driver.
[1]Not supported under Windows 98 Gold.	

function HidD_GetAttributes retrieves a pointer to a structure containing the Vendor ID, Product ID, and device release number.

Visual C++

The HIDD_ATTRIBUTES structure contains information about the device:

```
typedef struct _HIDD_ATTRIBUTES {
   ULONG   Size;
   USHORT  VendorID;
   USHORT  ProductID;
   USHORT  VersionNumber;
} HIDD_ATTRIBUTES, *PHIDD_ATTRIBUTES;
```

This is the function's declaration:

```
BOOLEAN
  HidD_GetAttributes(
    IN HANDLE HidDeviceObject,
    OUT PHIDD_ATTRIBUTES Attributes
    );
```

This is the code to retrieve the structure:

```
BOOLEAN Result;
HIDD_ATTRIBUTES Attributes;

// Set the Size member to the number of bytes
// in the structure.
Attributes.Size = sizeof(Attributes);
Result = HidD_GetAttributes
  (DeviceHandle,
  &Attributes);
```

The application can then compare the Vendor ID and Product ID to the desired values:

```
const unsigned int VendorID = 0x0925;
const unsigned int ProductID = 0x1234;

if (Attributes.VendorID == VendorID) {
    if (Attributes.ProductID == ProductID) {
        // The Vendor ID and Product ID match.
    }
    else {
        // The Product ID doesn't match.
        // Close the handle.
    }
}
else {
    // The Vendor ID doesn't match.
    // Close the handle.
}
```

Visual Basic

The HIDD_ATTRIBUTES structure contains information about the device:

```
<StructLayout(LayoutKind.Sequential)> _
Public Structure HIDD_ATTRIBUTES
    Dim Size As Integer
    Dim VendorID As Short
    Dim ProductID As Short
    Dim VersionNumber As Short
End Structure
```

This is the declaration for the function:

```
<DllImport("hid.dll")> _
Function HidD_GetAttributes _
    (ByVal HidDeviceObject As Integer, _
    ByRef Attributes As HIDD_ATTRIBUTES) _
    As Boolean
End Function
```

This is the code to retrieve the structure:

```
Dim DeviceAttributes As HIDD_ATTRIBUTES
Dim MyVendorID as Short
Dim MyProductID as Short
Dim Result as BOOLEAN

' Set the Size property of DeviceAttributes to the
' number of bytes in the structure.

DeviceAttributes.Size =
    Marshal.SizeOf(myHID.DeviceAttributes)

Result = HidD_GetAttributes _
    (DeviceHandle, _
    DeviceAttributes)
```

The application can then compare the Vendor ID and Product ID to the desired values:

```
MyVendorID = &h0925
MyProductID = &h1234

If (DeviceAttributes.VendorID = MyVendorID) And _
    (DeviceAttributes.ProductID = MyProductID) Then

    Debug.WriteLine("My device detected")

Else

    Debug.WriteLine("Not my device")
    ' Close the handle.
```

Details

DeviceHandle is a handle returned by CreateFile. Before calling HidD_GetAttributes, the Size member of the DeviceAttributes must be set to the structure's size. If the function returns True, the DeviceAttributes structure filled without error. The application can then compare the retrieved values with the desired Vendor ID and Product ID and device release number.

If the attributes don't indicate the desired device, the application should use the CloseHandle API function to close the handle to the interface. The application can then move on to test the next HID in the device information set retrieved with SetupDiGetClassDevs as described in Chapter 10.

Getting a Pointer to a Buffer with Device Capabilities

Another way to find out more about a device is to examine its capabilities. You can do this for a device whose Vendor ID and Product ID matched the values you were looking for, or you can examine the capabilities for an unknown device.

The first task is to call HidD_GetPreparsedData to get a pointer to a buffer with information about the device's capabilities.

Visual C++

This is the function's declaration:

```
BOOLEAN
  HidD_GetPreparsedData(
    IN HANDLE HidDeviceObject,
    OUT PHIDP_PREPARSED_DATA *PreparsedData
    );
```

This is the code to call the function:

```
PHIDP_PREPARSED_DATA PreparsedData;

HidD_GetPreparsedData
  (DeviceHandle,
  &PreparsedData);
```

Visual Basic

This is the function's declaration:

```
<DllImport("hid.dll")> _
Function HidD_GetPreparsedData _
    (ByVal HidDeviceObject As Integer, _
    ByRef PreparsedData As IntPtr) _
    As Boolean
End Function
```

This is the code to call the function:

```
Dim PreparsedData As IntPtr

HidD_GetPreparsedData _
    (DeviceHandle, _
    PreparsedData)
```

Details

DeviceHandle is the handle returned by CreateFile. PreparsedData is a pointer to the buffer containing the data. The application doesn't need to access the data in the buffer directly. The code just needs to pass the pointer to another API function.

When finished using the PreparsedData buffer, the application should free system resources by calling HidD_FreePreparsedData as described later in this chapter.

Getting the Device's Capabilities

The HidP_GetCaps function returns a pointer to a structure that contains information about the device's capabilities. The structure contains the HID's Usage Pages, Usages, report lengths, and the number of button-capabilities structures, value-capabilities structures, and data indexes that identify specific controls and data items in Input, Output, and Feature reports. An application can use the capabilities information to identify a particular HID and learn about its reports and report data. Not every item in the structure applies to all devices.

Visual C++

This is the declaration for the HIDP_CAPS structure:

```
typedef struct _HIDP_CAPS
{
    USAGE    Usage;
    USAGE    UsagePage;
    USHORT   InputReportByteLength;
    USHORT   OutputReportByteLength;
    USHORT   FeatureReportByteLength;
    USHORT   Reserved[17];

    USHORT   NumberLinkCollectionNodes;

    USHORT   NumberInputButtonCaps;
    USHORT   NumberInputValueCaps;
    USHORT   NumberInputDataIndices;

    USHORT   NumberOutputButtonCaps;
    USHORT   NumberOutputValueCaps;
    USHORT   NumberOutputDataIndices;

    USHORT   NumberFeatureButtonCaps;
    USHORT   NumberFeatureValueCaps;
    USHORT   NumberFeatureDataIndices;
} HIDP_CAPS, *PHIDP_CAPS;
```

This is the function's declaration:

```
NTSTATUS
  HidP_GetCaps(
    IN PHIDP_PREPARSED_DATA PreparsedData,
    OUT PHIDP_CAPS Capabilities
    );
```

This is the code to call the function:

```
HIDP_CAPS Capabilities;

HidP_GetCaps
  (PreparsedData,
  &Capabilities);
```

Visual Basic

This is the declaration for the HIDP_CAPS structure:

```
<StructLayout(LayoutKind.Sequential)> _
Public Structure HIDP_CAPS
    Dim Usage As Short
    Dim UsagePage As Short
    Dim InputReportByteLength As Short
    Dim OutputReportByteLength As Short
    Dim FeatureReportByteLength As Short
    <MarshalAs _
        (UnmanagedType.ByValArray, _
        SizeConst:=17)> _
        Dim Reserved() As Short
    Dim NumberLinkCollectionNodes As Short
    Dim NumberInputButtonCaps As Short
    Dim NumberInputValueCaps As Short
    Dim NumberInputDataIndices As Short
    Dim NumberOutputButtonCaps As Short
    Dim NumberOutputValueCaps As Short
    Dim NumberOutputDataIndices As Short
    Dim NumberFeatureButtonCaps As Short
    Dim NumberFeatureValueCaps As Short
    Dim NumberFeatureDataIndices As Short
End Structure
```

This is the declaration for the function:

```
<DllImport("hid.dll")> _
Function HidP_GetCaps _
    (ByVal PreparsedData As IntPtr, _
    ByRef Capabilities As HIDP_CAPS) _
    As Boolean
End Function
```

This is the code to call the function:

```
Dim Capabilities As HIDP_CAPS

HidP_GetCaps _
    (PreparsedData, _
    Capabilities)
```

Details

PreparsedData is the pointer returned by HidD_GetPreparsedData. When the function returns, the application can examine and use whatever values are of interest in the Capabilities structure. For example, if you're looking for a joystick, you can look for a Usage Page of 01h and a Usage of 04h.

The report lengths are useful for setting buffer sizes for sending and receiving reports.

Getting the Capabilities of the Buttons and Values

The device capabilities aren't the only thing that an application can retrieve from a HID. The application can also get the capabilities of each button and value in a report.

HidP_GetValueCaps returns a pointer to an array of structures containing information about the values in a report. The NumberInputValueCaps property of the HIDP_CAPS structure is the number of structures returned by HidP_GetValueCaps.

The items in the structures include many values obtained from the HID's report descriptor, as described in Chapter 12. The items include the Report ID, whether a value is absolute or relative, whether a value has a null state, and logical and physical minimums and maximums. A LinkCollection identifier distinguishes between controls with the same Usage and Usage Page in the same collection.

In a similar way, the HidP_GetButtonCaps function can retrieve information about a report's buttons. The information is stored in a HidP_ButtonCaps structure.

An application that has no use for this information doesn't have to retrieve it.

Sending and Receiving Reports

All of the previous API functions are concerned with finding and learning about a device that matches what the application is looking for. On finding

Table 13-6: The transfer type used to send or receive a report can vary with the API function, operating system edition, and available endpoints.

Report Type	API Function	Transfer Type
Input	ReadFile	Interrupt IN
	HidD_GetInputReport	Control with Get_Report request
Output	WriteFile	Interrupt OUT if possible; otherwise Control with Set_Report request
	HidD_SetOutputReport	Control with Set_Report request
Feature IN	HidD_GetFeature	Control with Get_Report request
Feature OUT	HidD_SetFeature	Control with Set_Report request

a device of interest, the application and device are ready to exchange data in reports.

Table 13-3 listed the six API functions for exchanging reports. Table 13-6 shows that the transfer type the host uses varies with the report type and may also vary depending on the operating system and available endpoints.

Sending an Output Report to the Device

On obtaining a handle and learning the number of bytes in the report, an application can send an Output report to the HID. The application copies the data to send to a buffer and calls WriteFile. As Chapter 11 explained, the type of transfer the HID driver uses to send the Output report depends on the Windows edition and whether the HID interface has an interrupt OUT endpoint. The application doesn't have to know or care which transfer type the driver uses.

Visual C++

This is the function's declaration:

```
BOOL WriteFile(
  HANDLE hFile,
  LPCVOID lpBuffer,
  DWORD nNumberOfBytesToWrite,
  LPDWORD lpNumberOfBytesWritten,
  LPOVERLAPPED lpOverlapped
);
```

This the code to call the function:

```
BOOLEAN Result;

// The report data can reside in a byte array.
// The array size should equal at least the report
// length in bytes + 1.

CHAR OutputReport[3];

DWORD BytesWritten;

// The first byte in the buffer containing the report
// is the Report ID.

OutputReport[0]=0;

// Store data to send in OutputReport[] in the
// bytes following the Report ID.
// Example:

OutputReport[1]=79;
OutputReport[2]=75;

Result = WriteFile
  (DeviceHandle,
  OutputReport,
  Capabilities.OutputReportByteLength,
  &BytesWritten,
  NULL);
```

Visual Basic

This is the function's declaration:

```
<DllImport("kernel32.dll")> Function WriteFile _
    (ByVal hFile As Integer, _
    ByRef lpBuffer As Byte, _
    ByVal nNumberOfBytesToWrite As Integer, _
    ByRef lpNumberOfBytesWritten As Integer, _
    ByVal lpOverlapped As Integer) _
    As Boolean
End Function
```

This is the code to send an Output report to the HID:

```
Dim NumberOfBytesWritten As Integer
Dim OutputReportBuffer() As Byte
Dim ReportID as Integer
Dim Result as Boolean

ReDim OutputReportBuffer _
        (Capabilities.OutputReportByteLength - 1)

ReportID = 0
OutputReportBuffer(0) = ReportID

' Store data to send in OutputReportBuffer()
' in the bytes following the report ID.
' Example:

OutputReportBuffer(1) = 79
OutputReportBuffer(2) = 75

Result = WriteFile _
    (DeviceHandle, _
    OutputReportBuffer(0), _
    UBound(OutputReportBuffer) + 1, _
    NumberOfBytesWritten, _
    0)
```

Details

The hFile parameter is the handle returned by CreateFile. The lpBuffer parameter points to the buffer that contains the report data. The nNumberOfBytesToWrite parameter specifies how many bytes to write and should equal the OutputReportByteLength property of the HIDP_CAPS structure retrieved with HidP_GetCaps. This value equals the report size in bytes plus one byte for the Report ID, which is the first byte in the buffer. The buffer must be large enough to hold the Report ID and report data.

The lpOverlapped parameter is unused in this example, but WriteFile can use overlapped I/O as described in the following section on ReadFile. Overlapped I/O can prevent the application's thread from hanging if the HID's interrupt OUT endpoint NAKs endlessly. In normal operation, the endpoint should accept received data with little delay.

On success, the function returns True with NumberOfBytesWritten containing the number of bytes the function successfully wrote to the HID.

If the interface supports only the default Report ID of 0, the Report ID doesn't transmit on the bus, but the Report ID must always be present in the buffer the application passes to WriteFile.

When sending a report to an interrupt endpoint, WriteFile returns on success or an error. If the device NAKs the report data, WriteFile waits until the endpoint ACKs the data. When sending a report via the control endpoint, WriteFile returns on success, an error, or a timeout (if the endpoint continues to NAK the report data).

Probably the most common error returned by WriteFile in HID communications is *CRC Error*. This error indicates that the host controller attempted to send the report, but the device didn't respond as expected. In spite of the error message, the problem isn't likely to be due to an error detected in a CRC calculation. The error is more likely to be due to a firmware problem that is keeping the endpoint from accepting the report data. If WriteFile doesn't return at all, the interrupt OUT endpoint probably has not been configured to accept the report data.

Reading an Input Report from the Device

The complement to WriteFile is ReadFile. When the application has a handle to the HID interface and knows the number of bytes in the device's

Input report, the application can use ReadFile to read an Input report from a device.

To read a report, the application declares a buffer to hold the data and calls ReadFile. The buffer size should equal at least the size reported in the InputReportByteLength property of the HIDP_CAPS structure returned by HidP_GetCaps.

When called with non-overlapped I/O, ReadFile is a blocking call. If an application calls ReadFile when the HID's read buffer is empty, the application's thread waits until either a report is available, the user closes the application from the Task Manager, or the user removes the device from the bus. There are several approaches to keeping an application from hanging as it waits for a report. The device can continuously send reports. The application can attempt to read a report only after requesting one using an Output or Feature report. The application can use ReadFile with overlapped I/O and a timeout. The ReadFiles can also take place in a separate thread.

To ensure that the device always has data to send, you can write the firmware so that the IN endpoint is always enabled and ready to respond to a request for data. If there is no new data to send, the device can send the same data as last time, or the device can return a vendor-defined code that indicates there is nothing new to report. Or before each ReadFile, the application can send a report that prompts the firmware to provide a report to send to the host.

In an overlapped read, ReadFile returns immediately even if there is no report available, and the application can call WaitForSingleObject to retrieve the report. The advantage of WaitForSingleObject is the ability to set a timeout. If the data hasn't arrived when the timeout period has elapsed, the function returns a code that indicates a timeout and the application can try again or use the CancelIo function to cancel the read operation. This approach works well if reports are normally available without delay, but the application needs to regain control if for some reason there is no report.

To prevent long delays waiting for WaitForSingleObject to return, an application can set the timeout to zero and call the function repeatedly in a loop or periodically, triggered by a timer. The function returns immediately if no report is available, and the application can perform other tasks in the loop or between timeouts.

Another way to improve the performance of an application that is reading Input reports is to do the ReadFiles in a separate thread that notifies the main thread when a report is available. A .NET application can define an asynchronous delegate and use the BeginInvoke method to call a method that performs the ReadFiles in a different thread. BeginInvoke can specify a callback routine that executes in the application's main thread when the method that has called ReadFile returns, enabling the application to retrieve the returned report.

Visual C++

In addition to CreateFile, introduced in Chapter 10, an overlapped ReadFile uses these functions:

```
BOOL CancelIo
   (HANDLE hFile);

HANDLE CreateEvent
   (LPSECURITY_ATTRIBUTES lpEventAttributes,
   BOOL bManualReset,
   BOOL bInitialState,
   LPCTSTR lpName);

BOOL ReadFile
   (HANDLE hFile,
   LPVOID lpBuffer,
   DWORD nNumberOfBytesToRead,
   LPDWORD lpNumberOfBytesRead,
   LPOVERLAPPED lpOverlapped);

DWORD WaitForSingleObject
   (HANDLE hHandle,
   DWORD dwMilliseconds);
```

This is the code for doing an overlapped ReadFile:

```
CHAR        InputReportBuffer[3];
DWORD       BytesRead;
DWORD       Result;
HANDLE      hEventObject;
OVERLAPPED  HIDOverlapped;

hEventObject = CreateEvent
  ((LPSECURITY_ATTRIBUTES)NULL,
  FALSE,
  TRUE,
  "");

HIDOverlapped.hEvent = hEventObject;
HIDOverlapped.Offset = 0;
HIDOverlapped.OffsetHigh = 0;

// Set the first byte in the buffer to the Report ID.
InputReportBuffer[0] = 0;

ReadHandle=CreateFile
  (DetailData->DevicePath,
  GENERIC_READ|GENERIC_WRITE,
  FILE_SHARE_READ|FILE_SHARE_WRITE,
  (LPSECURITY_ATTRIBUTES)NULL,
  OPEN_EXISTING,
  FILE_FLAG_OVERLAPPED,
  NULL);

Result = ReadFile
  (ReadHandle,
  InputReportBuffer,
  Capabilities.InputReportByteLength,
  &BytesRead,
  (LPOVERLAPPED) &HIDOverlapped);

Result = WaitForSingleObject
  (hEventObject,
  3000);
```

```
switch (Result)
{
    case WAIT_OBJECT_0: {

        // Success;
        // Use the report data;

        break;
        }
    case WAIT_TIMEOUT: {

        // Timeout error;
        //Cancel the read operation.

        CancelIo(ReadHandle);
        break;
        }
    default: {

        // Undefined error;
        //Cancel the read operation.

        CancelIo(ReadHandle);
        break;
        }
    }
```

Visual Basic

These are the constants and structures used in an overlapped ReadFile:

```
Public Const FILE_FLAG_OVERLAPPED As Integer _
    = &H40000000
Public Const FILE_SHARE_READ As Short = &H1S
Public Const FILE_SHARE_WRITE As Short = &H2S
Public Const GENERIC_READ As Integer = &H80000000
Public Const GENERIC_WRITE As Integer = &H40000000
Public Const OPEN_EXISTING As Short = 3
Public Const WAIT_OBJECT_0 As Short = 0
Public Const WAIT_TIMEOUT As Integer = &H102
```

```
<StructLayout(LayoutKind.Sequential)> _
Public Structure OVERLAPPED
    Dim Internal As Integer
    Dim InternalHigh As Integer
    Dim Offset As Integer
    Dim OffsetHigh As Integer
    Dim hEvent As Integer
End Structure
```

In addition to CreateFile, introduced in Chapter 10, an overlapped ReadFile uses these functions:

```
<DllImport("kernel32.dll")> _
Function CancelIo _
    (ByVal hFile As Integer) _
    As Integer
End Function

<DllImport("kernel32.dll", CharSet:=CharSet.Auto)> _
Function CreateEvent _
    (ByRef SecurityAttributes _
        As SECURITY_ATTRIBUTES, _
    ByVal bManualReset As Integer, _
    ByVal bInitialState As Integer, _
    ByVal lpName As String) _
    As Integer
End Function

<DllImport("kernel32.dll")> _
Function ReadFile _
    (ByVal hFile As Integer, _
    ByRef lpBuffer As Byte, _
    ByVal nNumberOfBytesToRead As Integer, _
    ByRef lpNumberOfBytesRead As Integer, _
    ByRef lpOverlapped As OVERLAPPED) _
    As Integer
End Function

<DllImport("kernel32.dll")> _
Function WaitForSingleObject _
    (ByVal hHandle As Integer, _
    ByVal dwMilliseconds As Integer) _
    As Integer
End Function
```

This the code to do an overlapped ReadFile:

```
Dim EventObject As Integer
Dim HIDOverlapped As OVERLAPPED
Dim InputReportBuffer() As Byte
Dim NumberOfBytesRead As Integer
Dim Result As Integer
Dim Security As SECURITY_ATTRIBUTES
Dim Success As Boolean

Security.lpSecurityDescriptor = 0
Security.bInheritHandle = CInt(True)
Security.nLength = Len(Security)

EventObject = CreateEvent _
    (Security,
    CInt(False),
    CInt(True),
    "")

HIDOverlapped.Offset = 0
HIDOverlapped.OffsetHigh = 0
HIDOverlapped.hEvent = EventObject

' Set the first byte in the report buffer to the
' report ID.

InputReportBuffer(0) = 0;

ReadHandle = CreateFile _
    (DevicePathName, _
    GENERIC_READ Or GENERIC_WRITE, _
    FILE_SHARE_READ Or FILE_SHARE_WRITE, _
    Security, _
    OPEN_EXISTING, _
    FILE_FLAG_OVERLAPPPED, _
    0)

ReDim InputReportBuffer _
    (Capabilities.InputReportByteLength - 1)
```

```
Result = ReadFile _
    (ReadHandle, _
    InputReportBuffer(0), _
    Capabilities.InputReportByteLength, _
    NumberOfBytesRead, _
    HIDOverlapped)

Result = WaitForSingleObject _
    (EventObject, _
    3000)

Select Case Result
    Case WAIT_OBJECT_0

        ' Success
        ' Use the report data.

    Case WAIT_TIMEOUT

        ' Timeout error.
        ' Cancel the Read operation.

        CancelIo(ReadHandle)

    Case Else

        ' Undefined error.
        ' Cancel the Read operation.

        CancelIo(ReadHandle)

    End Select
```

Details

Before calling ReadFile for the first time, the application calls CreateEvent to create an event object that is set to the signaled state when the ReadFile operation completes. Overlapped I/O requires a handle obtained from a call to CreateFile with the dwFlagsAndAttributes parameter set to FILE_FLAG_OVERLAPPPED.

InputReportBuffer is a byte array that must be large enough to hold the report ID and the largest Input report defined in the HID's report descriptor.

The call to ReadFile passes the handle returned by CreateFile, the address of the first element in the InputReportBuffer array, the report's length from the Capabilities structure returned by HidP_GetCaps, an Integer to hold the number of bytes read, and an overlapped structure whose hEvent parameter is a handle to the event object. A call to ReadFile returns immediately. The application then calls WaitForSingleObject, which returns when a report has been read or on a timeout. The parameters passed to WaitForSingleObject are the event object and a timeout value in milliseconds.

If WaitForSingleObject returns success (WAIT_OBJECT_0), the first byte in InputReportBuffer is the report ID, and the following bytes are the report data read from the device. If the interface supports only the default report ID of zero, the report ID doesn't transmit on the bus but is always present in the buffer returned by ReadFile.

A call to ReadFile doesn't initiate traffic on the bus. The call just retrieves a report that the host previously requested in one of its periodic interrupt IN transfers. If there are no unread reports, ReadFile waits for a report to arrive. The host begins requesting reports when the HID driver is loaded during enumeration. The driver stores the reports in a ring buffer. When the buffer is full and a new report arrives, the oldest report is overwritten. A call to ReadFile reads the oldest report in the buffer. Under Windows 98 SE and later, an application can set the buffer size with the HidD_SetNumInputBuffers function. Different Windows editions have different default buffer sizes, ranging from 2 under Windows 98 Gold to 32 under Windows XP.

Each handle with READ access to the HID has its own Input buffer, so multiple applications can read the same reports.

If the application doesn't request reports as frequently as they're sent, some will be lost. One way to keep from losing reports is to increase the size of the report buffer passed to ReadFile. If multiple reports are available, ReadFile returns as many as will fit in the buffer. If you need to be absolutely sure not to lose a report, use Feature reports instead. Also see the tips in Chapter 3 about performing time-critical transfers.

The Idle rate introduced in Chapter 11 determines whether or not a device sends a report if the data hasn't changed since the last transfer. During enumeration, Windows' HID driver attempts to set the Idle rate to 0, which means that the HID won't send a report unless the report data has changed. There is no API call that enables applications to change the Idle rate. To prevent setting an Idle rate of zero, the HID can return a STALL to the Set_Idle request to inform the host the request isn't supported. Not all device controllers have hardware support for the Idle rate, though support can be implemented with a timer in firmware.

Whether or not Set_Idle is supported, the firmware can be programmed to send each report only once. After sending a report, the firmware can configure the endpoint to return NAK in response to IN token packets. When the device has new data to send, the firmware can configure the endpoint to send a report. Otherwise, the device will continue to send the same data every time the host polls the endpoint, and the application is likely to read the same report multiple times.

If ReadFile isn't returning, these are possible reasons:

- The HID's interrupt IN endpoint is NAKing the IN token packets because the endpoint hasn't been configured to send the report data. Remember that the endpoint's hardware interrupt typically triggers after data has been sent, so the device must prepare to send the initial report before the first interrupt.

- The number of bytes the endpoint is sending doesn't equal the number of bytes in the report (for the default report ID) or the number of bytes in the report + 1 (for other report IDs).

- The endpoint is sending report ID zero with the report, or the endpoint isn't sending a report ID greater than zero with the report.

Writing a Feature Report to the Device

To send a Feature report to a device, use the HidD_SetFeature function. The function sends a Set_Report request and a report in a control transfer.

Visual C++

This is the function's declaration:

```
BOOLEAN
  HidD_SetFeature(
    IN HANDLE HidDeviceObject,
    IN PVOID ReportBuffer,
    IN ULONG ReportBufferLength
    );
```

This is the code to call the function:

```
CHAR OutFeatureReportBuffer[3];
BOOLEAN Result;

// The first byte in the report buffer is the
// report ID:

OutFeatureReportBuffer[0]=0;

// Store data to send in FeatureReport[] in the
// bytes following the Report ID.
// Example:

OutFeatureReportBuffer[1]=79;
OutFeatureReportBuffer[2]=75;

Result = HidD_SetFeature
  (DeviceHandle,
  OutFeatureReportBuffer,
  Capabilities.FeatureReportByteLength);
```

Visual Basic

This is the function's declaration:

```
<DllImport("hid.dll")> _
Function HidD_SetFeature _
    (ByVal HidDeviceObject As Integer, _
    ByRef lpReportBuffer As Byte, _
    ByVal ReportBufferLength As Integer) _
    As Boolean
End Function
```

This is the code to call the function:

```
Dim OutFeatureReportBuffer _
    (Capabilities.FeatureReportByteLength - 1) as Byte
Dim Success As Boolean

'The first byte in the report buffer is the report ID:

OutFeatureReportBuffer(0) = 0

' Example report data following the report ID:

OutFeatureReportBuffer(1) = 55
OutFeatureReportBuffer(2) = 41

Success = HidD_SetFeature _
    (DeviceHandle, _
    OutFeatureReportBuffer(0), _
    Capabilities.FeatureReportByteLength)
```

Details

A byte array holds the report to send. The first byte in the array is the report ID. The length of the Feature report plus one byte for the report ID is in the HIDP_CAPS structure retrieved by HidP_GetCaps. HidD_SetFeature requires a handle to the HID, the address of the first element in the byte array, and length of the byte array.

The function returns True on success. If the device continues to NAK the report data, the function times out and returns.

A call to HidD_SetOutputReport works much the same way to send an Output report using a control transfer. The function passes a handle to the HID, a pointer to a byte array containing an Output report, and the number of bytes in the report plus one byte for the report ID.

Reading a Feature Report from a Device

To read a Feature report from a device, use the HidD_GetFeature API function. The function sends a Get_Feature request in a control transfer. The device returns the report in the Data stage.

Visual C++

This is the function's declaration:

```
BOOLEAN
  HidD_GetFeature(
    IN HANDLE HidDeviceObject,
    OUT PVOID ReportBuffer,
    IN ULONG ReportBufferLength
    );
```

This is the code to call the function:

```
BOOLEAN Result;
CHAR    InFeatureReportBuffer[3];

// The first byte in the report buffer is the report
// ID:

InFeatureReportBuffer[0]=0;

Result = HidD_GetFeature
  (DeviceHandle,
   InFeatureReportBuffer,
   Capabilities.FeatureReportByteLength)
```

Visual Basic

This is the function's declaration:

```
<DllImport("hid.dll")> Function HidD_GetFeature _
    (ByVal HidDeviceObject As Integer, _
    ByRef lpReportBuffer As Byte, _
    ByVal ReportBufferLength As Integer) _
    As Boolean
End Function
```

This is the code to call the function:

```
Dim InFeatureReportBuffer _
    (Capabilities.FeatureReportByteLength - 1) as Byte
Dim Success As Boolean

'The first byte in the report buffer is the report ID:

InFeatureReportBuffer(0) = 0

Success = HidD_GetFeature _
    (DeviceHandle, _
    InFeatureReportBuffer(0), _
    Capabilities.FeatureReportByteLength)
```

Details

A byte array holds the retrieved report. The first byte in the array is the report ID. The length of the Feature report plus one byte for the report ID is in the HIDP_CAPS structure retrieved by HidP_GetCaps. HidD_GetFeature requires a handle to the HID, the address of the first element in the byte array, and length of the byte array.

The function returns True on success. If the device continues to NAK in the Data stage of the transfer, the function times out and returns.

A call to HidD_GetInputReport works in much the same way to request an Input report using a control transfer. The function passes a handle to the HID, a pointer to a byte array to hold the Input report, and the number of bytes in the report plus one byte for the report ID.

Closing Communications

When finished communicating with a device, the application should call CloseHandle to close any handles opened by CreateFile, as described in Chapter 10. When finished using the PreparsedData buffer returned by HidD_GetPreparsedData, the application should call HidD_FreePreparsedData.

Visual C++

This is declaration for HidD_FreePreparsedData:

```
BOOLEAN
  HidD_FreePreparsedData(
    IN PHIDP_PREPARSED_DATA PreparsedData
    );
```

This is the code to call the function:

```
HidD_FreePreparsedData(PreparsedData);
```

Visual Basic

This is the declaration for HidD_FreePreparsedData:

```
<DllImport("hid.dll")> _
Function HidD_FreePreparsedData _
    (ByRef PreparsedData As IntPtr) _
    As Boolean
End Function
```

This is the code to call the function:

```
HidD_FreePreparsedData(PreparsedData)
```

14

Bulk Transfers for Any CPU

Chapter 6 introduced FTDI Chip's FT245BM and FT245BM device controllers, which enable just about any CPU with a parallel or asynchronous serial interface to communicate with a USB host. The chips handle enumeration and other tasks with no USB-specific programming required. This chapter presents two example applications plus some tips on designing with these controllers.

Two Projects

Both example applications interface to Microchip PICMicro 16F877 microcontrollers. The first example uses an FT232BM, which has an asynchronous serial interface. The second example uses an FT245BM, which has a parallel interface. The firmware is written for microEngineering Labs' PicBasic Pro Basic compiler, but can be adapted to other languages.

As you'll see, writing device firmware and host applications for these chips requires very little knowledge of USB. An understanding of USB can help you understand the devices' abilities and limits, however.

Asynchronous Serial Interface

The FT232BM has a USB port and an asynchronous serial interface that can connect to an external CPU.

The Circuit

Figure 14-1 shows an example circuit. A DLP Design's DLP-232M module contains the FT232BM chip, an EEPROM for storing configuration data, and a USB connector. I built the circuit using microEngineering Labs, Inc.'s LAB-X2 board, which has a 40-pin DIP socket for the PICMicro 16F877 microcontroller, a power-supply regulator, and a 40-pin header that provides access to the '877's port pins. You can use just about any FT232BM circuit based on FTDI Chip's example schematic and any CPU with an asynchronous serial port. If you use the LAB-X2 board, remove the MAX232 chip from its socket (because the '877's serial-port pins connect to the '232BM instead), and switches S1 and S2 on the board won't be available if you use hardware handshaking.

To send data to the host computer, the '877's firmware writes serial data to its TX output, which connects to the DLP-232M's RXD input. This pin in turn connects to RXD on the '232BM. On receiving data at RXD, the '232BM sends the data out its USB port to the host computer.

On receiving USB data from the host, the '232BM writes the data to its TXD output, which connects to TXD on the DLP-232M and to the RX input on the '877. The microcontroller's firmware reads the data received at RX.

The circuit has two optional LEDs that flash when the '232BM is sending data to the PC or receiving data from the PC.

The example circuit includes connections for hardware handshaking. With the '232BM and the '877 configured to use hardware handshaking, the

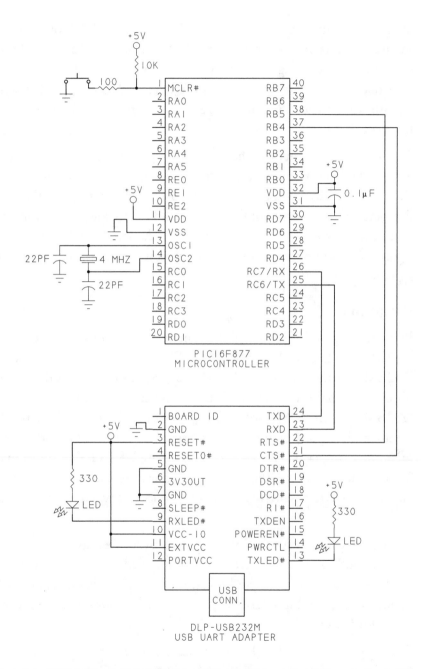

Figure 14-1: FTDI Chip's FT232BM USB UART can interface to just about any CPU with an asynchronous serial port.

'232BM transmits only when the '877 has brought RTS low, and the '877 should transmit only when the '232BM has brought RTS# low. If the corresponding handshaking signal is high, the sender should wait. Most microcontrollers (including the '877) don't have dedicated pins for serial-port handshaking but can use any spare port pins monitored and controlled by firmware.

As shown, the circuits use their own +5V power supply. To use bus power for the DLP-USB232M, connect VCC-IO, EXTVCC, and RESET# to PORTVCC. Circuits that use bus power must draw no more than 100 milliamperes until the host configures the USB device and must limit their current in the Suspend state, as described in Chapter 16. FTDI Chip provides information on how to ensure that a bus-powered device meets USB's power specifications.

Program Code

Programming a CPU for asynchronous serial communications with a '232BM requires no knowledge of USB protocols. The link between the '232BM and the device's CPU is an asynchronous serial link. The device's CPU doesn't have to know anything about the communications between the '232BM and the USB host. The program code will vary depending on whether the device contains a hardware UART/USART and on the programming language. The '877 has a hardware USART that transmits on the TX pin and receives on the RX pin. An interrupt can cause a routine to execute when a byte has arrived at the serial port and when a byte has transmitted.

Listing 14-1 demonstrates communications between an '877 and '232BM in PicBasic Pro. The '877 reads a byte received from the host, increments the byte, and sends the byte back to the host. For handshaking, the code defines one port bit (PORTB.4) as the RTS output and one port bit (PORTB.5) as the CTS input.

The program brings RTS low to indicate that the '877 is ready to receive a byte. RTS connects to the '232BM's CTS# input. On receiving a byte from the PC and determining that CTS# is low, the '232BM writes the byte to

```
' Registers that relate to serial communications:

' Automatically clear any receive overflow errors.
DEFINE HSER_CLROERR 1

' Set the baud rate.
DEFINE HSER_BAUD 2400

' Enable the serial receiver.
DEFINE HSER_RCSTA 90h

' Enable the serial transmitter.
DEFINE HSER_TXSTA 20h

' Handshaking bits. Use any spare port bits.
RTS                   VAR     PORTB.4
CTS                   VAR     PORTB.5

error                 VAR     BYTE
byte_was_received     VAR     BIT
serial_in             VAR     BYTE
serial_out            VAR     BYTE

' The RTS output connects to the '232BM's RTS# output.
' The CTS input connects to the '232BM's CTS# input.
OUTPUT RTS
INPUT  CTS

' On detecting a hardware interrupt, jump to interrupt_service.
ON INTERRUPT GOTO interrupt_service

' Enable global and peripheral interrupts.
INTCON = %11000000

' Enable the serial receive peripheral interrupt.
PIE1 = %00100000

' Tell the '232BM it's OK to send a byte.
byte_was_received = 0
RTS = 0
```

Listing 14-1: PicBasic Pro code to enable a PICMicro 16F877 to communicate with an FTDI Chip FT232BM. (Sheet 1 of 3)

```
' The main program loop.
loop:

    ' Find out if a serial byte was received.
    if byte_was_received = 1 then

        ' Find out if the '232BM is ready to receive a byte.
        if CTS = 0 then

            ' Increment the received byte.
            If (serial_in = 255) then
                serial_out = 0
            else
                serial_out = (serial_in + 1)
            endif

            ' Write the incremented byte to the serial port.
            HSEROUT [serial_out]

            ' Prepare to receive another byte.
            byte_was_received = 0
            RTS = 0
        endif
    endif

GOTO loop
```

Listing 14-1: PicBasic Pro code to enable a PICMicro 16F877 to communicate with an FTDI Chip FT232BM. (Sheet 2 of 3)

```
' Disable interrupt processing in the interrupt-service routine.
DISABLE INTERRUPT
interrupt_service:

    ' This routine executes on detecting a hardware interrupt.

    ' Find out if a byte was received on the serial port.
    if ((PIR1 & %00100000) = %00100000) then

        ' Set RTS high to prevent receiving more serial data.
        RTS = 1

        ' Find out if there was a framing error.
        error = (RCSTA & %000000100)

        ' Store the byte in serial_in.
        ' This also clears any framing-error flag.
        HSERIN [serial_in]

        ' If a byte was received without error,
        ' set byte_was_received = 1 to tell the main program loop
        ' that it should send a byte to the serial port.
        ' Otherwise, set CTS= 0 to enable receiving another byte.

        if error = 0 then
            byte_was_received = 1
        else
            RTS = 0
        endif
    endif

RESUME

' Re-enable interrupt processing.
ENABLE INTERRUPT
```

Listing 14-1: PicBasic Pro code to enable a PICMicro 16F877 to communicate with an FTDI Chip FT232BM. (Sheet 3 of 3) the '877's RX input. The byte's arrival triggers an interrupt, and an interrupt-service routine reads the byte and sets a variable to inform the main program loop.

When the '232BM's RTS# output is low, the '232BM is ready to receive a byte. RTS# connects to CTS on the '877. After a byte has been received and CTS is low, the main program loop increments the received byte and writes the byte to the TX output. The '232BM sends the received byte on to the host via the chip's USB port. The '877 sets RTS low to inform the '232BM that it's OK to send another byte.

If the '232BM is installed using an INF file that specifies FTDI Chip's virtual COM port (VCP) drivers, the driver causes the operating system to create a virtual COM port for communicating with the device. To access the device, you can use any application that can communicate with COM-port devices, including the HyperTerminal accessory provided with Windows.

In the PC software, set the COM port's parameters to match what the microcontroller's circuit uses. For example, Listing 14-1 uses a Baud rate of 2400 bits/second and the default settings of 8 data bits, 1 Stop bit, and no parity. The PC doesn't use the COM-port parameters to communicate with the '232BM, but the driver passes the parameters to the '232BM in vendor-specific requests. The '232BM uses the parameters when communicating over its asynchronous serial interface.

The Host Programming section in this chapter has more about FTDIChip's VCP driver and the alternative D2XX Direct driver.

Parallel Interface

The FT245BM is similar to the '232BM, but with an 8-bit parallel interface in place of the '232BM's asynchronous serial interface.

The Circuit

Figure 14-2 shows an example circuit. A DLP Design's DLP-245M module contains the FT245BM chip, an EEPROM, and a USB connector. As with the previous circuit, I used microEngineering Labs' LAB-X2 board with a

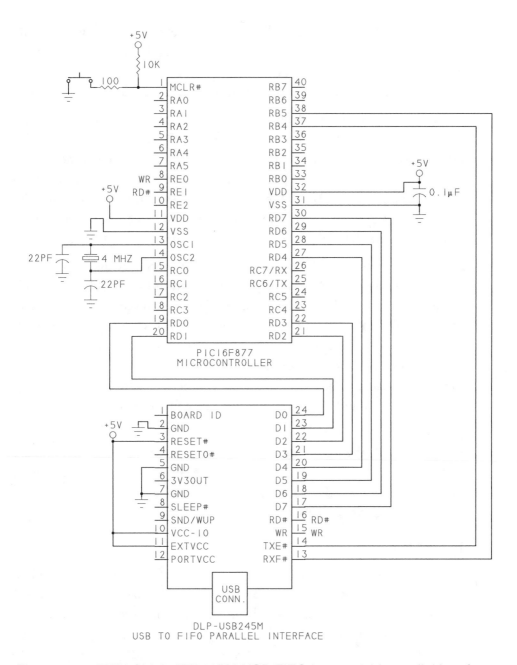

Figure 14-2: FTDI Chip's FT245BM USB FIFO has an 8-bit parallel interface.

PICMicro 16F877 microcontroller. You can use just about any FT245BM circuit based on FTDI Chip's example schematic and any CPU with a parallel I/O port and four additional spare port pins. If you use the LAB-X2 board, switches S1 and S2 on the board won't be available.

Figure 14-3 shows timing diagrams for reading and writing to the '245BM. When the PC has written a byte to the '245BM, the chip brings its RXF# output low to indicate that a byte is available. To read the byte, the external CPU brings the '245BM's RD# input low. The '245BM then places the byte on data pins D0–D7, and the external CPU can read the byte, bringing RD# high when the read operation is complete. When another byte is available for the external CPU to read, the '245BM brings RXF# low again.

To write a byte to the PC, the external CPU brings WR high and waits if necessary for the '245BM to bring its TXE# output low to indicate the chip is ready to receive a byte. The external CPU then places the byte on data pins D0–D7 and brings WR low, causing the '245BM to copy the byte into its transmit buffer and bring TXE# high. The chip sends the byte to the host over the USB port. The external CPU brings WR high to prepare for the next transfer. When ready to read another byte, the '245BM brings TXE# low again and the external CPU can write another byte to the data lines.

In Figure 14-2, the data port is Port D on the 16F877. The handshaking signals use bits on Port B and Port E. You can use any spare port pins to interface to the '245BM's data pins and status and control signals. The power connections are the same as for the '232BM.

Program Code

Listing 14-2 is PICBasic Pro code that waits to receive a byte from the host via the '245BM, increments the byte, and sends it back to the host. The firmware checks the state of RXF# before attempting to read a byte. Another option would be to use a hardware interrupt to cause the CPU to take action when RXF# goes low, indicating there is a byte available to be read. The firmware checks the state of TXE# before attempting to write a byte.

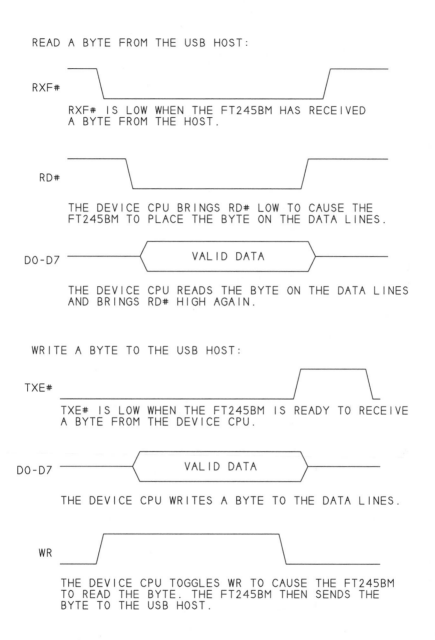

READ A BYTE FROM THE USB HOST:

RXF#

RXF# IS LOW WHEN THE FT245BM HAS RECEIVED
A BYTE FROM THE HOST.

RD#

THE DEVICE CPU BRINGS RD# LOW TO CAUSE THE
FT245BM TO PLACE THE BYTE ON THE DATA LINES.

D0-D7   VALID DATA

THE DEVICE CPU READS THE BYTE ON THE DATA LINES
AND BRINGS RD# HIGH AGAIN.

WRITE A BYTE TO THE USB HOST:

TXE#

TXE# IS LOW WHEN THE FT245BM IS READY TO RECEIVE
A BYTE FROM THE DEVICE CPU.

D0-D7   VALID DATA

THE DEVICE CPU WRITES A BYTE TO THE DATA LINES.

WR

THE DEVICE CPU TOGGLES WR TO CAUSE THE FT245BM
TO READ THE BYTE. THE FT245BM THEN SENDS THE
BYTE TO THE USB HOST.

Figure 14-3: In a read operation, the device CPU reads a byte from the
FT245BM. In a write operation, the device CPU writes a byte to the FT245BM.

```
' The PICMicro waits to receive a byte from the PC,
' increments the byte, and sends it back to the PC.

' An FT245BM provides the interface between a parallel port
' on the PICMicro and a USB port on the PC.

INPUTS              CON $FF
OUTPUTS             CON 0

' Parallel interface data bits.

data_port           VAR PORTD
data_port_direction VAR TRISD

' Parallel interface control outputs.
RD                  VAR PORTE.1
WR                  VAR PORTE.0

' Parallel interface status inputs.
RXF                 VAR PORTB.5
TXE                 VAR PORTB.4

data_in             VAR BYTE
data_out            VAR BYTE
read_or_write       VAR BIT

' Configure the control signals as outputs.

OUTPUT RD
OUTPUT WR

' Configure the status signals as inputs.

INPUT RXF
INPUT TXE

'Set RD and WR to their default (inactive) states.
RD = 1
WR = 0
```

Listing 14-2: PICBasic Pro code to enable a PICMicro 16F877 to read a byte from an FTDI FT245BM (Sheet 1 of 4).

```
' If read_or_write = 1,
' the PICMicro is waiting to receive a byte from the '245BM.
' If read_or_write = 0,
' the PICMicro is waiting to send a byte to the '245BM.

read_or_write = 1

'The main program loop.
loop:

    if (read_or_write = 1) then

        ' The PICMicro is waiting to receive a byte.
        ' Find out if a byte is available.

        if (RXF = 0) then

            ' RXF = 0, indicating the '245BM has a byte
            ' available to read.

            'Configure the data port's bits as inputs.
            data_port_direction = INPUTS

            ' Bring RD low to cause the '245BM to place a byte
            ' on the data port.
            RD = 0

            ' Store the byte in data_in.
            data_in = data_port

            ' Bring RD high.
            RD = 1

            ' Do something with the received byte.
            gosub process_received_data

        endif
```

Listing 14-2: PICBasic Pro code to enable a PICMicro 16F877 to read a byte from an FTDI FT245BM (Sheet 2 of 4).

```
    else

        ' The PICMicro is ready to send a byte.
        ' Find out if the '245BM is ready to receive a byte.

        if (TXE = 0) then

            ' TXE = 0, indicating that the '245BM is ready
            ' to receive a byte.

            ' Configure the data port's bits as outputs.
            data_port_direction = OUTPUTS

            ' Write the byte to the data port.
            data_port = data_out

            ' Bring WR high, then low, to cause the '245BM
            ' to read the byte.
            WR = 1
            WR = 0

            'The PICMicro is now ready to receive a byte.
            read_or_write = 1

        endif

    endif

GoTo loop
```

Listing 14-2: PICBasic Pro code to enable a PICMicro 16F877 to read a byte from an FTDI FT245BM (Sheet 3 of 4).

```
process_received_data:

    ' This example program increments the received byte
    ' and sets read_or_write = 0 to cause the PICMicro to send
    ' the byte back to the '245BM and thus on to the host.

    If (data_in = 255) then
        data_out = 0
    else
        data_out = (data_in + 1)
    endif

    ' The PICMicro is now ready to send a byte.
    read_or_write = 0

return
```

Listing 14-2: PICBasic Pro code to enable a PICMicro 16F877 to read a byte from an FTDI FT245BM (Sheet 4 of 4).

As with the previous circuit, PC applications can communicate with the '245BM circuit using FTDIChip's VCP driver or D2XX Direct driver.

Host Programming

When communicating with FTDI Chip's controllers, the VCP driver is a natural choice if you're upgrading an existing device that uses RS-232 or another asynchronous serial interface. FTDI Chip also provides the D2XX Direct driver, which enables applications to use vendor-specific functions to communicate with the '232BM and '245BM.

Reasons for using the D2XX driver include faster transfers, more control over communications with the external CPU, and the option to use Bit Bang mode.

Using the D2XX Direct Driver

Applications can communicate with the D2XX driver using either FTDI Chip's original Classic functions or an alternate set of functions that emulate Windows API functions.

Table 14-1 lists the Classic interface functions. The basic functions for exchanging data are FT_Open, FT_Read, FT_Write, and FT_Close. Additional functions enable configuring the controller and accessing the EEPROM. A few functions apply only to the '232BM's handshaking signals and serial-communication parameters.

An alternative to the Classic functions is the FT-Win32 API function set (Table 14-2). These functions emulate standard Win32 API functions such as CreateFile, ReadFile, and WriteFile. The functions are convenient if you have existing code that uses Win32 functions but want to use the D2XX driver. The FT-Win32 functions don't support setting the latency timer, EEPROM access, or Bit Bang mode.

An application should use either the Classic interface or the FT-Win32 interface, not both.

Selecting a Driver

Chapter 9 explained how Windows selects a driver for communicating with a device. The FTDI Chip controllers are a special case because they have two driver options and because the controllers can function using the default Vendor ID and Product ID. The defaults are your only option if your controller doesn't interface to an EEPROM. To avoid confusion about which driver the host should assign to the device, it's best to use an EEPROM with a unique Vendor ID/Product ID pair.

Although the '232BM and '245BM have different interfaces to their device CPUs, the two chips appear identical to the host computer. The host computer doesn't care what the device controller does with the data beyond the USB port. Devices that use both chips can use the same drivers and INF files. The '245BM can use the VCP driver even though it doesn't have the asynchronous serial interface found on conventional COM ports, and the

Table 14-1: Applications can use these Classic interface functions to communicate with devices that use FTDI Chip's D2XX direct driver. (Sheet 1 of 2)

Function	Purpose
FT_EE_Read	Read the EEPROM data in the FT_PROGRAM_DATA structure.
FT_EE_Program	Program the EEPROM with data in an FT_PROGRAM_DATA structure.
FT_EE_UARead	Read the EEPROM's user area.
FT_EE_UASize	Get the size of the EEPROM's user area.
FT_EE_UAWrite	Write to the EEPROM's user area.
FT_GetBitMode	In Bit Bang mode, read the bits.
FT_GetLatencyTimer	Get the value of the latency timer.
FT_GetModemStatus*	Get the states of modem status signals.
FT_GetQueueStatus	Get the number of characters in the receive buffer.
FT_GetStatus	Get the number of characters in the transmit and receive buffers and the event status.
FT_ListDevices	Get the number of connected devices and device strings.
FT_Open	Get a handle to access a device. Specifies the device by number.
FT_OpenEx	Get a handle to access a device. Specifies the device by serial number or description.
FT_Purge	Clear the transmit and receive buffers.
FT_Read	Read the specified number of bytes from the device.
FT_ResetDevice	Reset the device.
FT_SetBaudRate*	Set the baud rate, including non-standard rates.
FT_SetBitMode	Enable/disable Bit Bang mode and configure Bit Bang pins as inputs or outputs.
FT_SetBreakOff	Reset the Break condition.
FT_SetChars	Specify an event character and an error character.
FT_SetDataCharacteristics*	Set the number of bits per character, number of Stop bits, and parity.
FT_SetDTR*	Set DTR.
FT_SetEventNotification	Set conditions (character received or change in modem status) for an event notification.
FT_SetFlowControl*	Select a flow-control method.
FT_SetLatencyTimer	Set the latency timer (default = 16 milliseconds).

Table 14-1: Applications can use these Classic interface functions to communicate with devices that use FTDI Chip's D2XX direct driver. (Sheet 2 of 2)

Function	Purpose
FT_SetRTS*	Set RTS.
FT_SetTimeouts	Set timeouts for reading and writing to the device.
FT_SetUSBParameters	Set the USB maximum transfer size (default = 4096).
FT_Write	Write the specified bytes to the device.
*Not supported or needed by FT245BM (except SetBaudRate in Bit Bang mode).	

'232BM can use the D2XX driver even though it has an asynchronous serial interface that you might expect would use a COM-port driver.

Using Unique IDs

The most reliable way to be sure Windows assigns the driver you want is to assign your own Vendor ID and Product ID or use FTDI Chip's Vendor ID with a unique Product ID that you request from FTDI Chip. Store the IDs in an EEPROM that interfaces to the controller and place the IDs in an INF file for the driver you want to use. Then Windows will always know what driver to assign. (When assigning the driver, Windows will copy the INF file and rename it *oemxx.inf*, where *xx* is a unique number, so it won't matter if other vendors have also edited the INF file provided by FTDI Chip.)

Cautions When Using the Default IDs

If the device uses the default Vendor ID and Product ID, Windows may insist on selecting the driver for you, and you may not get the result you want, especially if your INF file isn't signed. (See Chapter 9 for more about signed drivers and INF files.) To avoid this problem when using the default IDs, during device installation, delete, move, or rename any signed INF files that specify the unwanted driver for the default IDs and disconnect from the Internet to prevent Windows from downloading a driver. You don't want to require end users to go to this much trouble when installing your device, however.

Table 14-2: As an alternative to the Classic functions, applications can use these FT-WIn32 functions, which emulate Windows API functions, to communicate with controllers that use FTDI Chip's D2XX direct driver.

Function	Purpose
FT_W32_ClearCommBreak	Clear the Break condition.
FT_W32_ClearCommError	Get the device status and information about a communications error.
FT_W32_CloseHandle	Close a handle obtained with FT_W32_CreateFile.
FT_W32_CreateFile	Obtain a handle to access a device. Specifies the device by serial number or description.
FT_W32_EscapeCommFunction*	Set or clear RTS, DTS, or Break.
FT_W32_GetCommModemStatus*	Get the states of modem status signals.
FT_W32_GetCommState	Get the communication parameters in a device control block.
FT_W32_GetCommTimeouts	Get the values of the read and write timeouts.
FT_W32_GetLastError	Get a status code for the last operation on the device. Success = non-zero; failure = zero.
FT_W32_GetOverlappedResult	Get the result of an overlapped operation.
FT_W32_PurgeComm	Terminate outstanding reads and/or writes and/or clear the read and/or write buffers.
FT_W32_ReadFile	Read the specified number of bytes from the device.
FT_W32_SetCommBreak	Put communications in the Break state.
FT_W32_SetCommMask	Specify events to monitor.
FT_W32_SetCommState*	Set the communication parameters in a device control block.
FT_W32_SetCommTimeouts	Set timeout values for reads and writes to the device.
FT_W32_SetupComm	Set the size of the read and write buffers.
FT_W32_WaitCommEvent	Wait for an event.
FT_W32_WriteFile	Write the specified bytes to the device.
*Not supported or needed by FT245BM.	

If you must use the default Vendor ID and Product ID, you can give each device a serial number to help distinguish the device from other devices with the same Vendor ID and Product ID. As Chapter 9 explained, Windows creates a hardware key for each device with a serial number and uses these entries to remember which driver to use. If there are no serial numbers,

Windows uses the physical port to identify the device, and the port can change as users remove and reattach devices. You could still run into problems, however, because you can't control the serial numbers of devices from other sources. So two devices that use the default Vendor ID and Product ID could end up with the same serial number.

Avoiding COM-port Proliferation

Windows by default creates a new COM port for every device that uses the VCP driver and has a serial number. If you're testing a batch of devices, you can quickly reach the maximum of 256 COM ports. To free up some port numbers, use Windows' Device Manager to uninstall devices you no longer need. Another solution (for in-house testing environments only!) is to edit *ftdibus.inf* to cause Windows to assign the VCP driver only to devices attached to a specified physical port or ports, and to cause Windows to create a single COM port for all of these devices, even if they have different serial numbers. FTDI Chip provides an application note with details about how to edit the INF file to accomplish this.

Performance Tips

When using FTDI Chip's controllers, there are several things you can do to get the best possible performance. The tips that follow show how to help data transfer as quickly as possible and how to prevent lost data.

Speed Considerations

In considering the rate of data transfer when using FTDI Chip's controllers, you need to consider both the transfer rate between the host computer and the device controller and the transfer rate between the device controller and the device's CPU.

Because the device controllers use bulk transfers, the amount of time required to transfer a specific amount of data between the host PC and the device controller can vary depending on how busy the bus is. The asynchronous serial and parallel interfaces can also slow things down if the transmitting end has to wait for the receiving end to indicate that it's ready to receive a byte. And of course the asynchronous serial interface can be no faster than the selected baud rate.

Using either the VCP or D2XX driver, an endpoint on a '232BM can transfer up to 3 Megabits/sec. This works out to 300 kilobytes/sec. assuming one Stop bit and one Start bit. To achieve this rate, the controller's asynchronous serial port must use a baud rate of 3 Megabits/sec.

A '245BM endpoint can transfer up to 300 kilobytes/sec. using the VCP driver and 1 Megabyte/sec. using the D2XX driver. For the fastest transfers, use the D2XX driver.

Minimizing Latency

For IN transfers of less than 62 data bytes, there are several ways to cause data to transfer more quickly. By default, the controller's bulk IN endpoint NAKs IN packets unless one of the following is true:

- The transmit buffer contains at least 62 bytes.
- At least 16 milliseconds has elapsed since the last IN packet was ACKed.
- An event character is enabled and was received by the device.
- For the '232BM only, CTS, DSR, DCD, or RI has changed state.

If any of the above is true, the controller returns two status bytes followed by the entire contents of the transmit buffer or 62 bytes, whichever is less.

For devices that must send less than 62 bytes to the host without delay, the D2XX driver has a function that can change the latency timer from its default value of 16 milliseconds. The allowed range is from 1 to 255 milliseconds. For the shortest latency, set the timer to 1, and the device will send status bytes and any data if at least 1 millisecond has elapsed since the last bulk IN packet was ACKed.

Event characters enable the host to request a device to send data immediately. The D2XX driver has a function that can define a character as a special event character. After receiving the event character, the controller sends status bytes and up to 62 data bytes in response to the next IN packet. The received event character is embedded in the data and the device firmware is responsible for recognizing and discarding the character if it's not part of the meaningful data.

A '232BM can also be prompted to send data by changing the state of one of its handshaking inputs. And of course any of the controllers can force the data to transmit by padding the transmit buffer so it contains 62 bytes.

Preventing Lost Data

The example programs in this chapter use handshaking to enable each end of the asynchronous serial or parallel link to indicate when it's OK to send data. Handshaking isn't needed if both ends of the link have buffers large enough to store received data until the CPU can read it. Devices like Parallax Inc.'s Basic Stamp, which can accept serial data only when executing a SerialIn statement, will almost certainly need handshaking to prevent missed data.

When a CPU writes asynchronous serial data to a '232BM, the chip stores the received data in a 384-byte transmit buffer and sends the data to the host in response to IN packets as described above. Because the interface uses bulk transfers, there's no guarantee of when the host will request the data. If the bus is busy or the host is occupied with other tasks, USB communications with the device may have to wait. If the transmit buffer is full and the CPU continues to send data to the '232BM, data will be lost. Handshaking provides a way for the '232BM to let the device's CPU know when it's OK to send data. At the host, an application can usually reserve a generous buffer to hold data until the application can use it.

In the other direction, application software on the host writes data to a buffer. The host's driver sends the data in the buffer to the '232BM in OUT bulk transfers. The '232BM can store up to 128 bytes received from the host. If the buffer is full, the '232BM returns NAKs in response to attempts to send more data. The '232BM sends the data received from the host to the device's CPU via the asynchronous serial link. The CPU and related circuits that receive the data from the '232BM may have a very small buffer or no buffer at all. If there is a chance that the '232BM will write data faster than the CPU can deal with it, handshaking can prevent lost data.

The '232BM supports three handshaking methods. The example programs use the RTS# and CTS# pins. The DTR# and DSR# pins can be used in the same way. A circuit can also use both pairs as defined in the TIA/EIA-232 standard. A third option is Xon/Xoff software handshaking, which uses dedicated codes embedded in the data to request stopping and starting transmissions.

The '245BM has the same buffers as the '232BM. The chip supports handshaking via the RXF# and TXE# pins, which enable each end to indicate when it's ready to receive data, and by the RD# and WR signals, which indicate when a read or write operation is complete.

EEPROM Programming

The D2XX Direct Driver enables application software to read and write to an EEPROM that connects to a '232BM or '245BM over a Microwire synchronous serial interface.

EEPROM Data

An EEPROM is required if you want to customize any of a variety of device characteristics, including the Vendor ID, Product ID, or support for remote wakeup. Listing 14-3 shows a C structure that contains the values an application can write to an EEPROM using the D2XX driver and FT_EE_Program function.

An EEPROM can also store data in a user area. Host applications can read and write to this area, but the device's CPU can access the user area only when the USB controller is in the Reset state.

Editing the Data

FTDI Chip provides an MPROG utility that enables storing a new Vendor ID, Product ID, serial number, and other information in an EEPROM that interfaces to a '232BM or '245BM. A complication is that the utility requires the D2XX driver to be assigned to the controller, yet Windows may balk at assigning the D2XX driver to a device that uses the default IDs. To

```
typedef struct ft_program_data {

    DWORD Signature1;              // Header - must be 0x00000000
    DWORD Signature2;              // Header - must be 0xFFFFFFFF
    DWORD Version;                 // Header - FT_PROGRAM_DATA version
                                   //   0 = original,
                                   //   1 = contains FT2232C extensions
    WORD VendorId;                 // Vendor ID (0x0403)
    WORD ProductId;                // Product ID (0x6001)
    char *Manufacturer;            // Pointer to Manufacturer string
                                   //   ("FTDI")
    char *ManufacturerId;          // Pointer to Manufacturer ID string
                                   //   ("FT")
    char *Description;             // Pointer to Device descr. string
                                   //   ("USB HS Serial Converter")
    char *SerialNumber;            // Pointer to Serial Number string
                                   //   ("FT000001" if fixed, or NULL)
    WORD MaxPower;                 // Max. required bus current (mA) (44)
    WORD PnP;                      // Plug and Play:
                                   //   disabled (0), enabled (1)
    WORD SelfPowered;              // power source: bus (0), self (1)
    WORD RemoteWakeup;             // remote wakeup available:
                                   //   no (0), yes (1)
    //
    // Rev4 (-BM series) extensions
    //
    UCHAR Rev4;                    // Chip series:
                                   //   -BM series (0), other (non-zero)
    UCHAR IsoIn;                   // IN endpoint:
                                   //   bulk (0), isochronous (non-zero)
    UCHAR IsoOut;                  // OUT endpoint:
                                   //   bulk (0), isochronous (non-zero)
    UCHAR PullDownEnable;          // pull-down mode:
                                   //   not enabled (0), enabled (1)
    UCHAR SerNumEnable;            // serial number:
                                   // enabled (non-zero), not enabled (0)
    UCHAR USBVersionEnable;        // USBVersion enabled?
                                   //   yes (non-zero), no (0)
    WORD USBVersion;               // USB version (BCD) (0x0200 = USB2.0)
```

Listing 14-3: The EEPROM data structure for an FTDI Chip device. Bold text indicates default values. Adapted from FTDI Chips' D2XX Programmer's Guide. (Sheet 1 of 2)

```
// FT2232C extensions

UCHAR Rev5;               // FT2232C chip? yes (non-zero), no (0)
UCHAR IsoInA;             // "A" channel IN endpoint:
                          // bulk (0), isochronous (non-zero)
UCHAR IsoInB;             // "B" channel IN endpoint:
                          // bulk (0), isochronous (non-zero)
UCHAR IsoOutA;            // "A" channel OUT endpoint:
                          // bulk (0), isochronous (non-zero)
UCHAR IsoOutB;            // "B" channel OUT endpoint:
                          // bulk (0), isochronous (non-zero)
UCHAR PullDownEnable5;    // pull-down mode:
                          // not enabled (0), enabled (1)
UCHAR SerNumEnable5;      // serial number:
                          // enabled (non-zero), not enabled (0)
UCHAR USBVersionEnable5;  // USBVersion enabled?
                          // yes (non-zero), no (0)
WORD USBVersion5;         // USB version (BCD) (0x0200 = USB2.0)
UCHAR AIsHighCurrent;     // "A" channel is high current?
                          // yes (non-zero), no (0)
UCHAR BIsHighCurrent;     // "B" channel is high current?
                          // yes (non-zero), no (0)
UCHAR IFAIsFifo;          // "A" channel is 245 FIFO?
                          // yes (non-zero), no (0)
UCHAR IFAIsFifoTar;       // "A" channel is 245 FIFO CPU target?
                          // yes (non-zero), no (0)
UCHAR IFAIsFastSer;       // "A" channel is Fast Serial?
                          // yes (non-zero), no (0)
UCHAR AIsVCP;             // "A" channel uses VCP driver?
                          // yes (non-zero), no (0)
UCHAR IFBIsFifo;          // "B" channel is 245 FIFO?
                          // yes (non-zero), no (0)
UCHAR IFBIsFifoTar;       // "B" channel is 245 FIFO CPU target?
                          // yes (non-zero), no (0)
UCHAR IFBIsFastSer;       // "B" channel is Fast Serial?
                          // yes (non-zero), no (0)
UCHAR BIsVCP;             // "B" channel uses VCP driver?
                          // yes (non-zero), no (0)
} FT_PROGRAM_DATA, *PFT_PROGRAM_DATA;
```

Listing 14-3: The EEPROM data structure for an FTDI Chip device. Bold text indicates default values. Adapted from FTDI Chips' D2XX Programmer's Guide. (Sheet 2 of 2) enable running MPROG on a device that has the default Vendor ID and Product ID and uses the VCP driver, FTDI Chip provides an application that changes the Product ID to a special "D2XX Recovery" Product ID (6006h) and an INF file that specifies the D2XX driver for devices with that Product ID. You can then run MPROG and store your final Vendor ID and/or Product ID in the EEPROM. An alternative is to use other methods to program the EEPROMs before interfacing them to the controllers.

15

Hubs: the Link between Devices and the Host

Every USB peripheral must connect to a hub. As Chapter 1 explained, a hub is an intelligent device that provides attachment points for devices and manages each device's connection to the bus. Devices that plug directly into a PC connect to the root hub. Other devices connect to external hubs downstream from the root hub.

A hub's main jobs are managing its devices' connections and power and passing traffic to and from the host. Managing the connections includes helping to get newly attached devices up and communicating and blocking communications from misbehaving devices so they don't interfere with other communications on the bus. Managing power includes providing the requested bus current to attached devices. The hub's role in passing traffic to and from the host depends on the speed of the host, the device, and the

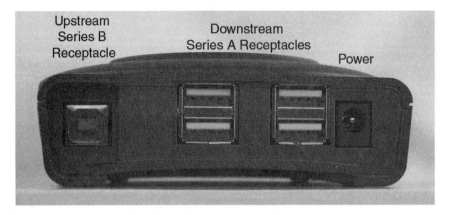

Figure 15-1: A hub has one upstream port and one or more downstream ports.

hubs between them. A hub may just repeat what it receives or it may convert the traffic to a different speed and manage transactions with the device.

This chapter presents essentials about hub communications. You don't need to know every detail about hubs in order to design a USB peripheral. Host applications and device drivers and device firmware don't have to know or care how many hubs are between the host and a device. But some understanding of what the hub does can help in understanding how devices are detected and communicate on the bus.

Hub Basics

Each external hub has one port, or attachment point, that connects in the upstream direction (toward the host) (Figure 15-1). This upstream port may connect directly to the host's root hub, or the port may connect to a downstream port on another external hub. Each hub also has one or more ports downstream from the host. Most downstream ports have a connector for attaching a cable. An exception is a hub that is part of a compound device whose ports connect to functions embedded in the device. Hubs with one, two, four, and seven downstream ports are common. A hub may be self-powered or bus-powered. As Chapter 16 explains, bus-powered hubs are limited because you can't attach high-power devices to them.

Every external hub has a hub repeater and a hub controller. (Figure 15-2). The hub repeater is responsible for passing USB traffic between the host's root hub or another upstream hub and whatever downstream devices are attached and enabled. The hub controller manages communications between the host and the hub repeater. State machines control the hub's response to events at the hub repeater and upstream and downstream ports. (The timing requirements are too strict to be handled by firmware.) A 2.0 hub also has one or more transaction translators and routing logic that enable low- and full-speed devices to communicate on a high-speed bus.

The host's root hub is a special case. The host controller performs many of the functions that the hub repeater and hub controller perform in an external hub, so a root hub may contain little more than routing logic and downstream ports.

The Hub Repeater

The hub repeater re-transmits, or repeats, the packets it receives, sending them on their way either upstream or downstream with minimal changes. The hub repeater also detects when a device is attached and removed, establishes the connection of a device to the bus, detects bus faults such as over-current conditions, and manages power to the device.

The hub repeater in a 2.0 hub has two modes of operation depending on the upstream bus speed. When the hub connects upstream to a full-speed bus segment, the repeater functions as a low- and full-speed repeater. When the hub connects upstream to a high-speed bus segment, the repeater functions as a high-speed repeater. The repeaters in 1.x hubs always function as low- and full-speed repeaters.

The Low- and Full-speed Repeater

The hub repeater in a 1.x hub handles low- and full-speed traffic. A 2.0 hub also uses this type of repeater when its upstream port connects to a full-speed bus. In this case, the 2.0 hub doesn't send or receive high-speed traffic but instead functions identically to a 1.x hub.

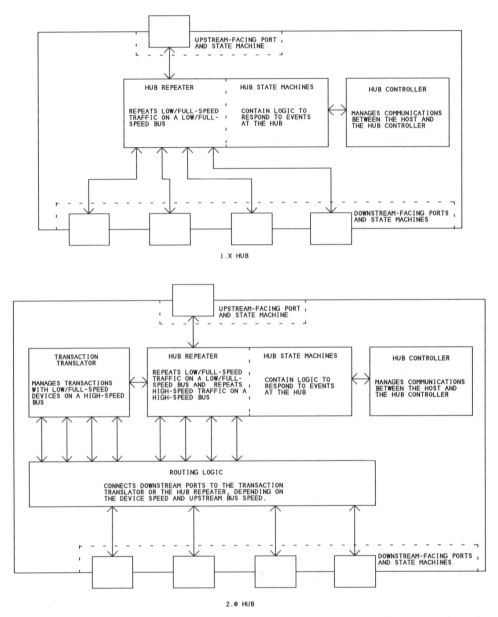

Figure 15-2: A 2.0 hub contains one or more transaction translators and routing logic that enable a hub on a high-speed bus to communicate with low- and full-speed devices. In a 1.x hub, the hub repeater is routed directly to the downstream ports.

A 1.x hub repeats all low- and full-speed packets received from the host (including data that has passed through one or more additional hubs) to all enabled, full-speed, downstream ports. Enabled ports include all ports with attached devices that are ready to receive communications from the hub. Devices with ports that aren't enabled include devices that the host controller has stopped communicating with due to errors or other problems, devices in the Suspend state, and devices that aren't yet ready to communicate because they have just been attached or are in the process of exiting the Suspend state.

The hub repeater doesn't translate, examine the contents of, or process the traffic to or from full-speed ports in any way. The hub repeater just regenerates the edges of the signal transitions and passes them on.

Low-speed devices never see full-speed traffic. A 1.x hub repeats only low-speed packets to low-speed devices. The hub identifies a low-speed packet by the PRE packet identifier that precedes the packet. The hub repeats the low-speed packets, and only these packets, to any enabled low-speed ports. The hub also repeats low-speed packets to its full-speed downstream ports, because a full-speed port may connect to a hub that in turn connects to a low-speed device. To give the hubs time to make their low-speed ports ready to receive data, the host adds a delay of at least four full-speed bit widths between the PRE packet and the low-speed packet.

Compared to full speed, traffic in a low-speed cable segment varies not only in speed, but also in edge rate and polarity. The hub nearest to a low-speed device uses low speed's edge rate and polarity when communicating with the device. When communicating upstream, the hub uses full-speed's faster edge rate and an inverted polarity compared to low speed. The hub repeater converts between the edge rates and polarities as needed. Chapter 18 has more on the signal polarities, and Chapter 19 has more about edge rates.

The High-speed Repeater

A 2.0 hub uses a high-speed repeater when the hub's upstream port connects to a high-speed bus segment. When this is the case, the hub sends and receives all upstream traffic at high speed, even if the traffic is to or from a low- or full-speed device. The path that traffic takes through a hub with a high-speed repeater depends on the speeds of the attached devices. Routing logic in the hub determines whether traffic to or from a downstream port passes through a transaction translator.

Unlike a low- and full-speed repeater, a high-speed repeater re-clocks received data to minimize accumulated jitter. In other words, instead of just repeating received transitions, a high-speed repeater extracts the data and uses its own local clock to time the transitions when retransmitting. The edge rate and polarity are unchanged. An elasticity buffer allows for small differences between the two clock frequencies. When the buffer is half full, the received data begins to be clocked out.

High-speed devices don't use the transaction translator. Traffic is routed from the receiving port on the hub, through the high-speed repeater, to the hub's transmitting port.

For traffic to and from low- and full-speed devices, the high-speed repeater communicates with the transaction translator that manages the transactions with the devices. Traffic received from upstream is routed to the high-speed repeater, then passes through the transaction translator, which communicates at the appropriate speed with the downstream ports. In the other direction, traffic from low- and full-speed devices is routed to the transaction translator, which processes the received data and takes appropriate action as described in the next section.

The Transaction Translator

Every 2.0 hub must have a transaction translator to manage communications with low- and full-speed devices. The transaction translator communicates upstream at high speed but enables 1.x devices to communicate at low and full speeds in exactly the same way as they do with 1.x hosts. The transaction translator stores received data and then forwards the data on toward its destination at a different speed.

The transaction translator frees bus time by enabling other bus communications to occur while a device is completing a low- or full-speed transaction.

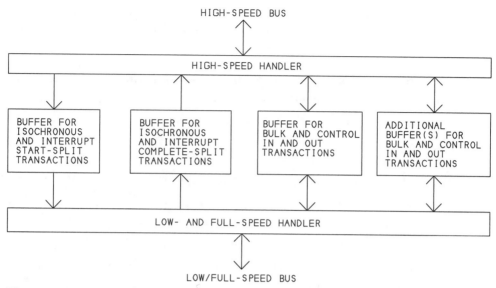

Figure 15-3: A transaction translator contains a high-speed handler for upstream traffic, buffers for storing information in split transactions, and a low- and full-speed handler for downstream traffic to low- and full-speed devices.

Transaction translators can also enable low- and full-speed devices to use more bandwidth than they would have on a shared 1.x bus.

Sections

The transaction translator contains three sections (Figure 15-3). The high-speed handler communicates with the host at high speed. The low/full-speed handler communicates with devices at low and full speeds. Buffers store data used in transactions with low- and full-speed devices. Each transaction translator has to have at least four buffers: one for interrupt and isochronous start-split transactions, one for interrupt and isochronous complete-split transactions, and two or more for control and bulk transfers.

Managing Split Transactions

When a 2.0 host on a high-speed bus wants to communicate with a low- or full-speed device, the host initiates a start-split transaction with the 2.0 hub that is nearest the device and communicating upstream at high speed. One or more start-split transactions contain the information the hub needs to complete the transaction with the device. The transaction translator stores the information received from the host and completes the start-split transaction with the host.

On completing a start-split transaction, the hub performs the function of a host controller in carrying out the transaction with the device. The transaction translator initiates the transaction in the token phase, sends data or stores returned data or status information as needed in the data phase, and sends or receives a status code as needed in the handshake phase. The hub uses low or full speed, as appropriate, in its communications with the device.

After the hub has had time to exchange data with the device, in all transactions except isochronous OUTs, the host initiates one or more complete-split transactions to retrieve the information returned by the device and stored in the transaction translator's buffer. The hub performs these transactions at high speed.

Figure 15-4 shows the transactions that make up a split transaction. Table 15-1 compares the structure and contents of transactions with low- and full-speed devices at different bus speeds.

In explaining how split transactions work, I'll start with bulk and control transfers, which don't have the timing constraints of interrupt and isochronous transfers. In the start-split transaction, the 2.0 host sends the start-split token packet (SSPLIT), followed by the usual low- or full-speed token packet, and any data packet destined for the device. The 2.0 hub that is nearest the device and communicating upstream at high speed returns ACK or NAK. The host is then free to use the bus for other transactions. The device knows nothing about the transaction yet.

On returning ACK in a start-split transaction, the hub has two responsibilities. The hub must complete the transaction with the device. And the hub must continue to handle any other bus traffic received from the host or other attached devices.

To complete the transaction, the hub converts the packet or packets received from the host to the appropriate speed, sends them to the device and stores the data or handshake returned by the device. Depending on the transac-

1. THE HOST INITIATES AND COMPLETES THE START-SPLIT TRANSACTION WITH THE HUB.

2. THE HUB INITIATES AND COMPLETES THE TRANSACTION WITH THE DEVICE.

3. THE HOST INITIATES AND COMPLETES THE COMPLETE-SPLIT TRANSACTION WITH THE HUB.

Figure 15-4: In a transfer that uses split transactions, the host communicates at high speed with a 2.0 hub, and the hub communicates at low or full speed with the device. Isochronous transactions may use multiple start-split or complete-split transactions.

tion, the device may return data, a handshake, or nothing. For IN transactions, the hub returns a handshake to the device. To the device, the transaction has proceeded at the expected low or full speed and is now complete. The device has no knowledge that it's a split transaction. The host hasn't yet received the device's response.

While the hub is completing the transaction with the device, the host may initiate other bus traffic that the device's hub must handle as well. The two functions are handled by separate hardware modules within the hub. When the host thinks the hub has had enough time to complete the transaction with the device, the host begins a complete-split transaction with the hub.

In a complete-split transaction, the host sends a complete-split token packet (CSPLIT), followed by a low- or full-speed token packet to request the data

Table 15-1: When a low- or full-speed device has a transaction on a high-speed bus, the host uses start-split (SSPLIT) and complete-split (CSPLIT) transactions with the 2.0 hub nearest the device. The hub is responsible for completing the transaction at low or full speed and reporting back to the host.

Bus Speed	Transaction Type	Transaction Phase		
		Token	Data	Handshake
Low/Full-speed communications with the device	Setup, OUT	PRE if low speed, LS/FS token	PRE if low speed, data	status (except for isochronous)
	IN	PRE if low speed, LS/FS token	data or status	PRE if low speed, status (except for isochronous)
High-speed communications between the 2.0 hub and host in transactions with a low- or full-speed device	Setup, OUT (isochronous OUT has no CSPLIT transaction)	SSPLIT, LS/FS token	data	status (bulk and control only)
		CSPLIT, LS/FS token	–	status
	IN	SSPLIT, LS/FS token	–	status (bulk and control only)
		CSPLIT, LS/FS token)	data or status	–

or status information the hub has received from the device. The hub returns the information. The transfer is now complete at the host. The host doesn't return an ACK to the hub. If the hub doesn't have the packet ready to send, the hub returns a NYET status code, and the host retries later. The device has no knowledge of the complete-split transaction.

In split transactions in interrupt and isochronous transfers, the process is similar, but with more strictly defined timing. The goal is to transfer data to the host as soon as possible after the device has data available to send, and to transfer data to the device just before the device is ready to receive new data. To achieve this timing, isochronous transactions with large packets use multiple start splits or complete splits, transferring a portion of the data in each.

Unlike with bulk and control transfers, the start-split transactions in interrupt and isochronous transfers have no handshake phase, just the start-split token followed by an IN, OUT, or Setup token and data for OUT or Setup transactions.

In an interrupt transaction, the hub schedules the start split in the microframe just before the earliest time that the hub is expected to begin the transaction with the device. For example, assume that the microframes in a frame are numbered in sequence, Y0 through Y7. If the start split is in Y0, the transaction with the device may occur as early as Y1. The device may have data or a handshake response to return to the host as early as Y2. The results of previous transactions and bit stuffing can affect when the transaction with the device actually occurs, so the host schedules time for three complete-split transactions, in Y2, Y3, and Y4. If the hub doesn't yet have the information to return in a complete split, the hub returns a NYET status code and the host retries.

Full-speed isochronous transactions can transfer up to 1023 bytes. To ensure that the data transfers just in time, or as soon as the device has data to send or is ready to receive data, transactions with large packets use multiple start splits or complete splits, with up to 188 bytes of data in each. This is the maximum amount of full-speed data that fits in a microframe. A single transaction's data can require up to eight start-split or complete-split transactions.

In an isochronous IN transaction, the host schedules complete-split transactions in every microframe where the host expects that the device will have at least a portion of the data to return. Requesting the data in smaller chunks ensures that the host receives the data as quickly as possible. The host doesn't have to wait for all of the data to transfer from the device at full speed before beginning to retrieve the data.

In an isochronous OUT transaction, the host sends the data in one or more start-split transactions. The host schedules the transactions so the hub's buffer will never be empty but will contain as few bytes as possible. Each SPLIT packet contains bits to indicate the data's position in the low- or full-speed data packet (beginning, middle, end, or all). There is no complete-split transaction.

Bandwidth Use of Low- and Full-speed Devices

Because a 2.0 hub acts as a host controller in managing transactions, low- and full-speed devices share 1.x bandwidth only with devices that use the same transaction translator. So if two full-speed devices connect to their own 2.0 hubs on a high-speed bus, each device can use all of the full-speed bandwidth it wants. When the hub converts to high speed, the 1.x communications will use little of the high-speed bandwidth.

However, for bulk transactions, the extra transaction with the host in each split transaction can slow the rate of data transfer with a full-speed device on a busy bus that is also carrying high-speed bulk traffic.

Many hubs provide one transaction translator for all ports, but a single hub can also have a transaction translator for each port that connects to a low- or full-speed device.

The Hub Controller

The hub controller manages communications between the host and the hub. The communications include enumeration along with other communications and actions due to events at downstream ports.

As it does for all devices, the host enumerates a newly detected hub to find out its abilities. The hub descriptor retrieved during enumeration tells the host how many ports the hub has. After enumerating the hub, the host requests the hub to report whether there are any devices attached. If so, the host enumerates these as well.

The host finds out if a device is attached to a port by sending the hub-class request Get_Port_Status. This is similar to a Get_Status request, but sent to a hub with a port number in the Index field. The hub returns two 16-bit values that indicate whether a device is attached as well as other information, such as whether the device is low power or in the Suspend state.

The hub controller is also responsible for disabling any port that was responsible for loss of bus activity or babble. Loss of bus activity occurs when a packet doesn't end with the expected End-of-Packet signal. Babble occurs when a device continues to transmit beyond the End-of-Packet signal.

In addition to Endpoint 0, which all devices must have for control transfers, each hub must have a Status Change endpoint configured for interrupt IN transfers. The host polls this endpoint to find out if there have been any changes at the hub. On each poll, the hub controller returns either a NAK if there have been no changes, or data that indicates a specific port or the hub itself as the source of the change. If there is a change, the host sends requests to find out more about the change and to take whatever action is needed. For example, if the hub reports the attachment of a new device, the host attempts to enumerate it.

Speed

An external 2.0 hub's downstream ports must support all three speeds. In the upstream direction, if a 2.0 hub's upstream segment is high speed, the hub communicates at high speed. Otherwise, the hub communicates upstream at low and full speeds.

A 1.x hub's upstream port must support low- and full-speed communications. All downstream ports with connectors must support both low- and full-speed communications. 1.x hubs never support high speed.

Filtering Traffic according to Speed

Low-speed devices aren't capable of receiving full-speed data, so hubs don't repeat full-speed traffic to low-speed devices. This behavior is necessary because a low-speed device would try to interpret the full-speed traffic as low-speed data and might even mistakenly see what looks like valid data. Full- or high-speed data on a low-speed cable could also cause problems due to radiated electromagnetic interference (EMI). In the other direction, hubs receive and repeat any low-speed data upstream.

Low- and full-speed devices aren't capable of receiving high-speed data, so 2.0 hubs don't repeat high-speed traffic to these devices, including 1.x hubs.

Detecting Device Speed

On attachment, every device must support either low or full speed. A hub detects whether an attached device is low or full speed by detecting which

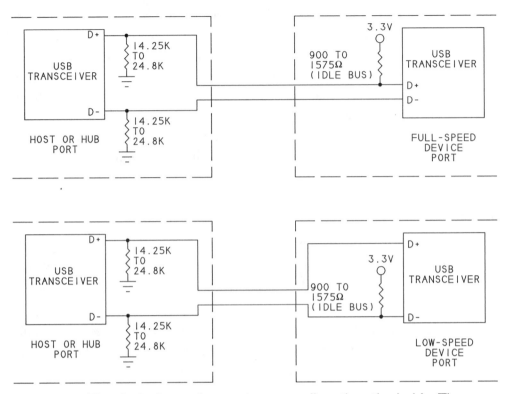

Figure 15-5: The device's port has a stronger pull-up than the hub's. The location of the pull-up tells the hub whether the device is low or full speed. High-speed devices are full speed at attachment.

signal line is more positive on an idle line. Figure 15-5 illustrates. As Chapter 4 explained, the hub has a pull-down resistor of 14.25 to 24.8 kilohms on each of the port's two signal lines, D+ and D-. A newly attached device has a pull-up resistor of 900 to 1575 ohms on either D+ for a full-speed device or D- for a low-speed device. When a device is attached to a port, the line with the pull-up is more positive than the hub's logic-high input threshold. The hub detects the voltage, assumes a device is attached, and detects the speed by which line is pulled up.

After detecting a full-speed device, a 2.0 hub determines whether the device supports high speed by using the high-speed detection handshake. The handshake occurs during the Reset state that the hub initiates during enumeration. If the handshake succeeds, the device removes its pull-up and communications are at high speed. A 1.x hub ignores the attempt to handshake, and the failure of the handshake informs the device that it must use full speed. Chapter 18 has more details about the handshake.

Maintaing an Idle Bus

Start-of-Frame packets keep full- and high-speed devices from entering the Suspend state on an otherwise idle bus. When there is no data on a full-speed bus, the host continues to send a Start-of-Frame packet once per frame, and all hubs pass these packets on to their full-speed devices. When there is no data on a high-speed bus, the host continues to send a Start-of-Frame packet once per microframe, and all hubs pass these packets on to their high-speed devices. A full-speed device that connects to a 2.0 hub that communicates upstream at high speed will also receive a Start-of-Frame once per frame.

Low-speed devices don't see the Start-of-Frame packets. Instead, at least once per frame, hubs must send their low-speed devices a low-speed End-of-Packet (EOP) signal (defined in Chapter 18). This signal functions as a keep-alive signal that keeps a device from entering the Suspend state on a bus with no low-speed activity. A host can also request a hub to suspend the bus at a single port. Chapter 16 has more on how hubs manage the Suspend state.

How Many Hubs in Series?

USB was designed for connecting to peripherals over short to moderate distances. But that hasn't stopped users from wondering just how far a USB peripheral can be from its host.

The USB 2.0 specification doesn't give a maximum length for cable segments, but the maximum allowed propagation delay limits the length to about 5 meters for full and high speed and 3 meters for low speed. You can increase the distance between a device and its host by using a series of hubs, each with a 5-meter cable.

The number of hubs you can connect in series is limited by the electrical properties of the hubs and cables and the resulting delays in propagating signals along the cable and through a hub. The limit is five hubs in series, with the hubs and the final device each using a 5-meter cable. The result is a device that is 30 meters from its host. If the device is low speed, the limit is 28 meters because the device's cable can be no more than 3 meters. Chapter 19 has more about extending the distance between a USB device and its host beyond these limits.

The Hub Class

Hubs are members of the Hub class, which is the only class defined in the main USB specification.

Hub Descriptors

A 1.x hub has a series of five descriptors: device, hub class, configuration, interface, and endpoint. A 2.0 hub has more descriptors because it must support all speeds and because the hub may offer a choice of using one or multiple transaction translators.

A 2.0 hub's descriptors include the device_qualifier descriptor and the other_speed_configuration_descriptor required for all high-speed-capable devices. The device_qualifier descriptor contains an alternate value for bDeviceProtocol in the device descriptor. The hub uses the alternate value when it switches between high and full speeds.

The other_speed_configuration_descriptor specifies the number of interfaces supported by the configuration not currently in use and is followed by the subordinate descriptors for that configuration. A configuration that supports multiple transaction translators has two interface descriptors: one for use with a single transaction translator and an alternate setting for use with multiple transaction translators. The bInterfaceProtocal field specifies whether the interface setting supports one or multiple transaction translators.

Hub Values for the Standard Descriptors

The USB specification assigns class-specific values for some parameters in a hub's device, and interface descriptors. The specification also defines the endpoint descriptor for the hub's status-change endpoint:

The device descriptor has these values:

> bDeviceClass: HUB_CLASSCODE (09h).
>
> bDeviceSubClass: 0.
>
> bDeviceProtocol: 0 for low/full speed, 1 for high speed when the hub supports a single transaction translator, 2 for high speed when the hub supports multiple transaction translators.

These fields also apply to the Device_Qualifier_Descriptor in 2.0 hubs.

The interface descriptor has these values:

> bNumEndpoints: 1.
>
> bInterfaceClass: HUB_CLASSCODE (09h).
>
> bInterfaceSubClass: 0.
>
> bInterfaceProtocol: 0 for a low/full speed hub or a high-speed hub with a single transaction translator. For a hub that supports single and multiple transaction translators, 1 indicates a single transaction translator, and 2 indicates multiple transaction translators.

The endpoint descriptor for the status change endpoint has these values:

> bEndpointAddress: implementation-dependent, with bit 7 (direction) = IN (01h).
>
> wMaxPacketSize: implementation-dependent.
>
> bmAttributes: Transfer Type = Interrupt.
>
> bInterval: FFh for full speed, 0Ch for high speed.

The Hub Descriptor

Each hub must have a hub-class descriptor that contains the following fields:

Identifying the Descriptor

bDescLength. The number of bytes in the descriptor.

bDescriptorType. Hub Descriptor, 29h.

Hub Description

bNbrPorts. The number of downstream ports the hub supports.

wHubCharacteristics:

Bits 1 and 0 specify the power-switching mode. 00=Ganged; all ports are powered together. 01=Ports are powered individually. 1X: used only on 1.0 hubs with no power switching.

Bit 2 indicates whether the hub is part of a compound device (1) or not (0).

Bits 4 and 3 are the Overcurrent Protection mode. 00 = Global protection and reporting. 01=Protection and reporting for each port. 1X = No protection and reporting (for bus-powered hubs only).

Bits 6 and 5 are the Transaction Translator Think Time. These bits indicate the maximum number of full-speed bit times required between transactions on a low- or full-speed downstream bus. 00 = 8; 01 = 16; 10 = 24; 11 = 32. Applies to 2.0 hubs only.

Bit 7 indicates whether the hub supports Port Indicators (1) or not (0). Applies to 2.0 hubs only.

Bits 8 through 15 are reserved.

bPwrOn2PwrGood. The maximum delay between beginning the power-on sequence on a port and when power is available on the port. The value is in units of 2 milliseconds. (Set to 100 for a 200-millisecond delay.)

bHubContrCurrent. The maximum current required by the hub controller's electronics only, in milliamperes.

DeviceRemovable. Indicates whether the device(s) attached to the hub's ports are removable (0) or not (1). The number of bits in this value equals the number of ports on the hub + 1. Bit 0 is reserved. Bit 1 is for Port 1, bit 2 is for Port 2, and so on up.

PortPowerCtrlMask. All bits should be 1. This field is only for compatibility with 1.0 software. Each port has one bit, and the field should be padded with additional 1s so that the field's size in bits is a multiple of 8.

Table 15-2: The 2.0 hub class has 12 class-specific requests, while the 1.x hub class has 9. Many are hub-specific variants of USB's standard requests.

Request	USB Versions	bRequest	Data source	wValue	wIndex	Data Length (bytes) (Data stage)	Data (in the Data stage)
Clear Hub Feature	all	Clear_ Feature	no Data stage	feature	0	–	–
Clear Port Feature	all	Clear_ Feature	no Data stage	feature	port	–	–
Clear TT Buffer	2.0 only	Clear_TT _Buffer	no Data stage	device address, endpoint #	TT_port	–	–
Get Bus State	1.x only	Get_State	Hub	0	port	1	per-port bus state
Get Hub Descriptor	all	Get_ Descriptor	Hub	descriptor type & index	0 or language ID	descriptor length	descriptor
Get Hub Status	all	Get_ Status	Hub	0	0	4	hub status and change indicators
Get Port Status	all	Get_ Status	Hub	0	port	4	port status and change indicators
Get TT State	2.0 only	Get_TT State	hub	TT flags	port	TT state, length	TT state
Reset TT	2.0 only	Reset_TT	no Data stage	0	port	–	–
Set Hub Descriptor (optional)	all	Set_ Descriptor	host	descriptor type and index	0 or language ID	descriptor length	descriptor length
Set Hub Feature	all	Set_ Feature	no Data stage	feature	0	–	–
Set Port Feature	all	Set_ Feature	no Data stage	feature	port	–	–
Stop TT	2.0 only	Stop_TT	no Data stage	0	port	–	–

Hub-class Requests

All hubs accept or return data for seven of the USB's eleven standard requests. Some 2.0 hubs support an additional request. Of the other standard requests, one is optional and the other two are undefined for hubs. Like all devices, hubs must return STALL for unsupported requests.

Hubs respond in the standard way to Clear_Feature, Get_Configuration, Get_Descriptor, Get_Status, Set_Address, Set_Configuration, and Set_Feature requests. Set_Descriptor is optional and should return STALL if not supported. Only 2.0 hubs that support multiple transaction translators support Get_Interface and Set_Interface. A hub can't have an isochronous endpoint, so Synch_Frame is undefined for hubs.

The hub class defines eight hub-specific requests that build on the standard requests with hub-specific values. For example, a Get_Status request directed to a hub with Index = 0 causes the hub to return a value in a Data packet indicating whether the hub is using an external power supply and whether an over-current condition exists.

Table 15-2 shows the hub-specific requests. One request from the 1.x specification, Get_Bus_State, isn't included in the 2.0 spec. This request enables the host to read the states of D+ and D- at a specified port on the hub.

The host uses many of the hub-specific requests to monitor and control the status of the hub and its ports. Get_Hub_Status reads status bits in a hub. Set_Hub_Feature and Clear_Hub_Feature set and clear status bits in a hub. Table 15-3 shows the bits and their meanings. In a similar way, Get_Port_Status, Set_Port_Feature, and Clear_Port_Feature enable the host to read and control status bits for a selected port in a hub. Table 15-4 shows the bits and their meanings.

In 2.0 hubs, Set_Port_Feature can place a port in one of five Test Modes. Chapter 18 has more about these modes.

The four new requests in the 2.0 spec all relate to monitoring and controlling the transaction translator (TT). The requests enable the host to clear a buffer in the TT, stop the TT, retrieve the state of a stopped TT using a vendor-specific format, and restart the TT by resetting it.

Table 15-3: The host can monitor and control Status bits in a hub using Get_Hub_Status, Set_Hub_Feature, and Clear_Hub_Feature.

Field	Bit	Status Indicator	Meaning (0 state/1 state)
Hub Status	0	HUB_LOCAL_POWER	Local power supply is good/not active.
	1	HUB_OVER_CURRENT	An over-current condition exists/does not exist.
	2-15	reserved	Returns 0 when read.
Hub Change	0	C_HUB_LOCAL_POWER	Local power status has not changed/changed.
	1	C_HUB_OVER_CURRENT	Over-current status has not changed/changed.
	2-15	reserved	Returns 0 when read.

Port Indicators

The USB 2.0 specification defines optional indicators to indicate port status to the user. Many hubs have status LEDs. The specification assigns standard meanings to the LEDs' colors and blinking properties. Bit 7 in the wHub-Characteristics field in the hub descriptor indicates whether a hub has port indicators.

Each downstream port on a hub can have an indicator, which can be either a single bi-color green/amber LED or a separate LED for each color. The indicator tells the state of the hub's port, not the attached device. These are the meanings of the indicators to the user:

Green: fully operational

Amber: error condition

Blinking off/green: software attention required

Blinking off/amber: hardware attention required

Off: not operational

Table 15-4: The host can monitor and control Status bits at a port using Get_Port_Status, Set_Port_Feature, and Clear_Port_Feature.

Field	Bit	Status Indicator	Meaning (0 state/1 state)
Port Status	0	PORT_CONNECTION	A device is not present/present.
	1	PORT_ENABLE	The port is disabled/enabled.
	2	PORT_SUSPEND	The port is not/is in the Suspend state.
	3	PORT_OVERCURRENT	An over-current condition exists/does not exist.
	4	PORT_RESET	The hub is not/is asserting Reset at the port.
	5-7	reserved	Returns 0 when read.
	8	PORT_POWER	The port is/is not in the Powered Off state.
	9	PORT_LOW_SPEED	The attached device is full or high speed/low speed.
	10	PORT_HIGH_SPEED	The attached device is full speed/high speed. (2.0 hubs only)
	11	PORT_TEST	The port is not/is in the Port Test mode. (2.0 hubs only)
	12	PORT_INDICATOR	Port indicator displays default/software controlled colors. (2.0 hubs only)
	13-15	reserved	Returns 0 when read.
Port Status Change	0	C_PORT_CONNECTION	Connect status has not changed/changed.
	1	C_PORT_ENABLE	A Port Error condition does not/does exist.
	2	C_PORT_SUSPEND	Resume signaling is not/is complete.
	3	C_PORT_OVERCURRENT	The over-current condition has not/has changed.
	4	C_PORT_RESET	Reset processing is not/is complete.
	5-15	reserved	Returns 0 when read.

16

Managing Power

A convenient feature of USB is the ability for devices to draw power from the bus. Many devices can be entirely bus powered. But drawing power from the bus carries the responsibility to live within the limits of available power, including entering the low-power Suspend state when required.

This chapter will help you decide whether or not your design can use bus power. And whether your design is bus-powered or self-powered, you'll find out how to ensure that your design follows the USB specification's requirements for managing power.

Powering Options

Inside a typical PC is a power supply with amperes to spare. Many hubs have their own power supplies as well. Many USB peripherals can take advantage of these existing supplies rather than having to provide their own power sources.

The ability to draw power from the same cable that carries data to and from the PC has several advantages. Users no longer need an electrical outlet near the peripheral, and a peripheral can be physically smaller and lighter in weight without an internal power supply. A peripheral without a power supply costs less to manufacture and thus can sell for less. A bus-powered device can save energy because power supplies in PCs use efficient switching regulators rather than the cheap linear regulators in the "wall bugs" that many peripherals provide instead of an internal supply. (Most self-powered hubs use wall bugs, however.)

Before USB, most peripherals used the PC's RS-232 serial and printer ports. Neither of these includes a power-supply line. The ability to use bus power was so compelling that the designers of some peripherals that connect to these ports used schemes that borrow the small amount of current available from unused data or control outputs in the interface. With a super-efficient regulator, you can get a few milliamperes from a serial or parallel port to power a device. Another approach used by some peripherals was to kludge onto the keyboard connector, which has access to the PC's power supply. With USB, you don't have to resort to these tricks.

Voltages

The nominal voltage between the VBUS and GND wires in a USB cable is 5V, but the actual value can be a little more or quite a bit less. A device that uses bus power must be able to handle the variations.

These are the minimum and maximum voltages allowed at a hub's downstream ports:

Hub Type	Minimum Voltage	Maximum Voltage
High Power	4.75	5.25
Low Power	4.4	5.25

To allow for cable and other losses, devices should be able to function with supply voltages a few tenths of a volt less than the minimum available at the hub's connector. In addition, transient conditions can cause the voltage at a low-power hub's port to drop briefly to as low as 4.07V.

If components in a device need a higher voltage, the device can contain a step-up switching regulator. Most USB controller chips require a +5V or +3.3V supply. Components that use 3.3V are handy because the device can use an inexpensive low-dropout linear regulator to obtain 3.3V from VBUS.

Which Peripherals Can Use Bus Power?

Not every peripheral can take advantage of bus power. Although the bus can provide generous amounts of current in comparison to other interfaces, the current available from a PC's power supply or an external hub is limited. Figure 16-1's chart will help you decide whether a device can use bus power.

Advances in semiconductor technology have reduced the power required by many electronic devices. This is good news for designers of bus-powered devices. Thanks to CMOS processes used in chip manufacturing, lower supply voltages for components, and power-conserving modes in CPUs, you can do a lot with 100 milliamperes.

A device that requires up to 100 milliamperes can be bus powered from any host or hub. A device that requires up to 500 milliamperes can use bus power when attached to a self-powered hub or any host except some battery-powered hosts. No device should draw more than 100 milliamperes until the host has configured the device. And all devices must limit their power consumption when the bus is suspended.

Of course, some devices need to function when they're not attached to a host. A digital camera is an example. These devices need their own supplies. Self power can use batteries or power from a wall socket. To save battery power without requiring users to plug in a supply, a device can be designed to be bus-powered when connected to the bus and self-powered otherwise. Some battery-powered devices can recharge when attached to the bus.

A device in the Suspend state can draw very little current from the bus, so some devices will need their own supplies to enable operating when the bus is suspended.

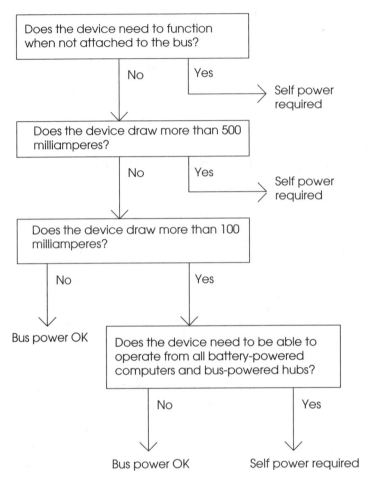

Figure 16-1: Not every device can use bus power alone. A device that uses bus power must also meet the USB specification's limits for Suspend current.

Power Needs

The USB specification defines a low-power device as one that draws up to 100 milliamperes from the bus, and a high-power device as one that draws up to 500 milliamperes from the bus. A self-powered device can draw up to 100 milliamperes from the bus and as much power as is available from the device's supply.

A high-power device must be able to enumerate at low power. On power-up, any device can draw up to 100 milliamperes from the bus until the device is configured during enumeration. After retrieving a configuration descriptor, the host examines the amount of current requested in bMaxPower, and if the current is available, the host sends a Set_Configuration request specifying the configuration. The device can then draw up to bMaxPower from the bus. In reality, hosts and hubs are likely to allocate either 100 or 500 milliamperes to a device rather than the precise amount requested in bMax-Power.

A self-powered device may also draw up to 100 milliamperes from the bus at any time that the bus isn't suspended. This capability enables the device's USB interface to function when the device's power supply is off so the host can detect and enumerate the device. Otherwise, if a device's pull-up is bus-powered but the rest of the interface is self-powered, the host will detect the device but won't be able to communicate with it.

These limits are absolute maximums, not averages. And remember that the bus's power-supply voltage can be as high as 5.25V, which may result in greater current consumption.

A device must never provide upstream power. Even the pull-up resistor must remain unpowered until VBUS is present. So self-powered devices must have a connection to VBUS to detect its presence even if the device never uses bus power.

Informing the Host

During enumeration, the host learns whether the device is self powered or bus powered and the maximum current the device will draw from the bus. As Chapter 4 explained, each device's configuration descriptor holds a bMaxPower value that specifies the maximum bus current the device requires. All hubs have over-current protection that prevents excessive current from flowing to a device.

If you connect a high-power device to a low-power hub, Windows displays a message informing you that the hub doesn't have enough power available and offering assistance. If the bus has a low-power device connected to a

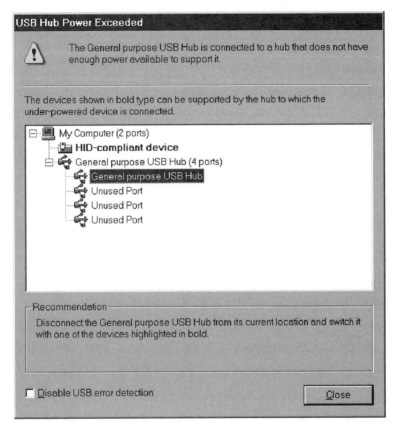

Figure 16-2: Windows warns users when they connect a high-power device to a low-power hub, and helps them find an alternate connection.

high-power port, Windows will recommend swapping the device with the high-power device (Figure 16-2).

A device can support both bus-powered and self-powered options, using self power when available and bus power (possibly with limited abilities) otherwise. When the power source changes, the host must re-enumerate the device. To enable forcing a re-enumeration, power to the device's bus pull-up resistor may be switched off briefly, then back on, to simulate a disconnect and re-connect. If the device doesn't have this ability, users will need to remove the device from the bus before attaching or removing the power supply. The device reports its use of bus or self power in response to a Get_Status (Device) request from the host.

Hub Power

Powering options for hubs are similar to the options for other devices, but hubs have some special considerations. A hub must also control power to its devices and monitor power consumption, taking action when the devices are using too much current and presenting a safety hazard.

Power Sources

Like other devices, all hubs except the root hub are self-powered or bus-powered. The root hub gets its power from the host.

If the host uses AC power from a wall socket or another external source, the root hub must be high power and capable of supplying 500 milliamperes to each port on the hub. If the host is battery-powered, the hub may supply either 500 or 100 milliamperes to each port on the hub. A hub that supplies 100 milliamperes is a low-power hub.

All of a bus-powered hub's downstream devices must be low power. The hub can draw no more than 500 milliamperes and the hub itself will use some of this, leaving less than 500 milliamperes for all attached devices combined.

Don't connect two bus-powered hubs in series. The upstream hub can guarantee no more that 100 milliamperes to each downstream port, and that doesn't leave enough current to power a second hub that also has one or more downstream ports, each requiring 100 milliamperes. An exception is a bus-powered compound device, which consists of a hub and one or more downstream, non-removable devices. In this case, the hub's configuration descriptor can report the maximum power required by the hub's electronics plus its non-removable device(s). The configuration descriptors for the non-removable device(s) report that the devices are self-powered with bMax-Power = 0. The hub descriptor indicates whether a hub's ports are removable.

Like other high-power, bus-powered devices, a bus-powered hub can draw up to 100 milliamperes until it's configured and up to 500 milliamperes after being configured. During configuration, the hub must manage the available current so its devices and the hub combined don't exceed the allowed current.

Like other self-powered devices, a self-powered hub may also draw up to 100 milliamperes from the bus so the hub interface can continue to function when the hub's power supply is off. If the hub's power is from an external source, such as AC power from a wall socket, the hub is high power and must be capable of supplying 500 milliamperes to each port on the hub. If the hub uses battery power, the hub may supply 100 or 500 milliamperes to each port on the hub.

Over-current Protection

As a safety precaution, hubs must be able to detect an over-current condition, which occurs when the current used by the total of all devices attached to the hub exceeds a preset value. When the port circuits on a hub detect an over-current condition, they limit the current at the port and the hub informs the host of the problem. Windows warns the user when a device exceeds the current limit of its hub port (Figure 16-3).

The USB 2.0 specification says only that the current that triggers the over-current actions must be less than 5 amperes. To allow for transient currents, the over-current value should be greater than the total of the maximum allowed currents for the devices. In the worst case, seven high-power, bus-powered downstream devices can legally draw up to 3.5 amperes. So a supply for a self-powered hub with up to seven downstream ports would provide much less than 5 amperes at all times unless something goes very wrong.

The USB specification allows a device to draw larger inrush currents when it attaches to the bus. This current is typically provided by the stored energy in a capacitor that is downstream from the over-current protection circuits so the protection circuits don't see the inrush current. If the inrush current is too large, the device will fail the USB-IF's compliance tests.

Figure 16-3: When a device exceeds the current limit of its hub's port, Windows warns the user and offers assistance.

Power Switching

A bus-powered hub must support power switching that can provide and cut off power to downstream ports in response to control requests. A single switch may control all ports, or the ports may switch individually. A self-powered hub must support switching to the Powered Off state and may also support power switching via control transfers.

Saving Power

The Suspend state reduces a device's use of bus power when the host has no reason to communicate with the device. A device must enter the Suspend state when there has been no activity on the bus for 3 milliseconds.

The USB specification limits the current that a suspended device can draw to a few milliamperes for high-power devices with remote wakeup enabled, and to much less than this amount for other devices. A device that needs to function even when the host has ceased communicating may need to be self-powered. However, many peripheral controllers can shut down and consume very little power while still being able to detect activity requiring attention on an I/O pin and wake up the host as needed.

Global and Selective Suspends

Most suspends are global, where the host stops communicating with the entire bus. When a PC detects no activity for a period of time, the PC enters a low-power state and stops sending Start-of-Frame packets on the bus. When a full-or high-speed device detects that no Start-of-Frame packet has arrived for 3 milliseconds, the device enters the Suspend state. Low-speed devices do the same when they haven't received a low-speed keep-alive signal for 3 milliseconds. A device must be in the Suspend state within 10 milliseconds of no bus activity.

A host may also request a selective suspend of an individual port. The host sends a Set_Port_Feature request to the a hub with the Index field set to a port number and the wValue field set to Port_Suspend. (See Chapter 15.) This request instructs the hub to stop sending any traffic, including Start-of-Frames or low-speed keep-alives, to the named port.

Current Limits for Suspended Devices

For all devices except high-power devices whose remote-wakup feature has been enabled, the USB 2.0 specification says that the device can draw no more than 500 *micro*amperes from the bus when in the Suspend state. This is very little current, and it includes the current through the device's bus

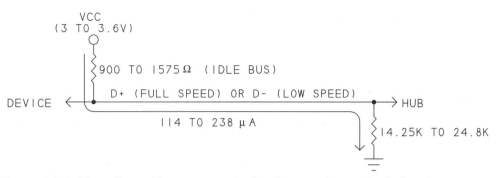

Figure 16-4: The allowed bus current in the Suspend state includes the current through the device's pull-up.

pull-up resistor. As Figure 16-4 shows, the pull-up current flows from the device's pull-up supply, which must be between 3.0 and 3.6V, through the device's pullup and the hub's pull-down, to ground. In the worst case, with a pull-up voltage of 3.6V and resistors that are the minimum allowed values, the pull-up current is 238 microamperes, leaving just 262 microamperes for everything else.

High-speed devices, which don't use pull-ups in normal communications, must switch to full speed and use a pull-up when entering the Suspend state. So high-speed devices have the same restriction on available current.

In compliance testing, however, the USB-IF has granted automatic waivers to low-power devices that consume up to 2.5 milliamperes in the Suspend state.

A high-power device that supports remote wakeup and whose remote-wakeup feature has been enabled by the host can draw up to 2.5 milliamperes from the bus when suspended, including current through the pull-up resistor. Every device connects as low power, so to comply with the USB specification, a device must meet the 500-microampere limit if the host suspends the device before configuring it as high power with remote wakeup enabled (assuming no waiver has been granted).

The limits are averages over intervals of up to 1 second, so brief currents can be greater. For example, a flashing LED that draws 20 milliamperes for one tenth of each second draws an average of 2 milliamperes per second.

A device should begin to enter the Suspend state after its bus segment has been in the Idle state for 3 milliseconds. The device must be in the Suspend state after its bus segment has been in the Idle state for 10 milliseconds.

Resuming Communications

When in the Suspend state, two actions can cause a device to enter the Resume state and restart communications. Any activity on the bus will cause the device to enter the Resume state. And if the device's remote wakeup feature is enabled by the host, the device itself may request a resume at any time.

To resume, the host places the bus in the Resume state (the K state, defined in Chapter 18) for at least 20 milliseconds. The host follows the Resume with a low-speed End-of-Packet signal. (Some hosts incorrectly send the End-of-Packet after just a few hundred microseconds.) The host then resumes sending Start-of-Frame packets and any other communications requested by the device driver.

A device causes a Resume by driving the upstream bus segment in the Resume state for between 1 and 15 milliseconds. The device then places its drivers in a high-impedance state to enable receiving traffic from the upstream hub. A device may initiate a Resume any time after the bus has been suspended for at least 5 milliseconds. The host-controller software must allow all devices at least 10 milliseconds to recover from a Resume.

Depending on a device's USB controller, monitoring the bus to determine whether to enter the Suspend state may require firmware support. The resume signaling is normally handled by the device's serial interface engine and requires no firmware support.

When a device uses bus power, the USB controller may need to control power to external circuits, removing power on entering the Suspend state and restoring power on resuming. A power switch with soft-start capability can prevent problems by limiting current surges when the switch turns on. Micrel Inc. has several power-distribution switches suitable for use with USB devices. Each switch contains one or more high-side MOSFET switches with soft-start capability.

Power Management under Windows

Recent PCs manage power according to the Advanced Configuration and Power Interface Specification (ACPI). The specification, first released in 1997, was developed by Hewlett-Packard, Intel, Microsoft, Phoenix Technologies, and Toshiba. Revision 3.0 was released in 2004. A system that implements ACPI power management enables the operating system to conserve power by shutting down components, including suspending the USB bus, when the computer is idle.

To implement ACPI, a PC must contain an ACPI controller. An ACPI BIOS provides tables that describe the power-management capabilities of system hardware and routines that the operating system can execute.

PCs support three low-power, or sleeping, states:

In the S1 state, the display is off and drives are powered down. USB buses are suspended, but VBUS remains powered.

In the S3 state, the PCI bus's main power supply is off and memory is not accessed, but system memory continues to be refreshed. Devices that can wake the system receive power from the PCI bus's auxiliary supply (Vaux). In older systems, USB's VBUS is not powered in the S3 state. In newer systems, VBUS is powered by Vaux.

In the S4 state, the system context is saved to disk and the system, including the USB bus, is powered off.

In Windows XP, you can view and change a system's power-management options in Control Panel > Power Options. In the Power Schemes tab (Figure 16-5), you can specify when the system goes into standby and hibernation. Hibernation is the S4 state. Standby is either S1 or S3. On a system that has no USB devices that can wake the system, the standby state is S3. On a system that has a USB keyboard, mouse, or another USB device that can wake the system, the standby state is S1 due to problems in using S3 with some (misbehaving) hardware. The problems include loss of VBUS in

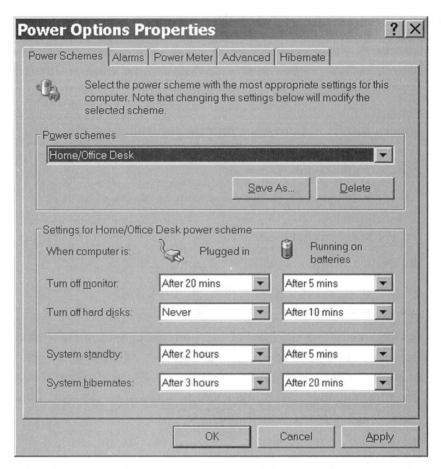

Figure 16-5: The Power Options Properties in Windows' Control Panel enable users to specify power-saving schemes that determine when USB devices must enter the Suspend state.

the S3 state, false device removal and arrival notifications on resuming, resetting of devices during suspend and resume, and failure to resume fully.

To enable or disable remote wakeup capability for a specific device that supports remote wakeup, in Windows' Device Manager, select the device, right-click, select Properties > Power Management, and check or uncheck *Allow this device to bring the computer out of standby.*

On some early Intel host controllers, a suspended root port didn't respond correctly to a remote wakeup. In addition, using remote wake-up requires work-arounds under Windows 98 Gold, Windows 98 SE, and Windows Me. With these operating systems, a device may wake up properly, but the device's driver isn't made aware of the wakeup so communications can't resume. A white paper from Intel titled *Understanding WDM Power Management* by Kosta Koeman (available from the USB-IF's Web site) details the problem and solutions. In short, a device using these operating systems shouldn't place itself in the Suspend state unless the host requests it, and the device driver requires extra code to ensure that the wake-up completes successfully. Windows 2000 and later don't have this problem.

Chapter 16

17

Testing and Debugging

In addition to the chip-specific development boards and debugging software described in Chapter 6, a variety of other hardware and software tools can help in testing and debugging USB devices and their host software. This chapter introduces tools available from the USB-IF and other sources. I also explain what's involved in passing the tests that required for devices and drivers to earn the Certified USB logo and the Windows logo.

Tools

Without a doubt the most useful tool for USB device developers is a protocol analyzer, which enables you to monitor USB traffic and other bus events. The analyzer collects data on the bus and decodes and displays the data you request in user-friendly formats. You can watch what happened during enumeration, detect and examine protocol and signaling errors, view data transferred during control, interrupt, bulk, and isochronous transfers, and focus on any aspect of a communication you specify.

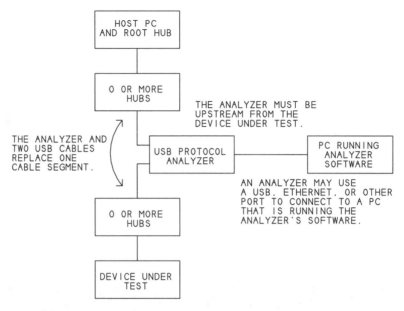

Figure 17-1: A hardware protocol analzyer monitors traffic between a device under test and the device's host. An interface to a PC (or logic analyzer) enables viewing the captured data.

A hardware analyzer is a combination of hardware and software, while a software analyzer consists only of software that runs on the device's host computer. The capabilities of the two types have much overlap, but each can also record and display information that isn't available to the other type.

Another useful tool is a traffic generator, which emulates a host or device and offers precise control over what the emulated host or device places on the bus.

Hardware Protocol Analyzers

A hardware protocol analyzer includes a piece of equipment that captures the signals in a cable segment without affecting the traffic in the segment. The analyzer connects in a cable segment upstream from the device under test (Figure 17-1). To enable viewing the captured traffic, the analyzer has another connection to a PC or logic analyzer. A connection to a PC can be via USB or another port type such as Ethernet. A few analyzers instead connect to logic analyzers from Agilent or Tektronix.

With a hardware analyzer, you can see the data in the cable down to the individual bytes that make up each packet. There's no question about what the host or device did or didn't send. For example, if the host sends an IN token packet, you can quickly see whether the device returned data or a NAK. You can view the packets in every stage of a control request. Time stamps enable you to see how often the host polls an endpoint.

Analyzers are available from a variety of vendors and with a range of prices. Ellisys' USB Explorer 200 is a relatively inexpensive yet very serviceable analyzer that supports all three bus speeds. In this chapter, I use the Explorer to illustrate the kinds of things you can do with an analyzer. Vendors are always updating and improving their products, so check for the latest information when you're ready to buy.

The Hardware

To use the Explorer, you must have two USB host controllers available. One communicates with the Explorer, and the other controls the bus being monitored. Both host controllers can be in the same PC, but for best performance, Ellisys recommends using two PCs.

The Explorer's back panel has a USB receptacle that connects to the PC that is running the Explorer's software. The PC detects the Explorer as a USB device that uses a vendor-specific driver provided by Ellisys.

Two USB receptacles on the front panel connect the analyzer in a cable segment upstream from the device being tested. One cable connects to the device being tested or a hub upstream from the device. The other cable connects to the host's root hub or another hub upstream from the analyzer.

The analyzer's circuits must capture the traffic as unobtrusively as possible. The host and device should detect no difference in the bus traffic when the analyzer is present. The two cables on the front panel and the analyzer's electronics must emulate an ordinary cable segment of 5 meters or less (3 meters or less for a low-speed segment). For these cables, Ellisys recommends using cables whose lengths together total 3 meters or less.

Item	Device	Endpoint	Status	Speed	Comment	Time
Enter text here	Ent...	Enter ...	Ent...	Ente...	Enter text here	Enter text here
Reset (4.0 s)						0.000 000 000
Suspended (159.2 ms)						3.954 854 458
Reset (11.0 ms)						4.114 037 395
GetDescriptor (Device)	0 (1)	0	OK	FS	8 bytes (12 01 00 02 00 00 00 08)	4.189 013 687
SETUP transaction	0 (1)	0	ACK	FS	8 bytes (80 06 00 01 00 00 40 00)	4.189 013 687
→ SETUP packet	0	0		FS		4.189 013 687
→ DATA0 packet				FS	8 bytes (80 06 00 01 00 00 40 00)	4.189 016 750
← ACK packet			ACK	FS		4.189 025 333
IN transaction	0 (1)	0	ACK	FS	8 bytes (12 01 00 02 00 00 00 08)	4.190 013 520
→ IN packet	0	0		FS		4.190 013 520
← DATA1 packet				FS	8 bytes (12 01 00 02 00 00 00 08)	4.190 016 625
→ ACK packet			ACK	FS		4.190 025 479
OUT transaction	0 (1)	0	ACK	FS	No data	4.192 013 250
→ OUT packet	0	0		FS		4.192 013 250
→ DATA1 packet				FS	No data	4.192 016 312
← ACK packet			ACK	FS		4.192 019 583
Reset (11.0 ms)						4.198 025 750
SetAddress (1)	0 (1)	0	OK	FS	No data	4.264 005 604
SETUP transaction	0 (1)	0	ACK	FS	8 bytes (00 05 01 00 00 00 00 00)	4.264 005 604
→ SETUP packet	0	0		FS		4.264 005 604
→ DATA0 packet				FS	8 bytes (00 05 01 00 00 00 00 00)	4.264 008 666
← ACK packet			ACK	FS		4.264 017 270
IN transaction	0 (1)	0	ACK	FS	No data	4.265 005 375
→ IN packet	0	0		FS		4.265 005 375
← DATA1 packet				FS	No data	4.265 008 458

Figure 17-2: Ellisys' USB Explorer 200 protocol analyzer includes Visual USB application software for viewing captured data. This example shows transactions and other events that occured when a device was attached downstream from the analyzer

The Software

Ellisys' Visual USB Analysis Software enables you to start and stop data logging and to save, view, and print the results. Figure 17-2 shows data captured by an analyzer. You can specify the amount, type, and format of data the displayed. For less detail, you can elect to hide the individual packets, repeated NAKs, and other information. Filters enable you to select the precise data to display. You can specify criteria such as a device or devices, endpoints, speeds, status codes, and control requests. The software displays only the traffic that meets the criteria you specify.

A Details pane provides more information about a request, transaction, packet, or other item in a row in the application's main window (Figure 17-3). A Data pane displays the individual bytes in hexadecimal and ASCII.

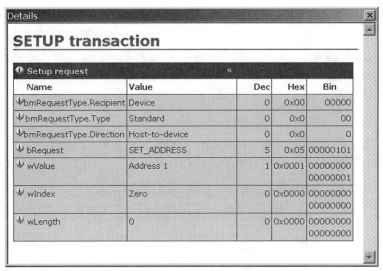

Figure 17-3: The Details pane in Ellisys' Visual USB software has more information about a request, transaction, packet, or other event.

You can also search for specific items, including events, token-packet types, traffic to and from a specific device or endpoint, and data.

Additional software modules add support for triggering on events, decoding class-specific information, and exporting captured data in text, XML, and other formats.

Software Protocol Analyzers

A software-only protocol analyzer runs on the host computer of the device being tested. You can view traffic to and from any device that connects to any of the computer's host controllers.

A software analyzer can display driver information that a hardware analyzer can't access. As Chapter 8 explained, Windows drivers communicate with USB devices using I/O Request Packets (IRPs) that contain USB Request Blocks (URBs). A software analyzer can show the IRPs and URBs that a driver has submitted and the responses received from a device.

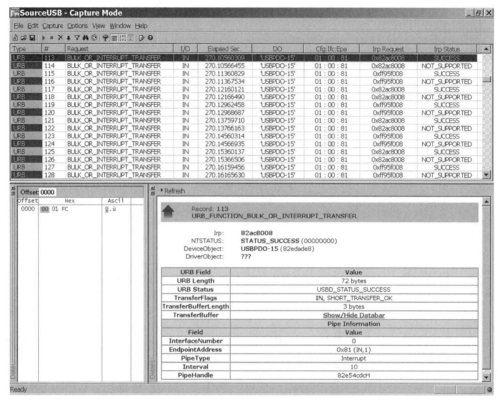

Figure 17-4: SourceUSB's application shows USB I/O requests at a host computer. These requests are for mouse communications.

But a software analyzer can't show anything that the host-controller or hub hardware handles on its own. For example, the analyzer won't show how many times an endpoint NAKed a transaction before returning an ACK or the precise time a transaction occurred on the bus.

Some software analyzers use a filter driver that loads when the operating system loads the driver for the device being monitored. Because the filter driver isn't loaded until the host has enumerated the device, the analyzer can't show the enumeration requests and other events that occur at device attachment.

Sourcequest, Inc.'s SourceUSB is a software analyzer that records USB I/O requests and other events, including enumeration requests. You can view the requests along with additional information about the system's host controllers, the devices on the host controllers' buses, and the drivers assigned to each host controller and device. Figure 17-4 shows logged requests and additional information about the request in the selected row.

The SourceUSB application can also display a tree of all of the system's host controllers and their attached devices and provide information about the drivers assigned to each host controller and device. As with a hardware analyzer, you have great flexibility in selecting what information you want to log and view.

Another software-only analyzer is the SnoopyPro project, free with source code from *www.sourceforge.net*.

Traffic Generators

Sometimes it's useful to be able to control bus traffic and signaling beyond what you can do from host software and device firmware. Some higher-end protocol analyzers can also function as traffic generators that emulate a host or device and give you precise control over the traffic that the emulated host or device places on the bus. In addition to generating valid traffic, a traffic generator can introduce errors such as bit-stuff and CRC errors. Two protocol analyzers with these abilities are Catalyst Enterprises, Inc.'s SBAE-30 Analyzer/Exerciser and LeCroy Corporation's CATC USBTracer/Trainer. Another option is RPM Systems' Root 2 USB Test Host, which emulates a USB host and enables you to specify traffic to generate on the bus, control the bus voltage, and measure bus current.

Testing

The USB-IF and Microsoft offer testing opportunities for developers of USB devices and host software. Passing the tests can earn a product the right to display the Certified USB logo and/or the Microsoft Windows logo. A logo can give users confidence that a device is thoroughly tested and reliable. A driver that passes Microsoft's tests can be digitally signed, which gives users confidence that the driver will work without problems.

Compliance Testing

One advantage USB has over other interfaces is that the developers of the specification didn't stop with the release of the specification. The USB-IF remains involved in helping developers design and test USB products. The USB-IF's Web site has many useful documents and tools.

The USB-IF has also developed a compliance program that specifies and sponsors tests for peripherals, hubs, host systems, On-The-Go devices, silicon building blocks, cable assemblies, and connectors. When a product passes the tests, The USB-IF deems it to have "reasonable measures of acceptability" and adds the product to its Integrators List of compliant devices. On receiving a signed license agreement and payment, the USB-IF authorizes the product to display the Certified USB logo. Even if you don't plan to submit your device to formal compliance testing, you can use the tests to verify your device's performance.

To pass compliance testing, a device must meet the requirements specified in the appropriate checklists and pass tests of the device's responses to standard control requests, the ability to operate under all host types and with other devices on the bus, and electrical performance. All of the tests except the high-speed electrical tests are described in the document *Universal Serial Bus Implementers Forum Full and Low Speed Electrical and Interoperability Compliance Test Procedure*. The specifications, procedures, and tools for high-speed electrical tests are in additional documents and files on the USB-IF's Web site.

You can submit a device for compliance testing at a compliance workshop sponsored by the USB-IF or at one of the independent labs that the USB-IF authorizes to perform the tests. To save time and expense, you should perform the tests as fully as possible on your own before submitting a product for compliance testing

Checklists

The compliance checklists contain a series of questions about a product's specifications and behavior. There are checklists for peripherals, hubs, hub and peripheral silicon, and host systems. The Peripheral checklist covers

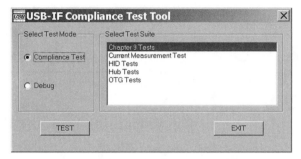

Figure 17-5: The USB Command Verifier utility includes several test suites.

mechanical design, device states and signals, operating voltages, and power consumption. You need to be able to answer yes to every question in the checklist. Accompanying each question is a reference to a section in the USB specification with more information.

Device Framework

The Device Framework tests verify that a device responds correctly to standard control requests. The USB Command Verifier (USBCV) software utility performs the tests. The document *USB Command Verifier Compliance Test Specification* describes the tests. The USBCV software and test-specification document are available from the USB-IF's Web site.

The USBCV software requires a PC with a USB 2.0 host controller. In addition, any low- or full-speed devices being tested must connect to the host via an external USB 2.0 hub. When you run USBCV, the software replaces the host-controller's driver with its own test-stack driver. On exiting USBCV, the software restores the original driver. The stack switching was tested using Microsoft's host-controller driver, and the USB-IF recommends running the software only on hosts that are using Microsoft's driver.

The software has several test suites: Chapter 9, Current Measurement, HID, Hub, and OTG (Figure 17-5).

In the Chapter 9 tests, the host issues the standard control requests defined in Chapter 9 of the USB specification and performs additional checks on the information returned by a device (Figure 17-6). For example, on retriev-

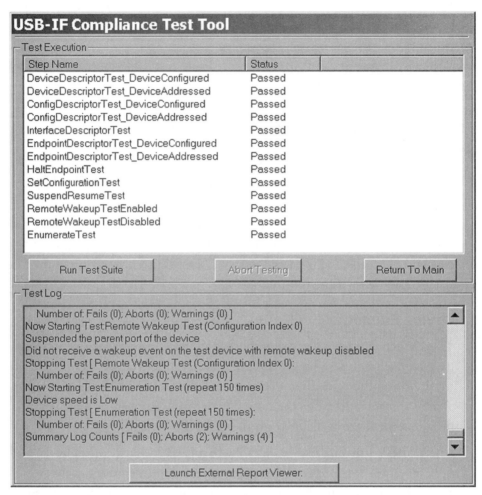

USB-IF Compliance Test Tool

Test Execution

Step Name	Status
DeviceDescriptorTest_DeviceConfigured	Passed
DeviceDescriptorTest_DeviceAddressed	Passed
ConfigDescriptorTest_DeviceConfigured	Passed
ConfigDescriptorTest_DeviceAddressed	Passed
InterfaceDescriptorTest	Passed
EndpointDescriptorTest_DeviceConfigured	Passed
EndpointDescriptorTest_DeviceAddressed	Passed
HaltEndpointTest	Passed
SetConfigurationTest	Passed
SuspendResumeTest	Passed
RemoteWakeupTestEnabled	Passed
RemoteWakeupTestDisabled	Passed
EnumerateTest	Passed

Run Test Suite   Abort Testing   Return To Main

Test Log

```
    Number of: Fails (0); Aborts (0); Warnings (0) ]
Now Starting Test:Remote Wakeup Test (Configuration Index 0)
Suspended the parent port of the device
Did not receive a wakeup event on the test device with remote wakeup disabled
Stopping Test [ Remote Wakeup Test (Configuration Index 0):
    Number of: Fails (0); Aborts (0); Warnings (0) ]
Now Starting Test:Enumeration Test (repeat 150 times)
Device speed is Low
Stopping Test [ Enumeration Test (repeat 150 times):
    Number of: Fails (0); Aborts (0); Warnings (0) ]
Summary Log Counts [ Fails (0); Aborts (2); Warnings (4) ]
```

Launch External Report Viewer.

Figure 17-6: USBCV's Chapter 9 tests check the device's responses to the control requests defined in Chapter 9 of the USB specification.

ing a device descriptor, the software checks to see that the bMaxPacketSize0 value is valid for the device's speed and that the bDeviceClass value is either a value for a standard class or 0FFh (vendor-defined). The software requests the device descriptor when the device is in the default, address, and configured states, at both full and high speeds if the device supports both, and in every supported configuration.

The Chapter 9 tests also include these tests:

- Enumerate the device multiple times with different addresses.
- Verify that all bulk and interrupt endpoints can be halted and unhalted with Set_Feature and Clear_Feature requests.
- Ensure that the device returns STALL in response to receiving a request for an unsupported descriptor type.
- Ensure that the device returns STALL in response to receiving a Set_Feature request for an unsupported feature.
- Suspend and resume the device.
- If the device supports remote wakeup, suspend the device and request the user to perform an action to wake the device.

Every device must pass all of the Chapter 9 tests.

The Current Measurement test suite pauses with the device in the unconfigured and configured states to enable you to measure the bus current the device is drawing in each state. In the unconfigured state, the device should draw no more than 100 milliamperes. When configured, the device should draw no more than the amount specified in the bMaxPower field of the configuration descriptor for the currently active configuration.

Additional test suites provide tests for hubs, HID-class devices, and devices that return On-The-Go (OTG) descriptors.

The software has two modes. Compliance Test mode runs an entire test suite. Debug mode enables selecting and running a single test within a suite and offers more control, such as selecting a configuration to use when running a test.

Interoperability Tests

The interoperability tests emulate a user's experience by testing a product with different host controllers and with a variety of other USB devices in use. The device must be tested under both EHCI/UHCI and EHCI/OHCI hosts and under hubs that do and don't support high speed. To enable testing both implementations of the S3 Sleep state, the device must be tested both under a host that maintains VBUS on entering the S3 state and under a host that removes VBUS on entering the S3 state. Devices are tested under all of these conditions:

- The bus is carrying control, bulk, interrupt, and isochronous transfers.
- There are five external hubs between the device and host.
- The device is 30 meters from the host (28 meters for low-speed devices).
- The bus is carrying full- and high-speed traffic.

For performing the tests, the test specification defines a Gold Tree that contains a variety of hubs and other devices on the bus with the device under test. As of revision 1.3 of the test specification, the Gold Tree contains these devices:

- Video camera: high speed, uses isochronous transfers, high power, bus powered.
- Mass storage device: high speed, uses bulk transfers, self powered.
- Flash media drive: high speed, uses bulk transfers, bus powered.
- Keyboard: low speed HID.
- Mouse: low speed HID.
- Seven hubs: five hubs that support all three bus speeds including one hub with multiple transaction translators; two hubs that support low and full speeds only.

The devices attach to the host in the configuration shown in Figure 17-7. The test specification names products that have been shown to have no interoperability problems of their own. You can use these or equivalent devices.

On attachment, the host must enumerate and install the driver for the device (with user assistance to identify the driver's location if appropriate). The device must operate properly while the other devices in the Gold Tree are also operating. In addition, the device must continue to operate properly after each of these actions:

- Detach the device and reattach it to the same port.
- Detach the device and attach it to a different port.

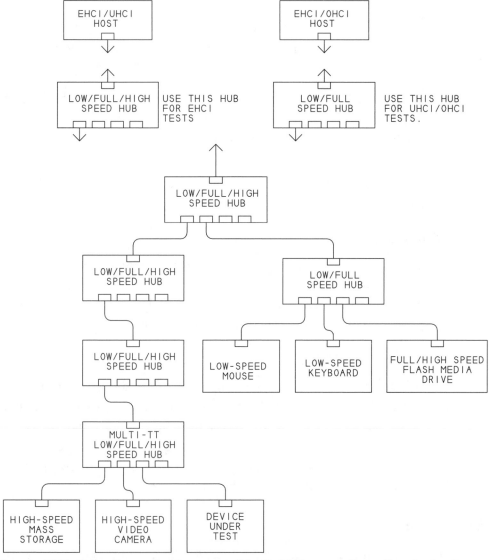

Figure 17-7: Compliance testing uses this Gold Tree configuration for testing how a device behaves in a system where other USB devices are in use.

- Do a warm boot. (Start > Shutdown > Restart.)
- Do a cold boot. (Start > Shutdown > Shutdown. Turn on the PC.)
- When the device is active, place the system in the S1 Sleep state and resume.
- When the device is idle, place the system in the S1 Sleep state and resume.
- When the device is active, place the system in the S3 Sleep state and resume.

A high-speed device must also be fully functional at full speed. The test specification has more details about the tests.

Waivers

A device can earn a USB Logo without passing every test. At its discretion, the USB-IF may grant a waiver of a requirement. For example, waivers have been granted for devices that should consume only 500 microamperes in the Suspend state but actually consume up to 2.5 milliamperes.

The Certified USB Logo

A device that passes compliance testing is eligible to display the official Certified USB logo. The logo indicates if a device supports high speed and/or USB On-The-Go (Figure 17-8). To use the logo, you must sign the USB-IF Trademark License Agreement. If you're not a member of the USB-IF, you also must pay a logo administration fee ($1500 at this writing). The logo is different from the USB icon described in Chapter 19.

WHQL Testing

For devices and drivers that will be used on Windows PCs, Microsoft offers Windows Hardware Quality Labs (WHQL) testing. The tests identify devices and drivers that "meet a baseline definition of platform features and quality goals that ensure a good Windows experience for the end user." When a device has passed WHQL tests, the device's packaging and marketing materials can display a *Designed for Microsoft Windows* logo. In

Figure 17-8: Devices that pass compliance testing can display one of the Certified USB logos. The logo indicates if the device supports high speed and/or USB On-The-Go.

Microsoft's online Windows Catalog of compatible devices, qualified devices show the logo in their listings. As Chapter 9 explained, a driver that passes WHQL testing has a digital signature that identifies the driver as a trusted driver.

The Windows Logo Program

To earn the Windows logo, a device must install and uninstall properly without interfering with other system components, and the device must interoperate well with other system components. Windows XP and Windows Server 2003 have different tests and logos. A device can qualify for multiple logos. Earning the Windows logo for a device requires performing the following steps:

- Pass the appropriate compatibility tests in the Windows Hardware Compatibility Test (HCT) kit provided by Microsoft.

- Use Microsoft's HCT Submission Review Utility to create a report that contains test logs of the compatibility tests.

- Submit the hardware, test logs, drivers (if any), user documentation, other configuration utilities or accessories as needed, and fee. The hardware is submitted to a Windows Quality Online Services test location. At this writing, the fee for most devices is $250 per operating system.

Microsoft's Web site has the latest information and downloads relating to WHQL testing.

Digital Signatures

To earn the Windows logo, a device must use a digitally signed driver. The driver may be one of the drivers included with the operating system or the vendor may supply the driver. To obtain a digital signature, a driver must pass WHQL testing and the vendor must provide a VeriSign Digital Code Signing ID obtained from *www.verisign.com*. At this writing, a VeriSign ID costs $400. Microsoft uses cryptographic technology to digitally sign the driver's catalog (*.cat*) file and returns the signed file to the vendor

The device's INF file references the catalog file. The signature enables Windows to detect if the driver has been modified since it passed WHQL testing. Each INF file has its own catalog file. A single INF file can support multiple devices. Any change in an INF file, including adding a new Product ID or device release number, requires obtaining a new digital signature.

For most USB devices, the INF file of a signed driver must include a device identification string that contains the device's VID and PID. An INF file that uses a compatible ID to identify the device only by class (and optional subclass and protocol) won't pass the WHQL tests, except for printers.

Your driver must be signed if you want it included in Microsoft's Windows Update. This feature of Windows makes it easy for users to update drivers installed on their systems. In some cases Windows Update can also find a driver for a newly installed device. A driver available via Windows Update must meet additional requirements to ensure that Windows can easily identify, download, and install the driver.

Under Windows Server 2003 and later, some devices can use an alternate way to obtain a digital signature. If WHQL doesn't have a test program for the driver's setup class, a vendor can use Microsoft's code-signing tools to generate an Authenticode signature for the driver.

18

Signals and Encoding

You can design and program a USB peripheral without knowing all of the details about how the data is encoded on the bus. But understanding something about these topics can help in understanding the capabilities and limits of your devices.

This chapter presents the essentials of the USB's encoding and data formats. The USB specification has the details.

Bus States

The USB specification defines bus states that correspond either to signal voltages on the bus or conditions that these voltages signify. Different cable segments on a bus may be in different states at the same time. For example, in response to a request from the host, a hub might place one of its downstream ports in the Reset state while its other ports are in the Idle state. Low/full speed and high speed each have different defined bus states, though with many similarities.

Low-speed and Full-speed Bus States

Low and full speed support the same bus states, though some are defined differently depending on the speed of the cable segment. A low-speed segment is a segment between a low-speed device and its nearest hub. A full-speed segment is any other segment that carries data at low- or full-speed bit rates.

Differential 0 and Differential 1

When transferring data, the two states on the bus are Differential 0 and Differential 1. A Differential 0 exists when D+ is a logic low and D- is a logic high. A Differential 1 exists when D+ is a logic high and D- is a logic low.Chapter 19 has details about the voltages that define logic low and high.

The Differential 0s and 1s don't translate directly into voltage levels, but instead indicate either a change in logic level, no change in logic level, or a bit stuff, as explained later in this chapter.

Single-Ended Zero

The Single-Ended-Zero (SE0) state occurs when both D+ and D- are logic low. The bus uses the SingleEnded-Zero state when entering the End-of-Packet, Disconnect, and Reset states.

Single-Ended One

The complement of the Single-Ended Zero is the Single-Ended One (SE1). This state occurs when both D+ and D- are logic high. This is an invalid bus state and should never occur.

Data J and Data K

In addition to the Differential 1 and 0 states, which are defined by voltages on the lines, USB also defines two Data bus states, J and K. These are defined by whether the bus state is Differential 1 or 0 and whether the cable segment is low or full speed:

Bus State	Data State	
	Low Speed	Full Speed
Differential 0	J	K
Differential 1	K	J

Defining the J and K states in this way makes it possible to use one terminology to describe an event or logic state even though the voltages on low- and full-speed lines differ. For example, a Start-of-Packet state exists when the bus changes from Idle to the K state. On a full-speed segment, the state occurs when D- becomes more positive than D+, while on a low-speed segment, the state occurs when D+ becomes more positive than D-.

Idle

In the Idle state, no drivers are active. On a full-speed segment, D+ is more positive than D-, while on a low-speed segment, D- is more positive than D+. Shortly after device attachment, a hub determines whether a device is low or full speed by checking the voltages on the Idle bus at the device's port.

Resume

When a device is in the Suspend state, the Data K state at the device's port signifies a resume from Suspend.

Start-of-Packet

The Start-of-Packet (SOP) bus state exists when the lines change from the Idle state to the K data state. Every transmitted low- or full-speed packet begins with a Start of Packet.

End-of-Packet

The End-of-Packet (EOP) state exists when a receiver has been in the Single-Ended-Zero state for at least one bit time, followed by a Data J state for at least one bit time. A receiver may optionally define a shorter minimum time for the Data J state. At the driver, the Single-Ended Zero is approximately two bit widths. Every transmitted low- or full-speed packet ends with an End of Packet.

Disconnect

A downstream port is in the Disconnect state when a Single-Ended Zero has lasted for at least 2.5 microseconds.

Connect

A downstream port enters the Connect state when the bus has been in the Idle state for at least 2.5 microseconds and no more than 2.0 milliseconds.

Reset

When a Single-Ended Zero has lasted for 10 milliseconds, the device must be in the Reset state. A device may enter the Reset state after the Single-Ended Zero has lasted for as little as 2.5 microseconds. A full-speed device that is capable of high-speed communications performs the high-speed handshake during the Reset state.

On exiting the Reset state, a device must be operating at its correct speed and must respond to communications directed to the default address (00h).

High-speed Bus States

Many of the high-speed bus states are similar to those for low and full speed. A few are unique to high speed, and some low- and full-speed bus states have no equivalent at high speed.

High-speed Differential 0 and Differential 1

The two bus states that exist when transferring high-speed data are High-speed Differential 0 and High-speed Differential 1. As with low and full speeds, a High-speed Differential 0 exists when D+ is a logic low and D- is a logic high, and a High-speed Differential 1 exists when D+ is a logic high and D- is a logic low. The voltage requirements differ at high speed, however, and high speed has additional requirements for AC differential levels.

High-speed Data J and Data K

The definitions for High-speed Data J and Data K states are identical to those for full-speed J and K:

Bus State	Data State, High Speed
Differential 0	K
Differential 1	J

Chirp J and Chirp K

The Chirp J and Chirp K bus states are present only during the high-speed detection handshake. The handshake occurs when a 2.0 hub has placed a downstream bus segment in the Reset state. Chirp J and Chirp K are defined as DC differential voltages. In a Chirp J, D+ is more positive than D-, and in a Chirp K, D- is more positive than D+.

A high-speed device must use full speed on attaching to the bus. The high-speed detection handshake enables a high-speed device to tell a 2.0 hub that the device supports high speed and to transition to high-speed communications.

As Chapter 4 explained, shortly after detecting device attachment, a device's hub places a device's port and bus segment in the Reset state. When a high-speed-capable device detects the Reset, the device sends a Chirp K to the hub for 1 to 7 milliseconds. A 2.0 hub that is communicating upstream at high speed detects the Chirp K and in response, sends an alternating sequence of Chirp Ks and Js. The sequence continues until shortly before the Reset state ends. At the end of Reset, the hub places the port in the High-speed Enabled state.

On detecting the Chirp K and Chirp J sequence, the device disconnects its full-speed pull-up, enables its high-speed terminations, and enters the high-speed Default state.

A 1.x hub ignores the device's Chirp K. The device doesn't see the answering sequence and knows that communications must take place at full speed.

High-speed Squelch

The High-speed Squelch state indicates an invalid signal. High-speed receivers must include circuits that detect the Squelch state, indicated by a differential bus voltage of 100 millivolts or less.

High-speed Idle

In the High-speed Idle state, no high-speed drivers are active and the low/full-speed drivers assert Single-Ended Zeroes. Both D+ and D- are between -10 and +10 millivolts.

Start of High-speed Packet

A Start-of-High-speed-Packet (HSSOP) exists when a segment changes from the High-speed Idle state to the High-speed Data K state. Every high-speed packet begins with a Start of High-speed Packet.

End of High-speed Packet

An End-of-High-speed-Packet (HSEOP) exists when the bus changes from the High-speed Data K or Data J state to the High-speed Idle state. Every high-speed packet ends with an End of High-speed Packet.

High-speed Disconnect

Removing a high-speed device from the bus also removes the high-speed line terminations at the device. The removal of the terminations causes the differential voltage at the hub to double. A differential voltage of 625 millivolts or more on the data lines indicates the High-speed Disconnect state. A 2.0 hub contains circuits that detect this voltage.

Data Encoding

All data on the bus is encoded. The encoding format, called *Non-Return to Zero Inverted (NRZI) with bit stuffing*, ensures that the receiver remains synchronized with the transmitter without the overhead of sending a separate clock signal or Start and Stop bits with each byte.

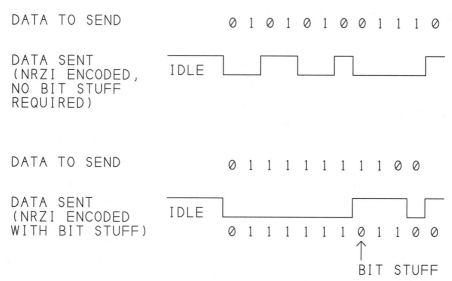

DATA TO SEND   0 1 0 1 0 1 0 0 1 1 1 0

DATA SENT
(NRZI ENCODED,   IDLE
NO BIT STUFF
REQUIRED)

DATA TO SEND   0 1 1 1 1 1 1 1 1 0 0

DATA SENT
(NRZI ENCODED   IDLE
WITH BIT STUFF)
                   0 1 1 1 1 1 1 0 1 1 0 0
                                   ↑
                                BIT STUFF

Figure 18-1: In NRZI encoding, a 0 causes a change and a 1 causes no change. Bit stuffing adds a 0 after six consecutive 1s.

If you use an oscilloscope or logic analyzer to view USB data on the bus, you'll find that unlike some other interfaces, reading the bits isn't as easy as matching voltage levels to logic levels.

Instead of defining logic 0s and 1s as voltages, NRZI encoding defines logic 0 as a voltage change, and logic 1 as a voltage that remains the same. Figure 18-1 shows an example. Each logic 0 results in a change from the previous state. Each logic 1 results in no change in the voltages. The bits transmit least-significant-bit (LSB) first.

Fortunately, the available USB hardware does all of the encoding and decoding automatically, so device developers and programmers don't have to worry about it. The encoded data makes it difficult to interpret the data on an oscilloscope or logic analyzer, but as Chapter 17 showed, the solution is to use a protocol analyzer that decodes the data for you.

Staying Synchronized

When two devices exchange data, the receiving device needs a way to know when each bit is available to be read. With the RS-232 interface, the transmitter and receiver each have their own clock reference, and both must agree on a bit rate for exchanging data. Each transmitted word begins with a transition from the Idle state to a Start bit. The receiver synchronizes to this transition and then uses timing circuits and the agreed-on bit rate to read each bit in the middle of each bit time. The Stop bit returns the link to the Idle state so the next Start bit can be detected. If the transmitter's and receiver's clocks differ by up to a few percent, the receiver will still be able to read ten or eleven bits before a new Start bit resynchronizes the clocks. But adding a Start and Stop bit to each data byte adds 25 percent overhead. A 9600-bps link with 8 data bits and one Start and Stop bit transmits only 7680 data bits (960 bytes) per second.

Another approach used by SPI, I²C, and Microwire interfaces is to send a clock signal along with the data. The receiver detects the bits either on detecting a rising or falling edge or a high or low logic level, depending on the protocol. Sending a clock requires an extra signal line, however, and a noise glitch on the clock line can cause misread data.

The NRZI encoding used in USB communications requires no Start and Stop bits or clock line. Instead, USB uses two other techniques to remain synchronized: bit stuffing and SYNC fields. Each adds some overhead to each transaction, but the amount is minimal with large packets.

Bit Stuffing

Bit stuffing is required because the receiver synchronizes on transitions. If the data is all 0s, there are plenty of transitions. But if the data contains a long string of 1s, the lack of transitions could cause the receiver to get out of sync.

If data has six consecutive 1s, the transmitter stuffs, or inserts, a 0 (represented by a transition) after the sixth 1. This ensures at least one transition for every seven bit widths. The receiver detects and discards any bit that follows six consecutive 1s.

Bit stuffing can increase the number of transmitted bits by up to 17 percent. In practice the average is much less. The bit-stuffing overhead for random data is just 0.8 percent, or one stuff bit per 125 data bits.

SYNC Field

Bit stuffing alone isn't enough to ensure that the transmitting and receiving clocks in a transfer are synchronized. Because devices and the host don't share a clock, the receiving device has no way of knowing exactly when a transmitting device will send a transition that marks the beginning of a new packet. A single transition isn't enough to ensure that the receiver will remain synchronized for the duration of a packet.

To keep things synchronized, each packet begins with a SYNC field to enable the receiving device to align, or synchronize, its clock to the transmitted data. For low and full speeds, the SYNC pattern is eight bits: KJKJKJKK. The transition from Idle to the first K serves as a sort of Start bit that indicates the arrival of a new packet. There's one SYNC field per packet, rather than a Start bit for each byte.

For high speed, the SYNC pattern is 32 bits: fifteen KJ repetitions, followed by KK. A high-speed hub repeating a packet can drop up to four bits from the beginning of the sync field, so a SYNC field repeated by the fifth external hub series can be as short as 12 bits.

The alternating Ks and Js provide the transitions for synchronizing, and the final two Ks mark the end of the field. By the end of the SYNC pattern, the receiving device can determine precisely when each of the remaining bits in the packet will arrive. The price to pay for synchronizing is the addition of 8 to 32 bit times to each packet. Large packets are thus much more efficient than smaller ones.

End of Packet

An End-of-Packet signal returns the bus to the Idle state in preparation for the next SYNC field. The End-of-Packet signal is different for low/full and high speed.

The low- or full-speed End of Packet is a Single-Ended-Zero that lasts for two bit widths.

At high speed, the signal is more complicated. High-speed receivers treat any bit-stuff error as an End of Packet, so an End of High-speed Packet must cause a bit-stuff error.

For all high-speed packets except Start-of-Frame packets, the End of High-speed Packet is an encoded byte of 01111111, without bit stuffing. If the preceding bit was a J, the End of High-speed Packet is KKKKKKKK. The initial 0 causes the first bit to be a change of state from J to K, and the following 1s mean that the rest of the bits don't change. If the preceding bit was a K, the End of High-speed Packet is JJJJJJJJ. The initial 0 causes the first bit to be a change of state from K to J, and the following 1s mean that the rest of the bits don't change. In either case, the sequence of seven 1s causes a bit stuff error.

In high-speed Start-of-Frame packets, the End of High-speed Packet is 40 bits. This allows a hub time to detect the doubled differential voltage that indicates that a device has been removed from the bus. The encoded byte begins with a zero, followed by 39 ones, which results in an End of High-speed Packet consisting of 40 Js or 40 Ks. As with low and full speeds, this sequence results in a bit-stuff error that the receiver treats as an End of Packet.

Timing Accuracy

A tradeoff of speed is more stringent timing requirements. USB's high speed has the most critical timing, followed by full speed and then low speed, which is quite tolerant of timing variations.

Devices typically derive their timing from a crystal. Many factors can affect a crystal's frequency, including initial accuracy, capacitive loading, aging of the crystal, supply voltage, and temperature. Crystal accuracy is typically specified as parts per million (ppm), which is the maximum number of cycles the crystal may vary in the time required for 1 million cycles at the rated frequency.

High speed's bit rate of 480 Megabits/sec. can vary no more than 0.05 percent, or 500 ppm. Full speed's bit rate of 12 Megabits/sec. can vary no more than 0.25 percent, or 2500 ppm. Low speed's bit rate of 1.5 Megabit/sec. can vary up to 1.5%, or 15,000 ppm. The greater tolerance for low speed means that low-speed devices can use inexpensive ceramic resonators instead of quartz crystals.

The data rate at a host or 2.0 hub must be within 0.05%, or 500 ppm, of the specified rate at all speeds. The frame intervals must be accurate as well, at 1 millisecond ±500 nanoseconds per frame or 125.0 ±62.5 microseconds per microframe. To maintain this accuracy, hubs must be able to adjust their frame intervals to match the host's. Each hub has its own timing source and synchronizes its transmissions to the host's Start-of-Frame signals in each frame or microframe.

The USB specification also defines limits for data jitter, or small variations in the timing of the individual bit transitions. The limits allow small differences in the rise and fall times of the drivers as well as clock jitter and other random noise.

Packet Format

As Chapter 2 explained, all USB data travels in packets, which are blocks of information with a defined format. The packets in turn contain fields, with each field type holding a particular type of information.

Fields

Table 18-1 lists the fields that packets contain and their purposes.

SYNC

Each packet begins with an 8-bit SYNC field, as described earlier. The SYNC Field serves as the Start-of-Packet delimiter.

Table 18-1: All USB traffic is in packets. Packets are made up of fields. The field type determines its contents.

Name	Size (bits)	Packet Types	Purpose
SYNC	8	all	Start-of-packet and synchronization
PID	8	all	Identify the packet type
Address	7	IN, OUT, Setup	Identify the function address
Endpoint	4	IN, OUT, Setup	Identify the endpoint
Frame Number	11	SOF	Identify the frame
Data	0 to 8192 (1024 bytes) for 2.0 hardware; 0 to 8184 (1023 bytes) for 1.x hardware	Data0, Data1	Data
CRC	5 or 16	IN, OUT, Setup, Data0, Data1	Detect errors

Packet Identifier

The packet identifier field (PID) is 8 bits. Bits 0 through 3 identify the type of packet and bits 4 through 7 are the one's complement of these bits, for use in error checking.

There are 16 defined PID codes for token, data, handshake and special packets. Chapter 2 introduced these codes. The lower two bits identify the PID type, and the upper two bits identify the specific PID.

Address

The address field is seven bits that identify the device the host is communicating with.

Endpoint

The endpoint field is four bits that identify an endpoint number within a device.

Frame Number

The frame-number field is eleven bits that identify the specific frame. The host sends this field in the Start-of-Frame packet that begins each frame or microframe. After 07FFh, the number rolls over to zero. A full-speed host maintains an 11-bit counter that increments once per frame. A high-speed host maintains a 14-bit counter that increments once per microframe. Only bits 3–13 of the microframe counter transmit in the frame number field, so the frame number increments once per frame, with eight microframes in sequence having the same frame number.

Data

The data field may range from 0 to 1024 bytes, depending on the transfer type, the bus's speed, and the amount of data in the transaction.

CRC

The CRC field is 5 bits for address and endpoint fields and 16 bits for data fields. The bits are used in error-checking. The transmitting hardware normally inserts the CRC bits and the receiving hardware does the required calculations; there's no need for program code to do it.

Inter-packet Delay

USB carries data from multiple sources, in both directions, on one pair of wires. Data can travel in just one direction at a time. To ensure that the previous transmitting device has had time to switch off its driver, the bus requires a brief delay between the end of one packet and the beginning of the next packet in a transaction. This delay time is limited, however, and devices must switch directions quickly.

The USB specification defines the delays differently for low/full and high speed. The delays are handled by the hardware and require no support in code.

Test Modes

For use in compliance testing, the USB 2.0 specification adds five new test modes that all host controllers, hubs, and high-speed-capable devices must support.

Entering and Exiting Test Modes

An upstream-facing port enters a test mode in response to a Set_Feature request with TEST_MODE in the wValue field. A downstream-facing port enters a test mode in response to the hub-class request Set_Port_Feature with PORT_TEST in the wValue field. In both cases, the wIndex field contains the port number and the test number. All downstream ports on a hub with a port to be tested must be in the suspended, disabled, or disconnected state.

An upstream-facing port exits the test mode when the device powers down and back up. A downstream-facing port exits the test mode when the hub is reset.

The Modes

These are the five test modes:

Test_SEO_NAK

Value. 01h.

Action. The transceiver enters and remains in high-speed receive mode. Upstream-facing ports respond to IN token packets with NAK.

Purpose. Test output impedance, low-level output voltage, and loading characteristics. Test device squelch-level circuits. Provide a stimulus-response test for basic functional testing.

Test_J

Value. 02h.

Action. The transceiver enters and remains in the High-speed Data J state.

Purpose. Test the high output drive level on D+.

Test_K

Value. 03h.

Action. The transceiver enters and remains in the High-speed Data K state.

Purpose. Test the high output drive level on D-.

Test_Packet

Value. 04h.

Action. Repetitively transmit the test packet defined by the USB specification.

Purpose. Test rise and fall times, eye pattern, jitter, and other dynamic waveform specifications.

Test_Force_Enable

Value. 05h.

Action. Enable downstream-facing hub ports in high-speed mode. Packets arriving at the upstream-facing port are repeated at the port being tested. The disconnect-detect bit can be polled while varying the loading on the port.

Purpose. Measure the disconnect-detection threshold.

Other Values

Test-mode values 06h through 3Fh are reserved for future standard tests. Value C0h through FFh are available for vendor-defined tests. All other values are reserved.

19

The Electrical Interface

All of the protocols and program code in the world are no use if the signals don't make it down the cable in good shape. The electrical interface plays an important part in making USB a reliable way to transfer information.

From a practical point of view, if you're using compliant cables and components, you don't need to know much about the electrical interface. But if you're designing USB transceivers or cables, printed-circuit boards with USB interfaces, or a protocol analyzer that must unobtrusively monitor the bus, you do need to understand the electrical interface and how it affects the components in your project.

This chapter presents the essentials about the electrical interface of the USB's drivers and receivers and details about the cables that carry the signals.

Transceivers and Signals

The electrical properties of the signals on a USB cable vary depending on the speed of the cable segment. Low-, full-, and high-speed signaling each have a different edge rate, which is a measure of the rise and fall times of the voltages on the lines and thus the amount of time required for an output to switch. The transceivers and supporting circuits that produce and detect the bus signals also vary depending on speed.

At any speed, the components that connect to a USB cable must be able to withstand the shorting of any line to any other line or the cable shield without component damage.

Cable Segments

A cable segment is a single physical cable that connects a device (which may be a hub) to an upstream hub (which may be the root hub at the host). The speed, edge rate, and polarity of the data in a segment depend on whether the segment is low, full, or high speed. Figure 19-1 illustrates.

Low-speed segments exist only between low-speed devices and their hubs. A low-speed segment carries only low-speed data, using low-speed's edge rate and inverted polarity compared to full speed.

A full-speed segment exists when the segment's downstream device is operating at full speed. The upstream device may be a 1.x or 2.0 hub (including the root hub). When the downstream device is a hub, the segment may also carry data to and from low-speed devices that are downstream from that hub. In this situation, the low-speed data on the full-speed segment uses low-speed's bit rate but full speed's polarity and edge rate. The hub that connects to the low-speed device converts between low and full speed's polarity and edge rates. Full-speed segments never carry data at high speed. If a high-speed-capable device connects to a 1.x hub, communications are at full speed. High-speed devices must at least respond to enumeration requests at full speed.

High-speed segments exist only where the host is USB 2.0, all upstream device(s) are 2.0 hubs, and the downstream device is high speed. When the

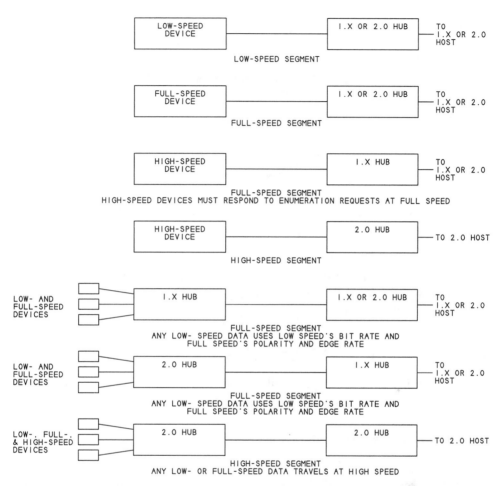

Figure 19-1: The speed of data in a segment depends on the capabilities of the device and its upstream hub.

downstream device is a hub, the segment may also carry data to and from low- and full-speed devices that are downstream from that hub. All data in a high-speed segment travels at high speed, and the transaction translator in a downstream hub converts between low or full speed and high speed as needed.

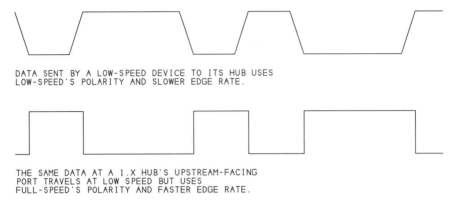

DATA SENT BY A LOW-SPEED DEVICE TO ITS HUB USES
LOW-SPEED'S POLARITY AND SLOWER EDGE RATE.

THE SAME DATA AT A 1.X HUB'S UPSTREAM-FACING
PORT TRAVELS AT LOW SPEED BUT USES
FULL-SPEED'S POLARITY AND FASTER EDGE RATE.

Figure 19-2: A 1.x hub converts between low- and full-speed's polarities and edge rates. (Not drawn to scale)

On attachment, all devices must communicate at low or full speed. When possible, a high-speed-capable device transitions from full to high speed shortly after the device is attached, during the high-speed handshake.

Low- and Full-speed Transceivers

The transceiver for low and full speeds has a simpler design compared to the transceiver for high speed.

Low- and Full-speed Differences

Low-speed data differs electrically from full speed in three ways. The bit rate is slower, at 1.5 Megabits/sec. compared to 12 Megabits/sec. for full speed. Low speed traffic's polarity is inverted compared to full speed. And low speed has a slower edge rate compared to full speed. Figure 19-2 illustrates. The slower edge rate reduces reflected voltages on the line and makes it possible to use cables that have less shielding and are thus cheaper to make and physically more flexible.

The transceiver's hardware doesn't care about the signal polarity. The transceiver just retransmits whatever logic levels are at its inputs. A driver that supports both speeds, such as a driver for a hub's downstream port, must be able to switch between the two edge rates.

The Circuits

Figure 19-3 shows port circuits and cable segments for low- and full-speed communications. Each transceiver contains a differential driver and receiver for sending and receiving data on the bus's twisted pair.

When transmitting data, the driver has two outputs that are 180 degrees out of phase: when one output is high, the other is low. A single driver can support both low and full speeds with a control input to select the full-speed or low-speed edge rate.

The differential receiver detects the voltage difference between the lines. A differential receiver has two inputs and defines logic levels in terms of the voltage difference between the inputs. Some differential interfaces, such as RS-485, define logic levels strictly as the difference between voltages on the two signal lines, with no reference to ground (though the interface requires a common ground connection). USB differs because it specifies absolute voltages in addition to a required voltage difference at the receivers. The differential receiver's output is a logic-high or logic-low voltage referenced to ground.

Each port also has two single-ended receivers that detect the voltages on D+ and D- with reference to signal ground. The logic states of the receivers' outputs indicate whether the bus is low or full speed or whether the bus is in the Single-Ended-Zero state.

The drivers' output impedances plus a 36-ohm series resistor at each driver's output act as source terminations that reduce reflected voltages when the outputs switch. The series resistors may be on-chip or external to the chip.

Pull-up and Pull-down Values

The pull-up resistor on D+ or D- at a device's upstream-facing port enables the hub to detect the device's speed. The hub's downstream-facing port has pull-down resistors on D+ and D-.

On devices with detachable cables, the pull-up resistors must connect to a voltage source of 3.0–3.6V. Devices with captive cables can instead use an

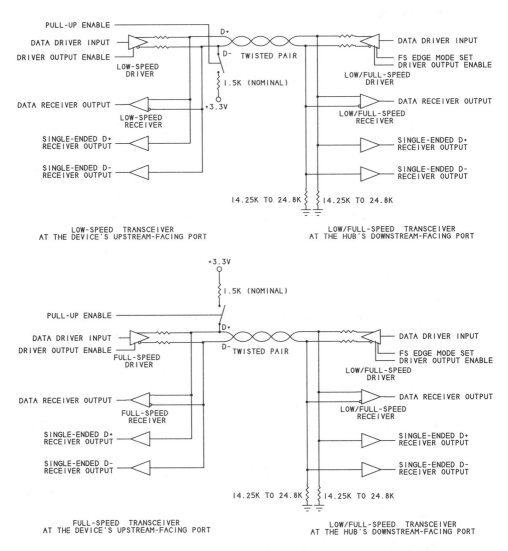

Figure 19-3: The downstream-facing ports on a 1.x hub must support both low and full speeds (except for ports with embedded or permanently attached devices). A device's upstream-facing port typically supports just one speed.

alternative means of termination, including connecting directly to VBUS. In selecting an alternatative means of termination, the designer is responsible for ensuring that all of the bus's signal levels meet the USB specification's requirements.

An Engineering Change Notice titled *Pull-up/pull-down resistors* revises the USB 2.0 specification by loosening the tolerances for pull-up and pull-down resistors that connect to a voltage source of 3.0–3.6V. The original values were 1.5 kilohms ±5% for the pull ups and 15 kilohms ±5% for the pull downs. The tolerances were loosened to make it easier to include the resistors on chip without requiring laser trimming of the values. Using the looser tolerances increases complexity slightly at upstream-facing ports because the device must switch between two pull-up values depending on whether the bus is idle or active. But overall, the result can be reduced cost to device manufacturers.

Table 19-1 shows the new values. Devices that use the old tolerances remain compliant, and devices that use the old tolerances can communicate with devices that use the new tolerances. To use the wider tolerances, a device must use one pull-up value when the bus is idle and switch to a higher value when the upstream device begins to transmit. The upper limit on the pull up for the idle bus ensures that the idle voltage is at least the required minimum of 2.7V. For the active bus, the lower limit is the same as the original lower limit and the upper limit ensures that the data line remains in a high state if the receiver interprets noise as a Start-of-Packet signal.

Using the new limits, the resistors can have tolerances as high as 27%. Examples of compliant values are 19 kilohms ±25% for the pull downs and 1200 and 2400 ohms ± 25% for the pull ups. A device can implement its pull up using two resistors in series, switching the second resistor into the circuit when the upstream device begins to transmit. A device must switch to the higher resistance within 0.5 bit time of detecting a J-to-K transition on the bus. To determine when to switch to the lower resistance, a device may use either or both of the following methods: on detecting a Single-ended Zero for more than 0.5 bit time or on detecting that the bus has been in the J state for more than 7 bit times. The ECN details a few hardware implications for designers of chips that use the wider tolerances.

Table 19-1: Values for the pull-up and pull-down resistors at the device and hub. The pull-up values assume that the pull up connects to a voltage source of 3– 3.6V, as required for devices with detachable cables.

Resistor	Bus State	Minimum (ohms)	Maximum (ohms)	Acceptable Value with 25% Tolerance
pull down	All	14,250	24,800	19k
pull up	Idle	900	1575	1.2k
	Active	1425	3090	2.4k
	Single-Ended Zero	900	<3090	2.4k

High-speed Transceivers

A high-speed device must support control requests at full speed, so the device must contain transceivers to support both full and high speeds and the logic to switch between them. A high-speed-capable device's upstream transceivers aren't allowed to support low speed. In an external 2.0 hub, the downstream transceivers at ports with user-accessible connectors must support all three speeds.

Why 480 Megabits per Second?

High speed's rate of 480 Megabits/sec. was chosen for several reasons. The frequency is slow enough to allow using the same cables and connectors as full speed. Components can use CMOS processes and don't require the advanced compensation used in high-speed digital signal processors. Tests of high-speed drivers showed 20 to 30 percent jitter at 480 Megabits/sec. Because receivers can be designed to tolerate 40 percent jitter, this bit rate allows a good margin of error. And 480 is an even multiple of 12, so a single crystal can support both full and high speed.

The use of separate drivers for high speed makes it easy to add high speed to the existing interface. Current-mode drivers were chosen because they're fast.

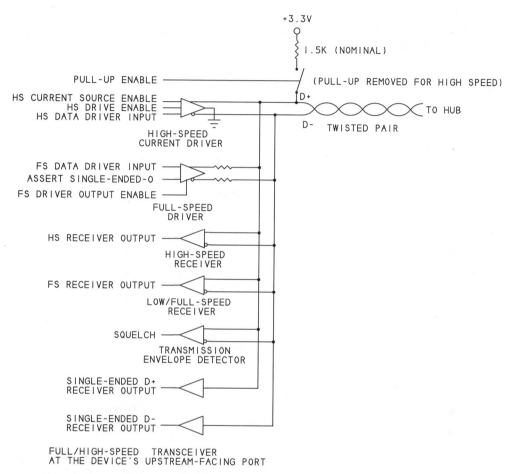

Figure 19-4: The upstream-facing port on a high-speed device must also support full-speed communications.

The Circuits

Figure 19-4 shows upstream-facing transceiver circuits in a high-speed-capable device, and Figure 19-5 shows downstream-facing transceiver circuits in a 2.0 hub.

High speed requires its own drivers, so a high-speed device must contain two sets of drivers. For receiving, a transceiver may use a single receiver to

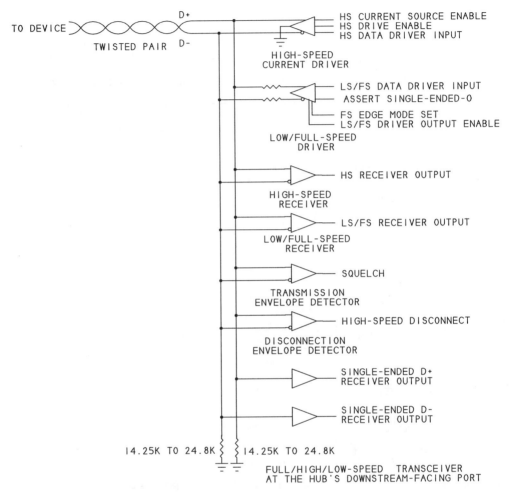

Figure 19-5: The downstream-facing ports on external 2.0 hubs must support all three speeds (except for ports with embedded or permanently attached devices).

handle all supported speeds or separate receivers for low/full speed and high speed.

When a high-speed driver sends data, a current source drives one line with the other line at ground. The current source may be active all the time or only when transmitting. A current source that is active all the time is easier to design but consumes more power. The USB specification requires devices to meet the signal-amplitude and timing requirements beginning with the first symbol in a packet. This requirement complicates the design of a current source that is active only when transmitting. If the driver instead keeps its current source active all the time, the driver can direct the current to ground when not transmitting on the bus.

In a high-speed-capable transceiver, the output impedance of the full-speed drivers has tighter tolerance compared to full-speed-only drivers (45 ohms ±10%, compared to 36 ohms ±22%). The change is required because the high-speed bus uses the full-speed drivers as electrical terminations on the cable. Full-speed drivers that aren't part of a high-speed transceiver don't require a change in output impedance.

When the high-speed drivers are active, the full-speed drivers bring both data lines low (the Single-ended-Zero state). Each driver and its series resistor then function as a 45-ohm termination to ground. Because there is a driver at each end of the cable segment, there is a termination at both the source and the load. This double termination quiets the line more effectively than the source-only series terminations in full-speed segments. Using the full-speed drivers as terminations means no extra components are required.

The USB specification provides eye-pattern templates that show the required high-speed transmitter outputs and receiver sensitivity. High-speed receivers must also meet new specifications that require the use of a differential time-domain reflectometer (TDR) to measure impedance characteristics.

All high-speed receivers must include a differential envelope detector to detect the Squelch (invalid signal) state, indicated by a differential bus voltage of 100 millivolts or less. The downstream ports on all 2.0 hubs must also include a high-speed-disconnect detector that detects when a device has been removed from the bus.

Other new responsibilities for high-speed-capable devices include managing the switch from full to high speed and handling new protocols for entering and exiting the Suspend and Reset states.

Switching Speeds

In a low- or full-speed device, a pull-up resistor on one of the signal lines indicates device speed. When a low- or full-speed device is attached or removed from the bus, the voltage change due to the pull up informs the hub of the change. High-speed-capable devices always attach at full speed, so hubs detect attachment of high-speed-capable devices in the same way.

As Chapter 18 explained, the switch to high speed occurs after the device has been detected, during the Reset sent by the hub. A high-speed-capable device must support the high-speed handshake that informs the hub that the device is capable of high speed. When switching to high speed, the device removes its pull up from the bus.

Detecting Removal of a High-speed Device

A 2.0 hub must also detect the removal of a high-speed device. Because the device has no pull up at high speed, the hub has to use a different method to detect the removal. When a device is removed from the bus, the differential terminations are removed, and the removal causes the differential voltage at the hub's port to double. On detecting the doubled voltage, the hub knows the device has been removed.

The hub detects the voltage by measuring the differential bus voltage during the extended End of High-speed Packet (HSEOP) in each high-speed Start-of-Frame Packet (HSSOP). A differential voltage of at least 625 millivolts indicates a disconnect.

Suspending and Resuming at High Speed

As Chapter 16 explained, devices must enter the low-power Suspend state when the bus has been in the Idle state for at least 3 milliseconds and no more than 10 milliseconds. When the bus has been idle for 3 milliseconds, a high-speed device switches to full speed. The device then checks the state of the full-speed bus to determine whether the host is requesting a Suspend or Reset. If the bus state is Single-Ended Zero, the host is requesting a Reset, so the device prepares for the high-speed-detect handshake. If the bus state is Idle, the device enters the Suspend state. The device must return to high speed on exiting the Suspend state.

Signal Voltages

Chapter 18 introduced USB's bus states. The voltages that define the states vary depending on the speed of the cable segment. The differences in the specified voltages at the transmitter and receiver mean that a signal can have some noise or attenuation and the receiver will still see the correct logic level.

Low and Full Speeds

Table 19-2 shows the driver output voltages for low/full and high speeds. At low and full speeds, a Differential 1 exists at the driver when the D+ output is at least 2.8V and the D- output is no greater than 0.3V referenced to the driver's signal ground. A differential 0 exists at the driver when D- is at least 2.8V and D+ is no greater than 0.3V referenced to the driver's signal ground.

At a low- or full-speed receiver, a differential 1 exists when D+ is at least 2V referenced to the receiver's signal ground, and the difference between D+ and D- is greater than 200 millivolts. A differential 0 exists when D- is at least 2V referenced to the receiver's signal ground, and the difference between D- and D+ is greater than 200 millivolts. However, a receiver may optionally have less stringent definitions that require only a differential voltage greater than 200 millivolts, ignoring the requirement for one line to be at least 2V.

Table 19-2: High speed requires different drivers and has different output specifications, compared to low and full speed. The receiver specifications differ as well.

Parameter	Low/Full Speed (V)	High Speed (V)
Vout low minimum	0	-0.010
Vout low maximum	0.3	0.010
Vout high minimum	2.8	0.360V
Vout high maximum	3.6	0.440V
Vin low maximum	0.8	Limits are defined by the eye-pattern templates in the USB specification
Vin high minimum	2.0	

High Speed

At high speed, a differential 1 exists at the driver when the D+ output is at least 0.36V and the D- output is no greater than 0.01V referenced to the driver's signal ground. A differential 0 exists at the driver when D- is at least 0.36V and D+ is no greater than 0.01V referenced to the driver's signal ground.

At a high-speed receiver, the input must meet the requirements shown in the eye-pattern templates in the USB specification. The eye patterns specify maximum and minimum voltages, rise and fall times, maximum jitter in a transmitted signal, and the maximum jitter a receiver must tolerate. The USB specification has details about how to make the measurements.

Cables

The USB 2.0 specification includes detailed requirements for cables. The requirements help to ensure that any compliant cable will be able to carry the bus's digital signals without errors due to noise in the cable without large amounts of noise radiating from the cable.

Conductors

USB cables have four conductors: VBUS, GND, D+ and D-.

VBUS is the +5V supply.

GND is the ground reference for VBUS as well as for D+ and D-.
D+ and D- are the differential signal pair.

Chapter 16 described the voltage and current limits for VBUS.

Cables to be used in full- or high-speed segments have different requirements compared to cables for low-speed segments. Table 19-3 compares the two cable types. A low-speed segment is a cable segment between a low-speed device and its hub. Any additional upstream segments between hubs are considered to be full- or high-speed segments.

The USB 2.0 specification tightened the requirements for low-speed cables. A 1.1-compliant low-speed cable required no shielding at all. A 2.0-compliant low-speed cable must have the same inner shield and drain wire required for full speed. The USB specification also recommends, but doesn't require, a braided outer shield and a twisted pair for data, as on full- and high-speed cables.

Full- and high-speed segments can use the same cables. When the USB 2.0 specification was under development, an Engineering Change Notice to the 1.x specification added new requirements to ensure that full-speed cables would also work at high speed. The 2.0 specification also includes these requirements. The requirements describe what was typically found in compliant full-speed cables, so most providers with compliant cables had no changes to make to their products.

In a full/high-speed cable, the signal wires must have a differential characteristic impedance of 90 ohms. This value is a measure of the input impedance of an infinite, open line and determines the initial current on the lines when the outputs switch. The characteristic impedance for a low-speed cable isn't defined because the slower edge rates mean that the initial current doesn't affect the logic states seen by the receiver.

The USB specification lists requirements for the cable's conductors, shielding, and insulation. These are the major requirements for full/high-speed cables:

Data wires: twisted pair, #28 AWG.
Power and ground: non-twisted, #20 to #28 AWG.

Table 19-3: The requirements for cables and related components differ for full/high-speed cables and cables that attach to low-speed devices.

Specification	Low Speed	Full/High Speed
Maximum length (meters)	3	5
Inner shield and drain wire required?	yes (new in USB 2.0)	yes
Braided outer shield required?	no, but recommended	yes
Twisted pair required?	no, but recommended	yes
Common-mode impedance (ohms)	not specified	30 ±30%
Differential Characteristic impedance (ohms)	not specified	90
Cable skew (picoseconds)	< 100	
Wire gauge (AWG#)	20 –28	
DC resistance, plug shell to plug shell (ohms)	0.6	
Cable delay	18 nanosecs. (one way)	5.2 nanoseconds/meter
pull up location at the device	D-	D+
Detachable cable OK?	no	yes
Captive cable OK?	yes	

Drain wire: stranded, tinned copper wire, #28 AWG

Inner shield: aluminum metallized polyester

Outer shield: braided, tinned copper

The USB specification also lists requirements for the cable's durability and performance.

A low-speed device can use a full-speed cable if the cable meets all of the low-speed cable requirements. These include *not* using any standard USB connector type at the device end and a maximum length of 3 meters.

Connectors

The USB specifications define four plug types for USB cables. USB 2.0 defines the Series-A plug for the upstream end of the cable and the Series-B plug for the downstream end of the cable. Each plug type has a mating receptacle type. (Figure 19-6). Because the Series-B connectors were bulky for some devices, a new mini-B connector was defined in an Engineering Change Notice titled *Mini-B connector*. A mini-B receptacle is less than half the height of a Series-B receptacle. Any device can use a mini-B receptacle instead of a Series-B receptacle. The On-The-Go supplement adds a mini-A plug as an option for connecting to On-The-Go hosts. Figure 19-7 shows all four plug types. Chapter 20 has more about On-The-Go connectors.

All of the connectors are keyed so you can't insert a plug upsidedown. The signal connections are recessed slightly to ensure that the power lines con-

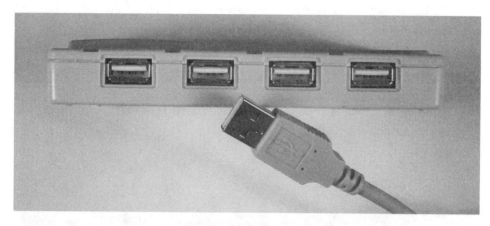

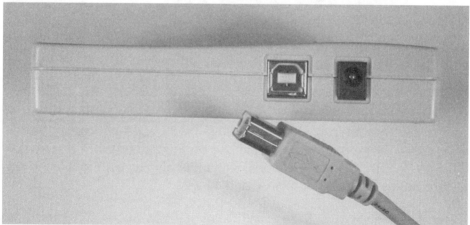

Figure 19-6: The Series-A plug (top) is on the upstream end of the cable and mates with a Series-A receptacle on a hub or the host. The Series-B plug (bottom) is on the downstream end of the cable and mates with a Series-B receptacle on the device.

nect first when a cable is attached. The receptacle should be mounted so the USB icon on the top of the plug is visible when a plug is attached.

The USB icon can identify a USB plug or receptacle (Figure 19-8). A "+" added to the icon indicates that a downstream-facing port supports high speed. Don't confuse the icon with the USB logo described in Chapter 17.

All of the connectors have connections for the bus's two signal wires, the V$_{BUS}$ supply, and ground. The mini-A and mini-B plugs have an additional ID pin. On-The-Go devices use the ID pin to identify a device's default

Figure 19-7: The USB specifications define four plug types. From left to right, they are Series A, Series B, mini-A, and mini-B.

Figure 19-8: The USB icon identifies a USB plug or receptacle. A "+" indicates support for high speed.

mode (host or function). The USB 2.0 specification gives the following pin and color assignments for the cable and connectors:

Series A or Series B pin	Mini-B pin	Conductor	Cable Wire
1	1	VBUS (+5V)	red
2	2	D-	white
3	3	D+	green
4	5	GND	black
-	4	ID	not connected
shell		shield	drain wire

Detachable and Captive Cables

The USB specification defines cables as being either detachable or captive. From the names, you might think that a detachable cable is one you can remove, while a captive cable is permanently attached to its downstream device. But in fact, a captive cable can be removable as long as its downstream connector is *not* one of the standard USB connector types.

A detachable cable must be full/high speed, with a Series-A plug for the upstream connection and a Series-B or mini-B plug for the downstream connection. A captive cable may be low or full/high speed. The upstream end has a Series-A plug. For the downstream connection, the cable can be permanently attached or removable with a non-standard connector type. The non-standard connector doesn't have to be hot pluggable, but the Series-A connector must be hot pluggable. Requiring low-speed cables to be captive eliminates the possibility of trying to use a low-speed cable in a full- or high-speed segment.

Cable Length

Version 1.0 of the USB specification gave maximum lengths for cable segments. A full-speed segment could be up to 5 meters and a low-speed segment could be up to 3 meters. Version 1.1 dropped the length limits in favor of a discussion of characteristics that limit a cable's ability to meet the interface's timing and voltage requirements. On full- and high-speed cables, the limits are due to signal attenuation, cable propagation delay (the amount of time it takes for a signal to travel from driver to receiver), and the voltage drops on the VBUS and GND wires. On low-speed cables, the length is limited by the rise and fall times of the signals, the capacitive load presented by the segment, and the voltage drops on the VBUS and GND wires.

The original limits of 3 and 5 meters are still good guidelines. A 2.0-compliant 5-meter cable will work at full and high speeds. Compliant cables of these lengths are readily available. Chapter 16 explained how the length limits translate to a maximum distance of 30 meters between a host and its peripheral, assuming the use of five hubs and six 5-meter cable segments.

The USB specification prohibits extension cables, which would extend the length of a segment by adding a second cable in series. An extension cable for the upstream side of a cable would have a Series-A plug on one end and a Series-A receptacle on the other, while an extension cable for the downstream side would have a Series-B plug and receptacle.

Prohibiting extension cables eliminates the temptation to stretch a segment beyond the interface's electrical limits. Extension cables are available, but just because you can buy one doesn't mean that it's a good idea or that the cable will work. Instead, buy a single cable of the length you need and add hubs as needed.

An exception is an active extension cable that contains a hub, a downstream port, and a cable. This type of cable works fine because it contains the required hub. Depending on the attached devices, the hub may need its own power supply. Chapter 20 discusses two cable adapters that are approved for use only with On-The-Go devices.

An option for longer distances is to use a standard USB cable that connects to a device that translates between USB and Ethernet, RS-485, or another interface designed for use over long distances. The remote device would then need to support the long-distance interface, rather than USB.

Another option enables you to place a USB device anywhere in a local Ethernet network. Two products that use this approach are the AnywhereUSB hub from Inside Out Networks, Inc. and the USB Server from Keyspan. The hub/server contains one or more host controllers that communicate with the host PC over an Ethernet connection using the Internet Protocol (IP). The hub/server can attach to any Ethernet port in the PC's local network. The device drivers are on the PC. The PC can use the hub/server to access many devices that use bulk and interrupt transfers, with some increased latency due to the additional protocol layer.

Ensuring Signal Quality

The USB specifications for drivers, receivers, and cable design ensure that virtually all data transfers occur without errors. Requirements that help to ensure signal quality include the use of balanced lines and shielded cables, twisted pairs required for full/high-speed cables, and slower edge rates required for low-speed drivers.

Sources of Noise

Noise can enter a wire in many ways, including by conductive, common-impedance, magnetic, capacitive, and electromagnetic coupling. If a noise voltage is large enough and is present when the receiver is attempting to detect a transmitted bit, the noise can cause the receiver to misread the received logic level. Very large noise voltages can damage components.

Conductive and common-impedance coupling require ohmic contact between the signal wire and the wire that is the source of the noise. Conductive coupling occurs when a wire brings noise from another source into a circuit. For example, a noisy power-supply line can carry noise into the circuit the supply powers. Common-impedance coupling occurs when two circuits share a wire, such as a ground return.

The other types of noise coupling result from interactions between the electric and magnetic fields of the wires themselves and signals that couple into the wires from outside sources, including other wires in the interface. Capacitive and inductive coupling can cause crosstalk, where signals on one wire enter another wire. Capacitive coupling, also called electric coupling, occurs when two wires carry charges at different potentials, resulting in an electric field between the wires. The strength of the field and the resulting capacitive coupling varies with the distance between the wires. Inductive, or magnetic, coupling occurs because current in a wire causes the wire to emanate a magnetic field. When the magnetic fields of two wires overlap, the energy in each wire's field induces a current in the other wire. When wires are greater then 1/6 wavelength apart, the captive and inductive coupling is considered together as electromagnetic coupling. An example of electromagnetic coupling is when a wire acts as a receiving antenna for radio waves.

Balanced Lines

One way that USB eliminates noise is with the balanced lines that carry the bus's differential signals. Balanced lines are electrically quiet. Noise that couples into the interface is likely to couple equally into both signal wires. At a differential receiver, which detects only the difference between the two wires' voltages, any noise that is common to both wires cancels out.

In contrast, in the unbalanced, single-ended lines used by RS-232 and other interfaces, the receiver detects the difference between a signal wire and a ground line shared by other circuits. The ground line is likely to be carrying noise from a number of sources, and the receiver sees this noise when it detects the difference between the signal voltage and ground.

Twisted Pairs

In a full/high-speed USB cable, the two signal wires must form a twisted pair. Twisted pairs are recommended, but not required, for low-speed cables. A twisted pair is two insulated conductors that spiral around each other with a twist every few inches (Figure 19-9). The twisting reduces noise in two ways: by reducing the amount of noise in the wires and by canceling whatever noise does enter the wires. Twisting is most effective at eliminating low-frequency, magnetically coupled signals such as 60-Hz power-line noise.

Twisting reduces noise by minimizing the area between the conductors. The magnetic field that emanates from a circuit is proportional to the area between the conductors. Twisting the conductors around each other reduces the total area between them. The tighter the twists, the smaller the area. Reducing the area shrinks the magnetic field emanating from the wires and thus reduces the amount of noise coupling into the field.

A twisted pair tends to cancel any noise that enters the wires because the conductors swap physical positions with each twist. Any noise that magnetically couples into the wires reverses polarity with each twist. The result is that the noise present in one twist is cancelled by a nearly equal, opposite

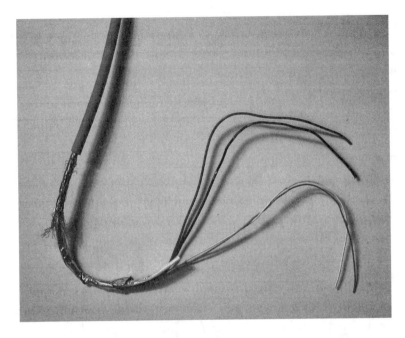

Figure 19-9: A full/high-speed USB cable contains a twisted pair for data, VBUS and GND wires, and aluminum metallized polyester and braided copper shields.

noise signal in the next twist. Of course, the twists aren't perfectly uniform, so the canceling isn't perfect, but noise is much reduced.

Shielding

Metal shielding prevents noise from entering or emanating from a cable. Shielding is most effective at blocking noise due to capacitive, electromagnetic, and high-frequency magnetic coupling. The USB 2.0 specification requires both low-speed and full/high-speed cables to be shielded, though the requirements differ.

In a full/high-speed cable, an aluminum metallized polyester shield surrounds the four conductors. Around this shield is an outer shield of braided, tinned copper wire. Between the shields and contacting both is a copper drain wire. The outside layer is a polyvinyl chloride jacket. The shield terminates at the connector plug.

A low-speed cable has the same requirements except that the braided outer shield is recommended but not required. The 1.x specification required no shielding for low-speed cables on the premise that the slower rise and fall times made shielding unnecessary. The shielding requirement was added in USB 2.0 not because the USB interface is noisy in itself, but because the cables are likely to attach to computers that are noisy internally. Shielding helps to keep the cable from radiating this noise and helps the cable pass FCC tests. The downside is that 2.0-compliant low-speed cables are more expensive to make and physically less flexible.

Edge Rates

Low speed's slower data rate enables the drivers to use slower edge rates that reduce both the reflected voltages seen by receivers and the noise that emanates from the cable.

When a digital output switches, a mismatch between the line's characteristic impedance and the load presented by the receiver can cause reflected voltages that affect the voltage at the receiver. If the reflections are large enough and last long enough, the receiver may misread a transmitted bit.

In low-speed cables, the slower edge rate ensures that any reflections have died out by the time the output has finished switching. The slow edge rate also means that the signals contain less high-frequency energy and thus the noise emanated by the cables is less.

Isolated Interfaces

Galvanic isolation can be useful in preventing electrical noise and power surges from coupling into a circuit. Circuits that are galvanically isolated from each other have no ohmic connection. Typical methods of isolation include using a transformer that transfers power by magnetic coupling and optoisolators that transfer digital signals by optical coupling.

USB devices should require no additional protection in offices, classrooms, and similar environments. For industrial environments or anywhere that devices require additional protection, USB's timing requirements and use of a single pair of wires for both directions make it difficult to completely isolate a USB device from its host. It is feasible, however, to isolate the circuits that a device controller connects to. For example, in a motor controller with a USB interface, the motor and control circuits can be isolated from the USB controller and bus.

Another option is an isolated hub available from B & B Electronics. The hub has four low- and full-speed downstream ports with 2500 VAC of optical isolation between the upstream port and the downstream ports.

Wireless Links

For the same reasons that isolated USB interfaces are difficult to implement, replacing a USB cable with a wireless connection isn't a simple task. USB transactions involve communicating in both directions with tight timing requirements. For example, when a host sends a token and data packet in the Data stage of an interrupt OUT transaction, the device must respond quickly with ACK or another code in the handshake packet.

But the idea of a wireless connection for USB devices is so appealing that several technologies that incorporate USB in wireless devices are available and under development. In most implementations, the wireless links use conventional wired devices that serve as wireless bridges, or adapters. The bridge or adapter uses USB to communicate with the host and a wireless link to communicate with the peripheral. The peripheral contains a wireless bridge to convert between the wireless interface and the peripheral's circuits.

Cypress WirelessUSB

Cypress Semiconductor offers the WirelessUSB technology as a solution for low-speed devices, including HIDs, without cables. The obvious market is wireless keyboards, mice, and game controllers. With a wireless range of up to 50 meters, the technology might also find uses in building and home automation and industrial control. The wireless interface uses radio-frequency (RF) transmissions at 2.4 Gigahertz in the unlicensed Industrial, Scientific, and Medical (ISM) band.

A WirelessUSB system consists of a WirelessUSB bridge and one or more WirelessUSB devices (Figure 19-10). The bridge translates between USB and the wireless protocol and medium. The WirelessUSB device carries out the device's function (mouse, keyboard, game controller) and communicates with the bridge.

The bridge contains a USB-capable microcontroller and a WirelessUSB transceiver chip and antenna. The WirelessUSB device contains a Cypress PsOC or another microcontroller and a WirelessUSB transmitter or transceiver chip and antenna. A device with a transceiver is 2-way: the device can communicate in both directions. A device with just a transmitter is 1-way: the device can send data to the host but can't receive data or status information. In both the bridge and device, the transmitter and transceiver chips use the SPI synchronous serial interface to communicate with their microcontrollers.

In a 2-way system, when a device has data to send to the host, the device's microcontroller writes the data to the transceiver chip, which encodes the data and transmits it through the air to the bridge's transceiver. On receiving the data, the bridge returns an acknowledgement to the device, decodes the data, and sends the data to the host in conventional USB interrupt or control transfers. If the device doesn't receive an acknowledgement from the bridge, the device resends the data.

When the host has data to send to the device, the host writes the data to the bridge's USB controller, which ACKs the data (if not busy) and passes the data to the bridge's transceiver. The transceiver encodes the data and sends it over the air to the WirelessUSB device. The device returns an acknowledgement to the bridge. On receiving a NAK or no reply, the bridge retries the transmission.

In a 1-way system, a device sends data to the host in much the same way as in a 2-way system, except that the device receives no acknowledgements from the host. To help ensure that the bridge and host receive all transmitted data, the device sends its data multiple times. Sequence numbers enable the bridge to identify previously received data.

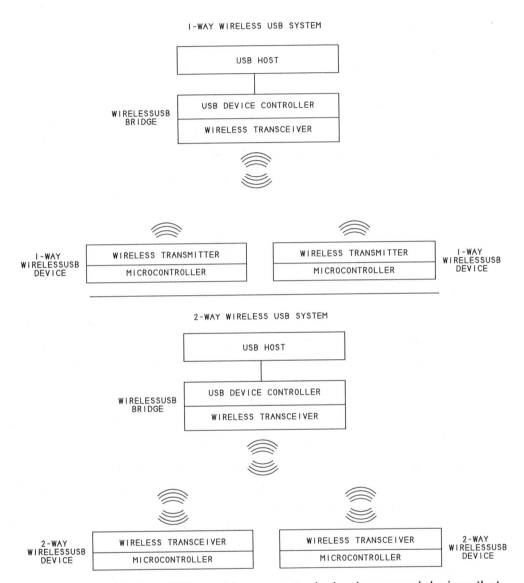

Figure 19-10: WirelessUSB provides a way to design low-speed devices that use a wireless interface.

With both systems, the host thinks it's communicating with an ordinary HID and has no knowledge of the wireless link.

A WirelessUSB link can have a data throughput of up to 62.5 kilobits/sec., but low-speed traffic is of course limited to the USB bandwidth available for low-speed control and interrupt transfers. A device and its bridge must use the same frequency/code pair. A single WirelessUSB bridge can use multiple frequency/code pairs to communicate with multiple devices.

For devices with human interfaces, communications between the wired and wireless interfaces must be fast enough so users don't perceive delays in response to keypresses, mouse movements, and similar actions. For faster performance, the microcontroller can use burst reads to read multiple registers in the WirelessUSB chip in sequence.

The Wireless USB Initiative

The mission of the Wireless USB Promoter Group is to specify a Wireless USB (WUSB) extension that can transmit at 480 Megabits/sec. over a distance of 3 meters (and at lower speeds over longer distances). Note that Wireless USB (WUSB) and Cypress' WirelessUSB have similar names but are different and unrelated technologies!

In Wireless USB, a conventional USB host can have a wired connection to a USB device that functions as a host wire adapter (HWA). The HWA can communicate with native WUSB devices and with device wire adapters (DWAs). A native WUSB device is a peripheral with Wireless USB support built in. A DWA connects to a conventional wired USB device and enables the wired device to communicate over the wireless link. Data on the wireless link is encrypted.

The members of the Wireless USB Promoter Group are Agere Systems, Hewlett Packard, Intel, Microsoft Corporation, NEC, Philips Semiconductors and Samsung Electronics. The specification is due for release in 2005.

Other Options

Other ways to use USB in wireless devices include various wireless bridges and a wireless networking option.

ZigBee is an inexpensive, low-power, RF interface suitable for building and industrial automation and other applications that transmit at up to 250 kilobits/sec. and over distances of up to 500 meters. DLP Design's DLP-RF1 USB/RF OEM Transceiver Module provides a way to monitor and control a Zigbee interface from a USB port. The module's USB controller is FTDI Chip's FT245BM. One or more DLP-RF2 RF OEM Transceiver Modules can communicate with the DLP-RF1.

The IrDA Bridge class described in Chapter 7 defines a way for a USB device to use bulk transfers to communicate over an infrared link.

Another option is a vendor-specific wireless bridge that uses infrared, RF, or other wireless modules designed for use in robotics and other low- to moderate-speed applications. The bridge functions as a wired USB device and supports a wireless interface. A remote device carries out the peripheral's function and also supports the wireless interface. Firmware in the bridge passes received wireless data to the host and passes received USB data to the device.

If you want to use an existing USB device wirelessly, you may be able to use the AnywhereUSB or Keyspan hub/server described earlier in this chapter with a wireless network interface between the host PC and the hub/server.

20

Dual-role Devices with USB On-The-Go

A USB host in a desktop system has many responsibilities, including supporting three bus speeds, managing communications with multiple devices, and providing up to 500 milliamperes to every device connected to the root hub. PCs and other desktop computers typically have the resources to implement a full USB host. But many smaller systems could benefit if they could function as hosts as well. For example, a camera could connect directly to a USB printer. A data-acquisition device could store its data in a USB drive. A PDA could interface to a USB keyboard and mouse. Two drives could exchange files.

An embedded system can incorporate a limited-capability host that supports communications with just one or a few devices. But for small systems, implementing even a limited-capability USB host can be challenging. The CPU may have limited resources, and battery-powered systems may be unable to provide the bus power that the host must make available. And a

USB device that also functions as a host requires two connectors: a Series-A receptacle for the host and a Series-B or mini-B receptacle for the device.

The On-The-Go (OTG) Supplement to the USB 2.0 Specification offers a an alternative for small devices that also want to function as hosts. The supplement defines a way for a USB device to function as a host with limited capabilities that are within the reach of many simpler devices. Version 1.0 of the On-The-Go supplement was released in 2001.

Device and Host in One

An OTG device is a dual-role device that can function both as a limited-capability host and as a USB peripheral. When functioning as a host, the OTG device can communicate with the devices in its targeted peripheral list. The list can be as limited as a single device or as extensive as a series of device types (keyboard, mouse, mass storage). The targeted peripherals can be any combination of other OTG devices and peripheral-only devices.

Capabilities and Limits

Table 20-1 compares the requirements of an On-The-Go device functioning as a host and a conventional, non-On-The-Go host. An OTG host doesn't have to support external hubs, multiple devices attached at the same time, or high and low speeds. The USB hosts in desktop systems support all three speeds and have multiple ports. The USB 2.0 specification doesn't forbid hosts with more limited capabilities, however.

Because On-The-Go communications often involve battery-powered devices, conserving power is important. For this reason, an OTG device functioning as a host is allowed to turn off the VBUS voltage when the bus is unused. Communications occur in sessions, with a session beginning when VBUS is above the session valid-threshold voltage and ending when VBUS falls below this voltage. The Session Request Protocol (SRP) enables a device to request a session even if VBUS isn't present.

The On-The-Go supplement defines new connector types in addition to the Series A, Series B, and mini-B plugs and receptacles defined in the USB 2.0

Table 20-1: Compared to a non-OTG host, an OTG device functioning as a host doesn't have to supply as much power and can use a single connector for host and peripheral functions.

Capability or Feature	Non-OTG Host	OTG Device Functioning as a Host
Communicate at high speed	Hosts in desktop systems support all three speeds. Hosts in embedded systems can support one or more speeds.	optional
Communicate at full speed		yes
Communicate at low speed		optional in host mode; not allowed in device mode
Allow external hubs	yes	optional
Provide targeted peripheral list	no	yes
Function as a peripheral	no	yes
Support Session Request Protocol	optional	yes
Support Host Negotiation Protocol	no	yes
Minimum available bus current per port	500 mA (100 mA if battery-powered)	8 mA
OK to turn off VBUS when unneeded?	no	yes
Connector	1 or more standard A	1 mini-AB

specification. The mini-A plug is a smaller alternative to the Series-A plug. The mini-AB receptacle can accept either a mini-A plug or a mini-B plug. Figure 20-1 shows mini-AB and mini-B receptacles. Every OTG device

Figure 20-1: A mini-AB receptacle (left) accepts a mini-A or mini-B plug. A mini-B receptacle (right) accepts only a mini-B plug.

must have a mini-AB receptacle. The only approved use for the mini-A receptacle is in an adapter that converts a mini-A plug to a Series-A plug.

On every approved USB cable, one end has a Series A or mini-A plug and the other end has a Series-B plug, a mini-B plug, a vendor-specific connector, or a permanent attachment to a device.

Every On-The-Go connection is between an A-device and a B-device. The A-device is defined by the type of plug inserted in the device's USB receptacle. The device with a Series A or mini-A plug is the A-device, and the device at the other end of the cable is the B-device. The A-device initially functions as the host, and the B-device initially functions as the peripheral. Two connected OTG devices can use a protocol to swap functions when needed, as described below. The A-device always provides the VBUS voltage and current, even when functioning as a peripheral.

Requirements for an OTG Device

An OTG device must provide all of the following:

- The ability to function as a full-speed peripheral. Support for high speed is optional. The peripheral must not use low speed.
- The ability to function as a host that can communicate with one or more full-speed devices. Support for low- and high-speed communications is optional. Support for hubs is optional.
- Support for the Host Negotiation Protocol, which enables two OTG devices to swap roles. (The host becomes the peripheral and the peripheral becomes the host.)
- The ability to initiate and respond to the Session Request Protocol, which enables a device to request communications with the host even if VBUS isn't present.
- Support for remote wakeup.
- One and only one Mini-AB receptacle, which can accept either a Mini-A plug or a Mini-B plug.
- The ability to provide at least 8 milliamperes of bus current when functioning as the A-device.

- A display or other way to communicate messages to users.
- A targeted peripheral list that names the devices the host can communicate with.

On-The-Go adds complexity by requiring hosts to support HNP and SRP and to be able to function as peripherals. On the other hand, On-The-Go reduces complexity by using a single connector for the host and device roles and by not requiring the host to supply large bus currents or support external hubs.

The following paragraphs describe the requirements for OTG devices in more detail.

Full-speed Device Capability

Any device that implements On-The-Go's limited-capability host must also be able to function as a USB peripheral. OTG host-only products aren't allowed. When functioning as a peripheral, an OTG device may support high speed and must not communicate at low speed.

Full-speed Host Capability

An OTG device functioning as a host must be able to communicate with one or more devices. The host must support full speed and may support low speed and/or high speed. The host does not have to support communications via hubs.

The Host Negotiation Protocol

The Host Negotiation Protocol (HNP) enables the B-device to request to function as a host. When connecting two OTG devices to each other, users don't have to worry about which end of the cable goes where. When necessary, the devices use HNP to swap roles.

When two OTG devices are connected to each other, the A-device enumerates the B-device in the same way that a standard USB host enumerates its devices. During enumeration, the A-device retrieves the B-device's OTG descriptor, which indicates whether the B-device supports HNP. If the B-device supports HNP, the A-device can send a Set_Feature request with a request code of hnp_enable. This request informs the B-device that it can use HNP to request to function as the host when the bus is suspended.

At any time after enumerating, if the A-device has no communications for the B-device, the A-device can suspend the bus. A B-device that supports HNP may then request to communicate. The B-device can use HNP in response to user input such as pressing a button, or firmware can initiate HNP without user intervention.

Standard hubs don't recognize HNP signaling. If there is a hub between the B-device and the A-device, the A-device must not send the hnp_enable request and the B-device can't use HNP.

This is the protocol the B-device uses to request to operate as the host:

1. The A-device suspends the bus.

2. If the devices were communicating at full speed, the B-device disconnects from the bus by switching off its pull-up resistor on D+. If the devices were communicating at high speed, the B-device switches on its pull-up resistor on D+ for 1 to 147 milliseconds, then switches the resistor off. The bus is then in the SE0 state.

3. The A-device detects the SE0 state and connects to the bus as a device by switching on its pull-up resistor on D+. The bus is in the J state.

4. The B-device detects the J state and resets the bus.

5. The B-device enumerates the A-device and can then perform other communications with the device.

When the B-device is finished communicating, it returns to its role as a peripheral using the following protocol:

1. The B-device suspends the bus and may switch on its pull-up resistor.

2. The A-device detects the suspended bus and switches off its pull-up resistor or removes VBUS to end the session.

3. If the B-device didn't switch on its pull-up resistor in Step 1, the B-device switches on its pull-up resistor to connect as a peripheral. The bus is in the J state.

4. If VBUS is present, the A-device detects the J state and resets the bus. The A-device can then enumerate and communicate with the B-device, suspend the bus, or end the session by removing VBUS.

The A-device and B-device must also control their pull-down resistors on D+ and D-. When idle or functioning as a host, an OTG device should switch on its pull-down resistors. When functioning as a peripheral, an OTG device should switch off its pull-down resistor on D+ only.

The Session Request Protocol

If the A-device has turned off the VBUS voltage, a B-device can use the Session Request Protocol (SRP) to request the host to restore VBUS and begin a new session. There are two SRP methods: data-line pulsing and VBUS pulsing. The B-device must try data-line pulsing first, followed by VBUS pulsing. An A-device that supports SRP must respond to one of the methods. OTG devices must support SRP both as an A-device and as a B-device. Other hosts and devices may support SRP, but aren't required to.

In data-line pulsing, the device turns on its pull-up resistor (on D+ or D-, depending on device speed) for 5 to 10 milliseconds.

In VBUS pulsing, the device must drive the VBUS line long enough for the host to detect the VBUS voltage but not long enough to damage a non-OTG host that isn't designed to withstand a voltage applied to VBUS. To meet this requirement, the B-device should drive VBUS until the voltage is greater than 2.1V if connected to a OTG device and less than 2.0V if connected to a non-OTG host. The device can do so because of the difference in capacitance at the two host types. On a non-OTG host, the VBUS capacitance is 96 microfarads or more, while on a OTG device, the VBUS capacitance is 6.5 microfarads or less.

To ensure that the VBUS current doesn't exceed 8 milliamperes even if the A-device drives VBUS while the B-device is pulsing VBUS, the B-device can use a voltage source greater than 3V with an output impedance greater than 281 ohms.

Within 5 seconds of detecting data-line pulsing or VBUS pulsing, the A-device must turn on VBUS and reset the bus.

Standard hubs don't recognize SRP signaling, so if there is a hub between the B-device and the A-device, the B-device can't use SRP. Any non-OTG USB peripheral also has the option to support SRP.

Support for Remote Wakeup

When VBUS is present and the bus is suspended, an OTG device can use remote wakeup to request communications from an OTG device or other USB host.

Cables and Connectors

If you see a mini-AB receptacle, you know you have an OTG device. Every OTG device must have one and only one Mini-AB receptacle, and any device with a mini-AB connector must function as a OTG device. The mini-AB receptacle can accept either a Mini-A plug or a Mini-B plug. A host or upstream hub connects to the mini-AB receptacle with a mini-B plug, a peripheral connects with a Mini-A plug, and an OTG device can connect using either plug type.

Figure 20-2 shows the cabling options. A cable that connects two OTG devices must have a mini-A plug on one end and a mini-B plug on the other end, and it doesn't matter which device has which plug. A cable that connects an OTG device and a peripheral-only device has a mini-A plug on one end, and the other end may have a B plug, a mini-B plug, or for captive cables, a vendor-specific connector or permanent attachment to the device.

The On-The-Go supplement allows cable adapters on devices with captive cables. To attach to a host or hub with A receptacles, a device with a mini-A plug on a captive cable can use an adapter that has a mini-A receptacle and a standard A plug. To attach to an OTG device, a device with an A plug on a captive cable can use an adapter that has a standard-A receptacle and a mini-A plug. These are the only approved cable adapters and the only approved use for the mini-A receptacle. To allow the use of adapters, all cables with mini-A connectors must have slightly shorter propagation delays (25 nanoseconds maximum) and a maximum length of 4.5 meters.

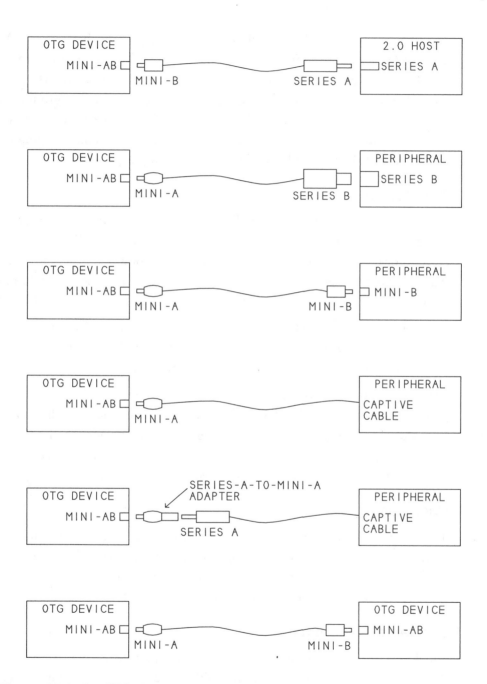

Figure 20-2: An OTG device might use any of these cable types to connect to hosts, peripherals, and other OTG devices.

In addition to D+, D-, VBUS and GND, the mini-A, mini-B, and mini-AB connectors have an ID pin. This pin enables an OTG device to determine whether a mini-A or mini-B plug is attached. In a mini-A plug, the ID pin is grounded. In a mini-B plug, the ID pin is open or connected to ground via a resistance greater than 100 kilohms. An OTG device typically has a pull-up resistor on the ID pin. If the pin is a logic low, the attached plug is a mini-A, and if the pin is a logic high, the attached plug is a mini-B.

Bus Current

The ability to draw up to 500 milliamperes from the bus is a convenience for users and a cost saver for device manufacturers. But providing this much current, or even the 100 milliamperes that battery-powered hosts must provide, can be a burden for an OTG device. And some peripherals, including battery-powered ones, may not need bus power at all.

For these reasons, an OTG device is required to supply only 8 milliamperes of bus current. OTG devices that need to supply more current to their peripherals are free to do so, up to 500 milliamperes.

Many OTG devices will need to supply more than 8 milliamperes. For example, a keyboard with a few LEDs could easily require 50 milliamperes from the host. A device whose targeted peripheral list includes an entire class (or a HID Usage, such as keyboards) should be sure that sufficient current is available to power any such device that users might attach.

User Messages

To prevent user frustration, every On-The-Go device must include and use a display or another way to communicate messages to users. For example, if a user connects an unsupported printer to a dual-role camera, a message of "Device not supported" would be helpful.

The Targeted Peripheral List

Every OTG device must have a targeted peripheral list that names all of the devices the host can communicate with. The On-The-Go supplement doesn't specify where the list must appear. Users will appreciate it if the information is easy to find!

The OTG Descriptor

During enumeration, a device that supports HNP or SRP must include an OTG Descriptor in the descriptors returned in response to a Get_Descriptor request for the Configuration descriptor.

Table 20-2 shows the fields of the descriptor. The bmAttributes field tells whether the device supports HNP and SRP. A device that supports HNP must support SRP. The A-device doesn't need to know in advance if a device supports SRP, but this information is included in the descriptor for use in compliance testing.

Feature Codes for HNP

The OTG supplement defines three codes for use in Set_Feature requests.

A code of b_hnp_enable (03h) informs the B-Device that it can use HNP. The A-device sends this request if all of the following are true: the A-device supports HNP, the A-device will respond to HNP when the bus is suspended, and the B-device connects directly to the A-device, with no hubs in between.

A code of a_hnp_support (04h) informs the B-device that the A-device supports HNP and the B-device is directly connected (no hubs), but the B-device isn't yet allowed to use HNP. The A-device can send this request before configuring the B-device. The A-device can then enable HNP at a later time, when the A-device is finished using the bus.

A code of a_alt_hnp_support (05h) notifies the B-device that the currently connected port does not support HNP, but that the A-device has an alternate port that does support HNP.

OTG Controller Chips

Several manufacturers offer controller chips designed for use in OTG devices. To function as a peripheral, the controller must include device-controller circuits similar to those in the controllers described in Chapter 6. As

Table 20-2: The OTG Descriptor indicates whether a device supports HNP and SRP.

Offset	Field	Size	Description
0	bLength	1	Descriptor length (3)
1	bDescriptorType	1	OTG (9)
2	bmAttributes	1	D2–D7: reserved, D1: 1 = HNP supported, 0 = HNP not supported D0: 1 = SNP supported, 0 = SNP not supported

with other device controllers, some OTG device controllers contain a CPU while others must interface to an external CPU.

To function as an OTG device, the controller (possibly with the help of external circuits) must have the ability to send SOF packets, schedule and initiate Setup, IN, and OUT transactions, provide VBUS, manage power, reset the bus, switch the pull-up and pull-down resistors as needed when changing roles, and detect the state of the ID pin. Some chips have internal charge pumps for supplying and controlling VBUS from a 3V supply.

A controller may also provide timers, status signals, or other hardware support for SRP and HNP signaling.

Philips ISP1362

Philips Semiconductor's ISP1362 is an interface-only chip for OTG devices. The chip contains an ISP1181B device controller (described in Chapter 6) and a host controller. Both controllers can communicate at full and low speeds. (The OTG device must use full speed when functioning as a peripheral.)

The controller interfaces to an external CPU using a 16-bit interface that can transfer data at up to 10 Megabytes/sec. The external CPU communicates with the controller by accessing its registers and buffer memory. The registers are compatible with the registers defined in the OHCI specification.

The Philips Transfer Descriptor (PTD) defines a format for exchanging information with the host controller's driver. The descriptor consists of a header that contains information such as the endpoint number, transaction type (Setup, IN, OUT), bus speed, toggle-bit value, and a completion code, followed by data.

The chip contains two USB ports. One port can function as the OTG port in a OTG device or as a host or device port for a non-On-The-Go host or device. The second port can function only as a host port and is not recommended for use in On-The-Go devices.

Philips provides host, peripheral, and OTG drivers for PCI platforms running Linux, Windows CE, DOS, and the FlexiUSB real-time operating system and for Intel PXA250/Arm architecture platforms running Linux or Windows CE.

If you need high speed, the ISP1761 is an OTG controller that supports high speed and can use a 16-bit or 32-bit CPU interface.

TransDimension TD242LP

Transdimension Inc.'s TD242LP is a physically small, low-power interface chip especially suited for compact and inexpensive dual-role products.

The controller interfaces to an external CPU using a 16-bit data bus that can transfer data at up to 22 Megabytes/sec.

The chip has two USB ports that can be configured in any of four modes. In Hardware HNP mode, one port is an OTG device port, the other is a non-OTG host port, and HNP is handled in hardware. Software HNP mode is the same except that HNP is handled in software. In Host Only mode, there is a single non-OTG host with two ports. In Function Host mode, one port is for a non-OTG host and the other is for a peripheral-only device. Both ports can operate at low and full speeds.

For reduced EMI, the chip can be clocked at 6 Megahertz rather than 48 Megahertz.

The Host Endpoint Transfer Descriptor defines a format for sending and receiving USB data. Information in the descriptor includes the endpoint number, transfer type, bus speed, direction, and a completion code.

Transdimension supplies a host-controller driver for Linux and Windows CE. Other operating systems can use USBLink drivers from SoftConnex.

Cypress CY7C67200 EZ-OTG

As the name suggests, Cypress Semiconductor's CY7C67200 EZ-OTG controller is designed for use in OTG devices. The chip contains a 16-bit CPU and can function in two modes. In stand-alone mode, the controller is the device's main CPU. Firmware can be stored in an I²C EEPROM or the controller can download its firmware from a USB host using the same method used by the EZ-USB chips described in Chapter 6. In coprocessor mode, the controller interfaces to an external CPU that manages USB communications and other tasks. The CPU can communicate via either a parallel Host Peripheral Interface at up to 16 Megabytes/sec., a high-speed asynchronous serial interface at up to 2 Megabaud, or a Serial Peripheral Interface (SPI) at up to 2 Megabits/sec.

The EZ-OTG has two USB ports and two serial interface engines that support low and full speeds. One port can function as an OTG device, a non-OTG host, or a peripheral-only device port. The other port can function as a non-OTG host or peripheral-only device port.

The controller contains a ROM BIOS that executes an Idle task consisting of an endless loop that waits for an interrupt, executes the tasks in the Idle chain, and repeats. Firmware can add tasks to the Idle chain or replace the entire Idle task with device-specific programming.

Firmware development can use the free GNU Toolset, which supports many CPUs and includes a C compiler, assembler, make utility, linker, debugger and other utilities. Cypress provides Frameworks C code for performing USB-related tasks and accessing other components in the controller.

A tutorial and many examples are in the free e-book, *USB Multi-Role Device Design By Example*, by John Hyde, available from *www.usb-by-example.com*.

A related chip, the CY7C67300 EZ-HOST, includes an interface to external memory, two ports for each of the two SIEs, memory expansion capabilities, and additional I/O features.

Philips ISP1261 Bridge Controller

Philips Semiconductor's ISP1261 is a bridge controller that takes a different approach to OTG design. With this controller and some additional firmware, an ordinary USB device can function as a "pseudo host" that can communicate with USB devices.

The ISP1261 adds some overhead, so it doesn't provide the most efficient communications, but the chip can offer a quick way to add host capability to a device. The controller can be integrated into a device or implemented as a separate dongle that attaches to a device's USB port. When implemented as a dongle, the bridge requires no hardware changes on the device, though the device must be able to store and run new firmware that communicates with the bridge controller.

The bridge contains a host port and host controller and an OTG port and OTG controller. The host port connects to the local device, and the OTG port connects to the remote host or device that the local device wants to communicate with. The host controller communicates with the local device, and the OTG controller communicates with the remote device. A Software Emulated OTG Controller (SEOC) Protocol Engine manages communications between the host controller and the OTG controller. A state machine implements the SEOC Protocol.

***

I hope you've found *USB Complete* to be useful. For more about USB developing, including device and host example code and links to product information, tutorials, articles, news, and updates, please visit my Web site at *www.Lvr.com.*

Jan Axelson

Index

Index